PERRINE'S
SOUND AND SENSE

An Introduction to Poetry

True ease in writing comes from art, not chance,
As those move easiest who have learned to dance.
'Tis not enough no harshness gives offense,
The sound must seem an echo to the sense.

ALEXANDER POPE
from *An Essay on Criticism*

NINTH EDITION

PERRINE'S
$\mathcal{S}$OUND AND $\mathcal{S}$ENSE

An Introduction to Poetry

THOMAS R. ARP
Southern Methodist University

HARCOURT BRACE COLLEGE PUBLISHERS

Fort Worth   Philadelphia   San Diego   New York   Orlando   Austin   San Antonio
Toronto   Montreal   London   Sydney   Tokyo

Publisher	Christopher P. Klein
Acquisitions Editor	John Meyers
Developmental Editor	Helen Triller
Project Editors	Elizabeth Cruce Alvarez
	Steve Welch
Art Director	Carol Kincaid
Production Manager	Jane Tyndall Ponceti

ISBN: 0-15-503028-0

Library of Congress Catalog Card Number: 96-77101

Harcourt Brace & Company may provide complimentary instructional aids and supplements
or supplement packages to those adopters qualified under our adoption policy. Please contact
your sales representative for more information. If as an adopter or potential user you receive
supplements you do not need, please return them to your sales representative or send them
to: Attn: Returns Department, Troy Warehouse, 465 South Lincoln Drive, Troy, MO 63379.

Address for Editorial Correspondence: Harcourt Brace College Publishers, 301 Commerce Street,
Suite 3700, Fort Worth, TX 76102.

Address for Orders: Harcourt Brace & Company, 6277 Sea Harbor Drive, Orlando, FL
32887-6777. 1-800-782-4479, or 1-800-433-0001 (in Florida).

Copyright Acknowledgments follow the Glossary and constitute a continuation of this
copyright page.

Printed in the United States of America

7   8   9   0   1   2   3   4   5   016   10   9   8   7   6   5   4   3   2

Preface

In the previous eight editions of this book, the preface has contained a brief introduction to the plan of the book and some expressions of gratitude. The ninth edition requires an expanded and more personal preface.

Most of the loyal users of this book and its predecessors will know that Laurence Perrine died in April 1995 after a protracted battle with Parkinson's disease. His death was a sad occasion for me, for his family, and I am sure for many who since 1956 have regarded *Sound and Sense* with high respect and esteem.

In 1977, a few years after I arrived at Southern Methodist University, I received a brief note from Laurence Perrine asking me to name a convenient day to join him for lunch off campus. I naturally panicked: what had I done that my senior colleague needed to move to neutral turf to counsel or chide me? We met at a cafeteria, filled our trays, and sat down, and instead of detailing my manifold shortcomings, Larry asked me if I would join him in revising *Sound and Sense*. My delight was even greater than my relief, and I accepted on the spot. From that point we worked together in producing the sixth, seventh, and eighth editions, and I graduated from being "with the assistance of" to co-author for the eighth.

Because of his health, Larry was not able to be as actively involved in this latest revision of the book, although as late as February 1995, he was still handing over to me copies of poems that he thought worth considering for the new edition. Over the years that we worked together, he expressed his confidence in my knowing how the book works, and how individual poems work in the book, and I hope that his confidence will be justified by the decisions I have made in this edition.

Through its many revisions, *Sound and Sense* has maintained its basic premises. It has presented to beginning students a balance of classic and contemporary works dealing with universal themes. With only two exceptions (the "title" poem by Alexander Pope and a brief excerpt from *Macbeth* used to illustrate allusion), the book has printed poems in their entirety. It has striven for conciseness and compactness (Larry always wanted a book to feel comfortable in the hand). It has presented the elements of poetry in a progression in which each new topic builds

on what preceded it, and has offered a step-by-step illustration of poetic techniques. The individual chapters gradually introduce the student to the elements of poetry, putting emphasis always on *how* and
why: How can the reader use these elements to get at the meaning of a
poem, to interpret it correctly, and to respond to it adequately? *Why*
does the poet use these elements? What values do they have for the
poet and for the reader?

In matters of theory, some issues are consciously simplified, but I
hope not compromised. The purpose of the book has always been to
give the beginning student something to understand and use. The first
assumptions of *Sound and Sense* are that poetry needs to be read carefully and thought about considerably and that, when so read, poetry
gives its readers continuing rewards in experience and understanding.

Each chapter is divided into two parts: a discussion of the topic indicated by the chapter title, with illustrative poems; and a relevant selection of poems with study questions for further illustration of the
topic. The division between the two parts of a chapter is visually indicated by a heavy line. The whole book is similarly divided into two
parts: Part One consists of the sixteen definitive chapters, and Part
Two contains poems for further reading, without study questions.

As in previous editions, three poets (Dickinson, Donne, and Frost)
are represented by a sufficient number of poems to support study of
them as individual artists.

The ninth edition differs from the eighth chiefly in the following
respects: while maintaining the desirable balance between traditional
and contemporary works, the number of poems by women and by
members of ethnic minorities (and the number of poets representing
these groups) has again been increased; the appendix on "Writing
about Poetry" has been augmented at the request of readers of the
eighth edition; and Chapter Twelve on "Rhythm and Meter" has been
extensively revised to take into account the increasing interest in nonmetrical verse. And I have felt free to do what Larry never did—I have
included three examples of his own limericks, a verse form of which
he was a master.

A book of such enduring usefulness grows through time and advice, and the debts to the helpful attention of others are now innumer-
able. With Larry, I wish to thank especially his wife Catherine. I have
also been given valued assistance by Ann Hayes of Carnegie Mellon
University and Robert Wallace of Case Western Reserve University.
But as the sole signatory, I must of course reserve most of my gratitude
for Laurence Perrine.

—T. R. A.

Professional Acknowledgments

The following instructors have offered helpful reactions and suggestions for this ninth edition of *Sound and Sense.*

Frank J. Albert
Community College of Beaver County

B. J. Alexander
Tarleton State University

Lillian H. Andon-Milligan
North Idaho College

Martha Atkins
Dyersburg State Community College

Donna Bauerly
Loras College

Richard R. Bollenbacher
Edison State Community College

Elaine C. Brookshire
Northeast Alabama State Community
College

Richard G. Brown
Ball State University

Robert A. Burns
Southeast Missouri State University

Susan McCann Butler
Thomas Nelson Community College

Norman E. Carlson
Western Michigan University

Nathan Anthony Cervo
Franklin Pierce College

Jan M. Chalupnik
Moorhead State University

Charlotte C. Crittenden
Georgia Southern University

Sharon Cupples
Stanly Community College

Elizabeth H. Davis
Southern Arkansas University, Magnolia

Margaret DeHart
Trinity Valley Community College

David C. Downing
Elizabethtown College

Richard Downing
Pasco-Hernando Community College,
North Campus

Kirby L. Duncan
Stephen F. Austin State University

John Early
Moorhead State University

Will Farrell
Mt. San Jacinto College

Marilyn Fontane
St. Louis College of Pharmacy

Geneva Frost
University of Maine, Machias

Kevin J. Gardner
Mount Vernon Nazarene College

C. Herbert Gilliland
U.S. Naval Academy

Rachel Hadas
Rutgers University, Newark

W. M. Hagen
Oklahoma Baptist University

John K. Hanes
Duquesne University

Carol Hansen
City College of San Francisco

Wayne E. Haskin
North Carolina State University, Raleigh

Donald Heidt
College of the Canyons

Jeff Henderson
University of Central Arkansas

Kathryn Henkins
Mt. San Antonio College

Jean Hodgin
North Shore Community College

Robert M. Hogge
Weber State University

Wayne P. Hubert
Chaffey Community College

Pamela Hudson
Hawaii Community College

O. Glade Hunsaker
Brigham Young University

Ruby T. Johnson
Wallace State College

James Jolly, Jr.
Shelton State Community College

Mary C. Jordan
Illinois Central College

Harvey Kassebaum
Cuyahoga Community College, West

David Kelly
Dyersburg State Community College

Dolores Keranen
University of Illinois, Chicago

Charlotte H. Kern
Northwestern Oklahoma State University

Sue L. Kimball
Methodist College

Patricia C. Knight
Amarillo College

Al Krahn
Milwaukee Area Technical College

Kenneth Paul Leisch
Danville Area Community College

William G. Leftwich III
U.S. Naval Academy

Eleanor Lyons
Indiana University, South Bend

Alexander J. Maxwell
Shoreline Community College

Thomas Carl Merriman
University of Texas—Pan American

Terry Miller
Indian River Community College

Virginia Ramey Mollenkott
William Paterson College

Phil Murdock
Ricks College

Caroline C. Nakamura
Kapiolani Community College

Elizabeth Nelson
St. Peter's College

Jane Neuburger
Cazenovia College

David M. Packard
John A. Logan College

Kathleen Parks
Antelope Valley College

Art Petersen
University of Alaska Southeast, Juneau

Lynn Pfannkuche
Lincoln Land Community College

Gloria Dibble Pond
Naugatuck Valley Community
Technical College

Norman Prinsky
Augusta College

Barbara Read
Kilgore College

Mary Roberti
Monroe County Community College

Horace S. Rockwood III
California University of Pennsylvania

Gordon K. W. Roeder
North Dakota State University,
Bottineau

Mary Rosa
University of St. Thomas

Alan Sandy
Sonoma State University

Karen Saupe
Calvin College

J. R. Scrutchins
Oklahoma Baptist University

Linda Rushton Selman
Southern Arkansas University, Magnolia

Sharon Shapiro
Naugatuck Valley Community
Technical College

Kathleen A. Sherfick
Albion College

Craig L. Shurtleff
Illinois Central College

Lynne Shuster
Erie Community College, North

Keith Slocum
Montclair State University

Diane Vanner Steinberg
University of St. Thomas

William Stephenson
Northland College

William Studebaker
College of Southern Idaho

Lou Suarez
Lorain County Community College

Mitchell E. Summerlin
John C. Calhoun Community College

Edwina Trentham
Asnuntuck Community Technical
College

Kathryn A. Walterscheid
St. Louis College of Pharmacy

John P. Weber
Cypress College

Cheryl Wotring
Middlesex Community College,
City Campus

CONTENTS

Chapter Six   Figurative Language 2

Symbol, Allegory   80

Chapter Seven   Figurative Language 3

Paradox, Overstatement, Understatement, Irony   101

Chapter Eight   Allusion   122

Chapter Nine   Meaning and Idea   133

Chapter Ten   Tone   146

Chapter Eleven   Musical Devices   163

Chapter Sixteen   Good Poetry and Great   251

Part 2   Poems for Further Reading   269

PART 1

The Elements of Poetry

CHAPTER ONE

What Is Poetry?

Poetry is as universal as language and almost as ancient. The most primitive peoples have used it, and the most civilized have cultivated it. In all ages and in all countries, poetry has been written, and eagerly read or listened to, by all kinds and conditions of people—by soldiers, statesmen, lawyers, farmers, doctors, scientists, clergy, philosophers, kings, and queens. In all ages it has been especially the concern of the educated, the intelligent, and the sensitive, and it has appealed, in its simpler forms, to the uneducated and to children. Why? First, because it has given pleasure. People have read it, listened to it, or recited it because they liked it—because it gave them enjoyment. But this is not the whole answer. Poetry in all ages has been regarded as important, not simply as one of several alternative forms of amusement, as one person might choose bowling, another chess, and another poetry. Rather, it has been regarded as something central to existence, something having unique value to the fully realized life, something that we are better off for having and without which we are spiritually impoverished. To understand the reasons for this, we need to have at least a provisional understanding of what poetry is—provisional, because people have always been more successful at appreciating poetry than at defining it.

Initially, poetry might be defined as a kind of language that says *more* and says it *more intensely* than does ordinary language. To understand this fully, we need to understand what poetry "says." For language is employed on different occasions to say quite different kinds of things; in other words, language has different uses.

Perhaps the commonest use of language is to communicate *information*. We say that it is nine o'clock, that we liked a certain movie, that George Washington was the first president of the United States, that bromine and iodine are members of the halogen group of chemical elements. This we might call the *practical* use of language; it helps us with the ordinary business of living.

But it is not primarily to communicate information that novels, short stories, plays, and poems are written. These exist to bring us a sense and a perception of life, to widen and sharpen our contacts with existence. Their concern is with *experience*. We all have an inner need to live more deeply and fully and with greater awareness, to know the experience of others, and to understand our own experience better. Poets, from their own store of felt, observed, or imagined experiences, select, combine, and reorganize. They create significant new experiences for their readers—significant because focused and formed—in which readers can participate and from which they may gain a greater awareness and understanding of their world. Literature, in other words, can be used as a gear for stepping up the intensity and increasing the range of our experience and as a glass for clarifying it. This is the *literary* use of language, for literature is not only an aid to living but a means of living.*

Suppose, for instance, that we are interested in eagles. If we want simply to acquire information about eagles, we may turn to an encyclopedia or a book of natural history. There we find that the family Falconidae, to which eagles belong, is characterized by imperforate nostrils, legs of medium length, a hooked bill, the hind toe inserted on a level parallel to the three front ones, and the claws roundly curved and sharp; that land eagles are feathered fully to the toes and sea-fishing eagles halfway to the toes; that their length is about three feet and their wingspan seven feet; that they usually build their nests on some inaccessible cliff; that the eggs are spotted and do not exceed three; and perhaps that the eagle's "great power of vision, the vast height to which it soars in the sky, the wild grandeur of its abode, have . . . commended it to the poets of all nations."†

But unless we are interested in this information only for practical purposes, we are likely to feel a little disappointed, as though we had grasped the feathers of the eagle but not its soul. True, we have learned many facts about the eagle, but we have missed somehow its

---

*A third use of language is as an instrument of persuasion. This is the use we find in advertisements, propaganda bulletins, sermons, and political speeches. These three uses of language—the practical, the literary, and the hortatory—are not sharply divided. They may be thought of as three points of a triangle; most actual specimens of written language fall somewhere within the triangle. Most poetry conveys some information, and some poetry has a design on the reader. But language becomes literature when the desire to communicate experience predominates.

†*Encyclopedia Americana* IX (1955) 473–74.

lonely majesty, its power, and the "wild grandeur" of its surroundings that would make the eagle a living creature rather than a mere museum specimen. For the living eagle we must turn to literature.

1. The Eagle

> He clasps the crag with crooked hands;
> Close to the sun in lonely lands,
> Ringed with the azure world, he stands.
>
> The wrinkled sea beneath him crawls;
> He watches from his mountain walls,   5
> And like a thunderbolt he falls.

> *Alfred, Lord Tennyson (1809–1892)*

QUESTIONS

1. What is peculiarly effective about the expressions "crooked hands," "Close to the sun," "Ringed with the azure world," "wrinkled," "crawls," and "like a thunderbolt"?
2. Notice the formal pattern of the poem, particularly the contrast of "he stands" in the first stanza and "he falls" in the second. Is there any other contrast between the two stanzas?

When "The Eagle" has been read well, readers will feel that they have enjoyed a significant experience and understand eagles better, though in a different way, than they did from the encyclopedia article alone. For while the article *analyzes* our experience of eagles, the poem in some sense *synthesizes* such an experience. Indeed, we may say the two approaches to experience—the scientific and the literary—complement each other. And we may contend that the kind of understanding we get from the second is at least as valuable as the kind we get from the first.

Literature, then, exists to communicate significant experience—significant because concentrated and organized. Its function is not to tell us *about* experience but to allow us imaginatively to *participate* in it. It is a means of allowing us, through the imagination, to live more fully, more deeply, more richly, and with greater awareness. It can do this in two ways: by *broadening* our experience—that is, by making us acquainted with a range of experience with which, in the ordinary course of events, we might have no contact—or by *deepening* our experience—that is, by making us feel more poignantly and more understandingly the everyday experiences all of us have. It enlarges our perspectives and breaks down some of the limits we may feel.

We can avoid two limiting approaches to poetry if we keep this conception of literature firmly in mind. The first approach always looks for a lesson or a bit of moral instruction. The second expects to find poetry always beautiful. Let us consider one of the songs from Shakespeare's *Love's Labor's Lost* (5.2).

2. Winter

When icicles hang by the wall,
And Dick the shepherd blows his nail,
And Tom bears logs into the hall,
And milk comes frozen home in pail,
When blood is nipped and ways be foul,   5
Then nightly sings the staring owl,
"Tu-whit, tu-who!"
     A merry note,
     While greasy Joan doth keel° the pot.   skim

When all aloud the wind doth blow,   10
And coughing drowns the parson's saw,
And birds sit brooding in the snow,
And Marian's nose looks red and raw,
When roasted crabs° hiss in the bowl,   crab apples
Then nightly sings the staring owl,   15
"Tu-whit, tu-who!"
     A merry note,
     While greasy Joan doth keel the pot.

William Shakespeare (1564–1616)

QUESTIONS

1. Vocabulary: *saw* (11), *brooding* (12).
2. Is the owl's cry really a "merry" note? How are this adjective and the verb "sings" employed?
3. In what way does the owl's cry contrast with the other details of the poem?

In this poem Shakespeare communicates the quality of winter life around a sixteenth-century English country house. But he does not do so by telling us flatly that winter in such surroundings is cold and in many respects unpleasant, though with some pleasant features too (the adjectives *cold, unpleasant,* and *pleasant* are not even used in the poem). Instead, he provides a series of concrete homely details that suggest these qualities and enable us, imaginatively, to experience this winter life ourselves. The shepherd blows on his fingernails to warm his hands; the milk freezes in the pail between the cowshed and the kitchen; the cook is slovenly and unclean, "greasy" either from spattered cooking fat or from her own sweat as she leans over the hot fire; the roads are muddy; the folk listening to the parson have colds; the birds "sit brooding in the snow"; and the servant girl's nose is raw from cold. But pleasant things are in prospect. Tom is bringing in logs for the fire, the hot cider or ale is ready for drinking, and the soup or stew will soon be ready. In contrast to all these familiar details of country life is the mournful and eerie note of the owl.

Obviously the poem contains no moral. If we limit ourselves to looking in poetry for some lesson, message, or noble truth about life, we are bound to be disappointed. This limited approach sees poetry as a kind of sugarcoated pill—a wholesome truth or lesson made palatable by being put into pretty words. What this narrow approach really wants is a sermon—not a poem, but something inspirational. Yet "Winter," which has appealed to readers for nearly four centuries, is not inspirational and contains no moral preachment.

Neither is the poem "Winter" beautiful. Though it is appealing in its way and contains elements of beauty, there is little that is really beautiful in red, raw noses, coughing in chapel, nipped blood, foul roads, and greasy cooks. Yet the second limiting approach may lead us to feel that poetry deals exclusively with beauty—with sunsets, flowers, butterflies, love, God—and that the one appropriate response to any poem is, after a moment of awed silence, "Isn't that beautiful!" But this narrow approach excludes a large proportion of poetry. The function of poetry is sometimes to be ugly rather than beautiful. And poetry may deal with common colds and greasy cooks as legitimately as with sunsets and flowers. Consider another example:

3. Dulce et Decorum Est

Bent double, like old beggars under sacks,
Knock-kneed, coughing like hags, we cursed through sludge,
Till on the haunting flares we turned our backs,

And towards our distant rest began to trudge.
Men marched asleep. Many had lost their boots,   5
But limped on, blood-shod. All went lame, all blind;
Drunk with fatigue; deaf even to the hoots
Of gas-shells dropping softly behind.

Gas! GAS! Quick, boys!—An ecstasy of fumbling,
Fitting the clumsy helmets just in time,   10
But someone still was yelling out and stumbling
And flound'ring like a man in fire or lime.—
Dim through the misty panes and thick green light,
As under a green sea, I saw him drowning.

In all my dreams before my helpless sight   15
He plunges at me, guttering, choking, drowning.

If in some smothering dreams, you too could pace
Behind the wagon that we flung him in,
And watch the white eyes writhing in his face,
His hanging face, like a devil's sick of sin,   20
If you could hear, at every jolt, the blood
Come gargling from the froth-corrupted lungs
Bitter as the cud
Of vile, incurable sores on innocent tongues,—
My friend, you would not tell with such high zest   25
To children ardent for some desperate glory,
The old lie: *Dulce et decorum est*
Pro patria mori.

Wilfred Owen (1893–1918)

QUESTIONS

1. The Latin quotation, from the Roman poet Horace, means "It is sweet and becoming to die for one's country." What is the poem's comment on this statement?
2. List the elements of the poem that seem not beautiful and therefore "unpoetic." Are there any elements of beauty in the poem?
3. How do the comparisons in lines 1, 14, 20, and 23–24 contribute to the effectiveness of the poem?
4. What does the poem gain by moving from plural pronouns and the past tense to singular pronouns and the present tense?

Poetry takes all life as its province. Its primary concern is not with beauty, not with philosophical truth, not with persuasion, but with experience. Beauty and philosophical truth are aspects of experience, and the poet is often engaged with them. But poetry as a whole is concerned with all kinds of experience—beautiful or ugly, strange or common, noble or ignoble, actual or imaginary. One of the paradoxes of human existence is that all experience—even painful experience—can be enjoyable when transmitted through the medium of art. In real life, death and pain and suffering are not pleasurable, but in poetry they may be. In real life, getting soaked in a rainstorm is not pleasurable, but in poetry it can be. In actual life, if we cry, usually we are unhappy; but if we cry in a movie, we are manifestly enjoying it. We do not ordinarily like to be terrified in real life, but we sometimes seek movies or books that will terrify us. We find some value in all intense living. To be intensely alive is the opposite of being dead. To be dull, to be bored, to be imperceptive is in one sense to be dead. Poetry comes to us bringing life and therefore pleasure. Moreover, art focuses and organizes experience so as to give us a better understanding of it. And to understand life is partly to be master of it.

There is no sharp distinction between poetry and other forms of imaginative literature. Although some beginning readers may believe that poetry can be recognized by the arrangement of its lines on the page or by its use of rime and meter, such superficial signs are of little worth. The Book of Job in the Bible and Melville's *Moby Dick* are highly poetical, but the familiar verse that begins: "Thirty days hath September, / April, June, and November . . ." is not. The difference between poetry and other literature is only one of degree. Poetry is the most condensed and concentrated form of literature. It is language whose individual lines, either because of their own brilliance or because they focus so powerfully on what has gone before, have a higher voltage than most language. It is language that grows frequently incandescent, giving off both light and heat.

Ultimately, therefore, poetry can be recognized only by the response made to it by a practiced reader, someone who has acquired some sensitivity to poetry. But there is a catch here. We are not all equally experienced readers. To some readers, poetry may often seem dull and boring, a fancy way of writing something that could be said more simply. So might a color-blind person deny that there is such a thing as color.

The act of communication involved in reading poetry is like the act of communication involved in receiving a message by radio. Two devices are required: a transmitting station and a receiving set. The completeness of the communication depends on both the power and clarity of the transmitter and the sensitivity and tuning of the receiver.

When a person reads a poem and no experience is received, either the poem is not a good poem or the reader is not properly tuned. With new poetry, we cannot always be sure which is at fault. With older poetry, if it has acquired critical acceptance—has been enjoyed by generations of good readers—we may assume that the receiving set is at fault. Fortunately, the fault is not irremediable. Though we cannot all become expert readers, we can become good enough to find both pleasure and value in much good poetry, or we can increase the amount of pleasure we already find in poetry and the number of kinds of poetry in which we find it. The purpose of this book is to help you increase your sensitivity and range as a receiving set.

Poetry, finally, is a kind of multidimensional language. Ordinary language—the kind that we use to communicate information—is one-dimensional. It is directed at only part of the listener, the understanding. Its one dimension is intellectual. Poetry, which is language used to communicate experience, has at least four dimensions. If it is to communicate experience, it must be directed at the *whole* person, not just at your understanding. It must involve not only your intelligence but also your senses, emotions, and imagination. To the intellectual dimension, poetry adds a sensuous dimension, an emotional dimension, and an imaginative dimension.

Poetry achieves its extra dimensions—its greater pressure per word and its greater tension per poem—by drawing more fully and more consistently than does ordinary language on a number of language resources, none of which is peculiar to poetry. These various resources form the subjects of a number of the following chapters. Among them are connotation, imagery, metaphor, symbol, paradox, irony, allusion, sound repetition, rhythm, and pattern. Using these resources and the materials of life, the poet shapes and makes a poem. Successful poetry is never effusive language. If it is to come alive it must be as cunningly put together and as efficiently organized as a tree. It must be an organism whose every part serves a useful purpose and cooperates with every other part to preserve and express the life that is within it.

---

4. Spring

> When daisies pied and violets blue,
>   And lady-smocks all silver-white,
> And cuckoo-buds of yellow hue

Do paint the meadows with delight,
The cuckoo then, on every tree,   5
Mocks married men; for thus sings he,
    "Cuckoo!
Cuckoo, cuckoo!" O word of fear,
Unpleasing to a married ear!

When shepherds pipe on oaten straws,   10
    And merry larks are plowmen's clocks,
When turtles tread, and rooks, and daws,
    And maidens bleach their summer smocks,
The cuckoo then, on every tree,
Mocks married men; for thus sings he,   15
    "Cuckoo!
Cuckoo, cuckoo!" O word of fear,
Unpleasing to a married ear!

William Shakespeare (1564–1616)

QUESTIONS

1. Vocabulary: *pied* (1), *lady-smocks* (2), *oaten straws* (10), *turtles* (12), *tread* (12), *rooks* (12), *daws* (12).
2. This song is a companion piece to "Winter." In what respects are the two poems similar? How do they contrast? What details show that this poem, like "Winter," was written by a realist, not simply by a man carried away with the beauty of spring?
3. The word "cuckoo" is "unpleasing to a married ear" because it sounds like *cuckold.* Cuckolds were a frequent butt of humor in earlier English literature. If you do not know the meaning of the word, look it up. How does this information help to shape the tone of the poem? Is it solemn? Light and semihumorous?

5. The Whipping

The old woman across the way
    is whipping the boy again
and shouting to the neighborhood
    her goodness and his wrongs.

Wildly he crashes through elephant-ears,   5
    pleads in dusty zinnias,
while she in spite of crippling fat
    pursues and corners him.

She strikes and strikes the shrilly circling
    boy till the stick breaks   10

in her hand. His tears are rainy weather
to woundlike memories:

My head gripped in bony vise
    of knees, the writing struggle
to wrench free, the blows, the fear   15
    worse than blows that hateful

Words could bring, the face that I
    no longer knew or loved . . .
Well, it is over now, it is over,
    and the boy sobs in his room,   20

And the woman leans muttering against
    a tree, exhausted, purged—
avenged in part for lifelong hidings
    she has had to bear.

Robert Hayden (1913–1980)

QUESTIONS

1. What similarities connect the old woman, the boy, and the speaker? Can
   you say that one of them is the main subject of the poem?
2. Does this poem express any beauty? What human truth does it embody?
   Could you argue against the claim that "it is over now, it is over" (19)?

6. The Computation

For the first twenty years since yesterday
    I scarce believed thou couldst be gone away;
For forty more I fed on favors past,
    And forty on hopes that thou wouldst they might last.
Tears drowned one hundred, and sighs blew out two;   5
    A thousand, I did neither think nor do,
Or not divide, all being one thought of you.
    Or, in a thousand more, forgot that too.
Yet call not this long life; but think that I
    Am, by being dead, immortal. Can ghosts die?   10

John Donne (1572–1631)

QUESTIONS

1. Who is the "I" of the poem? Who is the "thou" or "you"? How long have
   they been separated—literally? Figuratively?

2. Are the numbers in this "mathematical" poem used vaguely or precisely? What reasons can you find for their choice and arrangement?
3. Explain how, in the last two lines, the speaker undermines the series of overstatements just completed with another equally hyperbolic claim. Is he really dead? Of what did he "die"?

7. Hawk Roosting

I sit in the top of the wood, my eyes closed.
Inaction, no falsifying dream
Between my hooked head and hooked feet:
Or in sleep rehearse perfect kills and eat.

The convenience of the high trees!   5
The air's buoyancy and the sun's ray
Are of advantage to me;
And the earth's face upward for my inspection.

My feet are locked upon the rough bark.
It took the whole of Creation   10
To produce my foot, my each feather:
Now I hold Creation in my foot

Or fly up, and revolve it all slowly—
I kill where I please because it is all mine.
There is no sophistry in my body: 15
My manners are tearing off heads—

The allotment of death.
For the one path of my flight is direct
Through the bones of the living.
No arguments assert my right: 20

The sun is behind me.
Nothing has changed since I began.
My eye has permitted no change.
I am going to keep things like this.

Ted Hughes (b. 1930)

QUESTIONS

1. Vocabulary: *sophistry* (15).
2. Who is the speaker of this poem? Characterize his "personality." What do his errors in summing up his situation contribute to your characterization?
3. What are the similarities and differences between this poem and "The Eagle" (No. 1)?

8. Ballad of Birmingham

(On the bombing of a church in Birmingham, Alabama, 1963)

"Mother dear, may I go downtown
Instead of out to play,
And march the streets of Birmingham
In a Freedom March today?"

"No, baby, no, you may not go,   5
For the dogs are fierce and wild,
And clubs and hoses, guns and jails
Aren't good for a little child."

"But, mother, I won't be alone.
Other children will go with me,   10
And march the streets of Birmingham
To make our country free."

"No, baby, no, you may not go,
For I fear those guns will fire.
But you may go to church instead   15
And sing in the children's choir."

She has combed and brushed her night-dark hair,
And bathed rose petal sweet,
And drawn white gloves on her small brown hands,
And white shoes on her feet.   20

The mother smiled to know her child
Was in the sacred place,
But that smile was the last smile
To come upon her face.

For when she heard the explosion,   25
Her eyes grew wet and wild.
She raced through the streets of Birmingham
Calling for her child.

She clawed through bits of glass and brick,
Then lifted out a shoe.   30
"O, here's the shoe my baby wore,
But, baby, where are you?"

Dudley Randall (b. 1914)

QUESTIONS

1. This poem is based on a historical incident. Throughout 1963, Birmingham, Alabama, was the site of demonstrations and marches protesting the

racial segregation of schools and other public facilities. Although they were intended as peaceful protests, these demonstrations often erupted in violence as police attempted to disperse them with fire hoses and police dogs. On the morning of September 15, 1963, a bomb exploded during Sunday School at the 16th Street Baptist Church. Four children were killed and 14 were injured. How does the poem differ from what you would expect to find in a newspaper account of such an incident? In an encyclopedia entry? In a speech calling for the elimination of racial injustice?
2. What do the details in the fifth stanza (17–20) contribute to the effect of the poem? Is "She" (17) the mother or the child?
3. What characteristics does this poem share with "Edward" (No. 180), which is a traditional folk ballad? Why do you think this twentieth-century poet chose to write in a form that alludes to that tradition?
4. What purpose does the poem have beyond simply telling a story? How does the irony help achieve that purpose?

9. The Red Wheelbarrow

so much depends
upon

a red wheel
barrow

glazed with rain   5
water

beside the white
chickens.

William Carlos Williams (1883–1963)

QUESTIONS

1. The speaker asserts that "so much depends upon" the objects he refers to, leading the reader to ask: *How much and why?* This glimpse of a farm scene implies one kind of answer. What is the importance of the wheelbarrow, rain, and chicken to a farmer? To all of us?
2. What further importance can you infer from the references to color, shape, texture, and the juxtaposition of objects? Does the poem itself have a shape? What two ways of observing and valuing the world does the poem imply?

10. The Pasture

I'm going out to clean the pasture spring;
I'll only stop to rake the leaves away
(And wait to watch the water clear, I may):
I shan't be gone long. —You come too.

I'm going out to fetch the little calf   5
That's standing by the mother. It's so young
It totters when she licks it with her tongue.
I shan't be gone long. —You come too.

Robert Frost (1874–1963)

QUESTIONS

1. Who and what kind of person is the speaker? Who is addressed?
2. Frost characteristically strove to capture the speech rhythms and language of the speaking voice in poems retaining a metrical form. In what
   lines is he particularly successful at this?
3. Originally the initial poem in Frost's second volume of verse, "The Pasture"
   was subsequently placed as the initial poem in his collections of his verse.
   What additional meaning does the poem acquire from this positioning?

11. Terence, this is stupid stuff*

"Terence, this is stupid stuff:
You eat your victuals fast enough;
There can't be much amiss, 'tis clear,
To see the rate you drink your beer.
But oh, good Lord, the verse you make,   5
It gives a chap the belly-ache.
The cow, the old cow, she is dead;
It sleeps well, the horned head:
We poor lads, 'tis our turn now
To hear such tunes as killed the cow.   10
Pretty friendship 'tis to rhyme
Your friends to death before their time
Moping melancholy mad:
Come, pipe a tune to dance to, lad."

Why, if 'tis dancing you would be,   15
There's brisker pipes than poetry.
Say, for what were hop-yards meant,
Or why was Burton built on Trent?
Oh many a peer of England brews
Livelier liquor than the Muse,   20

*Whenever a heading duplicates the first line of the poem or a substantial portion
thereof, with only the first word capitalized, it is probable that the poet left the poem
untitled and that the anthologist has substituted the first line or part of it as an editorial
convenience. Such a heading is not referred to as the title of the poem.

And malt does more than Milton can
To justify God's ways to man.
Ale, man, ale's the stuff to drink
For fellows whom it hurts to think:
Look into the pewter pot   25
To see the world as the world's not.
And faith, 'tis pleasant till 'tis past:
The mischief is that 'twill not last.
Oh I have been to Ludlow fair
And left my necktie God knows where,   30
And carried half-way home, or near,
Pints and quarts of Ludlow beer:
Then the world seemed none so bad,
And I myself a sterling lad;
And down in lovely muck I've lain,   35
Happy till I woke again.
Then I saw the morning sky:
Heigho, the tale was all a lie;
The world, it was the old world yet,
I was I, my things were wet,   40
And nothing now remained to do
But begin the game anew.

   Therefore, since the world has still
Much good, but much less good than ill,
And while the sun and moon endure   45
Luck's a chance, but trouble's sure,
I'd face it as a wise man would,
And train for ill and not for good.
'Tis true, the stuff I bring for sale
Is not so brisk a brew as ale: 50
Out of a stem that scored the hand
I wrung it in a weary land.
But take it: if the smack is sour,
The better for the embittered hour;
It should do good to heart and head   55
When your soul is in my soul's stead;
And I will friend you, if I may,
In the dark and cloudy day.

   There was a king reigned in the East:
There, when kings will sit to feast,   60
They get their fill before they think
With poisoned meat and poisoned drink.
He gathered all that springs to birth
From the many-venomed earth;

First a little, thence to more,   65
He sampled all her killing store;
And easy, smiling, seasoned sound,
Sate the king when healths went round.
They put arsenic in his meat
And stared aghast to watch him eat;   70
They poured strychnine in his cup
And shook to see him drink it up:
They shook, they stared as white's their shirt:
Them it was their poison hurt.
—I tell the tale that I heard told.   75
Mithridates, he died old.

A. E. Housman (1859–1936)

QUESTIONS

1. The poem opens with the speaker quoting another person whose remarks he then refutes. What is the relationship between the two? Of what has the other person been complaining? What request has he made of the speaker?
2. Hops (17) and "malt" (21) are principal ingredients of beer and ale. Burton-upon-Trent (18) is an English city famous for its breweries. Milton (21), in the invocation of his epic poem *Paradise Lost,* declares that his purpose is to "justify the ways of God to men." What, in Terence's eyes, is the efficacy of liquor in helping one live a difficult life? What is the "stuff" *he* brings "for sale" (49)?
3. "Mithridates" (76) was a king of Pontus and a contemporary of Julius Caesar; his "tale" is told in Pliny's *Natural History.* The poem is structured by its line spacing into four verse paragraphs. What is the connection of this last verse paragraph with the rest of the poem? What is the function of each of the other three?
4. Essentially, Terence assesses the value of three possible aids for worthwhile living. What are they? Which does Terence consider the best? What six lines of the poem best sum up his philosophy?
5. This poem is the second last in Housman's book *A Shropshire Lad.* The last poem also concerns poetry and its place in the world. May we consider Terence in this poem a surrogate for Housman?
6. Many people like reading material that is cheerful and optimistic; they argue that "there's enough suffering and unhappiness in the world already." What, for Housman, is the value of pessimistic and tragic literature?

12. Ars Poetica

A poem should be palpable and mute
As a globed fruit,

Dumb
As old medallions to the thumb,

Silent as the sleeve-worn stone   5
Of casement ledges where the moss has grown—

A poem should be wordless
As the flight of birds.

                                         *

A poem should be motionless in time
As the moon climbs,   10

Leaving, as the moon releases
Twig by twig the night-entangled trees,

Leaving, as the moon behind the winter leaves,
Memory by memory the mind—

A poem should be motionless in time   15
As the moon climbs.

                                         *

A poem should be equal to:
Not true.

For all the history of grief
An empty doorway and a maple leaf.   20

For love
The leaning grasses and two lights above the sea—

A poem should not mean
But be.

                                    Archibald MacLeish (1892–1982)

QUESTIONS

1. How can a poem be "wordless" (7)? How can it be "motionless in time"
   (15)?
2. The Latin title, literally translated "The Art of Poetry," is a traditional title
   for works on the philosophy of poetry. What is *this* poet's philosophy of
   poetry? What does he mean by saying that a poem should not "mean"
   (23) and should not be "true" (18)?

CHAPTER TWO

Reading the Poem

The primary purpose of this book is to develop your ability to understand and appreciate poetry. Here are some preliminary suggestions:

1. Read a poem more than once. A good poem will no more yield its full meaning on a single reading than will a Beethoven symphony on a single hearing. Two readings may be necessary simply to let you get your bearings. And if the poem is a work of art, it will repay repeated and prolonged examination. One does not listen to a good piece of music once and forget it; one does not look at a good painting once and throw it away. A poem is not like a newspaper, to be hastily read and cast into the wastebasket. It is to be hung on the wall of one's mind.

2. Keep a dictionary by you and use it. It is futile to try to understand poetry without troubling to learn the meanings of the words of which it is composed. You might as well attempt to play tennis without a ball. One of your primary purposes while in college should be to build a good vocabulary, and the study of poetry gives you an excellent opportunity. A few other reference books also will be invaluable. Particularly desirable are a good book on mythology (your instructor can recommend one) and a Bible.

3. Read so as to hear the sounds of the words in your mind. Poetry is written to be heard: its meanings are conveyed through sound as well as through print. Every word is therefore important. The best way to read a poem is just the opposite of the best way to read a newspaper. One reads a newspaper as rapidly as possible; one should read a poem as slowly as possible. When you cannot read a poem aloud, lip-read it: form the words with your tongue and mouth even though you do not utter them. With ordinary reading material, lip-reading is a bad habit; with poetry, it is a good habit.

4. Always pay careful attention to what the poem is saying. Though you should be conscious of the sounds of the poem, you should never be so exclusively conscious of them that you pay no

attention to what the poem means. For some readers, reading a poem is like getting on board a rhythmical roller coaster. The car starts, and off they go, up and down, paying no attention to the landscape flashing past them, arriving at the end of the poem breathless, with no idea of what it has been about.* This is the wrong way to read a poem. One should make the utmost effort to follow the thought continuously and to grasp the full implications and suggestions. Because a poem says so much, several readings may be necessary, but on the very first reading you should determine the subjects of the verbs, the antecedents of the pronouns, and other normal grammatical facts.

5. Practice reading poems aloud. When you find one you especially like, make friends listen to it. Try to read it to them in such a way that they will like it too. (a) Read it affectionately, but not affectedly. The two extremes oral readers often fall into are equally deadly. One is to read as if one were reading a tax report or a railroad timetable, unexpressively, in a monotone. The other is to elocute, with artificial flourishes and vocal histrionics. It is not necessary to put emotion into reading a poem. The emotion is already there. It only wants a fair chance to get out. It will express *itself* if the poem is read naturally and sensitively. (b) Of the two extremes, reading too fast offers greater danger than reading too slow. Read slowly enough that each word is clear and distinct and that the meaning has time to sink in. Remember that your friends do not have the advantage, as you do, of having the text before them. Your ordinary rate of reading will probably be too fast. (c) Read the poem so that the rhythmical pattern is felt but not exaggerated. Remember that poetry, with few exceptions, is written in sentences, just as prose is, and that punctuation is a signal as to how it should be read. Give all grammatical pauses their full due. Do not distort the natural pronunciation of words or a normal accentuation of the sentence to fit into what you have decided is its metrical pattern. One of the worst ways to read a poem is to read it ta-DUM ta-DUM ta-DUM with an exaggerated emphasis on every other syllable. On the other hand, it should not be read as if it were prose. An important test of your reading will be how you handle the end of a line that lacks line-ending punctuation. A frequent mistake of the beginning reader is to treat each line as if it were a complete thought, whether grammatically complete or not, and to drop the voice at the end of it. A frequent mistake of the sophisticated reader is to take a running start upon approaching the end of a line and fly over

---

*Some poems encourage this type of reading. When this is so, usually the poet has not made the best use of rhythm to support sense.

it as if it were not there. The line is a rhythmical unit, and its end should be observed whether there is punctuation or not. If there is no punctuation, you ordinarily should observe the end of the line by the slightest of pauses or by holding on to the last word in the line just a little longer than usual, without dropping your voice. In line 12 of the following poem, you should hold on to the word "although" longer than if it occurred elsewhere in the line. But do not lower your voice on it: it is part of the clause that follows in the next stanza.

13. The Man He Killed

Had he and I but met
By some old ancient inn,
We should have sat us down to wet
Right many a nipperkin!°   half-pint cup

But ranged as infantry,   5
And staring face to face,
I shot at him as he at me,
And killed him in his place.

I shot him dead because—
Because he was my foe,   10
Just so: my foe of course he was;
That's clear enough; although

He thought he'd 'list, perhaps,
Off-hand-like—just as I—
Was out of work—had sold his traps—°   belongings 15
No other reason why.

Yes; quaint and curious war is!
You shoot a fellow down
You'd treat, if met where any bar is,
Or help to half-a-crown.   20

Thomas Hardy (1840–1928)

QUESTIONS

1. Vocabulary: *half-a-crown* (20).
2. In informational prose the repetition of a word like "because" (9–10) would be an error. What purpose does the repetition serve here? Why does the speaker repeat to himself his "clear" reason for killing a man (10–11)? The word "although" (12) gets more emphasis than it would ordinarily because it comes not only at the end of a line but at the end of

a stanza. What purpose does this emphasis serve? Can the redundancy of "old ancient" (2) be poetically justified?
3. Poetry has been defined as "the expression of elevated thought in elevated language." Comment on the adequacy of this definition in the light of Hardy's poem.

One starting point for understanding a poem at the simplest level, and for clearing up misunderstanding, is to paraphrase its content or part of its content. To **paraphrase** a poem means to restate it in different language, so as to make its prose sense as plain as possible. The paraphrase may be longer or shorter than the poem, but it should contain all the ideas in the poem in such a way as to make them clear to a puzzled reader, and to make the central idea, or **theme,** of the poem more accessible.

14. A Study of Reading Habits

When getting my nose in a book
Cured most things short of school,
It was worth ruining my eyes
To know I could still keep cool,
And deal out the old right hook   5
To dirty dogs twice my size.

Later, with inch-thick specs,
Evil was just my lark:
Me and my cloak and fangs
Had ripping times in the dark.   10
The women I clubbed with sex!
I broke them up like meringues.

Don't read much now: the dude
Who lets the girl down before
The hero arrives, the chap   15
Who's yellow and keeps the store,
Seem far too familiar. Get stewed:
Books are a load of crap.

Philip Larkin (1922–1985)

QUESTIONS

1. The three stanzas delineate three stages in the speaker's life. Describe each.
2. What kind of person is the speaker? What kinds of books does he read? May we identify him with the poet?

3. Contrast the speaker's advice in stanza 3 with Terence's counsel in "Terence, this is stupid stuff" (No. 11). Are A. E. Housman and Philip Larkin at odds in their attitudes toward drinking and reading? Discuss.

Larkin's poem may be paraphrased as follows:

There was a time when reading was one way I could avoid almost all my troubles—except for school. It seemed worth the danger of ruining my eyes to read stories in which I could imagine myself maintaining my poise in the face of threats and having the boxing skill and experience needed to defeat bullies who were twice as big as I.

Later, already having to wear thick glasses because my eyesight had become so poor, I found my delight in stories of sex and evil: imagining myself with Dracula cloak and fangs, I relished vicious nocturnal adventures. I fancied myself a rapist who beat and tortured his delectable, vulnerable victims, leaving them broken and destroyed!

I don't read much any more because now I can identify myself only with the flawed secondary characters, such as the flashy dresser who wins the heroine's confidence and then betrays her in a moment of crisis before the cowboy hero comes to her rescue, or the cowardly storekeeper who cringes behind the counter at the first sign of danger. Getting drunk is better than reading—books are just full of useless lies.

Notice that in a paraphrase, figurative language gives way to literal language; similes replace metaphors and normal word order supplants inverted syntax. But a paraphrase retains the speaker's use of first, second, and third person, and the tenses of verbs. Though it is neither necessary nor possible to avoid using some of the words found in the original, a paraphrase should strive for plain, direct diction. And since a paraphrase is prose, it does not maintain the length and position of poetic lines.

A paraphrase is useful only if you understand that it is the barest, most inadequate approximation of what the poem really "says" and is no more equivalent to the poem than a corpse is to a person. After you have paraphrased a poem, you should endeavor to see how far short of the poem it falls, and why. In what respects does Larkin's poem say more, and say it more memorably, than the paraphrase?

Does the phrase "full of useless lies" capture the impact of "a load of crap"? Furthermore, a paraphrase may fall far short of revealing the theme of a poem. "A Study of Reading Habits" represents a man summing up his reading experience and evaluating it—but in turn the poem itself evaluates *him* and his defects. A statement of the theme of the poem might be this: A person who turns to books as a source of self-gratifying fantasies may, in the course of time, discover that escapist reading no longer protects him from his awareness of his own reality, and he may out of habit have to find other, more potent, and perhaps more self-destructive means of escaping.

To aid us in the understanding of a poem, we may ask ourselves a number of questions about it. Two of the most important are *Who is the speaker?* and *What is the occasion?* A cardinal error of some readers is to assume that a speaker who uses the first person pronouns (*I, my, mine, me*) is always the poet. A less risky course would be to assume always that the speaker is someone other than the poet. Poems, like short stories, novels, and plays, belong to the world of fiction, an imaginatively conceived world that at its best is "truer" than the factually "real" world that it reflects. When poets put themselves or their thoughts into a poem, they present a *version* of themselves; that is, they present a person who in many ways is *like* themselves but who, consciously or unconsciously, is shaped to fit the needs of the poem. We must be very careful, therefore, about identifying anything in a poem with the biography of the poet.

However, caution is not prohibition. Sometimes events or ideas in a poem will help us to understand some episodes in the poet's life. More importantly for us, knowledge of the poet's life may help us understand a poem. There can be little doubt, when all the evidence is in, that "Terence, this is stupid stuff" (No. 11) is Housman's defense of the kind of poetry he writes, and that the six lines in which Terence sums up his beliefs about life and the function of poetry closely echo Housman's own beliefs. On the other hand, it would be folly to suppose that Housman ever got drunk at "Ludlow fair" and once lay down in "lovely muck" and slept all night in a roadside ditch.

We may well think of every poem, therefore, as being to some degree *dramatic*—that is, the utterance not of the person who wrote the poem but of a fictional character in a particular situation that may be inferred. Many poems are expressly dramatic. The fact that Philip Larkin was a poet and novelist, and for many years the chief administrator of a university library, underscores the wide gap between the author and speaker of "A Study of Reading Habits."

In "The Man He Killed" the speaker is a soldier; the occasion is his having been in battle and killed a man—obviously for the first time in his life. We can tell a good deal about him. He is not a career soldier: he enlisted only because he was out of work. He is a working-man: he speaks a simple and colloquial language ("nipperkin," " 'list," "off-hand-like," "traps"). He is a friendly, kindly sort who enjoys a neighborly drink of ale in a bar and will gladly lend a friend a half crown when he has it. He has known what it is to be poor. In any other circumstances he would have been horrified at taking a human life. It gives him pause even now. He is trying to figure it out. But he is not a deep thinker and thinks he has supplied a reason when he has only supplied a name: "I killed the man . . . because he was my foe." The critical question, of course, is *why* was the man his "foe"? Even the speaker is left unsatisfied by his answer, though he is not analytical enough to know what is wrong with it. Obviously this poem is expressly dramatic. We need know nothing about Thomas Hardy's life (he was never a soldier and never killed a man) to realize that the poem is dramatic. The internal evidence of the poem tells us so.

A third important question that we should ask ourselves upon reading any poem is *What is the central purpose of the poem?** The purpose may be to tell a story, to reveal human character, to impart a vivid impression of a scene, to express a mood or an emotion, or to convey vividly some idea or attitude. Whatever the purpose is, we must determine it for ourselves and define it mentally as precisely as possible. Only by relating the various details in the poem to the central purpose or theme can we fully understand their function and meaning. Only then can we begin to assess the value of the poem and determine whether it is a good one or a poor one. In "The Man He Killed" the central purpose is quite clear: it is to make us realize more keenly the irrationality of war. The puzzlement of the speaker may be our puzzlement. But even if we are able to give a more sophisticated answer than his as to why men kill each other, we ought still to have a greater awareness, after reading the poem, of the fundamental irrationality in war that makes men kill who have no grudge against each other and who might under different circumstances show each other considerable kindness.

---

*Our only reliable evidence of the poem's purpose, of course, is the poem itself. External evidence, when it exists, though often helpful, may also be misleading. Some critics have objected to the use of such terms as "purpose" and "intention" altogether; we cannot know, they maintain, what was *attempted* in the poem; we can know only what was *done*. We are concerned, however, not with the *poet's* purpose, but with the *poem's* purpose; that is, with the theme (if it has one), and this is determinable from the poem itself.

15. Is my team plowing

"Is my team plowing,
    That I was used to drive
And hear the harness jingle
    When I was man alive?"

Aye, the horses trample,   5
    The harness jingles now;
No change though you lie under
    The land you used to plow.

"Is football playing
    Along the river shore,   10
With lads to chase the leather,
    Now I stand up no more?"

Aye, the ball is flying,
    The lads play heart and soul;
The goal stands up, the keeper   15
    Stands up to keep the goal.

"Is my girl happy,
    That I thought hard to leave,
And has she tired of weeping
    As she lies down at eve?"   20

Aye, she lies down lightly,
    She lies not down to weep:
Your girl is well contented.
    Be still, my lad, and sleep.

"Is my friend hearty,   25
    Now I am thin and pine;
And has he found to sleep in
    A better bed than mine?"

Yes, lad, I lie easy,
    I lie as lads would choose;   30
I cheer a dead man's sweetheart,
    Never ask me whose.

A. E. Housman (1859–1936)

QUESTIONS

1. What is meant by "whose" in line 32?
2. Is Housman cynical in his observation of human nature and human life?

3. The word *sleep* in the concluding stanzas suggests three different meanings. What are they? How many meanings are suggested by the word *bed*?

Once we have answered the question *What is the central purpose of
the poem?* we can consider another question, equally important to full
understanding: *By what means is that purpose achieved?* It is important
to distinguish means from ends. A student on an examination once
used the poem "Is my team plowing" as evidence that A. E. Housman
believed in immortality because in it a man speaks from the grave.
This is as much a misconstruction as to say that Thomas Hardy in
"The Man He Killed" joined the army because he was out of work.
The purpose of Housman's poem is to communicate poignantly a
certain truth about human life: Life goes on after our deaths pretty
much as it did before—our dying does not disturb the universe. Further, it dramatizes that irrational sense of betrayal and guilt that may
follow the death of a friend. The poem achieves this purpose by means
of a fanciful dramatic framework in which a dead man converses with
his still-living friend. The framework tells us nothing about whether
Housman believed in immortality (as a matter of fact, he did not). It
is simply an effective means by which we *can* learn how Housman felt
a man's death affected the life he left behind. The question *By what
means is that purpose achieved?* is partially answered by describing the
poem's dramatic framework, if it has any. The complete answer requires an accounting of various resources of communication that we
will discuss in this book.

The most important preliminary advice we can give for reading
poetry is to maintain always, while reading it, the utmost mental alertness. The most harmful idea one can get about poetry is that its purpose is to soothe and relax and that the best place to read it is lying in
a hammock with a cool drink while low music plays in the back-
ground. You *can* read poetry lying in a hammock, but only if you
refuse to put your mind in the same attitude as your body. Its purpose
is not to soothe and relax but to arouse and awake, to shock us into
life, to make us more alive. Poetry is not a substitute for a sedative.

An analogy can be drawn between reading poetry and playing
tennis. Both offer great enjoyment if the game is played hard. Good
tennis players must be constantly on the tips of their toes, concentrat-
ing on their opponent's every move. They must be ready for a drive to
the right or left, a lob overhead, or a drop shot barely over the net.
They must be ready for topspin or underspin, a ball that bounces
crazily to the left or right. They must jump for the high ones and run

for the long ones. And they will enjoy the game almost exactly in proportion to the effort they put into it. The same is true of reading poetry. Great enjoyment is there, but this enjoyment demands a mental effort equivalent to the physical effort one puts into tennis.

The reader of poetry has one advantage over the tennis player: poets are not trying to win matches. They may expect the reader to stretch for their shots, but they *want* the reader to return them.

GENERAL EXERCISES FOR ANALYSIS AND EVALUATION

Most of the poems in this book are accompanied by study questions that are by no means exhaustive. The following is a list of questions that you may apply to any poem. You may be unable to answer many of them until you have read further into the book.

1. Who is the speaker? What kind of person is the speaker?
2. Is there an identifiable audience for the speaker? What can we know about it (her, him, or them)?
3. What is the occasion?
4. What is the setting in time (hour, season, century, and so on)?
5. What is the setting in place (indoors or out, city or country, land or sea, region, nation, hemisphere)?
6. What is the central purpose of the poem?
7. State the central idea or theme of the poem in a sentence.
8. a. Outline the poem so as to show its structure and development, or
   b. Summarize the events of the poem.
9. Paraphrase the poem.
10. Discuss the diction of the poem. Point out words that are particularly well chosen and explain why.
11. Discuss the imagery of the poem. What kinds of imagery are used? Is there a structure of imagery?
12. Point out examples of metaphor, simile, personification, and metonymy, and explain their appropriateness.
13. Point out and explain any symbols. If the poem is allegorical, explain the allegory.
14. Point out and explain examples of paradox, overstatement, understatement, and irony. What is their function?
15. Point out and explain any allusions. What is their function?
16. What is the tone of the poem? How is it achieved?
17. Point out significant examples of sound repetition and explain their function.
18. a. What is the meter of the poem?
    b. Copy the poem and mark its scansion.
19. Discuss the adaptation of sound to sense.
20. Describe the form or pattern of the poem.
21. Criticize and evaluate the poem.

16. Break of Day

'Tis true, 'tis day; what though it be?
Oh, wilt thou therefore rise from me?
Why should we rise because 'tis light?
Did we lie down because 'twas night?
Love which in spite of darkness brought us hither   5
Should, in despite of light, keep us together.

Light hath no tongue, but is all eye;
If it could speak as well as spy,
This were the worst that it could say:
That, being well, I fain would stay,   10
And that I loved my heart and honor so,
That I would not from him that had them go.

Must business thee from hence remove?
Oh, that's the worst disease of love;
The poor, the foul, the false, love can   15
Admit, but not the busied man.
He which hath business and makes love, doth do
Such wrong as when a married man doth woo.

John Donne (1572–1631)

QUESTIONS

1. Who is the speaker? Who is addressed? What is the situation? Can the speaker be identified with the poet?
2. Explain the comparison in line 7. To whom does "I" (10–12) refer? Is "love" (15) the subject or object of "can admit"?
3. Summarize the arguments used by the speaker to keep the person addressed from leaving. What is the speaker's scale of value?
4. Are the two persons married or unmarried? Justify your answer.

17. There's been a death in the opposite house

There's been a death in the opposite house
As lately as today.
I know it by the numb look
Such houses have alway.

The neighbors rustle in and out,   5
The doctor drives away.
A window opens like a pod,
Abrupt, mechanically;

Somebody flings a mattress out—
The children hurry by;   10
They wonder if it died on that—
I used to when a boy.

The minister goes stiffly in
As if the house were his,
And he owned all the mourners now,   15
And little boys besides;

And then the milliner, and the man
Of the appalling trade,
To take the measure of the house.

There'll be that dark parade   20

Of tassels and of coaches soon.
It's easy as a sign,
The intuition of the news
In just a country town.

Emily Dickinson (1830–1886)

QUESTIONS

1. What can we know about the speaker in the poem?
2. By what signs does the speaker "intuit" that a death has occurred? Explain them stanza by stanza. What does it mean that the speaker must intuit rather than simply *know* that death has taken place?
3. Comment on the words "appalling" (18) and "dark" (20).
4. What shift in the poem is signaled by the separation of line 20 from the end of stanza 5?
5. What is the speaker's attitude toward death?

18. When in Rome

Mattie dear
the box is full
take
whatever you like
to eat   5
    (an egg
    or soup
      . . . there ain't no meat.)
there's endive there
and   10

cottage cheese
        (whew! if I had some
        black-eyed peas . . .)
there's sardines
on the shelves   15
and such
but
don't
get my anchovies
they cost   20
too much!
        (me get the
        anchovies indeed!
        what she think, she got—
        a bird to feed?)   25
there's plenty in there
to fill you up.
        (yes'm. just the
        sight's
        enough!   30

Hope I lives till I get
home
I'm tired of eatin'
what they eats in Rome . . .)

Mari Evans

QUESTIONS

1. Who are the two speakers? What is the situation? Why are the second speaker's words enclosed in parentheses?
2. What are the attitudes of the two speakers toward one another? What is the attitude of each to herself?
3. What implications have the title and the last two lines?

19. The River-Merchant's Wife: A Letter

While my hair was still cut straight across my forehead
I played about the front gate, pulling flowers.
You came by on bamboo stilts, playing horse,
You walked about my seat, playing with blue plums,
And we went on living in the village of Chokan: 5
Two small people, without dislike or suspicion.

At fourteen I married My Lord you.
I never laughed, being bashful.
Lowering my head, I looked at the wall.
Called to, a thousand times, I never looked back.   10

At fifteen I stopped scowling,
I desired my dust to be mingled with yours
Forever and forever and forever.
Why should I climb the lookout?

At sixteen you departed,   15
You went into far Ku-to-yen, by the river of swirling eddies,
And you have been gone five months.
The monkeys make sorrowful noise overhead.

You dragged your feet when you went out.
By the gate now, the moss is grown, the different mosses,   20
Too deep to clear them away!
The leaves fall early this autumn, in wind.
The paired butterflies are already yellow with August
Over the grass in the West garden;
They hurt me. I grow older.   25
If you are coming down through the narrows of the river Kiang,
Please let me know beforehand,
And I will come out to meet you
                    As far as Cho-fu-sa.

                                        Ezra Pound (1885–1972)

QUESTIONS

1. Trace the stages in the speaker's life. Why do you suppose the husband
   departed? How do the small details provide clues about the woman's
   emotional states in each of the stages? For example, how does "pulling
   flowers" (2) give insight into the life of a child?
2. This poem is a translated adaptation of a poem by the Chinese poet Li
   Po (701–762). What does the indirect method of presenting the events
   contribute to your responses to the poem? What would you say is the
   central purpose?

20. The Mill

> The miller's wife had waited long,
>   The tea was cold, the fire was dead;
> And there might yet be nothing wrong

In how he went and what he said:
"There are no millers any more,"   5
  Was all that she had heard him say;
And he had lingered at the door
  So long that it seemed yesterday.

Sick with a fear that had no form
  She knew that she was there at last;   10
And in the mill there was a warm
  And mealy fragrance of the past.
What else there was would only seem
  To say again what he had meant;
And what was hanging from a beam   15
  Would not have heeded where she went.

And if she thought it followed her,
  She may have reasoned in the dark
That one way of the few there were
  Would hide her and would leave no mark: 20
Black water, smooth above the weir
  Like starry velvet in the night,
Though ruffled once, would soon appear
  The same as ever to the sight.

Edwin Arlington Robinson (1869–1935)

QUESTIONS

1. What is the meaning of the husband's remark in line 5? What has the husband's occupation been, and what historical developments would lead him to make that remark?
2. What does the miller's wife find in the mill in stanza 2? What does she do in stanza 3? Why?
3. Distinguish means from ends: is it the central purpose of this poem to relate the events, or to reveal the thoughts of the wife? Poets, especially modern poets, are sometimes accused of being perversely obscure. Certainly this poem tells its story in a roundabout way—by hints and implications rather than by direct statements. What is the justification for this "obscurity"?
4. What details of the poem especially bring it to life as experience?

21. Mirror

I am silver and exact. I have no preconceptions.
Whatever I see I swallow immediately
Just as it is, unmisted by love or dislike.

I am not cruel, only truthful—
The eye of a little god, four-cornered.   5
Most of the time I meditate on the opposite wall.
It is pink, with speckles. I have looked at it so long
I think it is a part of my heart. But it flickers.
Faces and darkness separate us over and over.

Now I am a lake. A woman bends over me,   10
Searching my reaches for what she really is.
Then she turns to those liars, the candles or the moon.
I see her back, and reflect it faithfully.
She rewards me with tears and an agitation of hands.
I am important to her. She comes and goes.   15
Each morning it is her face that replaces the darkness.
In me she has drowned a young girl, and in me an old woman
Rises toward her day after day, like a terrible fish.

                                              Sylvia Plath (1932–1963)

QUESTIONS

1. Who is the speaker? What is the central purpose of the poem, and by
   what means is it achieved?
2. In what ways is the mirror like and unlike a person (stanza 1)? In what
   ways is it like a lake (stanza 2)?
3. What is the meaning of the last two lines?

22. The Subalterns

"Poor wanderer," said the leaden sky,
    "I fain would lighten thee,
But there are laws in force on high
    Which say it must not be."

"I would not freeze thee, shorn one," cried   5
    The North, "knew I but how
To warm my breath, to slack my stride;
    But I am ruled as thou."

"Tomorrow I attack thee, wight,"
    Said Sickness. "Yet I swear   10
I bear thy little ark no spite,
    But am bid enter there."

"Come hither, Son," I heard Death say;
    "I did not will a grave

Should end thy pilgrimage today,   15
But I, too, am a slave!"

We smiled upon each other then,
    And life to me had less
Of that fell look it wore ere when
    They owned their passiveness.   20

Thomas Hardy (1840–1928)

QUESTIONS

1. Vocabulary: *subalterns* (title), *wight* (9), *ark* (11), *fell* (19), *owned* (20).
2. Paraphrase the last stanza, and explain the psychological reaction it displays.
3. Contrast the language and sentence structures of this poem to those of "The Man He Killed" (No. 13). Is there any reason to suppose that either of these poems reflects the poet's own manner of speaking? Explain.

EXERCISE

Here are three definitions of poetry, all framed by poets themselves. Which definition best fits the poems you have so far read? Discuss.

1. Poetry is Transfiguration, the transfiguration of the Actual or the Real into the Ideal, at a lofty elevation, through the medium of melodious or nobly sounding verse.   *Alfred Austin*

2. The art of poetry is simply the art of electrifying language with extraordinary meaning.   *Lascelles Abercrombie*

3. A poem consists of all the purest and most beautiful elements in the poet's nature, crystalized into the aptest and most exquisite language, and adorned with all the outer embellishment of musical cadence or dainty rhyme.   *Grant Allen*

CHAPTER THREE

Denotation and Connotation

A primary distinction between the practical use of language and the literary use is that in literature, especially in poetry, a *fuller* use is made of individual words. To understand this, we need to examine the composition of a word.

The average word has three component parts: sound, denotation, and connotation. It begins as a combination of tones and noises, uttered by the lips, tongue, and throat, for which the written word is a notation. But it differs from a musical tone or a noise in that it has a meaning attached to it. The basic part of this meaning is its **denotation** or denotations: that is, the dictionary meaning or meanings of the word. Beyond its denotations, a word may also have connotations. The **connotations** are what it suggests beyond what it expresses: its overtones of meaning. It acquires these connotations from its past history and associations, from the way and the circumstances in which it has been used. The word *home,* for instance, by denotation means only a place where one lives, but by connotation it suggests security, love, comfort, and family. The words *childlike* and *childish* both mean "characteristic of a child," but *childlike* suggests meekness, innocence, and wide-eyed wonder, while *childish* suggests pettiness, willfulness, and temper tantrums. If we list the names of different coins—nickel, peso, lira, shilling, sen, doubloon—the word *doubloon,* to four out of five readers, immediately will suggest pirates, though a dictionary definition includes nothing about pirates. Pirates are part of its connotation.

Connotation is very important in poetry, for it is one of the means by which the poet can concentrate or enrich meaning—say more in fewer words. Consider, for instance, the following short poem:

23. There is no frigate like a book

> There is no frigate like a book
> To take us lands away,
> Nor any coursers like a page

Of prancing poetry.
This traverse may the poorest take   5
Without oppress of toll.
How frugal is the chariot
That bears the human soul!

Emily Dickinson (1830–1886)

In this poem Emily Dickinson is considering the power of a book or of poetry to carry us away, to take us from our immediate surroundings into a world of the imagination. To do this she has compared literature to various means of transportation: a boat, a team of horses, a wheeled land vehicle. But she has been careful to choose kinds of transportation and names for them that have romantic connotations. "Frigate" suggests exploration and adventure; "coursers," beauty, spirit, and speed; "chariot," speed and the ability to go through the air as well as on land. (Compare "Swing Low, Sweet Chariot" and the myth of Phaëthon, who tried to drive the chariot of Apollo, and the famous painting of Aurora with her horses, once hung in almost every school.) How much of the meaning of the poem comes from this selection of vehicles and words is apparent if we were to substitute *steamship* for "frigate," *horses* for "coursers," and *streetcar* for "chariot."

QUESTIONS

1. What is lost if *miles* is substituted for "lands" (2) or *cheap* for "frugal" (7)?
2. How is "prancing" (4) peculiarly appropriate to poetry as well as to coursers? Could the poet without loss have compared a book to coursers and poetry to a frigate?
3. Is this account appropriate to all kinds of poetry or just to certain kinds? That is, was the poet thinking of poems like Wilfred Owen's "Dulce et Decorum Est" (No. 3) or of poems like Coleridge's "Kubla Khan" (No. 211) and Keats's "La Belle Dame sans Merci" (No. 247)?

Just as a word has a variety of connotations, so may it have more than one denotation. If we look up the word *spring* in the dictionary, for instance, we will find that it has between twenty-five and thirty distinguishable meanings: It may mean (1) a pounce or leap, (2) a season of the year, (3) a natural source of water, (4) a coiled elastic wire, and so forth. This variety of denotation, complicated by additional tones of connotation, makes language confusing and difficult to use. Any person using words must be careful to define precisely by context the denotation that is intended. But the difference between the writer using language to communicate and the poet is this: the practical writer will always attempt to confine words to one denotation at a time; the poet will often take advantage of the fact that the word has more than one meaning by using it to mean more than one thing at the same time. Thus when Edith Sitwell in one of her poems writes, "This is the time of the wild spring and the mating of the tigers,"* she uses the word "spring" to denote both a season of the year and a sudden leap (and she uses "tigers" rather than *deer* or *birds* because it has a connotation of fierceness and wildness that the others lack). The two denotations of "spring" are also appropriately possessed of contrasting connotations: the season is positive in its implications, while a sudden leap may connote the pouncing of a beast of prey. Similarly, in "Mirror" (No. 21), the word "swallow" in line 2 denotes both accepting without question and consuming or devouring, and so connotes both an inability to think on the one hand, and obliteration or destruction on the other.

24. When my love swears that she is made of truth

> When my love swears that she is made of truth,
> I do believe her, though I know she lies,
> That she might think me some untutored youth,
> Unlearnèd in the world's false subtleties.
> Thus vainly thinking that she thinks me young,   5
> Although she knows my days are past the best,
> Simply I credit her false-speaking tongue;
> On both sides thus is simple truth supprest.
> But wherefore says she not she is unjust?°   unfaithful
> And wherefore say not I that I am old?   10
> Oh, love's best habit is in seeming trust,
> And age in love loves not to have years told:
> Therefore I lie with her and she with me,
> And in our faults by lies we flattered be.

William Shakespeare (1564–1616)

QUESTIONS

1. How old is the speaker? How old is his beloved? What is the nature of their relationship?

Collected Poems (New York: Vanguard, 1954) 392.

2. How is the contradiction in line 2 to be resolved? In lines 5–6? Who is lying to whom?
3. How do "simply" (7) and "simple" (8) differ in meaning? The words "vainly" (5), "habit" (11), "told" (12), and "lie" (13) all have double denotative meanings. What are they?
4. What is the tone of the poem—that is, the attitude of the speaker toward his situation? Should line 11 be taken as an expression of (a) wisdom, (b) conscious rationalization, or (c) self-deception? In answering these questions, consider both the situation and the connotations of all the important words beginning with "swears" (1) and ending with "flattered" (14).

A frequent misconception of poetic language is that poets seek always the most beautiful or noble-sounding words. What they really seek are the most *meaningful* words, and these vary from one context to another. Language has many levels and varieties, and poets may choose from all of them. Their words may be grandiose or humble, fanciful or matter-of-fact, romantic or realistic, archaic or modern, technical or everyday, monosyllabic or polysyllabic. Usually a poem will be pitched pretty much in one key: the words in Emily Dickinson's "There is no frigate like a book" (No. 23) and those in Thomas Hardy's "The Man He Killed" (No. 13) are chosen from quite different areas of language, but both poets have chosen the words most meaningful for their own poetic context. It is always important to determine the level of diction employed in a poem, for it may provide clear insight into the purpose of the poem by helping to characterize the speaker. Sometimes a poet may import a word from one level or area of language into a poem composed mostly of words from a different level or area. If this is done clumsily, the result will be incongruous and sloppy; if it is done skillfully, the result will be a shock of surprise and an increment of meaning for the reader. In fact, the many varieties of language open to poets provide their richest resource. Their task is one of constant exploration and discovery. They search always for the secret affinities of words that allow them to be brought together with soft explosions of meaning.

25. Pathedy of Manners

At twenty she was brilliant and adored,
Phi Beta Kappa, sought for every dance;
Captured symbolic logic and the glance
Of men whose interest was their sole reward.

She learned the cultured jargon of those bred   5
To antique crystal and authentic pearls,
Scorned Wagner, praised the Degas dancing girls,
And when she might have thought, conversed instead.

She hung up her diploma, went abroad,
Saw catalogues of domes and tapestry,   10
Rejected an impoverished marquis,
And learned to tell real Wedgwood from a fraud.

Back home her breeding led her to espouse
A bright young man whose pearl cufflinks were real.
They had an ideal marriage, and ideal   15
But lonely children in an ideal house.

I saw her yesterday at forty-three,
Her children gone, her husband one year dead,
Toying with plots to kill time and re-wed
Illusions of lost opportunity.   20

But afraid to wonder what she might have known
With all that wealth and mind had offered her,
She shuns conviction, choosing to infer
Tenets of every mind except her own.

A hundred people call, though not one friend,   25
To parry a hundred doubts with nimble talk.
Her meanings lost in manners, she will walk
Alone in brilliant circles to the end.

Ellen Kay (b. 1931)

QUESTIONS

1. The title alludes to the type of drama called "comedy of manners" and coins a word combining the suffix -*edy* with the Greek root *path*- (as in *pathetic, sympathy, pathology*). How does the poem narrate a story with both comic and pathetic implications? For what might the central character be blamed? What arouses our pity for her?
2. Explore the multiple denotations and the connotations attached to each denotation of "brilliant" (both in 1 and 28), "interest" and "reward" (4), "cultured" and "jargon" (5), "circles" (28).
3. Why are the poet's words more effective than these possible synonyms: "captured" (3) rather than *learned;* "conversed" (8) rather than *chatted, gossiped,* or *talked;* "catalogues" (10) rather than *volumes* or *multitudes;* "espouse" (13) rather than *marry?* Discuss the momentary ambiguity presented by the word "re-wed" (19).

4. At what point in the poem does the speaker shift from language that represents the way the woman might have talked about herself to language that reveals how the speaker judges her? Point out examples of both kinds of language.

People using language only to convey information are usually indifferent to the sounds of the words and are hampered by their connotations and multiple denotations. They would rather confine each word to a single, exact meaning. They use, one might say, a fraction of the word and throw away the rest. Poets, on the other hand, use as much of the word as possible. They are interested in connotation and use it to enrich and convey meaning. And they may rely on more than one denotation.

The purest form of practical language is scientific language. Scientists need a precise language to convey information precisely. The existence of multiple denotations and various overtones of meaning hinders them from accomplishing their purpose. Their ideal language would be a language with a one-to-one correspondence between word and meaning; that is, every word would have only one meaning, and for every meaning there would be only one word. Since ordinary language does not fulfill these conditions, scientists have invented languages that do. A statement in one of these languages may look like this:

$$SO_2 + H_2O = H_2SO_3$$

In such a statement the symbols are entirely unambiguous; they have been stripped of all connotation and of all denotations but one. The word *sulfurous,* if it occurred in poetry, might have all kinds of connotations: fire, smoke, brimstone, hell, damnation. But H_2SO_3 means one thing and one thing only: sulfurous acid.

The ambiguity and multiplicity of meanings possessed by words are an obstacle to the scientist but a resource to the poet. Where the scientist wants singleness of meaning, the poet wants richness of meaning. Where the scientist requires and has invented a strictly one-dimensional language in which every word is confined to one denotation, the poet needs a multidimensional language and creates it partly by using a multidimensional vocabulary, in which the dimensions of connotation and sound are added to the dimension of denotation.

The poet, we may say, plays on a many-stringed instrument and sounds more than one note at a time.

The first task in reading poetry, therefore, as in reading any kind of literature, is to develop a sense of language, a feeling for words. One needs to become acquainted with their shape, their color, and their flavor. There are two ways of doing this: extensive use of the dictionary and extensive reading.

EXERCISES

1. Which word in each group has the most "romantic" connotations: (a) horse, steed, nag; (b) king, ruler, tyrant, autocrat; (c) Chicago, Pittsburgh, Samarkand, Birmingham?
2. Which word in each group is the most emotionally connotative: (a) female parent, mother, dam; (b) offspring, children, progeny; (c) brother, sibling?
3. Arrange the words in each of the following groups from most positive to most negative in connotation: (a) skinny, thin, gaunt, slender; (b) prosperous, loaded, moneyed, opulent; (c) brainy, intelligent, eggheaded, smart.
4. Of the following, which should you be less offended at being accused of: (a) having acted foolishly, (b) having acted like a fool?
5. In any competent piece of writing, the possible multiple denotations and connotations of the words used are controlled by context. The context screens out irrelevant meanings while allowing the relevant meanings to pass through. What denotation has the word *fast* in the following contexts: fast runner, fast color, fast living, fast day? What are the varying connotations of these four denotations of *fast?*
6. Explain how, in the following examples the denotation of the word *white* remains the same, but the connotations differ: (a) The young princess had blue eyes, golden hair, and a breast as white as snow; (b) Confronted with the evidence, the false princess turned as white as a sheet.

26. Naming of Parts

Today we have naming of parts. Yesterday,
We had daily cleaning. And tomorrow morning,
We shall have what to do after firing. But today,
Today we have naming of parts. Japonica
Glistens like coral in all of the neighboring gardens,   5
    And today we have naming of parts.

This is the lower sling swivel. And this
Is the upper sling swivel, whose use you will see,
When you are given your slings. And this is the piling swivel,
Which in your case you have not got. The branches   10
Hold in the gardens their silent, eloquent gestures,
    Which in our case we have not got.

This is the safety-catch, which is always released
With an easy flick of the thumb. And please do not let me
See anyone using his finger. You can do it quite easy   15
If you have any strength in your thumb. The blossoms
Are fragile and motionless, never letting anyone see
    Any of them using their finger.

And this you can see is the bolt. The purpose of this
Is to open the breech, as you see. We can slide it   20
Rapidly backwards and forwards: we call this
Easing the spring. And rapidly backwards and forwards
The early bees are assaulting and fumbling the flowers:
    They call it easing the Spring.

They call it easing the Spring: it is perfectly easy   25
If you have any strength in your thumb: like the bolt,
And the breech, and the cocking-piece, and the point of balance,
Which in our case we have not got; and the almond-blossom
Silent in all of the gardens and the bees going backwards and forwards,
    For today we have naming of parts.   30

Henry Reed (1914–1986)

QUESTIONS

1. Who is the speaker (or speakers) in the poem, and what is the situation?
2. What basic contrasts are represented by the trainees and by the gardens?
3. What is it that trainees "have not got" (28)? How many meanings have
   the phrases "easing the spring" (22) and "point of balance" (27)?
4. What differences in language and rhythm do you find between the lines
   that involve the "naming of parts" and those that describe the gardens?
5. Does the repetition of certain phrases throughout the poem have any special function or does it merely create a kind of refrain?
6. What statement does the poem make about war as it affects men and
   their lives?

27. Cross

My old man's a white old man
And my old mother's black.
If ever I cursed my white old man
I take my curses back.

If ever I cursed my black old mother   5
And wished she were in hell,

I'm sorry for that evil wish
And now I wish her well.

My old man died in a fine big house.
My ma died in a shack.   10
I wonder where I'm gonna die,
Being neither white nor black?

Langston Hughes (1902–1967)

QUESTIONS

1. What different denotations does the title have? What connotations are linked to each of them?
2. The language in this poem, such as "old man" (1, 3, 9), "ma" (10), and "gonna" (11), is plain, and even colloquial. Is it appropriate to the subject? Why or why not?

28. The world is too much with us

The world is too much with us; late and soon,
Getting and spending, we lay waste our powers:
Little we see in nature that is ours;
We have given our hearts away, a sordid boon!
This sea that bares her bosom to the moon,   5
The winds that will be howling at all hours,
And are up-gathered now like sleeping flowers,
For this, for everything, we are out of tune;
It moves us not. —Great God! I'd rather be
A pagan suckled in a creed outworn;   10
So might I, standing on this pleasant lea,
Have glimpses that would make me less forlorn;
Have sight of Proteus rising from the sea;
Or hear old Triton blow his wreathèd horn.

William Wordsworth (1770–1850)

QUESTIONS

1. Vocabulary: *boon* (4), *Proteus* (13), *Triton* (14). What two relevant denotations has "wreathèd" (14)?
2. Explain why the poet's words are more effective than these possible alternatives: *earth* for "world" (1); *selling and buying* for "getting and spending" (2); *exposes* for "bares" (5); *dozing* for "sleeping" (7); *posies* for "flowers"

(7); *nourished* for "suckled" (10); *visions* for "glimpses" (12); *sound* for "blow" (14).
3. Should "Great God!" (9) be considered as a vocative (term of address) or an expletive (exclamation)? Or something of both?
4. State the theme (central idea) of the poem in a sentence.

29. Eldorado

Gaily bedight,
A gallant knight,
In sunshine and in shadow,
Had journeyed long,
Singing a song,   5
In search of Eldorado.

But he grew old—
This knight so bold—
And o'er his heart a shadow
Fell, as he found   10
No spot of ground
That looked like Eldorado.

And, as his strength
Failed him at length,
He met a pilgrim shadow—   15
"Shadow," said he,
"Where can it be—
This land of Eldorado?"

"Over the Mountains
Of the Moon,   20
Down the Valley of the Shadow,
Ride, boldly ride,"
The shade replied,—
"If you seek for Eldorado!"

Edgar Allan Poe (1809–1849)

QUESTIONS

1. Eldorado (or El Dorado) was a legendary land of fabulous gold sought in South America by early Spanish explorers. In the poem is this land literal or symbolic—that is, is the quest portrayed as material or spiritual, unworthy or worthy?
2. The word "shadow" has different meanings (both denotative and connotative) in each stanza. Trace and account for the changes of meaning.

3. What is the meaning of the shade's reply in the last stanza? (What does the phrase "Valley of the Shadow" call to mind?) What is the central purpose of the poem?
4. The language used in this poem differs markedly from that used in "A Study of Reading Habits" (No. 14) and "Cross" (No. 27). Describe and illustrate the differences. How do they affect your responses to the themes of these poems?

30. A Hymn to God the Father

Wilt thou forgive that sin where I begun,
    Which is my sin though it were done before?
Wilt thou forgive those sins through which I run,°   ran
    And do them still, though still I do deplore?
      When thou hast done, thou hast not done,   5
      For I have more.

Wilt thou forgive that sin by which I won
    Others to sin, and made my sin their door?
Wilt thou forgive that sin which I did shun
    A year or two, but wallowed in a score?   10
      When thou hast done, thou hast not done,
      For I have more.

I have a sin of fear, that when I have spun
    My last thread, I shall perish on the shore;
Swear by thyself that at my death thy Sun   15
    Shall shine as it shines now, and heretofore;
      And having done that, thou hast done.
      I have no more.

John Donne (1572–1631)

QUESTIONS

1. In 1601, John Donne at 29 secretly married Anne More, age 17, infuriating her upper-class father, who had him imprisoned for three days. Because of the marriage, Donne lost his job as private secretary to an important official at court, and probably ruined his chances for the career at court that he desired. It was, however, a true love match. In 1615 Donne entered the church. In 1617 his wife, then 33, died after bearing twelve children. In 1621 he was appointed Dean of St. Paul's Cathedral in London and quickly won a reputation for his eloquent sermons. His religious poems differ markedly in tone from the often cynical, sometimes erotic poems of his youth. The foregoing poem was probably written during a severe illness in 1623. Is this information of any value to a reader of the poem?

2. What sin is referred to in lines 1–2? What is meant by "when I have spun / My last thread" (13–14)? By "I shall perish on the shore" (14)?
3. How do the puns on "done" (5, 11, 17), "more" (6, 12, 18), and "Sun" (15) give structure and meaning to the poem? Explain the relevance of the meanings generated by the puns.

31. One Art

The art of losing isn't hard to master;
so many things seem filled with the intent
to be lost that their loss is no disaster.

Lose something every day. Accept the fluster
of lost door keys, the hour badly spent.   5
The art of losing isn't hard to master.

Then practice losing farther, losing faster:
places, and names, and where it was you meant
to travel. None of these will bring disaster.

I lost my mother's watch. And look! my last, or   10
next-to-last, of three loved houses went.
The art of losing isn't hard to master.

I lost two cities, lovely ones. And, vaster,
some realms I owned, two rivers, a continent.
I miss them, but it wasn't a disaster.   15

—Even losing you (the joking voice, a gesture
I love) I shan't have lied. It's evident
the art of losing's not too hard to master
though it may look like (*Write* it!) like disaster.

Elizabeth Bishop (1911–1979)

QUESTIONS

1. What various denotations of "lose" and its derivative forms are relevant to the context? What connotations are attached to the separate denotative meanings?
2. Explain how "owned" (14) and "lost" (13) shift the meanings of possessing and losing.
3. What seems to be the purpose of the speaker in the first three tercets (three-line units)? How is the advice given there supported by the personal experiences related in the next two tercets?
4. The concluding quatrain (four-line unit) contains direct address to a person, as well as a command the speaker addresses to herself. How do these details reveal the real purpose of the poem? *Can* all kinds of losses be mastered with "one art of losing"?

CHAPTER FOUR

Imagery

Experience comes to us largely through the senses. Our experiences of a spring day, for instance, may consist partly of certain emotions we feel and partly of certain thoughts we think, but most of it will be a cluster of sense impressions. It will consist of *seeing* blue sky and white clouds, budding leaves and daffodils; of *hearing* robins and bluebirds singing in the early morning; of *smelling* damp earth and blossoming hyacinths; and of *feeling* a fresh wind against one's cheek. A poet seeking to express the experience of a spring day therefore provides a selection of sense impressions. So in "Spring" (No. 4) Shakespeare gives us "daisies pied" and "lady-smocks all silver-white" and "merry larks" and the song of the cuckoo and maidens bleaching their summer smocks. Had he not done so, he might have failed to evoke the emotions that accompany these sensations. The poet's language, then, is more *sensuous* than ordinary language. It is more full of imagery.

Imagery may be defined as the representation through language of sense experience. Poetry appeals directly to our senses, of course, through its music and rhythms, which we actually hear when it is read aloud. But indirectly it appeals to our senses through imagery, the representation to the imagination of sense experience. The word *image* perhaps most often suggests a mental picture, something seen in the mind's eye—and *visual* imagery is the kind of imagery that occurs most frequently in poetry. But an image may also represent a sound (*auditory imagery*); a smell (*olfactory imagery*); a taste (*gustatory imagery*); touch, such as hardness, softness, wetness, or heat and cold (*tactile imagery*); an internal sensation, such as hunger, thirst, fatigue, or nausea (*organic imagery*); or movement or tension in the muscles or joints (*kinesthetic imagery*). If we wish to be scientific, we could extend this list further, for psychologists no longer confine themselves to five or even six senses, but for purposes of discussing poetry the preceding classification should ordinarily be sufficient.

32. Meeting at Night

The gray sea and the long black land;
And the yellow half-moon large and low;
And the startled little waves that leap
In fiery ringlets from their sleep,
As I gain the cove with pushing prow,   5
And quench its speed i' the slushy sand.

Then a mile of warm sea-scented beach;
Three fields to cross till a farm appears;
A tap at the pane, the quick sharp scratch
And blue spurt of a lighted match,   10
And a voice less loud, through its joys and fears,
Than the two hearts beating each to each!

Robert Browning (1812–1889)

"Meeting at Night" is a poem about love. It makes, one might say, a number of statements about love: being in love is a sweet and exciting experience; when one is in love everything seems beautiful, and the most trivial things become significant; when one is in love one's sweetheart seems the most important thing in the world. But the poet actually *tells* us none of these things directly. He does not even use the word *love* in his poem. His business is to communicate experience, not information. He does this largely in two ways. First, he presents us with a specific situation, in which a lover goes to meet his sweetheart. Second, he describes the lover's journey so vividly in terms of sense impressions that the reader virtually sees and hears what the lover saw and heard and seems to share his anticipation and excitement.

Every line in the poem contains some image, some appeal to the senses: the gray sea, the long black land, the yellow half-moon, the startled little waves with their fiery ringlets, the blue spurt of the lighted match—all appeal to our sense of sight and convey not only shape but also color and motion. The warm sea-scented beach appeals to the senses of both smell and touch. The pushing prow of the boat on the slushy sand, the tap at the pane, the quick scratch of the match, the low speech of the lovers, and the sound of their hearts beating—all appeal to the sense of hearing.

33. Parting at Morning

> Round the cape of a sudden came the sea,
> And the sun looked over the mountain's rim:
> And straight was a path of gold for him,
> And the need of a world of men for me.

Robert Browning (1812–1889)

QUESTIONS

1. This poem is a sequel to "Meeting at Night." "[H]im" (3) refers to the sun. Does the last line mean that the lover needs the world of men or that the world of men needs the lover? Or both?
2. Does the sea *actually* come suddenly around the cape or *appear* to? Why does Browning mention the *effect* before its *cause* (the sun looking over the mountain's rim)?
3. Do these poems (32 and 33), taken together, suggest any larger truths about love? Browning, in answer to a question, said that the second part is the man's confession of "how fleeting is the belief (implied in the first part) that such raptures are self-sufficient and enduring—as for the time they appear."

The sharpness and vividness of any image will ordinarily depend on how specific it is and on the poet's use of effective detail. The word *hummingbird,* for instance, conveys a more definite image than does *bird,* and *ruby-throated hummingbird* is sharper and more specific still. However, to represent something vividly a poet need not describe it completely. One or two especially sharp and representative details will often serve, inviting the reader's imagination to fill in the rest. Tennyson in "The Eagle" (No. 1) gives only one visual detail about the eagle itself—that he clasps the crag with "crooked hands"—but this detail is an effective and memorable one. Robinson in "The Mill" (No. 20) withholds specific information about the life that the miller and his wife had shared, but the fact that she smells "a warm / And mealy fragrance of the past" when she enters the mill speaks volumes about her sense of loss. Browning, in "Meeting at Night," calls up a whole scene with "A tap at the pane, the quick sharp scratch / And blue spurt of a lighted match."

Since imagery is a peculiarly effective way of evoking vivid experience, and since it may be used to convey emotion and suggest ideas as well as to cause a mental reproduction of sensations, it is an invaluable resource of the poet. In general, the poet will seek concrete or image-bearing words in preference to abstract or non-image-bearing words. We cannot evaluate a poem, however, by the amount or quality of its imagery alone. Sense impression is only one of the elements of experience. Poetry may attain its ends by other means. We should never judge any single element of a poem except in reference to the total intent of that poem.

34. Spring

Nothing is so beautiful as spring—
    When weeds, in wheels, shoot long and lovely and lush;
    Thrush's eggs look little low heavens, and thrush
Through the echoing timber does so rinse and wring
The ear, it strikes like lightnings to hear him sing;   5
    The glassy peartree leaves and blooms, they brush
    The descending blue; that blue is all in a rush
With richness; the racing lambs too have fair their fling.

What is all this juice and all this joy?
    A strain of the earth's sweet being in the beginning   10
In Eden garden. —Have, get, before it cloy,

    Before it cloud, Christ, lord, and sour with sinning,
Innocent mind and Mayday in girl and boy,
    Most, O maid's child, thy choice and worthy the winning.

Gerard Manley Hopkins (1844–1889)

QUESTIONS

1. The first line makes an abstract statement. How is this statement brought to carry conviction?
2. The sky is described as being "all in a rush / With richness" (7–8). In what other respects is the poem "rich"?
3. To what two things does the speaker compare the spring in lines 9–14? In what ways are the comparisons appropriate?
4. Lines 11–14 might be made clearer by paraphrasing them thus: "Christ, lord, child of the Virgin: save the innocent mind of girl and boy before sin taints it, since it is most like yours and worth saving." Why are Hopkins's lines more effective, both in imagery and in syntax?

35. The Widow's Lament in Springtime

Sorrow is my own yard
where the new grass
flames as it has flamed
often before but not
with the cold fire   5
that closes round me this year.
Thirtyfive years
I lived with my husband.
The plumtree is white today
with masses of flowers.   10
Masses of flowers
load the cherry branches
and color some bushes
yellow and some red
but the grief in my heart   15
is stronger than they
for though they were my joy
formerly, today I notice them
and turned away forgetting.
Today my son told me   20
that in the meadows,
at the edge of the heavy woods
in the distance, he saw
trees of white flowers.
I feel that I would like   25
to go there
and fall into those flowers
and sink into the marsh near them.

William Carlos Williams (1883–1963)

QUESTIONS

1. Why is springtime so poignant a time for this lament? What has been the
   speaker's previous experience at this time of year?
2. Why does the speaker's son tell her of the flowering trees "in the distance"? What does he want her to do? Contrast the two locations in the
   poem—"yard" versus "meadows," "woods," and "marsh." What does the
   widow desire?
3. Imagery may have degrees of vividness, depending on its particularity,
   concreteness, and specific detail. What is the result of the contrast between the vividness of lines 2–3 and the relative flatness of lines 13–14?
   How does the fact that "masses" (10, 11) appeals to two senses relate to
   the speaker's emotional condition?

36. I felt a funeral in my brain

I felt a funeral in my brain,
And mourners to and fro
Kept treading—treading—till it seemed
That sense was breaking through.

And when they all were seated,   5
A service, like a drum,
Kept beating—beating—till I thought
My mind was going numb.

And then I heard them lift a box
And creak across my soul   10
With those same boots of lead again.
Then space began to toll,

As all the heavens were a bell
And being, but an ear,
And I and silence, some strange race,   15
Wrecked, solitary, here.

And then a plank in reason broke
And I dropped down, and down,
And hit a world at every plunge,
And finished knowing, then.   20

Emily Dickinson (1830–1886)

QUESTIONS

1. What senses are being evoked by the imagery? Can you account for the
   fact that one important sense is absent from the poem?
2. In sequence, what aspects of a funeral and burial are represented in the
   poem? Is it possible to define the sequence of mental events that are being compared to them?
3. With respect to the funeral activities in stanzas 1–3, where is the speaker
   imaginatively located?
4. What finally happens to the speaker?

37. The Forge

All I know is a door into the dark.
Outside, old axles and iron hoops rusting;
Inside, the hammered anvil's short-pitched ring,

The unpredictable fantail of sparks
Or hiss when a new shoe toughens in water.   5
The anvil must be somewhere in the center,
Horned as a unicorn, at one end square,
Set there immovable: an altar
Where he expends himself in shape and music.
Sometimes, leather-aproned, hairs in his nose,   10
He leans out on the jamb, recalls a clatter
Of hoofs where traffic is flashing in rows;
Then grunts and goes in, with a slam and flick
To beat real iron out, to work the bellows.

Seamus Heaney (b. 1939)

QUESTIONS

1. What does the speaker mean when he says that "all" he knows is "a door into the dark" (1)? What more does he know, and how does he make his knowledge evident?
2. How do the images describing the blacksmith (10–11) relate to his attitude toward his work and toward the changing times?
3. The speaker summarizes the smith's world as "shape and music" (9), terms that suggest visual and auditory imagery. What do the contrasts between visual images contribute? The contrasts between auditory images?

38. After Apple-Picking

My long two-pointed ladder's sticking through a tree
Toward heaven still,
And there's a barrel that I didn't fill
Beside it, and there may be two or three
Apples I didn't pick upon some bough.   5
But I am done with apple-picking now.
Essence of winter sleep is on the night,
The scent of apples: I am drowsing off.
I cannot rub the strangeness from my sight
I got from looking through a pane of glass   10
I skimmed this morning from the drinking trough
And held against the world of hoary grass.
It melted, and I let it fall and break.
But I was well
Upon my way to sleep before it fell,   15
And I could tell
What form my dreaming was about to take.

Magnified apples appear and disappear,
Stem end and blossom end,
And every fleck of russet showing clear.   20
My instep arch not only keeps the ache,
It keeps the pressure of a ladder-round.
I feel the ladder sway as the boughs bend.
And I keep hearing from the cellar bin
The rumbling sound   25
Of load on load of apples coming in.
For I have had too much
Of apple-picking: I am overtired
Of the great harvest I myself desired.
There were ten thousand thousand fruit to touch,   30
Cherish in hand, lift down, and not let fall.
For all
That struck the earth,
No matter if not bruised or spiked with stubble,
Went surely to the cider-apple heap   35
As of no worth.
One can see what will trouble
This sleep of mine, whatever sleep it is.
Were he not gone,
The woodchuck could say whether it's like his   40
Long sleep, as I describe its coming on,
Or just some human sleep.

Robert Frost (1874–1963)

QUESTIONS

1. How does the poet convey so vividly the experience of "apple-picking"?
   Point out effective examples of each kind of imagery used. What emotional responses do the images evoke?
2. How does the speaker regard his work? Has he done it well or poorly?
   Does he find it enjoyable or tedious? Is he dissatisfied with its results?
3. The speaker predicts what he will dream about in his sleep. Why does he
   shift to the present tense (18) when he begins describing a dream he has
   not yet had? How sharply are real experience and dream experience differentiated in the poem?
4. The poem uses the word *sleep* six times. Does it, through repetition, come
   to suggest a meaning beyond the purely literal? If so, what attitude does
   the speaker take toward this second signification? Does he fear it? Does
   he look forward to it? What does he expect of it?
5. If sleep is symbolic (both literal and metaphorical), other details also may
   take on additional meaning. If so, how would you interpret (a) the ladder,
   (b) the season of the year, (c) the harvesting, (d) the "pane of glass" (10)?
   What denotations has the word "Essence" (7)?
6. How does the woodchuck's sleep differ from "just some human sleep" (42)?

39. Those Winter Sundays

Sundays too my father got up early
and put his clothes on in the blueblack cold,
then with cracked hands that ached
from labor in the weekday weather made
banked fires blaze. No one ever thanked him.   5

I'd wake and hear the cold splintering, breaking.
When the rooms were warm, he'd call,
and slowly I would rise and dress,
fearing the chronic angers of that house,

Speaking indifferently to him,   10
who had driven out the cold
and polished my good shoes as well.
What did I know, what did I know
of love's austere and lonely offices?

Robert Hayden (1913–1980)

QUESTIONS

1. Vocabulary: *offices* (14).
2. What kind of imagery is central to the poem? How is this imagery related
   to the emotional concerns of the poem?
3. How do the subsidiary images relate to the central images?
4. From what point in time does the speaker view the subject matter of the
   poem? What has happened to him in the interval?

40. The Letter

Bad news arrives in her distinctive hand.
The cancer has returned, this time
to his brain. Surgery impossible,
treatments under way. Hair loss, bouts
of sleeplessness and agitation at night,   5
exhaustion during the day.

I snap the blue leash onto the D-ring
of the dog's collar, and we cross
Route 4, then cut through the hayfield
to the pond road, where I let him run   10
along with my morbidity.

The trees have leafed out—only just—
and the air is misty with sap.

So green, so brightly, richly succulent,
this arbor over the road . . .   15
Sunlight penetrates in golden drops.

We come to the place where a neighbor
is taking timber from his land.
There's a smell of lacerated earth
and pine. Hardwood smells different.   20
His truck is gone.

Now you can see well up the slope,
see ledges of rock and ferns breaking forth
among the stumps and cast-aside limbs
and branches.   25

The place will heal itself in time, first
with weeds—goldenrod, cinquefoil, moth
mullein—then blackberries, sapling
pine, deciduous trees . . . But for now
the dog rolls, jovial, in the pungent   30
disturbance of wood and earth.

I summon him with a word, turn back,
and we go the long way home.

Jane Kenyon (1947–1995)

QUESTIONS

1. The first six lines refer directly to the title. What is the speaker's apparent emotional reaction in these lines? How do you account for the lack of imagery in them?
2. Lines 10–11 seem to offer a motive for the speaker's walk. As precisely as you can, explain that motive.
3. Explain the connotations of "morbidity" (11), "lacerated" (19), "heal" (26).
4. From line 12, the poem is rich with imagery. What senses are evoked, and what emotions are conveyed?

41. Cavalry Crossing a Ford

A line in long array where they wind betwixt green islands,
They take a serpentine course, their arms flash in the sun—hark to the
    musical clank,
Behold the silvery river, in it the splashing horses loitering stop to drink,
Behold the brown-faced men, each group, each person a picture, the
    negligent rest on the saddles,

Some emerge on the opposite bank, others are just entering the
   ford—while,   5
Scarlet and blue and snowy white,
The guidon flags flutter gaily in the wind.

Walt Whitman (1819–1892)

QUESTION

There is an old Chinese proverb: "One picture is worth more than a thousand words." Like most proverbs it expresses a partial truth. What advantages would this Civil War poem have over a photograph of the same scene? (*Hint:* What distances would be necessary between the camera and each of the visual details?) Would a movie camera with zoom lens suffice to capture the experience of this poem?

42. Reapers

Black reapers with the sound of steel on stones
Are sharpening scythes. I see them place the hones
In their hip-pockets as a thing that's done,
And start their silent swinging, one by one.
Black horses drive a mower through the weeds,   5
And there, a field rat, startled, squealing bleeds,
His belly close to ground. I see the blade,
Blood-stained, continue cutting weeds and shade.

Jean Toomer (1894–1967)

QUESTIONS

1. The poem presents two examples of cutting down vegetation. What contrasts are drawn between reaping and mowing? How does imagery reinforce those contrasts?
2. What is signified by the speaker's stating that the "horses drive" (5) the mowing machine rather than that a man is driving the team of horses?
3. For whom (or what) would the weeds represent "shade" (8)? Are the connotations of *shade* positive or negative in this context? How are the usual connotations of "rat" (6) altered in the poem? Characterize the speaker.

43. To Autumn

Season of mists and mellow fruitfulness,
   Close bosom-friend of the maturing sun;
Conspiring with him how to load and bless
   With fruit the vines that round the thatch-eaves run;

> To bend with apples the mossed cottage-trees,   5
>   And fill all fruit with ripeness to the core;
>   To swell the gourd, and plump the hazel shells
> With a sweet kernel; to set budding more,
>   And still more, later flowers for the bees,
>   Until they think warm days will never cease,   10
>   For summer has o'er-brimmed their clammy cells.
>
> Who hath not seen thee oft amid thy store?
>   Sometimes whoever seeks abroad may find
> Thee sitting careless on a granary floor,
>   Thy hair soft-lifted by the winnowing wind;   15
> Or on a half-reaped furrow sound asleep,
>   Drowsed with the fume of poppies, while thy hook
>   Spares the next swath and all its twinèd flowers:
> And sometimes like a gleaner thou dost keep
>   Steady thy laden head across a brook;   20
>   Or by a cider-press, with patient look,
>   Thou watchest the last oozings hours by hours.
>
> Where are the songs of spring? Ay, where are they?
>   Think not of them, thou hast thy music too,—
> While barred clouds bloom the soft-dying day,   25
>   And touch the stubble-plains with rosy hue;
> Then in a wailful choir the small gnats mourn
>   Among the river sallows, borne aloft
>   Or sinking as the light wind lives or dies;
> And full-grown lambs loud bleat from hilly bourn;   30
>   Hedge-crickets sing; and now with treble soft
>   The red-breast whistles from a garden-croft;
>   And gathering swallows twitter in the skies.

John Keats (1795–1821)

QUESTIONS

1. Vocabulary: *hook* (17), *barred* (25), *sallows* (28), *bourn* (30), *croft* (32).
2. How many kinds of imagery do you find in the poem? Give examples of each.
3. Are the images arranged haphazardly or are they carefully organized? In answering this question, consider (a) what aspect of autumn each stanza particularly concerns, (b) what kind of imagery dominates each stanza, and (c) what time of the season each stanza presents. Is there any progression in time of day?
4. What is autumn personified as in stanza 2? Is there any suggestion of personification in the other two stanzas?
5. Although the poem is primarily descriptive, what attitude toward transience and passing beauty is implicit in it?

CHAPTER FIVE

Figurative Language 1

Simile, Metaphor, Personification, Apostrophe, Metonymy

> Poetry provides the one permissible way
> of saying one thing and meaning another.
> ROBERT FROST

Let us assume that your brother has just come in out of a rainstorm and you say to him, "Well, you're a pretty sight! Got slightly wet, didn't you?" And he replies, "Wet? I'm drowned! It's raining cats and dogs, and my raincoat's like a sieve!"

You and your brother probably understand each other well enough; yet if you examine this conversation literally, that is to say unimaginatively, you will find that you have been speaking nonsense. Actually you have been speaking figuratively. You have been saying less than what you mean, or more than what you mean, or the opposite of what you mean, or something other than what you mean. You did not mean that your brother was a pretty sight but that he was a wretched sight. You did not mean that he got slightly wet but that he got very wet. Your brother did not mean that he got drowned but that he got drenched. It was not raining cats and dogs; it was raining water. And your brother's raincoat is so unlike a sieve that not even a child would confuse them.

If you are familiar with Molière's play *Le Bourgeois Gentilhomme*, you will remember how delighted M. Jourdain was to discover that he had been speaking prose all his life. Many people might be equally surprised to learn that they have been speaking a kind of subpoetry all their lives. The difference between their figures of speech and the poet's is that theirs are probably worn and trite, the poet's fresh and original.

On first examination, it might seem absurd to say one thing and mean another. But we all do it—and with good reason. We do it because we can say what we want to say more vividly and forcefully by figures than we can by saying it directly. And we can say more by figurative statement than we can by literal statement. Figures of speech offer another way of adding extra dimensions to language.

Broadly defined, a **figure of speech** is any way of saying something other than the ordinary way, and some rhetoricians have classified as many as 250 separate figures. For our purposes, however, a figure of speech is more narrowly definable as a way of saying one thing and meaning another, and we need to be concerned with no more than a dozen. **Figurative language**—language using figures of speech—is language that cannot be taken literally (or should not be taken literally only).

Metaphor and **simile** are both used as a means of comparing things that are essentially unlike. The only distinction between them is that in simile the comparison is *expressed* by the use of some word or phrase, such as *like, as, than, similar to, resembles,* or *seems;* in metaphor, the comparison is not expressed but is created when a figurative term is *substituted for* or *identified with* the literal term.

44. The Guitarist Tunes Up

With what attentive courtesy he bent
Over his instrument;
Not as a lordly conqueror who could
Command both wire and wood,
But as a man with a loved woman might,   5
Inquiring with delight
What slight essential things she had to say
Before they started, he and she, to play.

Frances Cornford (1886–1960)

QUESTIONS

Explore the comparisons. Do they principally illuminate the guitarist or the lovers or both? What one word brings the figurative and literal terms together?

45. The Hound

Life the hound
Equivocal
Comes at a bound

Either to rend me
Or to befriend me.   5
I cannot tell
The hound's intent
Till he has sprung
At my bare hand
With teeth or tongue.   10
Meanwhile I stand
And wait the event.

Robert Francis (1901–1987)

QUESTIONS

What does "Equivocal" (2) mean? Show how this is the key word in the poem.
What is the effect of placing it on a line by itself?

Metaphors may take one of four forms, depending on whether
the literal and figurative terms are respectively *named* or *implied*. In
the first form of metaphor, as in simile, *both* the literal *and* figurative
terms are *named*. In Francis's poem, for example, the literal term is
"life" and the figurative term is "hound." In the second form, the literal term is *named* and the figurative term is *implied*.

46. Bereft

Where had I heard this wind before
Change like this to a deeper roar?
What would it take my standing there for,
Holding open a restive door,
Looking down hill to a frothy shore?   5
Summer was past and day was past.
Somber clouds in the west were massed.
Out in the porch's sagging floor,
Leaves got up in a coil and hissed,
Blindly struck at my knee and missed.   10
Something sinister in the tone
Told me my secret must be known:
Word I was in the house alone
Somehow must have gotten abroad,
Word I was in my life alone,   15
Word I had no one left but God.

Robert Frost (1874–1963)

QUESTIONS

1. Describe the situation precisely. What time of day and year is it? Where is the speaker? What is happening to the weather?
2. To what are the leaves in lines 9–10 compared? How does that comparison reflect the state of mind of the speaker?
3. The word "hissed" (9) is onomatopoetic (see Glossary of Terms). How is its effect reinforced in the lines following?
4. Though lines 9–10 present the clearest example of the second form of metaphor, there are others. To what is the wind ("it") compared in line 3? Why is the door "restive" (4) and what does this do (figuratively) to the door? To what is the speaker's "life" (15) compared?
5. What is the tone of the poem? How reassuring is the last line?

In the third form of metaphor, the literal term is *implied* and the figurative term is *named.* In the fourth form, *both* the literal *and* figurative terms are *implied.* The following poem exemplifies both forms:

47. It sifts from leaden sieves

It sifts from leaden sieves,
It powders all the wood.
It fills with alabaster wool
The wrinkles of the road.

It makes an even face   5
Of mountain and of plain—
Unbroken forehead from the east
Unto the east again.

It reaches to the fence,
It wraps it rail by rail   10
Till it is lost in fleeces;
It deals celestial veil

To stump and stack and stem—
A summer's empty room—
Acres of joints where harvests were,   15
Recordless,° but for them.   unrecorded

It ruffles wrists of posts
As ankles of a queen,
Then stills its artisans like ghosts,
Denying they have been.   20

Emily Dickinson (1830–1886)

QUESTIONS

1. This poem consists essentially of a series of metaphors having the same literal term identified only as "It." What is "It"?
2. In several of these metaphors the figurative term is named—"alabaster wool" (3), "fleeces" (11), "celestial veil" (12). In two of them, however, the figurative term as well as the literal term is left unnamed. To what is "It" compared in lines 1–2? In lines 17–18?
3. Comment on the additional metaphorical expressions or complications contained in "leaden sieves" (1), "alabaster wool" (3), "even face" (5), "unbroken forehead" (7), "a summer's empty room" (14), "artisans" (19).

Metaphors of the fourth form, as one might guess, are comparatively rare. An extended example, however, is provided by Dickinson's "I like to see it lap the miles" (No. 191).

Using some examples from the previous four poems, the chart below provides a visual demonstration of the figures of comparison (simile and the four forms of metaphor).

		Poem Number	Literal Term	Figurative Term
Similes (*like, as, seems,* etc.)		44	**named** guitarist guitarist	**named** conqueror man with woman
Metaphors (*is, are,* etc.)	Form 1	45	**named** life	**named** hound
	Form 2	46	**named** leaves	**implied** [snake] hissed
	Form 3	47	**implied** it [snow]	**named** wool
	Form 4	47	**implied** it [snow]	**implied** [flour] sifts

Personification consists in giving the attributes of a human being to an animal, an object, or a concept. It is really a subtype of metaphor, an implied comparison in which the figurative term of the comparison is always a human being. When Sylvia Plath makes a mirror speak and think (No. 21), she is personifying an object. When Keats describes autumn as a harvester "sitting careless on a granary floor" or "on a half-reaped furrow sound asleep" (No. 43), he is personifying a season. Personifications differ in the degree to which they ask the reader actually to visualize the literal term in human form. In

Keats's comparison, we are asked to make a complete identification of autumn with a human being. In Sylvia Plath's, though the mirror speaks and thinks, we continue to visualize it as a mirror; similarly, in Frost's "Bereft" (No. 46), the "restive" door remains in appearance a door tugged by the wind. In Browning's reference to "the startled little waves" (No. 32), a personification is barely suggested; we would make a mistake if we tried to visualize the waves in human form or even, really, to think of them as having human emotions.*

48. Scholars

Logic does well at school;
And Reason answers every question right;
Poll-parrot Memory unwinds her spool;
And Copy-cat keeps Teacher well in sight:

The Heart's a truant; nothing does by rule;   5
Safe in its wisdom, is taken for a fool;
Nods through the morning on the dunce's stool;
And wakes to dream all night.

Walter de la Mare (1873–1956)

QUESTIONS

1. The title identifies the metaphorical context. What is it, and what language in the poem supports it? Is it the purpose of the poem to denigrate scholarly diligence?
2. Five of the capitalized "names" are personifications, and one is not. Which one, and why not?

Closely related to personification is **apostrophe,** which consists in addressing someone absent or dead or something nonhuman as if

---

*The various figures of speech blend into each other, and it is sometimes difficult to classify a specific example as definitely metaphor or symbol, symbolism or allegory, understatement or irony, irony or paradox. Often a given example may exemplify two or more figures at once. In "The Guitarist Tunes Up" (No. 44), "wire and wood" are metonymies (see page 62) for a guitar and are personified as subjects, slaves, or soldiers who could be commanded by a lordly conqueror. In "The world is too much with us" (No. 28), when the winds are described as calm, "like sleeping flowers," the flowers function as part of a simile and are personified as something that can sleep. The important consideration in reading poetry is not that we classify figures definitively but that we construe them correctly.

that person or thing were present and alive and could reply to what is being said. The speaker in A. E. Housman's "To an Athlete Dying Young" (No. 240) apostrophizes a dead runner. William Blake apostrophizes a tiger throughout his famous poem (No. 205) but does not otherwise personify it. Keats apostrophizes *and* personifies autumn (No. 43). Personification and apostrophe are both ways of giving life and immediacy to one's language, but since neither requires great imaginative power on the part of the poet—apostrophe especially does not—they may degenerate into mere mannerisms and are to be found as often in bad and mediocre poetry as in good. We need to distinguish between their effective use and their merely conventional use.

49. Western Wind

> Western wind, when wilt thou blow,
> The small rain down can rain?
> Christ! if my love were in my arms,
> And I in my bed again!
>
> *Anonymous (c. 1500)*

QUESTIONS

1. Paraphrase the first two lines. What do you conceive to be the speaker's situation?
2. What is the connection between the first two lines and the last two?

In contrast to the preceding figures that compare *unlike* things are two figures that rest on congruences or correspondences. **Synecdoche** (the use of the part for the whole) and **metonymy** (the use of something closely related for the thing actually meant) are alike in that both substitute some significant detail or aspect of an experience for the experience itself. Thus Shakespeare uses synecdoche when he says that the cuckoo's song is unpleasing to a "married ear" (No. 4), for he means a married *man*. Kay uses synecdoche when she refers to "catalogues of domes" (No. 25), because what she means is "enough domed buildings to fill a catalogue," and Housman's Terence (No. 11) uses synecdoche when he declares that "malt does more than Milton can / To justify God's ways to man," for "malt" means beer or ale, of which malt is an essential ingredient. On the other hand, when Terence advises "fellows whom it hurts to think" to "Look into the pewter pot / To see the world as the world's not," he is using metonymy, for by "pewter pot" he means the ale *in* the pot, not the pot itself, and by "world" he means human life and the conditions under which it is lived. Shakespeare uses metonymy when he says that the yellow cuckoo-buds "paint the meadows with delight" (No. 4), for he means with bright color that produces delight. Robert Frost uses metonymy in "'Out, Out—'" (No. 90) when he describes an injured boy holding up his cut hand "as if to keep / The life from spilling," for literally he means to keep the blood from spilling. In each case, however, the poem gains in vividness, meaning, or compactness. Kay, by substituting one architectural detail for whole buildings, suggests the superficiality and boredom of a person who looks at many but appreciates none. Shakespeare, by referring to bright color as "delight," evokes not only the visual effect but the emotional response it arouses. Frost tells us both that the boy's hand is bleeding and that his life is in danger.

Many synecdoches and metonymies, of course, like many metaphors, have become so much a part of the language that they no longer strike us as figurative; this is the case with *redhead* for a red-haired person, *hands* for manual workers, *highbrow* for a sophisticate, *tongues* for languages, and a boiling *kettle* for the water *in* the kettle. Such figures are often referred to as *dead metaphors* (where the word *metaphor* is itself a metonymy for all figurative speech). Synecdoche and metonymy are so much alike that it is hardly worthwhile to distinguish between them, and the latter term is increasingly used for both. In this book metonymy will be used for both figures—that is, for any figure in which a part or something closely related is substituted for the thing literally meant.

We said at the beginning of this chapter that figurative language often provides a more effective means of saying what we mean than does direct statement. What are some of the reasons for that effectiveness?

First, figurative language affords us imaginative pleasure. Imagination might be described in one sense as that faculty or ability of the mind that proceeds by sudden leaps from one point to another, that goes up a stair by leaping in one jump from the bottom to the top rather than by climbing up one step at a time.* The mind takes delight in these sudden leaps, in seeing likenesses between unlike things. We have all probably taken pleasure in staring into a fire and seeing castles and cities and armies in it, or in looking into the clouds and shaping

---

*It is also the faculty of mind that is able to "picture" or "image" absent objects as if they were present. It was with imagination in this sense that we were concerned in the chapter on imagery.

them into animals or faces, or in seeing a man in the moon. We name our plants and flowers after fancied resemblances: jack-in-the-pulpit, babies'-breath, Queen Anne's lace. Figures of speech are therefore satisfying in themselves, providing us with a source of pleasure in the exercise of the imagination.

Second, figures of speech are a way of bringing additional imagery into verse, of making the abstract concrete, of making poetry more sensuous. When Tennyson's eagle falls "like a thunderbolt" (No. 1), his swooping down for his prey is charged with energy, speed, and power; the simile also recalls that the Greek god Zeus was accompanied by an eagle and armed with lightning. When Emily Dickinson compares poetry to prancing coursers (No. 23), she objectifies imaginative and rhythmical qualities by presenting them in visual terms. When Robert Browning compares the crisping waves to "fiery ringlets" (No. 32), he starts with one image and transforms it into three. Figurative language is a way of multiplying the sense appeal of poetry.

Third, figures of speech are a way of adding emotional intensity to otherwise merely informative statements and of conveying attitudes along with information. If we say, "So-and-so is a rat" or "My feet are killing me," our meaning is as much emotional as informative. When Philip Larkin's pathetic escapist metaphorically compares books to "a load of crap" (No. 14), the vulgar language not only expresses his distaste for reading, but intensifies the characterization of him as a man whose intellectual growth was stunted. As this example shows, the use of figures may be a poet's means of revealing the characteristics of a speaker—*how* he or she expresses a thought will define the attitudes or qualities as much as *what* that thought is. When Frost's speaker in "Bereft" (No. 46) sees a striking snake in an eddy of leaves he shows that he is fearful. When Wilfred Owen compares a soldier caught in a gas attack to a man drowning under a green sea (No. 3), he conveys a feeling of despair and suffocation as well as a visual image.

Fourth, figures of speech are an effective means of concentration, a way of saying much in brief compass. Like words, they may be multidimensional. Consider, for instance, the merits of comparing life to a candle, as Shakespeare does in a passage from *Macbeth* (No. 91). Life is like a candle in that it begins and ends in darkness; in that while it burns, it gives off light and energy, is active and colorful; in that it gradually consumes itself, gets shorter and shorter; in that it can be snuffed out at any moment; in that it is brief at best, burning only for a short duration. Possibly your imagination can suggest other similarities. But at any rate, Macbeth's compact, metaphorical description of life as a "brief candle" suggests certain truths about life that would require dozens of words to state in literal language. At the same time it makes the abstract concrete, provides imaginative pleasure, and adds a degree of emotional intensity.

It is as important, when analyzing and discussing a poem, to decide what it is that the figures accomplish as it is to identify them. Seeing a personification or a simile should lead to the next questions: *What use is being made of this figure? How does it contribute to the experience of the poem?*

Obviously, if we are to read poetry well, we must be able to respond to figurative language. Every use of figurative language involves a risk of misinterpretation, though the risk is well worth taking. For the person who can interpret the figure, the dividends are immense. Fortunately all people have imagination to some degree, and imagination can be cultivated. By practice, one's ability to interpret figures of speech can be increased.

EXERCISE

Identify each of the following quotations as literal or figurative. If figurative, explain what is being compared to what and explain the appropriateness of the comparison. EXAMPLE: "Talent is a cistern; genius is a fountain." ANSWER: Metaphor. Talent = cistern; genius = fountain. Talent exists in finite supply; it can be used up. Genius is inexhaustible, ever renewing.

1. O tenderly the haughty day
   Fills his blue urn with fire.   *Ralph Waldo Emerson*
2. It is with words as with sunbeams—the more
   they are condensed, the deeper they burn.   *Robert Southey*
3. Joy and Temperance and Repose
   Slam the door on the doctor's nose.   *Anonymous*
4. The pen is mightier than the sword.   *Edward Bulwer-Lytton*
5. The strongest oaths are straw
   To the fire i' the blood.   *William Shakespeare*
6. The Cambridge ladies . . . live in furnished souls.   *e. e. cummings*
7. Dorothy's eyes, with their long brown lashes,
   looked very much like her mother's.   *Laetitia Johnson*
8. The tawny-hided desert crouches watching her.   *Francis Thompson*
9. Let us eat and drink, for tomorrow we shall die.   *Isaiah 22.13*
10. Let us eat and drink, for tomorrow we may die.
                                        Common misquotation of the above

50. Mind

Mind in its purest play is like some bat
That beats about in caverns all alone,
Contriving by a kind of senseless wit
Not to conclude against a wall of stone.

It has no need to falter or explore;   5
Darkly it knows what obstacles are there,
And so may weave and flitter, dip and soar
In perfect courses through the blackest air.

And has this simile a like perfection?
The mind is like a bat. Precisely. Save   10
That in the very happiest intellection
A graceful error may correct the cave.

Richard Wilbur (b. 1921)

QUESTIONS

1. A poet may use a variety of metaphors and similes in developing a subject
   or may, as Wilbur does here, develop a single figure at length (this poem
   is an example of an **extended simile**). Identify in this chapter a poem
   containing a variety of figures and define the advantages of each type of
   development.
2. Explore the similarities between the two things compared in this poem.
   In line 12, what is meant by "A graceful error" and by "correct the cave"?

51. I taste a liquor never brewed

I taste a liquor never brewed,
From tankards scooped in pearl;
Not all the vats upon the Rhine
Yield such an alcohol!

Inebriate of air am I,   5
And debauchee of dew,
Reeling, through endless summer days,
From inns of molten blue.

When landlords turn the drunken bee
Out of the foxglove's door,   10
When butterflies renounce their drams,
I shall but drink the more!

Till seraphs swing their snowy hats,
And saints to windows run,
To see the little tippler   15
Leaning against the sun!

Emily Dickinson (1830–1886)

QUESTIONS

1. Vocabulary: *debauchee* (6), *foxglove* (10).
2. In this **extended metaphor,** what is being compared to alcoholic intoxication? The clues are given in the variety of "liquors" named or implied—"air" (5), "dew" (6), and the nectar upon which birds and butterflies feed.
3. What figurative meanings have the following details: "tankards scooped in pearl" (2), "inns of molten blue" (8), "snowy hats" (13)?
4. The last stanza creates a sterotypical street scene in which neighbors observe the behavior of a drunkard. What do comic drunks lean against in the street? What unexpected attitude do the seraphs and saints display?

52. Metaphors

I'm a riddle in nine syllables,
An elephant, a ponderous house,
A melon strolling on two tendrils,
O red fruit, ivory, fine timbers!
This loaf's big with its yeasty rising.   5
Money's new-minted in this fat purse.
I'm a means, a stage, a cow in calf.
I've eaten a bag of green apples,
Boarded the train there's no getting off.

Sylvia Plath (1932–1963)

QUESTIONS

1. Like its first metaphor, this poem is a riddle to be solved by identifying the literal terms of its metaphors. After you have identified the speaker ("riddle," "elephant," "house," "melon," "stage," "cow"), identify the literal meanings of the related metaphors ("syllables," "tendrils," "fruit," "ivory," "timbers," "loaf," "yeasty rising," "money," "purse," "train"). How do you interpret line 8?
2. How does the form of the poem relate to its content? Is this poem a complaint?

53. Song: Go, lovely rose!

Go, lovely rose!
Tell her that wastes her time and me
That now she knows,
When I resemble her to thee,
How sweet and fair she seems to be.   5

Tell her that's young
And shuns to have her graces spied
That hadst thou sprung
In deserts where no men abide,
Thou must have uncommended died.   10

Small is the worth
Of beauty from the light retired.
Bid her come forth,
Suffer herself to be desired
And not blush so to be admired.   15

Then die! that she
The common fate of all things rare
May read in thee,
How small a part of time they share
That are so wondrous sweet and fair!   20

Edmund Waller (1607–1687)

QUESTIONS

1. Vocabulary: *resemble* (4), *suffer* (14).
2. The speaker addresses a rose, but his message is to a beautiful young
   woman. How might this indirect means of speaking to her increase the
   effect of his message? What is he asking her to do? What part does "time"
   play in the poem?
3. Rather than using apostrophe to compare his love to a rose, the speaker
   might have addressed her directly, making the comparison in a simile or
   a metaphor ("you are like a rose" or "you are a rose"), or he might have
   used an abstract third-person form ("she is like a rose" or "she is a rose").
   What does the poem gain from apostrophe?

54. Toads

Why should I let the toad *work*
Squat on my life?
Can't I use my wit as a pitchfork
And drive the brute off?

Six days of the week it soils   5
    With its sickening poison—
Just for paying a few bills!
    That's out of proportion.

Lots of folk live on their wits:
    Lecturers, lispers,   10
Losels,° loblolly-men,° louts—   scoundrels; bumpkins
    They don't end as paupers;

Lots of folk live up lanes
    With fires in a bucket,
Eat windfalls and tinned sardines—   15
    They seem to like it.

Their nippers° have got bare feet,   children
    Their unspeakable wives
Are skinny as whippets—and yet
    No one actually *starves*.   20

Ah, were I courageous enough
    To shout *Stuff your pension!*
But I know, all too well, that's the stuff
    That dreams are made on;

For something sufficiently toad-like   25
    Squats in me, too;
Its hunkers° are heavy as hard luck,   haunches
    And cold as snow,

And will never allow me to blarney
    My way to getting   30
The fame and the girl and the money
    All at one sitting.

I don't say, one bodies the other
    One's spiritual truth;
But I do say it's hard to lose either,   35
    When you have both.

Philip Larkin (1922–1985)

QUESTIONS

1. Two "toads" are described in the poem. Where is each located? How are
   they described? What are the antecedents of the pronouns "one" and "the
   other / One's" (33–34) respectively?
2. What characteristics in common have the people mentioned in lines
   9–12? Those mentioned in lines 13–20?

3. Explain the pun in lines 22–23 and the literary allusion it leads into. (If you don't recognize the allusion, check Shakespeare's *The Tempest*, Act 4, scene 1, lines 156–58).
4. The first "toad" is explicitly identified as "*work*" (1). The literal term for the second "toad" is not named. Why not? What do you take it to be?
5. What kind of person is the speaker? What are his attitudes toward work?

55. A Valediction: Forbidding Mourning

As virtuous men pass mildly away,
    And whisper to their souls to go,
While some of their sad friends do say,
    The breath goes now, and some say, no:

So let us melt, and make no noise,   5
    No tear-floods, nor sigh-tempests move;
'Twere profanation of our joys
    To tell the laity our love.

Moving of th' earth brings harms and fears,
    Men reckon what it did and meant,   10
But trepidation of the spheres,
    Though greater far, is innocent.

Dull sublunary lovers' love
    (Whose soul is sense) cannot admit
Absence, because it doth remove   15
    Those things which elemented it.

But we by a love so much refined,
    That ourselves know not what it is,
Inter-assurèd of the mind,
    Care less, eyes, lips, and hands to miss.   20

Our two souls therefore, which are one,
    Though I must go, endure not yet
A breach, but an expansion,
    Like gold to airy thinness beat.

If they be two, they are two so   25
    As stiff twin compasses are two;
Thy soul the fixed foot, makes no show
    To move, but doth, if th' other do.

And though it in the center sit,
    Yet when the other far doth roam,   30
It leans, and hearkens after it,
    And grows erect, as that comes home.

Such wilt thou be to me, who must
Like th' other foot, obliquely run;
Thy firmness makes my circle just,   35
And makes me end, where I begun.

John Donne (1572–1631)

QUESTIONS

1. Vocabulary: *valediction* (title), *mourning* (title), *profanation* (7), *laity* (8), *trepidation* (11), *innocent* (12), *sublunary* (13), *elemented* (16). Line 11 is a reference to the spheres of the Ptolemaic cosmology, whose movements caused no such disturbance as does a movement of the earth—that is, an earthquake.
2. Is the speaker in the poem about to die? Or about to leave on a journey? (The answer may be found in a careful analysis of the simile in the last three stanzas and by noticing that the idea of dying in stanza 1 is introduced in a simile.)
3. The poem is organized around a contrast of two kinds of lovers: the "laity" (8) and, as their implied opposite, the "priesthood." Are these terms literal or metaphorical? What is the essential difference between their two kinds of love? How, according to the speaker, does their behavior differ when they must separate from each other? What is the motivation of the speaker in this "valediction"?
4. Find and explain three similes and one metaphor used to describe the parting of true lovers. The figure in the last three stanzas is one of the most famous in English literature. Demonstrate its appropriateness by obtaining a drawing compass or by using two pencils to imitate the two legs.
5. What kind of language is used in the poem? Is the language consonant with the figures of speech?

56. To His Coy Mistress

Had we but world enough, and time,
This coyness, lady, were no crime.
We would sit down, and think which way
To walk, and pass our long love's day.
Thou by the Indian Ganges' side   5
Shouldst rubies find; I by the tide
Of Humber would complain. I would
Love you ten years before the Flood,
And you should, if you please, refuse
Till the conversion of the Jews.   10
My vegetable love should grow
Vaster than empires, and more slow;
An hundred years should go to praise

Thine eyes, and on thy forehead gaze;
Two hundred to adore each breast,   15
But thirty thousand to the rest;
An age at least to every part,
And the last age should show your heart.
For, lady, you deserve this state,
Nor would I love at lower rate.   20
   But at my back I always hear
Time's wingèd chariot hurrying near;
And yonder all before us lie
Deserts of vast eternity.
Thy beauty shall no more be found,   25
Nor, in thy marble vault, shall sound
My echoing song; then worms shall try
That long-preserved virginity,
And your quaint honor turn to dust,
And into ashes all my lust: 30
The grave's a fine and private place,
But none, I think, do there embrace.
   Now therefore, while the youthful hue
Sits on thy skin like morning dew,
And while thy willing soul transpires   35
At every pore with instant fires,
Now let us sport us while we may,
And now, like amorous birds of prey,
Rather at once our time devour
Than languish in his slow-chapped power.   40
Let us roll all our strength and all
Our sweetness up into one ball,
And tear our pleasures with rough strife
Thorough° the iron gates of life.   through
Thus, though we cannot make our sun   45
Stand still, yet we will make him run.

Andrew Marvell (1621–1678)

QUESTIONS

1. Vocabulary: *coy* (title), *Humber* (7), *transpires* (35). "Mistress" (title) has the now archaic meaning of *sweetheart;* "slow-chapped" (40) derives from *chap,* meaning *jaw.*
2. What is the speaker urging his sweetheart to do? Why is she being "coy"?
3. Outline the speaker's argument in three sentences that begin with the words *If, But,* and *Therefore.* Is the argument valid?
4. Explain the appropriateness of "vegetable love" (11). What simile in the third section contrasts with it and how? What image in the third section

contrasts with the distance between the Ganges and the Humber? Of what would the speaker be "complaining" by the Humber (7)?
5. Explain the figures in lines 22, 24, and 40 and their implications.
6. Explain the last two lines. For what is "sun" a metonymy?
7. Is this poem principally about love or about time? If the latter, what might making love represent? What philosophy is the poet advancing here?

57. Suum Cuique

> Wilt thou seal up the avenues of ill?
> Pay every debt, as if God wrote the bill.

Ralph Waldo Emerson (1803–1882)

QUESTIONS

1. The title is Latin: "to each his own." How would you interpret its relevance to the poem?
2. Discuss the metaphor in line 1 and the simile in line 2. Is "Pay every debt" literal or metaphorical? Or both?

58. after minor surgery

> this is the dress rehearsal
> when the body
> like a constant lover
> flirts for the first time
> with faithlessness   5
>
> when the body
> like a passenger on a long journey
> hears the conductor call out
> the name
> of the first stop   10
>
> when the body
> in all its fear and cunning
> makes promises to me
> it knows
> it cannot keep   15

Linda Pastan (b. 1932)

QUESTIONS

1. Explore the metaphor in line 1: if "this is the dress rehearsal" of a drama, what is the opening night? Explore the similes in the first two stanzas (for example, if the body is "like a constant lover," what is it flirting with, and what would "faithlessness" be?).
2. What is the effect of the shift in the third stanza from the use of similes to personification?

59. Dream Deferred

What happens to a dream deferred?

Does it dry up
like a raisin in the sun?
Or fester like a sore—
And then run?   5
Does it stink like rotten meat?
Or crust and sugar over—
like a syrupy sweet?

Maybe it just sags
like a heavy load.   10

Or does it explode?

Langston Hughes (1902–1967)

QUESTIONS

1. Of the six images, five are similes. Which is a metaphor? Comment on its position and its effectiveness.
2. Since the dream could be any dream, the poem is general in its implication. What happens to your understanding of it on learning that its author was a black American?

EXERCISES

1. Robert Frost has said that "poetry is what evaporates from all translations." Why might this be true? How much of a word can be translated?
2. Ezra Pound has defined great literature as "simply language charged with meaning to the utmost possible degree." Would this be a good definition of poetry? The word "charged" is roughly equivalent to *filled*. Why is "charged" a better word in Pound's definition?

CHAPTER SIX

Figurative Language 2

Symbol, Allegory

60. The Road Not Taken

Two roads diverged in a yellow wood,
And sorry I could not travel both
And be one traveler, long I stood
And looked down one as far as I could
To where it bent in the undergrowth;   5

Then took the other, as just as fair,
And having perhaps the better claim,
Because it was grassy and wanted wear;
Though as for that the passing there
Had worn them really about the same,   10

And both that morning equally lay
In leaves no step had trodden black.
Oh, I kept the first for another day!
Yet knowing how way leads on to way,
I doubted if I should ever come back.   15

I shall be telling this with a sigh
Somewhere ages and ages hence:
Two roads diverged in a wood, and I—
I took the one less traveled by,
And that has made all the difference.   20

Robert Frost (1874–1963)

QUESTIONS

1. Does the speaker feel that he has made the wrong choice in taking the road "less traveled by" (19)? If not, why will he "sigh" (16)? What does he regret?

2. Why will the choice between two roads that seem very much alike make such a big difference many years later?

A **symbol** may be roughly defined as something that means *more* than what it is. "The Road Not Taken," for instance, concerns a choice made between two roads by a person out walking in the woods. He would like to explore both roads. He tells himself that he will explore one and then come back and explore the other, but he knows that he will probably be unable to do so. By the last stanza, however, we realize that the poem is about something more than the choice of paths in a wood, for that choice would be relatively unimportant, whereas this choice, the speaker believes, is one that will make a great difference in his life and is one that he will remember "with a sigh . . . ages and ages hence." We must interpret his choice of a road as a symbol for any choice in life between alternatives that appear almost equally attractive but will result through the years in a large difference in the kind of experience one knows.

Image, metaphor, and symbol shade into each other and are sometimes difficult to distinguish. In general, however, an image means only what it is; the figurative term in a metaphor means something other than what it is; and a symbol means what it is and something more, too. A symbol, that is, functions literally and figuratively at the same time.* If I say that a shaggy brown dog was rubbing its back against a white picket fence, I am talking about nothing but a dog (and a picket fence) and am therefore presenting an image. If I say, "Some dirty dog stole my wallet at the party," I am not talking about a dog at all and am therefore using a metaphor. But if I say, "You can't teach an old dog new tricks," I am talking not only about dogs but about living creatures of any species and am therefore speaking symbolically. Images, of course, do not cease to be images when they become incorporated in metaphors or symbols. If we are discussing the sensuous qualities of "The Road Not Taken," we should refer to the two leaf-strewn roads in the yellow wood as an image; if we are discussing the significance of the poem, we talk about the roads as symbols.

The symbol is the richest and at the same time the most difficult of the poetic figures. Both its richness and its difficulty result from its

---

*This account does not hold for nonliterary symbols such as the letters of the alphabet and algebraic signs (the symbol ∞ for infinity or = for equals). With these, the symbol is meaningless except as it stands for something else, and the connection between the sign and what it stands for is purely arbitrary.

imprecision. Although the poet may pin down the meaning of a symbol to something fairly definite and precise, more often the symbol is so general in its meaning that it can suggest a great variety of specific meanings. It is like an opal that flashes out different colors when slowly turned in the light. The choice in "The Road Not Taken," for instance, concerns some choice in life, but what choice? Was it a choice of profession? A choice of residence? A choice of mate? It might be any, all, or none of these. We cannot determine what particular choice the poet had in mind, if any, and it is not important that we do so. It is enough if we see in the poem an expression of regret that the possibilities of life experience are so sharply limited. The speaker in the poem would have liked to explore both roads, but he could explore only one. The person with a craving for life, whether satisfied or dissatisfied with the choices he has made, will always long for the realms of experience that he had to forgo. Because the symbol is a rich one, the poem suggests other meanings too. It affirms a belief in the possibility of choice and says something about the nature of choice—how each choice narrows the range of possible future choices, so that we make our lives as we go, both freely choosing and being determined by past choices. Though not a philosophical poem, it obliquely comments on the issue of free will and determinism and indicates the poet's own position. It can do all these things, concretely and compactly, by its use of an effective symbol.

Symbols vary in the degree of identification and definition given them by their authors. In this poem Frost forces us to interpret the choice of roads symbolically by the degree of importance he gives it in the last stanza. Sometimes poets are much more specific in identifying their symbols. Sometimes they do not identify them at all. Consider, for instance, the next two poems.

61. A Noiseless Patient Spider

A noiseless patient spider,
I marked where on a little promontory it stood isolated,
Marked how to explore the vacant vast surrounding,
It launched forth filament, filament, filament, out of itself,
Ever unreeling them, ever tirelessly speeding them.   5

And you, O my soul where you stand,
Surrounded, detached, in measureless oceans of space,
Ceaselessly musing, venturing, throwing, seeking the spheres to
    connect them,

Till the bridge you will need be formed, till the ductile anchor hold,
Till the gossamer thread you fling catch somewhere, O my soul.   10

Walt Whitman (1819–1892)

In the first stanza the speaker describes a spider's apparently tire-less effort to attach its thread to some substantial support so that it can begin constructing a web. The speaker reveals his attentive inter-est by the hinted personification of the spider, and his sympathy with it is expressed in the overstatement of size and distance—he is trying to perceive the world as a spider sees it from a "promontory" sur-rounded by vast space. He even attributes a human motive to the spi-der: exploration, rather than instinctive web-building. Nevertheless, the first stanza is essentially literal—the close observation of an actual spider at its task. In the second stanza the speaker explicitly interprets the symbolic meaning of what he has observed: his soul (personified by apostrophe and by the capabilities assigned to it) is like the spider in its constant striving. But the soul's purpose is to find spiritual or in-tellectual certainties in the vast universe it inhabits. The symbolic meaning is richer than a mere comparison; while a spider's actual purpose is limited to its instinctive drives, the human soul strives for much more, in a much more complex "surrounding." And, of course, the result of the soul's symbolized striving is much more open-ended than is the attempt of a spider to spin a web, as the paradoxical lan-guage ("Surrounded, detached," "ductile anchor") implies. *Can* the human soul connect the celestial spheres?

QUESTIONS

1. In "The Hound" (No. 45) Robert Francis compares unpredictable human life to a hound. Whitman compares the striving human soul to a spider. Why is Francis's comparison a metaphor and Whitman's a symbol? What additional comparison does Whitman make to the soul's quest? What figure of speech is it?
2. In what ways are the spider and the soul contrasted? What do the contrasts contribute to the meaning of the symbol?
3. Can the questing soul represent human actions other than the search for spiritual certainties?

62. The Sick Rose

O Rose, thou art sick!
The invisible worm

That flies in the night,
In the howling storm,

Has found out thy bed   5
Of crimson joy,
And his dark secret love
Does thy life destroy.

William Blake (1757–1827)

QUESTIONS

1. What figures of speech do you find in the poem in addition to symbol?
   How do they contribute to its force or meaning?
2. Several symbolic interpretations of this poem are given below. Do you
   think of others?
3. Should symbolic meanings be sought for the night and the storm? If so,
   what meanings would you suggest?

In "A Noiseless Patient Spider" the symbolic meaning of the spider is identified and named. By contrast, in "The Sick Rose" no
meanings are explicitly indicated for the rose and the worm. Indeed,
we are not *compelled* to assign them specific meanings. The poem is
validly read as being about a rose that has been attacked on a stormy
night by a cankerworm.

The organization of "The Sick Rose" is so rich, however, and its
language so powerful that the rose and the worm refuse to remain
merely a flower and an insect. The rose, apostrophized and personified
in the first line, has traditionally been a symbol of feminine beauty
and love, as well as of sensual pleasures. "Bed" can refer to a woman's
bed as well as to a flower bed. "Crimson joy" suggests the intense
pleasure of passionate lovemaking as well as the brilliant beauty of a
red flower. The "dark secret love" of the "invisible worm" is more
strongly suggestive of a concealed or illicit love affair than of the feed-
ing of a cankerworm on a plant, though it fits that too. For all these
reasons the rose almost immediately suggests a woman and the worm
her secret lover—and the poem suggests the corruption of innocent
but physical love by concealment and deceit. But the possibilities do
not stop there. The worm is a common symbol or metonymy for
death; and for readers steeped in Milton (as Blake was) it recalls the
"undying worm" of *Paradise Lost,* Milton's metaphor for the snake (or
Satan in the form of a snake) that tempted Eve. Meanings multiply
also for the reader who is familiar with Blake's other writings. Thus
"The Sick Rose" has been variously interpreted as referring to the

destruction of joyous physical love by jealousy, deceit, concealment, or the possessive instinct; of innocence by experience; of humanity by Satan; of imagination and joy by analytic reason; of life by death. We cannot say what specifically the poet had in mind, nor need we do so. A symbol defines an *area* of meaning, and any interpretation that falls within that area is permissible. In Blake's poem the rose stands for something beautiful, or desirable, or good. The worm stands for some corrupting agent. Within these limits, the meaning is largely "open." And because the meaning is open, the reader is justified in bringing personal experience to its interpretation. Blake's poem, for instance, might remind someone of a gifted friend whose promise has been destroyed by drug addiction.

Between the extremes exemplified by "A Noiseless Patient Spider" and "The Sick Rose" a poem may exercise all degrees of control over the range and meaning of its symbolism. Consider another example.

63. Digging

Between my finger and my thumb
The squat pen rests; snug as a gun.

Under my window, a clean rasping sound
When the spade sinks into gravelly ground:
My father, digging. I look down   5

Till his straining rump among the flowerbeds
Bends low, comes up twenty years away
Stooping in rhythm through potato drills
Where he was digging.

The coarse boot nestled on the lug, the shaft   10
Against the inside knee was levered firmly.
He rooted out tall tops, buried the bright edge deep
To scatter new potatoes that we picked
Loving their cool hardness in our hands.

By God, the old man could handle a spade.   15
Just like his old man.

My grandfather cut more turf in a day
Than any other man on Toner's bog.
Once I carried him milk in a bottle
Corked sloppily with paper. He straightened up   20
To drink it, then fell to right away

Nicking and slicing neatly, heaving sods
Over his shoulder, going down and down
For the good turf. Digging.

The cold smell of potato mould, the squelch and slap   25
Of soggy peat, the curt cuts of an edge
Through living roots awaken in my head.
But I've no spade to follow men like them.

Between my finger and my thumb
The squat pen rests.   30
I'll dig with it.

Seamus Heaney (b. 1939)

QUESTIONS

1. Vocabulary: *drills* (8), *fell to* (21). In Ireland, "turf" (17) is a block of peat dug from a bog; when dried, it is used as fuel.
2. What emotional responses are evoked by the imagery?

On the literal level, this poem presents a writer who interrupts himself to have a look at his father digging in a flower garden below his window. He is reminded of his father twenty years earlier digging potatoes for harvesting, and by that memory he is drawn farther back to his grandfather digging peat from a bog for fuel. The memories are vivid and appealing and rich in imagery, but the writer is not like his forebears, he has "no spade to follow" their examples. And so, with a trace of regret, he decides that his writing will have to be his substitute for their manual tasks.

But the title and the emphasis on varieties of the same task carried out in several different ways over a span of generations alert the reader to the need to discover the further significance of this literal statement. The last line is metaphorical, comparing digging to writing (and thus is itself not symbolic, for on a literal level one cannot dig with a pen). The metaphor, however, suggesting that the writer will commit himself to exploring the kinds of memories in this poem, invites an interpretation of the literal forms of digging. We notice then that the father has been involved in two sorts—the practical, backbreaking task of digging up potatoes to be gathered by the children, and twenty years later the relatively easy chore of digging in flowerbeds so as to encourage the growth of ornamental plants. There is a progression represented in the father's activities, from the necessary and arduous earlier life to the leisurely growing of flowers. Farther back in time, the grandfather's labors were deeper, heavier, and more essential, cutting and digging the material that would be used for heating and cooking—cooking potatoes, we should assume. The grandfather digs deeper and deeper, always in quest of the best peat, "the good turf."

Symbolically, then, digging has meanings that relate to basic needs—for warmth, for sustenance, for beauty, and for the personal satisfaction of doing a job well. In the concluding metaphor, another basic need is implied, the need to remember and confront one's origins, to find oneself in a continuum of meaningful activities, to assert the relevance and importance of one's vocation. And it is not coincidental that an Irish poet should find symbolic meanings in a confluence of Irish materials—from peat bogs to potatoes to poets and writers, that long-beleaguered island has asserted its special and distinct identity. Nor is it coincidental that Heaney selected this to be the opening poem in his first book of poetry: "Digging" is what his poetry does.

Meanings ray out from a symbol, like the corona around the sun or like connotations around a richly suggestive word. But the very fact that a symbol may be so rich in meanings requires that we use the greatest tact in its interpretation. Although Blake's "The Sick Rose" might, because of personal association, remind us of a friend destroyed by drug addiction, it would be unwise to say that Blake uses the rose to symbolize a gifted person succumbing to drug addiction, for this interpretation is private, idiosyncratic, and narrow. The poem allows it, but does not itself suggest it.

Moreover, we should never assume that because the meaning of a symbol is more or less open, we may make it mean anything we choose. We would be wrong, for instance, in interpreting the choice in "The Road Not Taken" as some choice between good and evil, for the poem tells us that the two roads are much alike and that both lie "In leaves no step had trodden black." Whatever the choice is, it is a choice between two goods. Whatever our interpretation of a symbolic poem, it must be tied firmly to the facts of the poem. We must not let loose of the string and let our imaginations go ballooning up among the clouds. Because the symbol is capable of adding so many dimensions to a poem, it is a peculiarly effective resource for the poet, but it is also peculiarly susceptible to misinterpretation by the incautious reader.

Accurate interpretation of the symbol requires delicacy, tact, and good sense. The reader must maintain balance while walking a tightrope between too little and too much—between underinterpretation and overinterpretation. If the reader falls off, however, it is much more desirable to fall off on the side of too little. Someone who reads "The Road Not Taken" as being only about a choice between two roads in a wood has at least understood part of the experience that the poem communicates, but the reader who reads into it anything imaginable might as well discard the poem and simply daydream.

Above all, we should avoid the disease of seeing symbols everywhere, like a person with hallucinations, whether or not there are symbols there. It is better to miss a symbol now and then than to walk constantly among shadows and mirages.

64. To the Virgins, to Make Much of Time

Gather ye rosebuds while ye may,
    Old Time is still a-flying;
And this same flower that smiles today
    Tomorrow will be dying.

The glorious lamp of heaven, the Sun,   5
    The higher he's a-getting,
The sooner will his race be run,
    And nearer he's to setting.

That age is best which is the first,
    When youth and blood are warmer;   10
But being spent, the worse, and worst
    Times still succeed the former.

Then be not coy, but use your time;
    And while ye may, go marry;
For having lost but once your prime,   15
    You may forever tarry.

Robert Herrick (1591–1674)

QUESTIONS

1. The first two stanzas might be interpreted literally if the third and fourth stanzas did not force us to interpret them symbolically. What do the "rosebuds" symbolize (stanza 1)? What does the course of a day symbolize (stanza 2)? Does the poet narrow the meaning of the rosebud symbol in the last stanza or merely name *one* of its specific meanings?
2. How does the title help us interpret the meaning of the symbol? Why is "virgins" a more meaningful word than, for example, *maidens*?

3. Why is such haste necessary in gathering the rosebuds? True, the blossoms die quickly, but they are replaced by others. Who *really* is dying?
4. What are "the worse, and worst" times (11)? Why?
5. Why is the wording of the poem better than these possible alternatives: *blooms* for "smiles" (3); *course* for "race" (7); *used* for "spent" (11); *spend* for "use" (13)?

Allegory is a narrative or description that has a second meaning beneath the surface. Although the surface story or description may have its own interest, the author's major interest is in the ulterior meaning. When Pharoah in the Bible, for instance, has a dream in which seven fat kine are devoured by seven lean kine, the story does not really become significant until Joseph interprets its allegorical meaning: that Egypt is to enjoy seven years of fruitfulness and prosperity followed by seven years of famine. Allegory has been defined sometimes as an extended metaphor and sometimes as a series of related symbols. But it is usually distinguishable from both of these. It is unlike extended metaphor in that it involves a *system* of related comparisons rather than one comparison drawn out. It differs from symbolism in that it puts less emphasis on the images for their own sake and more on their ulterior meanings. Also, these meanings are more fixed. In allegory there is usually a one-to-one correspondence between the details and a single set of ulterior meanings. In complex allegories the details may have more than one meaning, but these meanings tend to be definite. Meanings do not ray out from allegory as they do from a symbol.

Allegory is less popular in modern literature than it was in medieval and Renaissance writing, and it is much less often found in short poems than in long narrative works such as *The Faerie Queene, Everyman,* and *Pilgrim's Progress.* It has sometimes, especially with political allegory, been used to disguise meaning rather than reveal it (or, rather, to disguise it from some people while revealing it to others). Though less rich than the symbol, allegory is an effective way of making the abstract concrete and has occasionally been used effectively even in fairly short poems.

65. Peace

Sweet Peace, where dost thou dwell? I humbly crave,
Let me once know.
I sought thee in a secret cave,

And asked if Peace were there.
A hollow wind did seem to answer, "No,   5
            Go seek elsewhere."

I did, and going did a rainbow note.
            "Surely," thought I,
        "This is the lace of Peace's coat;
            I will search out the matter."   10
But while I looked, the clouds immediately
            Did break and scatter.

Then went I to a garden, and did spy
            A gallant flower,
        The Crown Imperial. "Sure," said I,   15
        "Peace at the root must dwell."
But when I digged, I saw a worm devour
            What showed so well.

At length I met a reverend good old man,
            Whom when for Peace   20
        I did demand, he thus began:
            "There was a prince of old
At Salem dwelt, who lived with good increase
            Of flock and fold.

"He sweetly lived; yet sweetness did not save   25
            His life from foes.
        But after death out of his grave
            There sprang twelve stalks of wheat;
Which many wondering at, got some of those
            To plant and set.   30

"It prospered strangely, and did soon disperse
            Through all the earth,
        For they that taste it do rehearse
            That virtue lies therein,
A secret virtue, bringing peace and mirth   35
            By flight of sin.

"Take of this grain, which in my garden grows,
            And grows for you;
        Make bread of it; and that repose
            And peace, which everywhere   40
With so much earnestness you do pursue,
            Is only there."

George Herbert (1593–1633)

QUESTIONS

1. Vocabulary: *gallant* (14), *rehearse* (33), *virtue* (34). "Crown Imperial" (15) is a garden flower, fritillary; "Salem" (23) is Jerusalem.
2. Identify the "prince" (22), his "flock and fold" (24), the "twelve stalks of wheat" (28), the "grain" (37), and the "bread" (39).
3. Should the "secret cave" (stanza 1), the "rainbow" (stanza 2), and the flower "garden" (stanza 3) be understood merely as places where the speaker searched or do they have more precise meanings?
4. Who is the "reverend good old man" (19), and what is *his* garden (37)?

66. Fire and Ice

Some say the world will end in fire,
Some say in ice.
From what I've tasted of desire
I hold with those who favor fire.
But if it had to perish twice,   5
I think I know enough of hate
To say that for destruction ice
Is also great
And would suffice.

Robert Frost (1874–1963)

QUESTIONS

1. Who are "Some" (1–2)? To which two theories do lines 1–2 refer? (In answering, it might help you to know that the poem was published in 1920.)
2. What do "fire" and "ice" respectively symbolize? What two meanings has "the world"?
3. The poem ends with an *understatement* (see Chapter 7). How does it affect the tone of the poem?

67. Ulysses

It little profits that an idle king,
By this still hearth, among these barren crags,
Matched with an agèd wife, I mete and dole
Unequal laws unto a savage race,
That hoard, and sleep, and feed, and know not me.   5

I cannot rest from travel; I will drink
Life to the lees. All times I have enjoyed
Greatly, have suffered greatly, both with those
That loved me, and alone; on shore, and when
Through scudding drifts the rainy Hyades   10
Vext the dim sea. I am become a name;
For always roaming with a hungry heart
Much have I seen and known,—cities of men,
And manners, climates, councils, governments,
Myself not least, but honored of them all;   15
And drunk delight of battle with my peers,
Far on the ringing plains of windy Troy.
I am a part of all that I have met;
Yet all experience is an arch wherethrough
Gleams that untraveled world, whose margin fades   20
For ever and for ever when I move.
How dull it is to pause, to make an end,
To rust unburnished, not to shine in use!
As though to breathe were life! Life piled on life
Were all too little, and of one to me   25
Little remains; but every hour is saved
From that eternal silence, something more,
A bringer of new things; and vile it were
For some three suns to store and hoard myself,
And this gray spirit yearning in desire   30
To follow knowledge like a sinking star,
Beyond the utmost bound of human thought.

This is my son, mine own Telemachus,
To whom I leave the scepter and the isle—
Well-loved of me, discerning to fulfil   35
This labor, by slow prudence to make mild
A rugged people, and through soft degrees
Subdue them to the useful and the good.
Most blameless is he, centered in the sphere
Of common duties, decent not to fail   40
In offices of tenderness, and pay
Meet adoration to my household gods,
When I am gone. He works his work, I mine.

There lies the port; the vessel puffs her sail:
There gloom the dark, broad seas. My mariners,   45
Souls that have toiled, and wrought, and thought with me—
That ever with a frolic welcome took
The thunder and the sunshine, and opposed

Free hearts, free foreheads—you and I are old;
Old age hath yet his honor and his toil.   50
Death closes all; but something ere the end,
Some work of noble note, may yet be done,
Not unbecoming men that strove with Gods.
The lights begin to twinkle from the rocks;
The long day wanes; the slow moon climbs; the deep   55
Moans round with many voices. Come, my friends,
'Tis not too late to seek a newer world.
Push off, and sitting well in order smite
The sounding furrows; for my purpose holds
To sail beyond the sunset, and the baths   60
Of all the western stars, until I die.
It may be that the gulfs will wash us down;
It may be we shall touch the Happy Isles,
And see the great Achilles, whom we knew.
Though much is taken, much abides; and though   65
We are not now that strength which in old days
Moved earth and heaven, that which we are, we are:
One equal temper of heroic hearts,
Made weak by time and fate, but strong in will
To strive, to seek, to find, and not to yield.   70

Alfred, Lord Tennyson (1809–1892)

QUESTIONS

1. Vocabulary: *lees* (7), *Hyades* (10), *meet* (42).
2. Ulysses, king of Ithaca, is a legendary Greek hero, a major figure in Homer's *Iliad,* the hero of Homer's *Odyssey,* and a minor figure in Dante's *Divine Comedy.* After ten years at the siege of Troy, Ulysses set sail for home but, having incurred the wrath of the god of the sea, he was subjected to storms and vicissitudes and was forced to wander for another ten years, having many adventures and seeing most of the Mediterranean world before again reaching Ithaca, his wife, and his son. Once back home, according to Dante, he still wished to travel and "to follow virtue and knowledge." In Tennyson's poem, Ulysses is represented as about to set sail on a final voyage from which he will not return. Locate Ithaca on a map. Where exactly, in geographical terms, does Ulysses intend to sail (59–64)? (The Happy Isles were the Elysian fields, or Greek paradise; Achilles was another Greek prince, the hero of the *Iliad,* who was killed at the siege of Troy.)
3. Ulysses's speech is divided into three sections, beginning at lines 1, 33, and 44. What is the topic or purpose of each section? To whom, specifically, is the third section addressed? To whom, would you infer, are sections 1 and 2 addressed? Where do you visualize Ulysses as standing during his speech?
4. Characterize Ulysses. What kind of person is he as Tennyson represents him?

5. What way of life is symbolized by Ulysses? Find as many evidences as you can that Ulysses's desire for travel represents something more than mere wanderlust and wish for adventure.
6. Give two symbolic implications of the westward direction of Ulysses's journey.
7. Interpret lines 18–21 and 26–29. What metaphor is implied in line 23? What is symbolized by "The thunder and the sunshine" (48)? What do the two metonymies in line 49 stand for?

68. Curiosity

may have killed the cat; more likely
the cat was just unlucky, or else curious
to see what death was like, having no cause
to go on licking paws, or fathering
litter on litter of kittens, predictably.   5

Nevertheless, to be curious
is dangerous enough. To distrust
what is always said, what seems,
to ask odd questions, interfere in dreams,
leave home, smell rats, have hunches   10
do not endear cats to those doggy circles
where well-smelt baskets, suitable wives, good lunches
are the order of things, and where prevails
much wagging of incurious heads and tails.

Face it. Curiosity   15
will not cause us to die—
only lack of it will.
Never to want to see
the other side of the hill
or that improbable country   20
where living is an idyll
(although a probable hell)
would kill us all.
Only the curious
have, if they live, a tale   25
worth telling at all.

Dogs say cats love too much, are irresponsible,
are changeable, marry too many wives,
desert their children, chill all dinner tables
with tales of their nine lives.   30

Well, they are lucky. Let them be
nine-lived and contradictory,
curious enough to change, prepared to pay
the cat price, which is to die
and die again and again,   35
each time with no less pain.
A cat minority of one
is all that can be counted on
to tell the truth. And what cats have to tell
on each return from hell   40
is this: that dying is what the living do,
that dying is what the loving do,
and that dead dogs are those who do not know
that dying is what, to live, each has to do.

Alastair Reid (b. 1926)

QUESTIONS

1. On the surface this poem is a dissertation on cats. What deeper comments does it make? Of what are cats and dogs, in this poem, symbols?
2. In what different senses are the words *death, die,* and *dying* here used?
3. Compare and contrast this poem in meaning and manner with "Ulysses."

69. Discovery of the New World

The creatures that we met this morning
    marveled at our green skins
        and scarlet eyes.
They lack antennae
    and can't be made to grasp   5
        your proclamation that they are
our lawful food and prey and slaves,
        nor can they seem to learn
    their body-space is needed to materialize
        our oxygen absorbers—   10
which they conceive are breathing
        and thinking creatures whom they implore
at first as angels or (later) as devils
        when they are being snuffed out
            by an absorber swelling   15
                into their space.
Their history bled from one this morning

while we were tasting his brain
in holographic rainbows
which we assembled into quite an interesting   20
set of legends—
that's all it came to, though
the colors were quite lovely before we
poured them into our time;
the blue shift bleached away   25
meaningless circumstance and they would not fit
any of our truth-matrices—
there was, however,
a curious visual echo in their history
of our own coming to their earth;   30
a certain General Sherman
had said concerning a group of them
exactly what we were saying to you
about these creatures:
it is our destiny to asterize this planet,   35
and they will not be asterized,
so they must be wiped out.
We need their space and oxygen
which they do not know how to use,
yet they will not give up their gas unforced,   40
and we feel sure,
whatever our "agreements" made this morning,
we'll have to kill them all:
the more we cook this orbit,
the fewer next time around.   45
We've finished burning all their crops
and killed their cattle.
They'll have to come into our pens
and then we'll get to study
the way our heart attacks and cancers spread among them,   50
since they seem not immune to these.
If we didn't have this mission it might be sad
to see such helpless creatures die,
but never fear,
the riches of this place are ours   55
and worth whatever pain others may have to feel.
We'll soon have it cleared
as in fact it is already, at the poles.
Then we will be safe, and rich, and happy here forever.

Carter Revard (b. 1931)

QUESTIONS

1. Vocabulary: *asterize* (35) is a word coined from the common prefix *aster-*
   or *astro-;* what would you surmise it to mean? "[M]aterialize / our oxygen
   absorbers" (9–10) and "truth-matrices" (27) are similarly devised terms
   whose meanings you should easily infer. What does the poem gain from
   this stretching of normal language?
2. Who (or what) is the speaker? Who (or what) is being addressed, and for
   what purpose?
3. "[A] certain General Sherman," some of whose attitudes are adapted
   beginning in line 35, was William Tecumseh Sherman (1820–1891), the
   Union general who after the Civil War was sent on a mission to control
   the native Americans in the West. Sherman was both praised and criticized for his accomplishment but took pride in having confined so many
   "Indians" to reservations. How does this poem allegorize that aspect of
   American history?
4. Does this allegory have meaning beyond its reflection of history and its
   fanciful imagination of a future?

70. Hymn to God My God, in My Sickness

Since I am coming to that holy room
    Where, with thy choir of saints for evermore,
I shall be made thy music, as I come
    I tune the instrument here at the door,
    And what I must do then, think now before.   5

Whilst my physicians by their love are grown
    Cosmographers, and I their map, who lie
Flat on this bed, that by them may be shown
    That this is my southwest discovery,
    Per fretum febris,° by these straits to die,   through the 10
                                                    raging of fever
I joy that in these straits I see my west;
    For though those currents yield return to none,
What shall my west hurt me? As west and east
    In all flat maps (and I am one) are one,
    So death doth touch the resurrectiön.   15

Is the Pacific Sea my home? Or are
    The eastern riches? Is Jerusalem?
Anyan° and Magellan and Gibraltar,   Bering Strait
    All straits, and none but straits, are ways to them,
    Whether there Japhet dwelt, or Cham, or Shem.   20

We think that Paradise and Calvary,
  Christ's cross and Adam's tree, stood in one place;
Look, Lord, and find both Adams met in me;
  As the first Adam's sweat surrounds my face,
  May the last Adam's blood my soul embrace.   25

So, in his purple wrapped receive me, Lord;
  By these his thorns give me his other crown;
And as to others' souls I preached thy word,
  Be this my text, my sermon to mine own:
  Therefore that he may raise, the Lord throws down.   30

John Donne (1572–1631)

QUESTIONS

1. Vocabulary: *Cosmographers* (7).
2. For the last ten years of his life John Donne was Dean of St. Paul's Cathedral in London, and he is famous for his sermons (see lines 28–30) as well as his poems. According to his earliest biographer (though some scholars disagree), this poem was written eight days before Donne's death. What are "that holy room" (1) and "the instrument" (4)? What is the speaker doing in stanza 1?
3. During Donne's lifetime such explorers as Henry Hudson and Martin Frobisher sought a Northwest Passage to the East Indies to match Magellan's discovery in 1520 of a southwest passage through the straits that bear his name. Why is "southwest" more appropriate to the speaker's condition than "northwest"? In what ways is his raging fever like a strait? What different meanings of the word "straits" (10) are operative here? What do the straits symbolize?
4. In what ways does the speaker's body resemble a map?
5. Although the map is metaphorical, its parts are symbolic. What does the west symbolize? The east? The fact that west and east are one?
6. What meanings has the word "return" (12)? (Compare line 17.)
7. Japhet, Cham (or Ham), and Shem (20)—the sons of Noah—are in Christian legend the ancestors of the three races of man, roughly identifiable with the populations of Europe, Africa, and Asia. What must one go through, according to the speaker, to reach any place important? In what ways are the Pacific Ocean, the East Indies, and Jerusalem (16–17) each a fitting symbol for the speaker's own destination?
8. The locations of the garden of Eden and of Calvary (21) were identical according to early Christian scholars. How does this tie in with the poem's geographical symbolism? What connection is there between Adam's "sweat" (24) and Christ's "blood" (25)? Because Adam is said in the Bible to prefigure Christ (Romans 5:12–21), Christ is sometimes called the second Adam. How do the two Adams meet in the speaker? What do blood and sweat (together and separately) symbolize?

9. For what are "eastern riches" (17), "his purple" (26), and "his thorns" (27) respectively metonymies? What do "purple" and "thorns" symbolize? What is Christ's "other crown" (27)?
10. With what earlier paradoxes (see Chapter 7) in the poem does the paradox in the final line (very roughly paraphrased from Psalms 146.8) tie in? How does the poem explain human suffering and give it meaning?

71. Our journey had advanced

Our journey had advanced.
Our feet were almost come
To that odd fork in Being's road
"Eternity" by term.

Our pace took sudden awe.   5
Our feet reluctant led.
Before were cities, but between
The forest of the dead.

Retreat was out of hope,
Behind, a sealed route,   10
"Eternity's" white flag before,
And God at every gate.

Emily Dickinson (1830–1886)

QUESTIONS

1. Identify the "journey" (1), the "road" (3), the "forest" (8), and the speaker's destination in this allegory. What literal human experience is the subject of the poem?
2. Explain the implications of the plural forms: "Our" (1–2, 5–6), "cities" (7), "every gate" (12).
3. What is the underlying metaphor implied in the last stanza by "Retreat" (9), "flag" (11), "gate" (12)? Does the "white flag" signify surrender?

72.   Dust of Snow

The way a crow
Shook down on me
The dust of snow
From a hemlock tree

Has given my heart   5
A change of mood
And saved some part
Of a day I had rued.

Robert Frost (1874–1963)

73. Soft Snow

I walked abroad in a snowy day;
I asked the soft snow with me to play;
She played and she melted in all her prime,
And the winter called it a dreadful crime.

William Blake (1757–1827)

QUESTION

In what respects are the two preceding poems alike? In what respects are
they essentially different?

EXERCISES

1. Determine whether "sleep," in the following poems, is literal, a symbol, or
   a metaphor (or simile).
   a. "Stopping by Woods on a Snowy Evening" (No. 105)
   b. "The Chimney Sweeper" (No. 78)
   c. "Is my team plowing" (No. 15)
   d. "The Second Coming" (No. 298)
2. Shapiro's "The Fly" (No. 278) and Shaw's "Shut In" (No. 139) deal with
   a common subject. Which of them is symbolic? Explain your choice.
3. What does Blake's tiger symbolize (No. 205)?
4. Determine whether the following poems are predominantly symbolic or
   literal.
   a. "Because I could not stop for Death" (No. 151)
   b. "The Snow Man" (No. 283)
   c. "The Darkling Thrush" (No. 235)
   d. "Song: Go and catch a falling star" (No. 219)
   e. "Blackberry Eating" (No. 165)
   f. "Musée des Beaux Arts" (No. 202)
   g. "Richard Cory" (No. 271)
   h. "The Wild Swans at Coole" (No. 299)
   i. "Poem: As the cat" (No. 291)
   j. "To Waken an Old Lady" (No. 293)
   k. "Desert Places" (No. 224)
   l. "Never Again Would Birds' Song Be the Same" (No. 226)
   m. "Constantly risking absurdity" (No. 150)

CHAPTER SEVEN

Figurative Language 3

Paradox, Overstatement, Understatement, Irony

Aesop tells the tale of a traveler who sought refuge with a Satyr on a bitter winter night. On entering the Satyr's lodging, he blew on his fingers, and was asked by the Satyr why he did it. "To warm them up," he explained. Later, on being served a piping-hot bowl of porridge, he blew also on it, and again was asked why he did it. "To cool it off," he explained. The Satyr thereupon thrust him out of doors, for he would have nothing to do with a man who could blow hot and cold with the same breath.

A **paradox** is an apparent contradiction that is nevertheless somehow true. It may be either a situation or a statement. Aesop's tale of the traveler illustrates a paradoxical situation. As a figure of speech, paradox is a statement. When Alexander Pope wrote that a literary critic of his time would "damn with faint praise," he was using a verbal paradox, for how can a man damn by praising?

When we understand all the conditions and circumstances involved in a paradox, we find that what at first seemed impossible is actually entirely plausible and not strange at all. The paradox of the cold hands and hot porridge is not strange to anyone who knows that a stream of air directed upon an object of different temperature will tend to bring that object closer to its own temperature. And Pope's paradox is not strange when we realize that *damn* is being used figuratively, and that Pope means only that a too reserved praise may damage an author with the public almost as much as adverse criticism. In a paradoxical statement the contradiction usually stems from one of the words being used figuratively or with more than one denotation.

The value of paradox is its shock value. Its seeming impossibility startles the reader into attention and, by the fact of its apparent absurdity, underscores the truth of what is being said.

74. Much madness is divinest sense

Much madness is divinest sense
To a discerning eye,
Much sense, the starkest madness.
'Tis the majority
In this, as all, prevail: 5
Assent, and you are sane;
Demur, you're straightway dangerous
And handled with a chain.

Emily Dickinson (1830–1886)

QUESTIONS

1. This poem presents the two sides of a paradoxical proposition: that insanity is good sense, and that good sense is insane. How do the concepts implied by the words "discerning" (2) and "majority" (4) provide the resolution of this paradox?
2. How do we know that the speaker does not believe that the majority is correct? How do the last five lines extend the subject beyond a contrast between sanity and insanity?

Overstatement, understatement, and verbal irony form a continuous series, for they consist, respectively, of saying more, saying less, and saying the opposite of what one really means.

Overstatement, or *hyperbole*, is simply exaggeration, but exaggeration in the service of truth. It is not the same as a fish story. If you say, "I'm starved!" or "You could have knocked me over with a feather!" or "I'll die if I don't pass this course!" you do not expect to be taken literally; you are merely adding emphasis to what you really mean. (And if you say, "There were literally millions of people at the beach!" you are merely piling one overstatement on top of another, for you really mean, "There were figuratively millions of people at the beach," or, literally, "The beach was very crowded.") Like all figures of speech, overstatement may be used with a variety of effects. It may be humorous or grave, fanciful or restrained, convincing or unconvincing. When Tennyson says of his eagle (No. 1) that it is "*Close* to the sun in lonely lands," he says what appears to be literally true, though we know from our study of astronomy that it is not. When Kay reports that her character in "Pathedy of Manners" (No. 25) "Saw *catalogues* of domes" on her European trip she implies the superficiality of a person for whom visiting a few churches and palaces seemed like enough architecture to fill catalogues. When Frost says, at the conclusion of "The Road Not Taken" (No. 60),

> I shall be telling this with a sigh
> Somewhere *ages and ages hence*

we are scarcely aware of the overstatement, so quietly is the assertion made. Unskillfully used, however, overstatement may seem strained and ridiculous, leading us to react as Gertrude does to the player-queen's speeches in *Hamlet:* "The lady doth protest too much."

It is paradoxical that one can emphasize a truth either by over-stating it or by understating it. **Understatement,** or saying less than one means, may exist in what one says or merely in how one says it. If, for instance, upon sitting down to a loaded dinner plate, you say, "This looks like a nice snack," you are actually stating less than the truth; but if you say, with Artemus Ward, that a man who holds his hand for half an hour in a lighted fire will experience "a sensation of excessive and disagreeable warmth," you are stating what is literally true but with a good deal less force than the situation warrants.

75. The Sun Rising

> Busy old fool, unruly sun,
>   Why dost thou thus
> Through windows and through curtains call on us?
> Must to thy motions lovers' seasons run?
>   Saucy pedantic wretch, go chide   5
>   Late schoolboys and sour 'prentices,
>   Go tell court-huntsmen that the king will ride,
>   Call country ants to harvest offices;
> Love, all alike, no season knows, nor clime,
> Nor hours, days, months, which are the rags of time.   10
>
>   Thy beams so reverend and strong
>   Why shouldst thou think?
> I could eclipse and cloud them with a wink,
> But that I would not lose her sight so long;
>   If her eyes have not blinded thine,   15
>   Look, and tomorrow late tell me
>   Whether both th' Indias of spice and mine
>   Be where thou left'st them, or lie here with me.
> Ask for those kings whom thou saw'st yesterday,
> And thou shalt hear, "All here in one bed lay."   20

> She's all states, and all princes I;
>   Nothing else is.
> Princes do but play us; compared to this,
> All honor's mimic, all wealth alchemy.
>   Thou, sun, art half as happy as we,   25
>   In that the world's contracted thus;
>   Thine age asks ease, and since thy duties be
>   To warm the world, that's done in warming us.
> Shine here to us, and thou art everywhere;
> This bed thy center is, these walls thy sphere.   30

John Donne (1572–1631)

QUESTIONS

1. Vocabulary: *offices* (8), *alchemy* (24).
2. As precisely as possible, identify the time of day and the locale. What three "persons" does the poem involve?
3. What is the speaker's attitude toward the sun in stanzas 1 and 2? How and why does it change in stanza 3?
4. Does the speaker understate or overstate the actual qualities of the sun? Point out specific examples. Identify the overstatements in lines 9–10, 13, 15, 16–20, 21–24, 29–30. What do these overstatements achieve?
5. Line 17 introduces a geographical image referring to the East and West Indies, sources respectively of spices and gold. What relationship between the lovers and the rest of the world is expressed in lines 15–22?
6. Who is actually the intended listener for this extended apostrophe? What is the speaker's purpose? What is the poem's purpose?

76. Incident

> Once riding in old Baltimore
>   Heart-filled, head-filled with glee,
> I saw a Baltimorean
>   Keep looking straight at me.
>
> Now I was eight and very small,   5
>   And he was no whit bigger,
> And so I smiled, but he poked out
>   His tongue, and called me, "Nigger."
>
> I saw the whole of Baltimore
>   From May until December;   10
> Of all the things that happened there
>   That's all that I remember.

Countee Cullen (1903–1946)

QUESTION

What accounts for the effectiveness of the last stanza? Comment on the title.
Is it in key with the meaning of the poem?

Like paradox, **irony** has meanings that extend beyond its use
merely as a figure of speech.

Verbal irony, saying the opposite of what one means, is often
confused with sarcasm and with satire, and for that reason it may be
well to look at the meanings of all three terms. Sarcasm and satire
both imply ridicule, one on the colloquial level, the other on the literary
level. **Sarcasm** is simply bitter or cutting speech, intended to wound
the feelings (it comes from a Greek word meaning to tear flesh). **Satire**
is a more formal term, usually applied to written literature rather than
to speech and ordinarily implying a higher motive: it is ridicule (either
bitter or gentle) of human folly or vice, with the purpose of bringing
about reform or at least of keeping other people from falling into similar folly or vice. Irony, on the other hand, is a literary device or figure
that may be used in the service of sarcasm or ridicule or may not. It is
popularly confused with sarcasm and satire because it is so often used
as their tool; but irony may be used without either sarcastic or satiri-
cal intent, and sarcasm and satire may exist (though they do not usually) without irony. If, for instance, one of the members of your class
raises his hand on the discussion of this point and says, "I don't understand," and your instructor replies, with a tone of heavy disgust in
his voice, "Well, I wouldn't expect *you* to," he is being sarcastic but
not ironic; he means exactly what he says. But if, after you have done
particularly well on an examination, your instructor brings your test
papers into the classroom saying, "Here's some *bad* news for you: you
all got As and Bs!" he is being ironic but not sarcastic. Sarcasm, we
may say, is cruel, as a bully is cruel: it intends to give hurt. Satire is
both cruel and kind, as a surgeon is cruel and kind: it gives hurt in the
interest of the patient or of society. Irony is neither cruel nor kind: it is
simply a device, like a surgeon's scalpel, for performing any operation
more skillfully.

Though verbal irony always implies the opposite of what is said, it
has many gradations, and only in its simplest forms does it mean *only*
the opposite of what is said. In more complex forms it means both
what is said and the opposite of what is said, at once, though in different ways and with different degrees of emphasis. When Terence's critic,
in "Terence, this is stupid stuff" (No. 11) says, "*Pretty* friendship 'tis

to rhyme / Your friends to death before their time" (11–12), we may substitute the literal *sorry* for the ironic "pretty" with little or no loss of meaning. When Terence speaks in reply, however, of the pleasure of drunkenness—"And down in *lovely* muck I've lain, / Happy till I woke again" (35–36)—we cannot substitute *loathsome* for "lovely" without considerable loss of meaning for, while muck is actually extremely unpleasant to lie in, it may *seem* lovely to an intoxicated person. Thus two meanings—one the opposite of the other—operate at once.

Like all figures of speech, verbal irony runs the danger of being misunderstood. With irony, the risks are perhaps greater than with other figures for, if metaphor is misunderstood, the result may be simply bewilderment; but if irony is misunderstood, the reader goes away with exactly the opposite idea from what the user meant to convey. The results of misunderstanding if, for instance, you ironically called someone a villain, might be calamitous. For this reason the user of irony must be very skillful in its use, conveying by an altered tone, or by a wink of the eye or pen, that irony is intended; and the reader of literature must be always alert to recognize the subtle signs of irony.

No matter how broad or obvious the irony, a number of people in any large audience always will misunderstand. The humorist Artemus Ward used to protect himself against these people by writing at the bottom of his newspaper column, "This is writ ironical." But irony is most delightful and most effective when it is subtlest. It sets up a special understanding between writer and reader that may add either grace or force. If irony is too obvious, it sometimes seems merely crude. But if effectively used, it, like all figurative language, is capable of adding extra dimensions to meaning.

77. One Perfect Rose

> A single flow'r he sent me, since we met.
>   All tenderly his messenger he chose;
> Deep-hearted, pure, with scented dew still wet—
>   One perfect rose.
>
> I knew the language of the floweret;   5
>   "My fragile leaves," it said, "his heart enclose."
> Love long has taken for his amulet
>   One perfect rose.

Why is it no one ever sent me yet
   One perfect limousine, do you suppose?   10
Ah no, it's always just my luck to get
   One perfect rose.

Dorothy Parker (1893–1967)

QUESTIONS

1. Comment on the contrast in diction between stanzas 1–2 and 3.
2. At what or whom is this satire directed? For a partial answer, review
   "Song: Go, lovely rose!" (No. 53).

    The term *irony* always implies some sort of discrepancy or incongruity. In verbal irony the discrepancy is between what is said and what is meant. In other forms the discrepancy may be between appearance and reality or between expectation and fulfillment. These other forms of irony are, on the whole, more important resources for the poet than is verbal irony. Two types are especially important.

    In **dramatic irony*** the discrepancy is not between what the speaker says and what the speaker means but between what the speaker says and what the poem means. The speaker's words may be perfectly straightforward, but the author, by putting these words in a particular speaker's mouth, may be indicating to the reader ideas or attitudes quite opposed to those the speaker is voicing. This form of irony is more complex than verbal irony and demands a more complex response from the reader. It may be used not only to convey attitudes but also to illuminate character, for the author who uses it is indirectly commenting not only upon the value of the ideas uttered but also upon the nature of the person who utters them. Such comment may be harsh, gently mocking, or sympathetic.

---

*The term *dramatic irony,* which stems from Greek tragedy, often connotes something more specific and perhaps a little different from what I am developing here. It describes a speech or an action in a story that has much greater significance to the audience than to the character who speaks or performs it, because the audience possesses knowledge the character does not have, as when the enemies of Ulysses, in the *Odyssey,* wish good luck and success to a man who the reader knows is Ulysses himself in disguise, or as when Oedipus, in the play by Sophocles, bends every effort to discover the murderer of Laius so that he may avenge the death, not knowing, as the audience does, that Laius is the man whom he himself once slew. I have appropriated the term for a perhaps slightly different situation because no other suitable term exists. Both uses have the common characteristic—that the author conveys to the reader something different, or at least something more, than the character himself intends or understands.

78. The Chimney Sweeper

When my mother died I was very young,
And my father sold me while yet my tongue
Could scarcely cry " 'weep! 'weep! 'weep! 'weep!"
So your chimneys I sweep, and in soot I sleep.

There's little Tom Dacre, who cried when his head,   5
That curled like a lamb's back, was shaved; so I said,
"Hush, Tom! never mind it, for, when your head's bare,
You know that the soot cannot spoil your white hair."

And so he was quiet, and that very night,
As Tom was asleeping, he had such a sight!   10
That thousands of sweepers, Dick, Joe, Ned, and Jack,
Were all of them locked up in coffins of black.

And by came an Angel who had a bright key,
And he opened the coffins and set them all free;
Then down a green plain leaping, laughing, they run,   15
And wash in a river, and shine in the sun.

Then naked and white, all their bags left behind,
They rise upon clouds and sport in the wind;
And the Angel told Tom, if he'd be a good boy,
He'd have God for his father, and never want joy.   20

And so Tom awoke, and we rose in the dark,
And got with our bags and our brushes to work.
Though the morning was cold, Tom was happy and warm;
So if all do their duty they need not fear harm.

William Blake (1757–1827)

QUESTIONS

1. In the eighteenth century small boys, sometimes no more than four or
   five years old, were employed to climb up the narrow chimney flues and
   clean them, collecting the soot in bags. Such boys, sometimes sold to the
   master sweepers by their parents, were miserably treated by their masters
   and often suffered disease and physical deformity. Characterize the boy
   who speaks in this poem. How do his and the poet's attitudes toward his
   lot in life differ? How, especially, are the meanings of the poet and the
   speaker different in lines 3, 7–8, and 24?
2. The dream in lines 11–20, besides being a happy dream, can be interpreted allegorically. Point out possible significances of the sweepers' being
   "locked up in coffins of black" (12) and the Angel's releasing them with a
   bright key to play upon green plains.

A third type of irony, **irony of situation,** occurs when a discrepancy exists between the actual circumstances and those that would seem appropriate or between what one anticipates and what actually comes to pass. If a man and his second wife, on the first night of their honeymoon, are accidentally seated at the theater next to the man's first wife, we should call the situation ironic. When, in O. Henry's famous short story "The Gift of the Magi" a poor young husband pawns his most prized possession, a gold watch, in order to buy his wife a set of combs for her hair for Christmas, and his wife sells her most prized possession, her long brown hair, in order to buy a fob for her husband's watch, we call the situation ironic. When King Midas, in the famous fable, is granted his fondest wish, that anything he touch turn to gold, and then finds that he cannot eat because even his food turns to gold, we call the situation ironic. When Coleridge's Ancient Mariner finds himself in the middle of the ocean with "Water, water, everywhere," but not a "drop to drink," we call the situation ironic. In each case the circumstances are not what would seem appropriate or what we would expect.

Dramatic irony and irony of situation are powerful devices for poetry for, like symbol, they enable a poem to suggest meanings without stating them—to communicate a great deal more than is said. We have seen one effective use of irony of situation in "The Widow's Lament in Springtime" (No. 35). Another is in "Ozymandias," which follows.

Irony and paradox may be trivial or powerful devices, depending on their use. At their worst they may degenerate into mere mannerism and mental habit. At their best they may greatly extend the dimensions of meaning in a work of literature. Because irony and paradox demand an exercise of critical intelligence, they are particularly valuable as safeguards against sentimentality.

79. Ozymandias

I met a traveler from an antique land
Who said: Two vast and trunkless legs of stone
Stand in the desert . . . Near them, on the sand,
Half sunk, a shattered visage lies, whose frown,
And wrinkled lip, and sneer of cold command,   5
Tell that its sculptor well those passions read
Which yet survive, stamped on these lifeless things,
The hand that mocked them, and the heart that fed;
And on the pedestal these words appear:

"My name is Ozymandias, king of kings;   10
Look on my works, ye Mighty, and despair!"
Nothing beside remains. Round the decay
Of that colossal wreck, boundless and bare
The lone and level sands stretch far away.

Percy Bysshe Shelley (1792–1822)

QUESTIONS

1. "[S]urvive" (7) is a transitive verb with "hand" and "heart" as direct objects. Whose hand? Whose heart? What figure of speech is exemplified in "hand" and "heart"?
2. Characterize Ozymandias.
3. Ozymandias was an ancient Egyptian tyrant. This poem was first published in 1817. Of what is Ozymandias a *symbol?* What contemporary reference might the poem have had in Shelley's time?
4. What is the theme of the poem and how is it "stated"?

EXERCISE

Identify the figure in each of the following quotations as paradox, overstatement, understatement, or irony—and explain the use to which the figure is put (emotional emphasis, humor, satire, etc.).
1. Poetry is a language that tells us, through a more or less emotional reaction, something that cannot be said.   *Edwin Arlington Robinson*
2. Christians have burnt each other, quite persuaded
   That all the Apostles would have done as they did.   *Lord Byron*
3. A man who could make so vile a pun would not scruple to pick a pocket.
   John Dennis
4. Last week I saw a woman flayed, and you will hardly believe how much it altered her person for the worse.   *Jonathan Swift*
5. . . . Where ignorance is bliss, / 'Tis folly to be wise.   *Thomas Gray*
6. All night I made my bed to swim; with my tears I dissolved my couch.
   Psalms 6.6
7. Believe him, he has known the world too long,
   And seen the death of much immortal song.   *Alexander Pope*
8. Cowards die many times before their deaths;
   The valiant never taste of death but once.   *William Shakespeare*
9. . . . all men would be cowards if they durst.   *John Wilmot, Earl of Rochester*

80. Batter my heart, three-personed God

Batter my heart, three-personed God; for you
As yet but knock, breathe, shine, and seek to mend;

That I may rise and stand, o'erthrow me, and bend
Your force to break, blow, burn, and make me new.
I, like an usurped town, to another due,   5
Labor to admit you, but oh, to no end;
Reason, your viceroy in me, me should defend,
But is captived, and proves weak or untrue.
Yet dearly I love you and would be lovèd fain,°   gladly
But am betrothed unto your enemy;   10
Divorce me, untie or break that knot again,
Take me to you, imprison me, for I,
Except° you enthrall me, never shall be free,   unless
Nor ever chaste, except you ravish me.

John Donne (1572–1631)

QUESTIONS

1. In this sonnet (one in a group called "Holy Sonnets") the speaker addresses God in a series of metaphors and paradoxes. What is the paradox in the first quatrain? To what is the "three-personed God" metaphorically compared? To what is the speaker compared? Can the first three verbs of the parallel lines 2 and 4 be taken as addressed to specific "persons" of the Trinity (Father, Son, Holy Spirit)? If so, to which are "knock" and "break" addressed? "breathe" and "blow"? "shine" and "burn"? (What concealed pun helps in the attribution of the last pair? What etymological pun in the attribution of the second pair?)
2. To what does the speaker compare himself in the second quatrain? To what is God compared? Who is the usurper? What role does "Reason" (7) play in this political metaphor, and why is it a weak one?
3. To what does the speaker compare himself in the sestet (lines 9–14)? To what does he compare God? Who is the "enemy" (10)? Resolve the paradox in lines 12–13 by explaining the double meaning of "enthrall." Resolve the paradox in line 14 by explaining the double meaning of "ravish."

81. Sorting Laundry

Folding clothes,
I think of folding you
into my life.

Our king-sized sheets
like tablecloths   5
for the banquets of giants,

pillowcases, despite so many
washings, seams still
holding our dreams.

Towels patterned orange and green,   10
flowered pink and lavender,
gaudy, bought on sale,

reserved, we said, for the beach,
refusing, even after years,
to bleach into respectability.   15

So many shirts and skirts and pants
recycling week after week, head over heels
recapitulating themselves.

All those wrinkles
to be smoothed, or else   20
ignored; they're in style.

Myriad uncoupled socks
which went paired into the foam
like those creatures in the ark.

And what's shrunk   25
is tough to discard
even for Goodwill.

In pockets, surprises:
forgotten matches,
lost screws clinking on enamel;   30

paper clips, whatever they held
between shiny jaws, now
dissolved or clogging the drain;

well-washed dollars, legal tender
for all debts public and private,   35
intact despite agitation;

and, gleaming in the maelstrom,
one bright dime,
broken necklace of good gold

you brought from Kuwait,   40
the strangely tailored shirt
left by a former lover. . . .

If you were to leave me,
if I were to fold
only my own clothes,   45

the convexes and concaves
of my blouses, panties, stockings, bras
turned upon themselves,

a mountain of unsorted wash
could not fill   50
the empty side of the bed.

Elisavietta Ritchie (b. 1932)

QUESTIONS

1. Explain the metaphor in the first stanza. Where does the poem explicitly
   return to it? What psychological association connects lines 41–42 to
   line 43?
2. Explain how the length of the poem supports the overstatement in line
   49. What is the speaker's attitude toward the "you" in the poem, and toward her role as housekeeper?

82. The Unknown Citizen

(To JS/07/M/378 This Marble Monument Is Erected by the State)

He was found by the Bureau of Statistics to be
One against whom there was no official complaint,
And all the reports on his conduct agree
That, in the modern sense of an old-fashioned word, he was a saint,
For in everything he did he served the Greater Community.   5
Except for the War till the day he retired
He worked in a factory and never got fired,
But satisfied his employers, Fudge Motors Inc.
Yet he wasn't a scab or odd in his views,
For his Union reports that he paid his dues   10
(Our report on his Union shows it was sound),
And our Social Psychology workers found
That he was popular with his mates and liked a drink.
The Press are convinced that he bought a paper every day
And that his reactions to advertisements were normal in every way. 15
Policies taken out in his name prove that he was fully insured,
And his Health-card shows he was once in hospital but left it cured.
Both Producers Research and High-Grade Living declare
He was fully sensible to the advantages of the Installment Plan
And had everything necessary to the Modern Man,   20
A phonograph, a radio, a car and a frigidaire.
Our researchers into Public Opinion are content
That he held the proper opinions for the time of year;
When there was peace, he was for peace; when there was war, he went.
He was married and added five children to the population,   25
Which our Eugenist says was the right number for a parent of his
   generation,

And our teachers report that he never interfered with their education.
Was he free? Was he happy? The question is absurd:
Had anything been wrong, we should certainly have heard.

W. H. Auden (1907–1973)

QUESTIONS

1. Vocabulary: *scab* (9), *Eugenist* (26).
2. Explain the allusion and the irony in the title. Why was the citizen
   "unknown"?
3. This obituary of an unknown state "hero" was apparently prepared by a
   functionary of the state. Give an account of the citizen's life and character
   from Auden's own point of view.
4. What trends in modern life and social organization does the poem satirize?

83. Departmental

An ant on the tablecloth
Ran into a dormant moth
Of many times his size.
He showed not the least surprise.
His business wasn't with such.   5
He gave it scarcely a touch,
And was off on his duty run.
Yet if he encountered one
Of the hive's enquiry squad
Whose work is to find out God   10
And the nature of time and space,
He would put him onto the case.
Ants are a curious race;
One crossing with hurried tread
The body of one of their dead   15
Isn't given a moment's arrest—
Seems not even impressed.
But he no doubt reports to any
With whom he crosses antennae,
And they no doubt report   20
To the higher up at court.
Then word goes forth in Formic:
"Death's come to Jerry McCormic,
Our selfless forager Jerry.
Will the special Janizary   25
Whose office it is to bury
The dead of the commissary

Go bring him home to his people.
Lay him in state on a sepal.
Wrap him for shroud in a petal.   30
Embalm him with ichor of nettle.
This is the word of your Queen."
And presently on the scene
Appears a solemn mortician;
And taking formal position   35
With feelers calmly atwiddle,
Seizes the dead by the middle,
And heaving him high in air,
Carries him out of there.
No one stands round to stare.   40
It is nobody else's affair.

It couldn't be called ungentle.
But how thoroughly departmental.

Robert Frost (1874–1963)

QUESTIONS

1. Vocabulary: *dormant* (2), *Formic* (22), *Janizary* (25), *commissary* (27), *sepal* (29), *ichor* (31).
2. The poem is ostensibly about ants. Is it ultimately about ants? Give reasons to support your view that it is or is not.
3. What is the author's attitude toward the "departmental" (43) organization of ant society? How is it indicated? Could this poem be described as "gently satiric"? If so, in what sense?
4. Compare and contrast this poem with "The Unknown Citizen" in content and manner.

84. The State

When they killed my mother it made me nervous;
I thought to myself, it was *right*:
Of course she was crazy, and how she ate!
And she died, after all, in her way, for the State.
But I minded: how queer it was to stare   5
At one of them not sitting there.

When they drafted Sister I said all night,
"It's healthier there in the fields";
And I'd think, "Now I'm helping to win the War,"
When the neighbors came in, as they did, with my meals.   10

And I was, I was; but I was scared
With only one of them sitting there.

When they took my cat for the Army Corps
Of Conservation and Supply,
I thought of him there in the cold with the mice   15
And I cried, and I cried, and I wanted to die.
They were there, and I saw them, and that is my life.
Now there's nothing. I'm dead, and I want to die.

Randall Jarrell (1914–1965)

QUESTIONS

1. Point out examples of overstatement and understatement. Do they create verbal irony, or dramatic irony? Resolve the paradox in line 18.
2. Compare the purpose of this poem to that of "The Unknown Citizen" and "Departmental." In what ways are they similar? In what ways are they dissimilar?

85. Grace to Be Said at the Supermarket

That God of ours, the Great Geometer,
Does something for us here, where He hath put
(if you want to put it that way) things in shape,
Compressing the little lambs in orderly cubes,
Making the roast a decent cylinder,   5
Fairing the tin ellipsoid of a ham,
Getting the luncheon meat anonymous
In squares and oblongs with the edges bevelled
Or rounded (streamlined, maybe, for greater speed).

Praise Him, He hath conferred aesthetic distance   10
Upon our appetites, and on the bloody
Mess of our birthright, our unseemly need,
Imposed significant form. Through Him the brutes
Enter the pure Euclidean kingdom of number,
Free of their bulging and blood-swollen lives   15
They come to us holy, in cellophane
Transparencies, in the mystical body,

That we may look unflinchingly on death
As the greatest good, like a philosopher should.

Howard Nemerov (1920–1991)

QUESTIONS

1. In this poem "God" is a metaphor for meatpackers and the rest of those who are involved in the display of packaged meat products in the supermarkets. Does the poem satirize "us" for eating meat, or is it aimed at our denial of "our unseemly need" (12)?
2. How does meat in supermarket coolers suggest "the pure Euclidean kingdom of number" (14)?
3. Point out examples of overstatement, understatement, and paradox. Is the irony in this poem verbal or dramatic?

86. in the inner city

> in the inner city
> or
> like we call it
> home
> we think a lot about uptown   5
> and the silent nights
> and the houses straight as
> dead men
> and the pastel lights
> and we hang on to our no place   10
> happy to be alive
> and in the inner city
> or
> like we call it
> home   15

Lucille Clifton (b. 1936)

QUESTION

Is the irony in this poem verbal or dramatic?

87. Mr. Z

> Taught early that his mother's skin was the sign of error,
> He dressed and spoke the perfect part of honor;
> Won scholarships, attended the best schools,
> Disclaimed kinship with jazz and spirituals;
> Chose prudent, raceless views of each situation,   5
> Or when he could not cleanly skirt dissension,

Faced up to the dilemma, firmly seized
Whatever ground was Anglo-Saxonized.

In diet, too, his practice was exemplary:
Of pork in its profane forms he was wary;   10
Expert in vintage wines, sauces and salads,
His palate shrank from cornbread, yams and collards.

He was as careful whom he chose to kiss:
His bride had somewhere lost her Jewishness,
But kept her blue eyes; an Episcopalian   15
Prelate proclaimed them matched chameleon.
Choosing the right addresses, here, abroad,
They shunned those places where they might be barred;
Even less anxious to be asked to dine
Where hosts catered to kosher accent or exotic skin.   20

And so he climbed, unclogged by ethnic weights,
An airborne plant, flourishing without roots.
Not one false note was struck—until he died:
His subtly grieving widow could have flayed
The obit writers, ringing crude changes on a clumsy phrase: 25
"One of the most distinguished members of his race."

M. Carl Holman (1919–1988)

QUESTIONS

1. Vocabulary: *profane* (10), *kosher* (20), *exotic* (20), *ethnic* (21), *obit* (25).
2. Explain Mr. Z's motivation and the strategies he used to achieve his goal.
3. What is the author's attitude toward Mr. Z? Is he satirizing him or the society that produced him? Why does he not give Mr. Z a name?
4. What judgments on Mr. Z are implied by the metaphors in lines 16 and 22? Explain them.
5. What kind of irony is operating in the last line? As you reread the poem, where else do you detect ironic overtones?
6. What is Mr. Z's color?

88. Southern Cop

Let us forgive Ty Kendricks.
The place was Darktown. He was young.
His nerves were jittery. The day was hot.
The Negro ran out of the alley.
And so Ty shot.   5

Let us understand Ty Kendricks.
The Negro must have been dangerous,
Because he ran;
And here was a rookie with a chance
To prove himself a man.   10

Let us condone Ty Kendricks
If we cannot decorate.
When he found what the Negro was running for,
It was too late;
And all we can say for the Negro is   15
It was unfortunate.

Let us pity Ty Kendricks.
He has been through enough,
Standing there, his big gun smoking,
Rabbit-scared, alone,   20
Having to hear the wenches wail
And the dying Negro moan.

Sterling A. Brown (1901–1989)

QUESTIONS

1. Explain the poem in terms of irony and understatement. Is the irony verbal
   or dramatic? Trace the slight changes in the irony from stanza to stanza.
2. To what extent does the poem create sympathy for Ty Kendricks? How
   does it do so? Does that sympathy mean that we should "forgive" (1) or
   "condone" (11) his actions?

89. My Last Duchess

Ferrara

That's my last duchess painted on the wall,
Looking as if she were alive. I call
That piece a wonder, now; Fra Pandolf's hands
Worked busily a day, and there she stands.
Will 't please you sit and look at her? I said   5
"Fra Pandolf" by design, for never read
Strangers like you that pictured countenance,
The depth and passion of its earnest glance,
But to myself they turned (since none puts by
The curtain I have drawn for you, but I)   10
And seemed as they would ask me, if they durst,
How such a glance came there; so, not the first

Are you to turn and ask thus. Sir, 'twas not
Her husband's presence only, called that spot
Of joy into the Duchess' cheek; perhaps   15
Fra Pandolf chanced to say, "Her mantle laps
Over my lady's wrist too much," or, "Paint
Must never hope to reproduce the faint
Half-flush that dies along her throat." Such stuff
Was courtesy, she thought, and cause enough   20
For calling up that spot of joy. She had
A heart—how shall I say?—too soon made glad,
Too easily impressed; she liked whate'er
She looked on, and her looks went everywhere.
Sir, 'twas all one! My favor at her breast,   25
The dropping of the daylight in the West,
The bough of cherries some officious fool
Broke in the orchard for her, the white mule
She rode with round the terrace—all and each
Would draw from her alike the approving speech,   30
Or blush, at least. She thanked men—good! but thanked
Somehow—I know not how—as if she ranked
My gift of a nine-hundred-years-old name
With anybody's gift. Who'd stoop to blame
This sort of trifling? Even had you skill   35
In speech—which I have not—to make your will
Quite clear to such an one, and say, "Just this
Or that in you disgusts me; here you miss,
Or there exceed the mark"—and if she let
Herself be lessoned so, nor plainly set   40
Her wits to yours, forsooth, and made excuse—
E'en then would be some stooping; and I choose
Never to stoop. Oh, sir, she smiled, no doubt,
Whene'er I passed her; but who passed without
Much the same smile? This grew; I gave commands;   45
Then all smiles stopped together. There she stands
As if alive. Will 't please you rise? We'll meet
The company below, then. I repeat,
The Count your master's known munificence
Is ample warrant that no just pretense   50
Of mine for dowry will be disallowed;
Though his fair daughter's self, as I avowed
At starting, is my object. Nay, we'll go
Together down, sir. Notice Neptune, though,
Taming a sea-horse, thought a rarity,   55
Which Claus of Innsbruck cast in bronze for me!

Robert Browning (1812–1889)

QUESTIONS

1. Vocabulary: *officious* (27), *munificence* (49).
2. Ferrara is in Italy. The time is during the Renaissance, probably the sixteenth century. To whom is the Duke speaking? What is the occasion? Are the Duke's remarks about his last Duchess a digression, or do they have some relation to the business at hand?
3. Characterize the Duke as fully as you can. How does your characterization differ from the Duke's opinion of himself? What kind of irony is this?
4. Why was the Duke dissatisfied with his last Duchess? Was it sexual jealousy? What opinion do you get of the Duchess's personality, and how does it differ from the Duke's opinion?
5. What characteristics of the Italian Renaissance appear in the poem (marriage customs, social classes, art)? What is the Duke's attitude toward art? Is it insincere?
6. What happened to the Duchess? Should Browning have told us?

ADDITIONAL EXERCISE

Follow the instructions for the exercise on page 110, of which this is a continuation.

10. Whoe'er their crimes for interest only quit,
    Sin on in virtue, and good deeds *commit*.   *Edward Young*
11. No doubt but ye are the people, and wisdom shall die with you.
                                                        Book of Job, 12.1

12. One soul was ours, one mind, one heart devoted,
    That, wisely doting, asked not why it doted.   *Hartley Coleridge*
13. Give me my Romeo: and, when he shall die,
    Take him and cut him out in little stars,
    And he will make the face of heaven so fine
    That all the world will be in love with night,
    And pay no worship to the garish sun.   *Juliet,* in *Shakespeare*
14. Have not the Indians been kindly and justly treated? Have not the temporal things, the vain baubles and filthy lucre of this world, which were too apt to engage their worldy and selfish thoughts, been benevolently taken from them? And have they not instead thereof, been taught to set their affections on things above?   *Washington Irving*
15. There lives more faith in honest doubt,
    Believe me, than in half the creeds.   *Alfred, Lord Tennyson*

CHAPTER EIGHT

Allusion

The famous English diplomat and letter writer Lord Chesterfield once was invited to a great dinner given by the Spanish ambassador. At the conclusion of the meal the host rose and proposed a toast to his master, the king of Spain, whom he compared to the sun. The French ambassador followed with a health to the king of France, whom he likened to the moon. It was then Lord Chesterfield's turn. "Your excellencies have taken from me," he said, "all the greatest luminaries of heaven, and the stars are too small for me to make a comparison of my royal master; I therefore beg leave to give your excellencies— Joshua!"*

For a reader familiar with the Bible—that is, for one who recognizes the biblical allusion—Lord Chesterfield's story will come as a stunning revelation of his wit. For an **allusion**—a reference to something in history or previous literature—is, like a richly connotative word or a symbol, a means of suggesting far more than it says. The one word "Joshua," in the context of Chesterfield's toast, calls up in the reader's mind the whole biblical story of how the Israelite captain stopped the sun and the moon in order that the Israelites might finish a battle and conquer their enemies before nightfall.† The force of the toast lies in its extreme economy; it says so much in so little, and it exercises the mind of the reader to make the connection for himself.

The effect of Chesterfield's allusion is chiefly humorous or witty, but allusions may also have a powerful emotional effect. The essayist William Hazlitt writes of addressing a fashionable audience about the lexicographer Samuel Johnson. Speaking of Johnson's great heart and of his charity to the unfortunate, Hazlitt recounted how, finding a drunken prostitute lying in Fleet Street late at night, Johnson carried her on his broad back to the address she managed to give him. The audience, unable to face the picture of the famous dictionary-maker

---

*Samuel Shellabarger, *Lord Chesterfield and His World* (Boston: Little, Brown, 1951) 132.
†Joshua 10.12–14.

doing such a thing, broke out in titters and expostulations, whereupon Hazlitt simply said: "I remind you, ladies and gentlemen, of the parable of the Good Samaritan." The audience was promptly silenced.*

Allusions are a means of reinforcing the emotion or the ideas of one's own work with the emotion or ideas of another work or occasion. Because they may compact so much meaning in so small a space, they are extremely useful to the poet.

90. "Out, Out—"

The buzz-saw snarled and rattled in the yard
And made dust and dropped stove-length sticks of wood,
Sweet-scented stuff when the breeze drew across it.
And from there those that lifted eyes could count
Five mountain ranges one behind the other   5
Under the sunset far into Vermont.
And the saw snarled and rattled, snarled and rattled,
As it ran light, or had to bear a load.
And nothing happened: day was all but done.
Call it a day, I wish they might have said   10
To please the boy by giving him the half hour
That a boy counts so much when saved from work.
His sister stood beside them in her apron
To tell them "Supper." At the word, the saw,
As if to prove saws knew what supper meant,   15
Leaped out at the boy's hand, or seemed to leap—
He must have given the hand. However it was,
Neither refused the meeting. But the hand!
The boy's first outcry was a rueful laugh,
As he swung toward them holding up the hand   20
Half in appeal, but half as if to keep
The life from spilling. Then the boy saw all—
Since he was old enough to know, big boy
Doing a man's work, though a child at heart—
He saw all spoiled. "Don't let him cut my hand off—   25
The doctor, when he comes. Don't let him, sister!"
So. But the hand was gone already.
The doctor put him in the dark of ether.
He lay and puffed his lips out with his breath.
And then—the watcher at his pulse took fright.   30
No one believed. They listened at his heart.

*Jacques Barzun, *Teacher in America* (Boston: Little, Brown, 1945) 160.

Little—less—nothing!—and that ended it.
No more to build on there. And they, since they
Were not the one dead, turned to their affairs.

Robert Frost (1874–1963)

QUESTIONS

1. How does this poem differ from a newspaper account that might have dealt with the same incident?
2. To whom does "They" (33) refer? The boy's family? The doctor and medical attendants? Casual onlookers? Need we assume that all these people—whoever they are—turned immediately "to their affairs" (34)? Does the ending of this poem seem to you callous or merely realistic? Would a more tearful and sentimental ending have made the poem better or worse?
3. What figure of speech is used in lines 21–22?

Allusions vary widely in the burden put on them by the poet to convey meaning. Lord Chesterfield risked his whole meaning on his hearers' recognizing his allusion. Robert Frost in "'Out, Out—'" makes his meaning entirely clear even for the reader who does not recognize the allusion contained in the poem's title. His theme is the uncertainty and unpredictability of life, which may be ended accidentally at any moment, and the tragic waste of human potentiality that takes place when such premature deaths occur. A boy who is already "Doing a man's work" and gives every promise of having a useful life ahead of him is suddenly wiped out. There seems no rational explanation for either the accident or the death. The only comment to be made is, "No more to build on there."

Frost's title, however, is an allusion to one of the most famous passages in all English literature, and it offers a good illustration of how a poet may use allusion not only to reinforce emotion but also to help define his theme. The passage is that in *Macbeth* in which Macbeth has just been informed of his wife's death. A good many readers will recall the key phrase, "Out, out, brief candle!" with its underscoring of the tragic brevity and uncertainty of life. For some readers, however, the allusion will summon up the whole passage in Act 5, scene 5, in which this phrase occurs. Macbeth's words are:

91.   She should have died hereafter;
           There would have been a time for such a word.
           Tomorrow, and tomorrow, and tomorrow

Creeps in this petty pace from day to day
To the last syllable of recorded time;   5
And all our yesterdays have lighted fools
The way to dusty death. Out, out, brief candle!
Life's but a walking shadow, a poor player,
That struts and frets his hour upon the stage
And then is heard no more. It is a tale   10
Told by an idiot, full of sound and fury,
Signifying nothing.

Macbeth's first words underscore the theme of premature death. The boy also "should have died hereafter." The rest of the passage, with its marvelous evocation of the vanity and meaninglessness of life, expresses neither Shakespeare's philosophy nor, ultimately, Frost's, but it is Macbeth's philosophy at the time of his bereavement, and it is likely to express the feelings of us all when such tragic accidents occur. Life does indeed seem cruel and meaningless, "a tale / Told by an idiot," signifying nothing, when human life and potentiality are thus without explanation so suddenly ended.

QUESTION

Examine Macbeth's speech for examples of personification, apostrophe, and metonymy. How many metaphors for an individual human life does it present?

Allusions also vary widely in the number of readers to whom they will be familiar. Poets, in using an allusion, as in using a figure of speech, are always in danger of being misunderstood. What appeals powerfully to one reader may lose another reader altogether. But poets must assume a certain fund of common experience in readers. They could not even write about the ocean unless they could assume that readers have seen the ocean or pictures of it. In the same way poets assume a certain common fund of literary experience, most frequently of classical mythology, Shakespeare, or the Bible—particularly the King James Version. Poets are often justified in expecting a rather wide range of literary experience in readers, for the people who read poetry for pleasure are generally intelligent and well-read. But, obviously, beginning readers will not have this range, just as they will not know the meanings of as many words as will more mature readers. Students should therefore be prepared to look up certain allusions, just as they should be eager to look up in their dictionaries the meanings of unfamiliar words. They will find that every increase in knowledge broadens their base for understanding both literature and life.

---

92. in Just-

in Just-
spring   when the world is mud-
luscious the little
lame balloonman

whistles   far   and wee   5

and eddieandbill come
running from marbles and
piracies and it's
spring

when the world is puddle-wonderful   10

the queer
old balloonman whistles
far   and   wee
and bettyandisbel come dancing

from hop-scotch and jump-rope and   15

it's
spring
and
     the

               goat-footed   20

balloonMan   whistles
far
and
wee

                                        e. e. cummings (1894–1962)

QUESTION

Why is the balloonman called "goat-footed" (20)? How does the identification made by this mythological allusion enrich the meaning of the poem?

93. On His Blindness

When I consider how my light is spent
  Ere half my days in this dark world and wide,
  And that one talent which is death to hide
  Lodged with me useless, though my soul more bent
To serve therewith my Maker, and present   5
  My true account, lest he returning chide,
  "Doth God exact day-labor, light denied?"
  I fondly ask. But Patience, to prevent
That murmur, soon replies, "God doth not need
  Either man's work or his own gifts. Who best   10
  Bear his mild yoke, they serve him best. His state
Is kingly: thousands at his bidding speed,
  And post o'er land and ocean without rest;
  They also serve who only stand and wait."

John Milton (1608–1674)

QUESTIONS

1. Vocabulary: *spent* (1), *fondly* (8), *prevent* (8), *post* (13).
2. What two meanings has "talent" (3)? What is Milton's "one talent"?
3. The poem is unified and expanded in its dimensions by a biblical allusion that Milton's original readers would have recognized immediately. What is it? If you do not know, look up Matthew 25.14–30. In what ways is the situation in the poem similar to that in the parable? In what ways is it different?
4. What is the point of the poem?

94. Hero and Leander

Both robbed of air, we both lie in one ground,
Both whom one fire had burnt, one water drowned.

John Donne (1572–1631)

QUESTIONS

1. After looking up the story of Hero and Leander (if necessary), explain each of the four parts into which this epigram is divided by its punctuation. Which parts are literal? Which are metaphorical?
2. The subject of the poem is taken from Greek legend; its structure is based on Greek science. Explain.

95. Miniver Cheevy

Miniver Cheevy, child of scorn,
   Grew lean while he assailed the seasons;
He wept that he was ever born,
   And he had reasons.

Miniver loved the days of old   5
   When swords were bright and steeds were prancing;
The vision of a warrior bold
   Would set him dancing.

Miniver sighed for what was not,
   And dreamed, and rested from his labors;   10
He dreamed of Thebes and Camelot,
   And Priam's neighbors.

Miniver mourned the ripe renown
   That made so many a name so fragrant;
He mourned Romance, now on the town,   15
   And Art, a vagrant.

Miniver loved the Medici,
   Albeit he had never seen one;
He would have sinned incessantly
   Could he have been one.   20

Miniver cursed the commonplace
   And eyed a khaki suit with loathing;
He missed the medieval grace
   Of iron clothing.

Miniver scorned the gold he sought,   25
   But sore annoyed was he without it;
Miniver thought, and thought, and thought,
   And thought about it.

Miniver Cheevy, born too late,
   Scratched his head and kept on thinking;   30
Miniver coughed, and called it fate,
   And kept on drinking.

Edwin Arlington Robinson (1869–1935)

QUESTIONS

1. Vocabulary: *khaki* (22). The phrase "on the town" (15) means "on charity" or "down and out."

2. Identify Thebes, Camelot (11), Priam (12), and the Medici (17). What names and what sort of life does each call up? What does Miniver's love of these names tell about him?
3. Discuss the phrase "child of scorn" (1). What does it mean? In how many ways is it applicable to Miniver?
4. What is Miniver's attitude toward material wealth?
5. The phrase "rested from his labors" (10) alludes to the Bible *and* to Greek mythology. Explore the ironic effect of comparing Miniver to the Creator (Genesis 2.2) and to Hercules. Point out other examples of irony in the poem and discuss their importance.
6. Can we call this a poem about a man whose "fate" was to be "born too late"? Explain your answer.

96. Leda and the Swan

A sudden blow: the great wings beating still
Above the staggering girl, her thighs caressed
By the dark webs, her nape caught in his bill,
He holds her helpless breast upon his breast.

How can those terrified vague fingers push   5
The feathered glory from her loosening thighs?
And how can body, laid in that white rush,
But feel the strange heart beating where it lies?

A shudder in the loins engenders there
The broken wall, the burning roof and tower   10
And Agamemnon dead.
                          Being so caught up,
So mastered by the brute blood of the air,
Did she put on his knowledge with his power
Before the indifferent beak could let her drop?

William Butler Yeats (1865–1939)

QUESTIONS

1. What is the connection between Leda and "The broken wall, the burning roof and tower / And Agamemnon dead"? If you do not know, look up the myth of Leda and, if necessary, the story of Agamemnon.
2. How does this poem do more than evoke an episode out of mythology? What is the significance of the question asked in the last two lines? How would you answer it?

97. Leda's Sister and the Geese

All the boys always wanted her, so
it was no surprise about the swan-
man, god, whatever he was. That day

I was stuck at home, as usual, while
she got to moon around the lake   5
supposedly picking lilies for dye. Think *I*

would have let some pair of wings catch me,
bury me under the weight of the sky?
She came home whimpering, whined out

the whole story, said she was "sore afraid"   10
she'd got pregnant. Hunh. "Sore"
I'll bet, the size she described, and

pregnant figures: no guess who'll get
to help her with the kid or, Hera forbid,
more than one (twins run in our damned   15

family). "Never you mind, dear," Mother said.
"Your sister will take on your chores."
Sure. As though I wasn't already doing

twice as many of my own. So now
I clean, I spin, I weave, I bake,   20
fling crusts to feed these birds I wish

to Hades every day; while she sits smug
in a wicker chair, and eats sweetmeats,
and combs and combs that ratty golden hair.

Katharyn Howd Machan (b. 1952)

QUESTIONS

1. What does this humorous version of the Leda/Zeus story add to your
   perspective on that grand myth? How does the language create humor?
2. "[S]ore afraid" (10) is an allusion to Luke 2.9. How does the poem make
   use of it? What purpose is served by this vulgarized link between two inci-
   dences of divine birth?

98. An altered look about the hills

An altered look about the hills—
A Tyrian light the village fills—
A wider sunrise in the morn—

A deeper twilight on the lawn—
A print of a vermilion foot—   5
A purple finger on the slope—
A flippant fly upon the pane—
A spider at his trade again—
An added strut in chanticleer—
A flower expected everywhere—   10
An axe shrill singing in the woods—
Fern odors on untraveled roads—
All this and more I cannot tell—
A furtive look you know as well—
And Nicodemus's mystery   15
Receives its annual reply!

Emily Dickinson (1830–1886)

QUESTIONS

1. Vocabulary: *Tyrian* (2), *chanticleer* (9).
2. What does the list of natural changes indicate? How is that an answer to
   Nicodemus's questions to Jesus? (If you are not familiar with the allusion,
   see John 3.4.) Does the meaning of this poem concur or contrast with the
   meaning of the biblical passage?

99. Abraham to kill him

Abraham to kill him
Was distinctly told.
Isaac was an urchin,
Abraham was old.

Not a hesitation—   5
Abraham complied.
Flattered by obeisance,
Tyranny demurred.

Isaac, to his children
Lived to tell the tale.   10
Moral: with a mastiff
Manners may prevail.

Emily Dickinson (1830–1886)

QUESTIONS

1. Vocabulary: *obeisance* (7), *demurred* (8).
2. To whom or to what do "Tyranny" (8) and "mastiff" (11) refer? What
   figure of speech is each?

3. Who are Abraham and Isaac? What, in the context of the original story, does "demurred" mean? If you cannot answer these questions, read Genesis 22.1–18.
4. What is the reaction of the poet to this Bible story?

100. Jack, eating rotten cheese, did say

> Jack, eating rotten cheese, did say,
> Like Samson I my thousands slay;
> I vow, quoth Roger, so you do.
> And with the self-same weapon, too.

Benjamin Franklin (1706–1790)

QUESTION

If you cannot identify the allusion, see Judges 15.15–16.

101. A monkey sprang down from a tree

> A monkey sprang down from a tree
> And angrily cursed Charles D.
>   "I hold with the Bible,"
>   He cried. "It's a libel
> That man is descended from me!"

Laurence Perrine (1915–1995)

102. Two brothers devised what at sight

> Two brothers devised what at sight
> Seemed a bicycle crossed with a kite.
>   They predicted—rash pair!
>   It would fly through the air!
> And what do you know? They were Wright!

Laurence Perrine (1915–1995)

QUESTION

One of the two preceding allusive limericks is little more than a clever pun, the other poses a theme in a witty form. Which is which?

CHAPTER NINE

Meaning and Idea

103. Little Jack Horner

> Little Jack Horner
> Sat in a corner
> Eating a Christmas pie.
> He stuck in his thumb
> And pulled out a plum   5
> And said, "What a good boy am I!"

Anonymous

The meaning of a poem is the experience it expresses—nothing less. But readers who, baffled by a particular poem, ask perplexedly, "What does it *mean?*" are usually after something more specific than this. They want something they can grasp entirely with their minds. We may therefore find it useful to distinguish the **total meaning** of a poem—the experience it communicates (and which can be communicated in no other way)—from its **prose meaning**—the ingredient that can be separated out in the form of a prose paraphrase (see Chapter 2). If we make this distinction, however, we must be careful not to confuse the two kinds of meaning. The prose meaning is no more the poem than a plum is a pie or than a prune is a plum.

The prose meaning will not necessarily or perhaps even usually be an idea. It may be a story, a description, a statement of emotion, a presentation of human character, or some combination of these. "The Mill" (No. 20) tells a story; "The Eagle" (No. 1) is primarily descriptive; "Western Wind" (No. 49) is an expression of emotion; "My Last Duchess" (No. 89) is an account of human character. None of these poems is directly concerned with ideas. Message-hunters will be baffled and disappointed by poetry of this kind because they will not find what they are looking for, and they may attempt to read some idea into the poem that is really not there. Yet ideas are also part of human experience, and therefore many poems are concerned, at least partially, with presenting ideas. But with these poems message-hunting is an even more dangerous activity, for the message-hunters are likely to think that the whole object of reading the poem is to find the message—that the idea is really the only important thing in it. Like Little Jack Horner, they will reach in and pluck out the idea and say, "What a good boy am I!" as if the pie existed for the plum.

The idea in a poem is only part of the total experience that it communicates. The value and worth of the poem are determined by the value of the total experience, not by the truth or the nobility of the idea itself. This is not to say that the truth of the idea is unimportant, or that its validity should not be examined and appraised. But a good idea alone will not make a good poem, nor need an idea with which the reader does not agree ruin one. Good readers of poetry are receptive to all kinds of experience. They are able to make that "willing suspension of disbelief" that Coleridge characterized as constituting poetic faith. When one attends a performance of *Hamlet,* one is willing to forget for the time being that such a person as Hamlet never existed and that the events on the stage are fictions. Likewise, poetry readers should be willing to entertain imaginatively, for the time being, ideas they objectively regard as untrue. It is one way of better understanding these ideas and of enlarging the reader's own experience. The person who believes in God should be able to enjoy a good poem expressing atheistic ideas, just as the atheist should be able to appreciate a good poem in praise of God. The optimist should be able to find pleasure in pessimistic poetry, and the pessimist in optimistic poetry. The teetotaler should be able to enjoy *The Rubáiyát of Omar Khayyám,* and the winebibber a good poem in praise of austerity. The primary value of a poem depends not so much on the truth of the idea presented as on the power with which it is communicated and on its being made a convincing part of a meaningful total experience. We must feel that the idea has been truly and deeply *felt* by the poet, and that the poet is doing something more than merely moralizing. The plum must be made part of a pie. If the plum is properly combined with other ingredients and if the pie is well baked, it should be enjoyable even for persons who do not care for the type of plums from which it is made. Consider, for instance, the following two poems.

104. Loveliest of Trees

Loveliest of trees, the cherry now
Is hung with bloom along the bough,
And stands about the woodland ride
Wearing white for Eastertide.

Now, of my threescore years and ten,   5
Twenty will not come again,
And take from seventy springs a score,
It only leaves me fifty more.

And since to look at things in bloom
Fifty springs are little room,   10
About the woodlands I will go
To see the cherry hung with snow.

A. E. Housman (1859–1936)

QUESTIONS

1. Very briefly, this poem presents a philosophy of life. In a sentence, what is it?
2. How old is the speaker? Why does he assume that his life will be seventy years in length? What is surprising about the words "only" (8) and "little" (10)?
3. A good deal of ink has been spilt over whether "snow" (12) is literal or figurative. What do you say? Justify your answer.

105. Stopping by Woods on a Snowy Evening

Whose woods these are I think I know.
His house is in the village though;
He will not see me stopping here
To watch his woods fill up with snow.

My little horse must think it queer   5
To stop without a farmhouse near
Between the woods and frozen lake
The darkest evening of the year.

He gives his harness bells a shake
To ask if there is some mistake.   10
The only other sound's the sweep
Of easy wind and downy flake.

The woods are lovely, dark and deep,
But I have promises to keep,
And miles to go before I sleep,   15
And miles to go before I sleep.

Robert Frost (1874–1963)

QUESTIONS

1. How do these two poems differ in idea?
2. What contrasts are suggested between the speaker in the second poem
   and (a) his horse and (b) the owner of the woods?

Both of these poems present ideas, the first more or less explicitly, the second symbolically. Perhaps the best way to get at the idea of the second poem is to ask two questions. First, why does the speaker stop? Second, why does he go on? He stops, we answer, to watch the woods fill up with snow—to observe a scene of natural beauty. He goes on, we answer, because he has "promises to keep"—that is, he has obligations to fulfill. He is momentarily torn between his love of beauty and these other various and complex claims that life has upon him. The small conflict in the poem is symbolic of a larger conflict in life. One part of the sensitive, thinking person would like to give up his life to the enjoyment of beauty and art. But another part is aware of larger duties and responsibilities—responsibilities owed, at least in part, to other human beings. The speaker in the poem would like to satisfy both impulses. But when the two conflict, he seems to suggest, the "promises" must take precedence.

The first poem also presents a philosophy but it is an opposing one. For the twenty-year-old speaker, the appreciation of beauty is of such importance that he will make it his lifelong dedication, filling his time with enjoying whatever the seasons bring. The metaphor comparing white cherry blossoms to snow suggests that each season has its own special beauty, though the immediate season is spring. In a limited life, one should seek out and delight in whatever beauty is present. Thoughtful readers will have to choose between these two philosophies—to commit themselves to one or the other—but this commitment should not destroy for them their enjoyment of either poem. If it does, they are reading for plums and not for pies.

Nothing we have said so far in this chapter should be construed as meaning that the truth or falsity of the idea in a poem is a matter of no importance. *Other things being equal,* good readers naturally will, and properly should, value more highly the poem whose idea they feel to be more mature and nearer to the heart of human experience. Some ideas, moreover, may seem so vicious or so foolish or so beyond the pale of normal human decency as to discredit *by themselves* the poems in which they are found. A rotten plum may spoil a pie. But good readers strive for intellectual flexibility and tolerance, and are able to entertain sympathetically ideas other than their own. They often will like a poem whose idea they disagree with better than one with an idea they accept. And, above all, they will not confuse the prose meaning of any poem with its total meaning. They will not mistake plums for pies.

106. To a Waterfowl

Whither, midst falling dew,
While glow the heavens with the last steps of day,
Far, through their rosy depths, dost thou pursue
Thy solitary way?

Vainly the fowler's eye   5
Might mark thy distant flight to do thee wrong,
As, darkly painted on the crimson sky,
Thy figure floats along.

Seek'st thou the plashy brink
Of weedy lake, or marge of river wide,   10
Or where the rocking billows rise and sink
On the chafed ocean side?

There is a Power whose care
Teaches thy way along that pathless coast—
The desert and illimitable air—   15
Lone wandering, but not lost.

All day thy wings have fanned,
At that far height, the cold, thin atmosphere,
Yet stoop not, weary, to the welcome land,
Though the dark night is near.   20

And soon that toil shall end;
Soon shalt thou find a summer home, and rest,
And scream among thy fellows; reeds shall bend,
Soon, o'er thy sheltered nest.

Thou'rt gone, the abyss of heaven   25
Hath swallowed up thy form; yet, on my heart
Deeply has sunk the lesson thou hast given,
    And shall not soon depart.

He who, from zone to zone,
Guides through the boundless sky thy certain flight,   30
In the long way that I must tread alone,
    Will lead my steps aright.

William Cullen Bryant (1794–1878)

QUESTIONS

1. Vocabulary: *fowler* (5), *desert* (15), *stoop* (19).
2. What figure of speech unifies the poem?
3. Where is the waterfowl flying? Why? What is "that pathless coast" (14)?
4. What "Power" (13) "Guides" (30) the waterfowl to its destination? How
   does it do so?
5. What lesson does the poet derive from his observations?

107. Design

I found a dimpled spider, fat and white,
On a white heal-all, holding up a moth
Like a white piece of rigid satin cloth—
Assorted characters of death and blight
Mixed ready to begin the morning right,   5
Like the ingredients of a witches' broth—
A snow-drop spider, a flower like a froth,
And dead wings carried like a paper kite.

What had that flower to do with being white,
The wayside blue and innocent heal-all?   10
What brought the kindred spider to that height,
Then steered the white moth thither in the night?
What but design of darkness to appall?—
If design govern in a thing so small.

Robert Frost (1874–1963)

QUESTIONS

1. Vocabulary: *characters* (4), *snow-drop* (7).
2. The heal-all is a wildflower, usually blue or violet but occasionally white,
   found blooming along roadsides in the summer. It was once supposed to

have healing qualities, hence its name. Of what significance, scientific and poetic, is the fact that the spider, the heal-all, and the moth are all white? Of what poetic significance is the fact that the spider is "dimpled" and "fat" and like a "snow-drop," and that the flower is "innocent" and named "heal-all"?

3. The "argument from design"—that the manifest existence of design in the universe implies the existence of a Great Designer—was a favorite eighteenth-century argument for the existence of God. What twist does Frost give the argument? What answer does he suggest to the question in lines 11–12? How comforting is the apparent concession in line 14?

4. Contrast Frost's poem in content and emotional effect with "To a Water-fowl." Is it possible to like both?

108. The Indifferent

"I can love both fair and brown,
Her whom abundance melts, and her whom want betrays,
Her who loves loneness best, and her who masks and plays,
    Her whom the country formed, and whom the town,
        Her who believes, and her who tries,°   tests   5
        Her who still weeps with spongy eyes,
    And her who is dry cork and never cries;
    I can love her, and her, and you, and you;
    I can love any, so she be not true.°   faithful

"Will no other vice content you?   10
Will it not serve your turn to do as did your mothers?
Or have you all old vices spent, and now would find out others?
    Or doth a fear that men are true torment you?
        Oh, we are not; be not you so.
        Let me, and do you, twenty know.   15
    Rob me, but bind me not, and let me go.
    Must I, who came to travail thorough° you,   through
    Grow your fixed subject because you are true?"

Venus heard me sing this song,
And by love's sweetest part, variety, she swore   20
She heard not this till now, and that it should be so no more.
    She went, examined, and returned ere long,
        And said, "Alas, some two or three
        Poor heretics in love there be,
    Which think to 'stablish dangerous constancy,   25
    But I have told them, 'Since you will be true,
    You shall be true to them who are false to you.'"

                                        John Donne (1572–1631)

QUESTIONS

1. Vocabulary: *Indifferent* (title), *know* (15), *travail* (17).
2. Who is the speaker? To whom is he speaking? About what is he "indifferent"? What one qualification does he insist on in a lover? Why?
3. Of what vice does he accuse the women of his generation in line 10? How, in his opinion, do they differ from their mothers? Why?
4. Why does Venus investigate the speaker's complaint? Does her investigation confirm or refute his accusation? Who are the "heretics in love" (24) whom she discovers? What punishment does she decree for them?

109. Love's Deity

I long to talk with some old lover's ghost
    Who died before the god of love was born.
I cannot think that he who then loved most
    Sunk so low as to love one which did scorn.
But since this god produced a destiny,   5
And that vice-nature, custom, lets it be,
        I must love her that loves not me.

Sure, they which made him god meant not so much,
    Nor he in his young godhead practiced it.
But when an even flame two hearts did touch,   10
    His office was indulgently to fit
Actives to passives. Correspondency
Only his subject was. It cannot be
        Love till I love her that loves me.

But every modern god will° now extend   wants to 15
    His vast prerogative as far as Jove.
To rage, to lust, to write to, to commend,
    All is the purlieu of the god of love.
Oh, were we wakened by this tyranny
To ungod this child again, it could not be   20
        I should love her who loves not me.

Rebel and atheist too, why murmur I
    As though I felt the worst that Love could do?
Love might make me leave loving, or might try
    A deeper plague, to make her love me too,   25
Which, since she loves before, I am loath to see.
Falsehood is worse than hate, and that must be
        If she whom I love should love me.

John Donne (1572–1631)

QUESTIONS

1. Vocabulary: *vice-* (6), *even* (10), *purlieu* (18).
2. Who is the modern "god of love" (2)? Why is he called a "child" (20)? What did "they which made him god" (8) intend to be his duties? How has he gone beyond these duties? Why does the speaker long to talk with some lover's ghost who died before this god was born (1–2)?
3. What is the speaker's situation? Whom does the speaker call "Rebel and atheist" (22)? Why?
4. Why does the speaker rebuke himself for "murmuring" in the final stanza? What two things could Love do to him that have not been done already? Why are they worse? Explain the words "before" (26) and "Falsehood" (27). To which word in the first stanza does "hate" (27) correspond?
5. How does the speaker define "love" in this poem? Is he consistent in his use of the term? How does he differ from the speaker in "The Indifferent" in his conception of love?
6. How do you explain the fact that "Love's Deity" and "The Indifferent," though both by the same poet, express opposite opinions about the value of fidelity in love?

110. To the Mercy Killers

If ever mercy move you murder me,
I pray you, kindly killers, let me live.
Never conspire with death to set me free,
but let me know such life as pain can give.
Even though I be a clot, an aching clench,   5
a stub, a stump, a butt, a scab, a knob,
a screaming pain, a putrefying stench,
still let me live, so long as life shall throb.
Even though I turn such traitor to myself
as beg to die, do not accomplice me.   10
Even though I seem not human, a mute shelf
of glucose, bottled blood, machinery
to swell the lung and pump the heart—even so,
do not put out my life. Let me still glow.

Dudley Randall (b. 1914)

QUESTIONS

1. In form this is a Shakespearean sonnet (see page 328), consisting of three quatrains and a concluding couplet (units of 4, 4, 4, and 2 lines each); but in structure (organization of thought) it follows the Italian model of an octave and sestet (8- and 6-line units) in which the first eight lines

introduce a thought and the sestet produces some kind of counterthought. What "turn" of thought occurs at the end of line 8 in this sonnet?
2. Identify the paradox in line 2 that introduces the central topic of the poem. (It is also stated in the title, but line 2 states it more effectively because of its alliteration.)
3. Is the speaker advocating a universal standard of conduct or merely expressing his personal desire?

111. How Annandale Went Out

"They called it Annandale—and I was there
To flourish, to find words, and to attend:
Liar, physician, hypocrite, and friend,
I watched him; and the sight was not so fair
As one or two that I have seen elsewhere: 5
An apparatus not for me to mend—
A wreck, with hell between him and the end,
Remained of Annandale; and I was there.

"I knew the ruin as I knew the man;
So put the two together, if you can,   10
Remembering the worst you know of me.
Now view yourself as I was, on the spot—
With a slight kind of engine. Do you see?
Like this . . . You wouldn't hang me? I thought not."

Edwin Arlington Robinson (1869–1935)

QUESTIONS

1. George Annandale is the central character in two longish poems by Robinson. In one of these, after a visit to his closest friend (who is also his doctor), Annandale is maimed and almost killed in an automobile accident. The doctor hears "a sick crash in the street" and finds his friend in a condition for which there can be no healing and which will only entail intense suffering while he lives. This information, though not essential to understanding Robinson's sonnet, may make it easier. Who is the speaker? Whom is he addressing? Why?
2. Discuss the role of overstatement and understatement in the poem. Why does the speaker call himself a "Liar" and "hypocrite" (3)? What does he mean by lines 4–5? What does he mean by line 9? What nouns and pronouns does he use in referring to Annandale?
3. Why does he repeat "and I was there" (1, 8)? What meanings has "on the spot" (12)?
4. What is the "slight kind of engine" (13)? What gesture does he make with his hand in explaining it? What has he done—something legal or illegal? Moral or immoral? What is his motivation in revealing what he has done?

5. Does his auditor approve of his action? Does Robinson?
6. Compare or contrast the attitudes expressed in this poem and in "To the Mercy Killers."

112. The Caged Skylark

As a dare-gale skylark scanted in a dull cage
   Man's mounting spirit in his bone-house, mean house, dwells—
   That bird beyond the remembering his free fells;
This in drudgery, day-laboring-out life's age.

Though aloft on turf or perch or poor low stage,   5
   Both sing sometimes the sweetest, sweetest spells,
   Yet both droop deadly sometimes in their cells
Or wring their barriers in bursts of fear or rage.

Not that the sweet-fowl, song-fowl, needs no rest—
Why, hear him, hear him babble and drop down to his nest,   10
   But his own nest, wild nest, no prison.

Man's spirit will be flesh-bound when found at best,
But uncumbered: meadow-down is not distressed
   For a rainbow footing it nor he for his bones risen.

Gerard Manley Hopkins (1844–1889)

QUESTIONS

1. Vocabulary: *scanted* (1), *fells* (3). What meanings of "mean" (2) are appropriate here? "[T]urf" (5) is a piece of sod placed in a cage.
2. The speaker expresses a belief in the Christian doctrine of the resurrection of the body. According to this belief, the immortal soul, after death, will be ultimately reunited with the body; this body, however, will be a weightless, perfected, glorified body, not the gross imperfect body of mortal life. Express the analogy in the poem as a pair of mathematical statements of proportion (in the form $a:b = c:d$ and $e:f = g:h = i:j$), using the following terms: caged skylark, mortal body, meadow-down, cage, rainbow, spirit-in-life, nest, immortal spirit, wild skylark, resurrected body.
3. Discuss the image of the last two lines as a figure for weightlessness. Why would a shadow not have been as apt as a rainbow for this comparison?

113. No worst, there is none

No worst, there is none. Pitched past pitch of grief,
More pangs will, schooled at forepangs, wilder wring.
Comforter, where, where is your comforting?

Mary, mother of us, where is your relief?
My cries heave, herds-long; huddle in a main, a chief-   5
woe, world-sorrow; on an age-old anvil wince and sing—
Then lull, then leave off. Fury had shrieked "No ling-
ering! Let me be fell: force,° I must be brief."   perforce
O the mind, mind has mountains; cliffs of fall
Frightful, sheer, no-man-fathomed. Hold them cheap   10
May who ne'er hung there. Nor does long our small
Durance° deal with that steep or deep. Here! creep,   endurance
Wretch, under a comfort serves in a whirlwind: all
Life death does end and each day dies with sleep.

Gerard Manley Hopkins (1844–1889)

QUESTIONS

1. Vocabulary: *fell* (8). "Comforter" (3) refers to the Holy Spirit; "herds-long" and "huddle in a main" (5) evoke two images of flocks of sheep.
2. Examine the auditory and visual imagery.
3. What is gained by the failure to identify a particular cause of the speaker's pain and terror? Do the religious references in lines 3 and 4 and the pastoral images in line 5 suggest a context?
4. What are the emotional contrasts between this and the preceding poem, and how are they expressed? What lines in "The Caged Skylark" might allude to the ideas presented here? Determine the extent of the contrasts between them.

114. Alter! When the hills do

Alter! When the hills do.
Falter! When the sun
Question if his glory
Be the perfect one.

Surfeit! When the daffodil   5
Doth of the dew.
Even as herself, Sir,
I will of you.

Emily Dickinson (1830–1886)

QUESTIONS

Who is speaking to whom? What assertion does the speaker make?

115. We outgrow love

> We outgrow love like other things
> And put it in the drawer,
> Till it an antique fashion shows
> Like costumes grandsires wore.

Emily Dickinson (1830–1886)

QUESTIONS

1. To what is love metaphorically compared?
2. How does the assertion made in this poem differ from that in the preceding poem? Can you account for the difference?

EXERCISE

Explore the contrasting ideas in the following pairs of poems:
1. "Spring" (No. 4) and "Spring and All" (No. 292).
2. "Good Times" (No. 209) and "Nikki-Rosa" (No. 229).
3. "Low Barometer" (No. 206) and "Allegory of the Wolf Boy" (No. 230).
4. "The Dead" (No. 207) and "The Death of a Soldier" (No. 281).
5. "Woman Work" (No. 200) and "A Work of Artifice" (No. 263).
6. "To a Daughter Leaving Home" (No. 149) and "Offspring" (No. 253).
7. "Those Winter Sundays" (No. 39) and "Life with Father" (No. 254).

CHAPTER TEN

Tone

Tone, in literature, may be defined as the writer's or speaker's attitude toward his subject, his audience, or himself. It is the emotional coloring, or the emotional meaning, of the work and is an extremely important part of the full meaning. In spoken language it is indicated by the inflections of the speaker's voice. If, for instance, a friend tells you, "I'm going to get married today," the facts of the statement are entirely clear. But the emotional meaning of the statement may vary widely according to the tone of voice with which it is uttered. The tone may be ecstatic ("Hooray! I'm going to get married today!"); it may be incredulous ("I can't believe it! I'm going to get married today"); it may be despairing ("Horrors! I'm going to get married today"); it may be resigned ("Might as well face it. I'm going to get married today"). Obviously, a correct interpretation of the tone will be an important part of understanding the full meaning. It may even have rather important consequences. If someone calls you a fool, your interpretation of the tone may determine whether you roll up your sleeves for a fight or walk off with your arm around his shoulder. If a woman says "No" to a proposal of marriage, the man's interpretation of her tone may determine whether he asks her again or starts going with someone else.

In poetry tone is likewise important. We have not really understood a poem unless we have accurately sensed whether the attitude it manifests is playful or solemn, mocking or reverent, calm or excited. But the correct determination of tone in literature is a much more delicate matter than it is in spoken language, for we do not have the speaker's voice to guide us. We must learn to recognize tone by other means. Almost all of the elements of poetry help to indicate its tone: connotation, imagery, and metaphor; irony and understatement; rhythm, sentence construction, and formal pattern. There is therefore no simple formula for recognizing tone. It is an end product of all the elements in a poem. The best we can do is illustrate.

Robert Frost's "Stopping by Woods on a Snowy Evening" (No. 105) seems a simple poem, but it has always afforded trouble to beginning readers. A very good student, asked to interpret it, once wrote this: "The poem means that we are forever passing up pleasures to go onward to what we wrongly consider our obligations. We would like to watch the snow fall on the peaceful countryside, but we always have to rush home to supper and other engagements. Frost feels that the average person considers life too short to stop and take time to appreciate true pleasures." This student did a good job in recognizing the central conflict of the poem but went astray in recognizing its tone. Let's examine why.

In the first place, the fact that the speaker in the poem *does* stop to watch the snow fall in the woods immediately establishes him as a human being with more sensitivity and feeling for beauty than most. He is not one of the people of Wordsworth's sonnet (No. 28) who, "Getting and spending," have laid waste their powers and lost the capacity to be stirred by nature. Frost's speaker is contrasted with his horse, who, as a creature of habit and an animal without esthetic perception, cannot understand the speaker's reason for stopping. There is also a suggestion of contrast with the "owner" of the woods, who, if he saw the speaker stopping, might be as puzzled as the horse. (Who most truly "profits" from the woods—its absentee owner or the person who can enjoy its beauty?) The speaker goes on because he has "promises to keep." But the word "promises," though it may here have a wry ironic undertone of regret, has a favorable connotation: people almost universally agree that promises ought to be kept. If the poet had used a different term, say, "things to do," or "business to attend to," or "financial affairs to take care of," or "money to make," the connotations would have been quite different. As it is, the tone of the poem tells us that the poet is sympathetic to the speaker; Frost is endorsing rather than censuring the speaker's action. Perhaps we may go even further. In the concluding two lines, because of their climactic position, because they are repeated, and because "sleep" in poetry is often used figuratively to refer to death, there is a suggestion of symbolic interpretation: "and many years to live before I die." If we accept this interpretation, it poses a parallel between giving oneself up to contemplation of the woods and dying. The poet's total implication would seem to be that beauty is a distinctively human value that deserves its place in a full life but that to devote one's life to its pursuit, at the expense of other obligations and duties, is tantamount to one's death as a responsible being. The poet therefore accepts the choice the speaker makes, though not without a touch of regret.

Differences in tone, and their importance, can perhaps be studied best in poems with similar content. Consider, for instance, the following pair.

116. For a Lamb

I saw on the slant hill a putrid lamb,
Propped with daisies. The sleep looked deep,
The face nudged in the green pillow
But the guts were out for crows to eat.

Where's the lamb? whose tender plaint   5
Said all for the mute breezes.
Say he's in the wind somewhere,
Say, there's a lamb in the daisies.

Richard Eberhart (b. 1904)

QUESTION

What connotative force do these words possess: "putrid" (1), "guts" (4), "mute" (6), "lamb" (1), "daisies" (2), "pillow" (3), "tender" (5)? Give two relevant denotations of "a lamb in the daisies" (8).

117. Apparently with no surprise

Apparently with no surprise
To any happy flower,
The frost beheads it at its play
In accidental power.

The blond assassin passes on,   5
The sun proceeds unmoved
To measure off another day
For an approving God.

Emily Dickinson (1830–1886)

QUESTIONS

1. What is the "blond assassin" (5)?
2. What ironies are involved in this poem?

Both of these poems are concerned with natural process; both use contrast as their basic organizing principle—a contrast between life and death, innocence and destruction, joy and tragedy. But in tone the two poems are sharply different. The first is realistic and resigned; its tone is wistful but not pessimistic. The second, though superficially fanciful, is basically grim, almost savage; its tone is horrified. Let's examine the difference.

The title, "For a Lamb," invites associations of innocent, frolicsome youthfulness, with the additional force of traditional Christian usage. These expectations are shockingly halted by the word "putrid." Though the speaker tries to overcome the shock with the more comforting personification implied in "face" and "pillow," the truth is undeniable: the putrefying animal is food for scavengers. The second stanza comes to grips with this truth, and also with the speaker's desire that the lamb might still represent innocence and purity in nature. It mingles fact and desire by hoping that what the lamb represented is still "somewhere" in the wind, that the lamb is both lying in the daisy field and will, in nature's processes, be transformed into the daisies. The reader shares the speaker's sad acceptance of reality.

The second poem makes the same contrast between joyful innocence ("happy flower . . . at its play") and fearful destruction ("beheads it"). The chief difference would seem to be that the cause of destruction—"the blond assassin"—is specifically identified, while the lamb seems to have died in its sleep, pillowed as it is in grass and surrounded by flowers. But the metaphorical sleep is no less a death than that delivered by an assassin—lambs *do* die, and frost actually *does* destroy flowers. In the second poem, what makes the horror of the killing worse is that nothing else in nature is disturbed by it or seems even to notice it. The sun "proceeds unmoved / To measure off another day." Nothing in nature stops or pauses. The flower itself is not surprised. And even God—the God who we have been told is benevolent and concerned over the least sparrow's fall—seems to approve of what has happened, for He shows no displeasure, and He supposedly created the frost as well as the flower. Further irony lies in the fact that the "assassin" (the word's connotations are of terror and violence) is not dark but "blond," or white (the connotations here are of innocence and beauty). The destructive agent, in other words, is among the most exquisite creations of God's handiwork. The poet, then, is shocked by what has happened, and is even more shocked that nothing else in nature is shocked. What has happened seems inconsistent with a rule of benevolence in the universe. In her ironic reference to an "approving God," therefore, the poet is raising a dreadful question: are the forces that created and govern the universe actually benevolent? And if we think that the poet is unduly disturbed over the death of a flower, we may consider that what is true for the flower is true throughout nature. Death—even early or accidental death, in terrible juxtaposition with beauty—is its constant condition; the fate that befalls the flower befalls us all. In Dickinson's poem, that is the end of the process. In Eberhart's, the potentially terrible irony is directed into a bittersweet acceptance of both death and beauty as natural.

These two poems, then, though superficially similar, are basically as different as night and day. And the difference is primarily one of tone.

We have been discussing tone as if every poem could be distinguished by a single tone. But varying or shifting tones in a single poem are often a valuable means for achieving the poet's purpose, and indeed may create the dramatic structure of a poem. Consider the following.

118. Since there's no help

Since there's no help, come let us kiss and part;
Nay, I have done, you get no more of me,
And I am glad, yea, glad with all my heart
That thus so cleanly I myself can free;
Shake hands forever, cancel all our vows,   5
And when we meet at any time again,
Be it not seen in either of our brows
That we one jot of former love retain.
Now, at the last gasp of Love's latest breath,
When, his pulse failing, Passion speechless lies,   10
When Faith is kneeling by his bed of death,
And Innocence is closing up his eyes,
Now, if thou wouldst, when all have given him over,
From death to life thou mightst him yet recover.

Michael Drayton (1563–1631)

QUESTIONS

1. What difference in tone do you find between the first eight lines and the last six? In which part is the speaker more sincere? What differences in rhythm and language help to establish the difference in tone?

2. How many figures are there in the allegorical scene in lines 9–12? What
   do the pronouns "his" and "him" in lines 10–14 refer to? What is dying?
   Why? How might the person addressed still restore it from death to life?
3. Define the dramatic situation as precisely as possible, taking into consideration both the man's attitude and the woman's.

Accurately determining tone, whether it be the tone of a rejected
marriage proposal or of an insulting remark, is extremely important,
both when reading poetry and in real life. For the experienced reader
it will be instinctive and automatic. For the beginning reader it will require study. But beyond the general suggestions for reading that we
already have made, there are no specific instructions we can give.
Recognition of tone requires an increasing familiarity with the meanings and connotations of words, alertness to the presence of irony and
other figures, and, above all, careful reading. Poetry cannot be read
as one would skim a newspaper or a mystery novel looking merely
for facts.

119. The Coming of Wisdom with Time

> Though leaves are many, the root is one;
> Through all the lying days of my youth
> I swayed my leaves and flowers in the sun;
> Now I may wither into the truth.

> *William Butler Yeats (1865–1939)*

QUESTIONS

Is the poet exulting over a gain or lamenting over a loss? Is there a single
tone in this poem?

120. Crossing the Bar

> Sunset and evening star,
>   And one clear call for me!
> And may there be no moaning of the bar
>   When I put out to sea,

But such a tide as moving seems asleep,   5
    Too full for sound and foam,
When that which drew from out the boundless deep
    Turns again home.

Twilight and evening bell,
    And after that the dark!   10
And may there be no sadness of farewell
    When I embark;

For though from out our bourne of Time and Place
    The flood may bear me far,
I hope to see my Pilot face to face   15
    When I have crossed the bar.

Alfred, Lord Tennyson (1809–1892)

QUESTIONS

1. Vocabulary: *bourne* (13).
2. What two sets of figures does Tennyson use for approaching death? What is the precise moment of death in each set?
3. In troubled weather the wind and waves above the sandbar across a harbor's mouth make a moaning sound. What metaphorical meaning has the "moaning of the bar" (3) here? For what kind of death is the speaker wishing? Why does he want "no sadness of farewell" (11)?
4. What is "that which drew from out the boundless deep" (7)? What is "the boundless deep"? To what is it opposed in the poem? Why is "Pilot" (15) capitalized?

121. The Oxen

Christmas Eve, and twelve of the clock.
    "Now they are all on their knees,"
An elder said as we sat in a flock
    By the embers in hearthside ease.

We pictured the meek mild creatures where   5
    They dwelt in their strawy pen,
Nor did it occur to one of us there
    To doubt they were kneeling then.

So fair a fancy few would weave
    In these years! Yet, I feel,   10
If someone said on Christmas Eve,
    "Come; see the oxen kneel

"In the lonely barton° by yonder coomb°   farm; valley
　　Our childhood used to know,"
I should go with him in the gloom,   15
　　Hoping it might be so.

Thomas Hardy (1840–1928)

QUESTIONS

1. Is the simple superstition referred to in this poem opposed to, or identified with, religious faith? With what implications for the meaning of the poem?
2. What are "these years" (10) and how do they contrast with the years of the poet's boyhood? What event in intellectual history between 1840 and 1915 (the date Hardy composed this poem) was most responsible for the change?
3. Both "Crossing the Bar" and "The Oxen" in their last lines use a form of the verb *hope*. By fully discussing tone, establish the precise meaning of hope in each poem. What degree of expectation does it imply? How should the word be handled in reading Tennyson's poem aloud?

122. One dignity delays for all

One dignity delays for all,
One mitred afternoon.
None can avoid this purple,
None evade this crown.

Coach, it insures, and footmen,   5
Chamber, and state, and throng—
Bells, also, in the village,
As we ride grand along!

What dignified attendants!
What service when we pause!   10
How loyally at parting
Their hundred hats they raise!

How pomp surpassing ermine
When simple you and I
Present our meek escutcheon   15
And claim the rank to die!

Emily Dickinson (1830–1886)

QUESTIONS

1. Vocabulary: *mitred* (2), *state* (6), *escutcheon* (15).
2. What is the "dignity" that delays for all? What is its nature? What is being described in stanzas 2 and 3?
3. What figures of speech are combined in "our meek escutcheon" (15)? What does it represent metaphorically?

123. 'Twas warm at first like us

'Twas warm at first like us,
Until there crept upon
A chill, like frost upon a glass,
Till all the scene be gone.

The forehead copied stone,   5
The fingers grew too cold
To ache, and like a skater's brook
The busy eyes congealed.

It straightened—that was all.
It crowded cold to cold.   10
It multiplied indifference
As pride were all it could.

And even when with cords
'Twas lowered like a weight,
It made no signal, nor demurred,   15
But dropped like adamant.

Emily Dickinson (1830–1886)

QUESTIONS

1. Vocabulary: *adamant* (16).
2. What is "It" in the opening line? What is being described in the poem, and between which points in time?
3. How would you describe the tone of this poem? How does it contrast with that of the preceding poem?

124. The Apparition

When by thy scorn, O murderess, I am dead,
        And that thou thinkst thee free
From all solicitatiön from me,

Then shall my ghost come to thy bed,
And thee, feigned vestal, in worse arms shall see;   5
Then thy sick taper° will begin to wink,   candle
And he, whose thou art then, being tired before,
Will, if thou stir, or pinch to wake him, think
    Thou call'st for more,
And in false sleep will from thee shrink.   10
And then, poor aspen wretch, neglected, thou,
Bathed in a cold quicksilver sweat, wilt lie
    A verier° ghost than I.   truer
What I will say, I will not tell thee now,
Lest that preserve thee; and since my love is spent, 15
I had rather thou shouldst painfully repent,
Than by my threatenings rest still innocent.

             John Donne (1572–1631)

QUESTIONS

1. Vocabulary: *feigned* (5), *aspen* (11), *quicksilver* (12). Are the latter two words used literally or figuratively? Explain.
2. What has been the past relationship between the speaker and the woman addressed? How does a "solicitatïon" differ from a proposal? Why does he call her a "murderess"? What threat does he make against her?
3. In line 15 the speaker proclaims that his love for the woman "is spent." Does the tone of the poem support this contention? Discuss.
4. In line 5 why does the speaker use the word "vestal" instead of *virgin*? Does he believe her not to be a virgin? Of what is he accusing her? (In ancient Rome the vestal virgins tended the perpetual fire in the temple of Vesta. They entered this service between the ages of six and ten, and served for a term of thirty years, during which they were bound to virginity.)
5. The implied metaphor in line 1—that a woman who will not satisfy her lover's desires is "killing" him—was a cliché of Renaissance poetry. What original twist does Donne give it to make it fresh and new?
6. In the scene imagined by the speaker of his ghost's visit to the woman's bed, he finds her "in worse arms"—worse than whose? In what respect? By what will this other man have been "tired before"? Of what will he think she is calling for "more"? What is the speaker implying about himself and the woman in these lines?
7. Why (according to the speaker) will the woman *really* be trying to wake up her bedmate? Why, when she fails, will she be a "verier" ghost than the speaker?
8. What will the ghost say to her that he will not now reveal lest his telling it "preserve" her? Can we know? Does *he* know? Why does he make this undefined threat?
9. For what does the speaker say he wants the woman to "painfully repent"? Of what crime or sin would she remain "innocent" if he revealed now what his ghost would say? What is the speaker's real objective?

125. The Flea

Mark but this flea, and mark in this
How little that which thou deny'st me is;
It sucked me first, and now sucks thee,
And in this flea our two bloods mingled be;
Thou know'st that this cannot be said   5
A sin, nor shame, nor loss of maidenhead;
   Yet this enjoys before it woo,
    And pampered swells with one blood made of two,
    And this, alas, is more than we would do.

Oh stay, three lives in one flea spare,   10
Where we almost, yea more than married are.
This flea is you and I, and this
Our marriage bed and marriage temple is;
Though parents grudge, and you, we are met
And cloistered in these living walls of jet.   15
   Though use° make you apt to kill me,   habit
    Let not to that, self-murder added be,
    And sacrilege, three sins in killing three.

Cruel and sudden, hast thou since
Purpled° thy nail in blood of innocence?   crimsoned   20
Wherein could this flea guilty be,
Except in that drop which it sucked from thee?
Yet thou triumph'st and say'st that thou
Find'st not thyself, nor me, the weaker now.
'Tis true. Then learn how false fears be: 25
   Just so much honor, when thou yield'st to me,
    Will waste, as this flea's death took life from thee.

John Donne (1572–1631)

QUESTIONS

1. In many respects this poem is like a miniature play: it has two characters,
   dramatic conflict, dialogue (though we hear only one speaker), and stage
   action. The action is indicated by stage directions embodied in the dialogue. What has happened just *preceding* the first line of the poem? What
   happens *between* the first and second stanzas? What happens *between* the
   second and third? How does the female character behave and what does
   she say *during* the third stanza?
2. What has been the past relationship of the speaker and the woman? What
   has she denied him (2)? How has she habitually "kill[ed]" him (16)? Why
   has she done so? How does it happen that he is still alive? What is his objective in the poem?

3. According to a traditional Renaissance belief, the bloods of lovers "mingled" during sexual intercourse. What is the speaker's argument in stanza 1? Reduce it to paraphrase. How logical is it?
4. What do "parents grudge, and you" in stanza 2? What are the "living walls of jet" (15)? What three things will the woman kill by crushing the flea? What three sins will she commit (18)?
5. Why and how does the woman "triumph . . ." in stanza 3? What is the speaker's response? How logical is his concluding argument?
6. What action, if any, would you infer, follows the conclusion of the poem?
7. "The Apparition" and "The Flea" may both be classified as "seduction poems." How do they differ in tone?

126. Dover Beach

The sea is calm tonight,
The tide is full, the moon lies fair
Upon the straits;—on the French coast the light
Gleams and is gone; the cliffs of England stand,
Glimmering and vast, out in the tranquil bay.   5
Come to the window, sweet is the night-air!
Only, from the long line of spray
Where the sea meets the moon-blanched land,
Listen! you hear the grating roar
Of pebbles which the waves draw back, and fling,   10
At their return, up the high strand,
Begin, and cease, and then again begin,
With tremulous cadence slow, and bring
The eternal note of sadness in.

Sophocles long ago   15
Heard it on the Aegean, and it brought
Into his mind the turbid ebb and flow
Of human misery; we
Find also in the sound a thought,
Hearing it by this distant northern sea.   20

The Sea of Faith
Was once, too, at the full, and round earth's shore
Lay like the folds of a bright girdle furled.
But now I only hear
Its melancholy, long, withdrawing roar,   25
Retreating, to the breath
Of the night-wind, down the vast edges drear
And naked shingles° of the world.   pebbled beaches

Ah, love, let us be true
To one another! for the world, which seems   30
To lie before us like a land of dreams,
So various, so beautiful, so new,
Hath really neither joy, nor love, nor light,
Nor certitude, nor peace, nor help for pain;
And we are here as on a darkling plain   35
Swept with confused alarms of struggle and flight,
Where ignorant armies clash by night.

Matthew Arnold (1822–1888)

QUESTIONS

1. Vocabulary: *strand* (11), *girdle* (23), *darkling* (35). Identify the physical locale of the cliffs of Dover and their relation to the French coast; identify
   the Aegean and Sophocles.
2. As precisely as possible, define the implied scene: What is the speaker's
   physical location? Whom is he addressing? What is the time of day and
   the state of the weather?
3. Discuss the visual and auditory images of the poem and their relation to
   illusion and reality.
4. The speaker is lamenting the decline of religious faith in his time. Is he
   himself a believer? Does he see any medicine for the world's maladies?
5. Discuss in detail the imagery in the last three lines. Are the "armies" figurative or literal? What makes these lines so effective?
6. What term or terms would you choose to describe the overall tone of
   the poem?

127. Church Going

Once I am sure there's nothing going on
I step inside, letting the door thud shut.
Another church: matting, seats, and stone,
And little books; sprawlings of flowers, cut
For Sunday, brownish now; some brass and stuff   5
Up at the holy end; the small neat organ;
And a tense, musty, unignorable silence,
Brewed God knows how long. Hatless, I take off
My cycle-clips in awkward reverence,

Move forward, run my hand around the font.   10
From where I stand, the roof looks almost new—
Cleaned, or restored? Someone would know: I don't.
Mounting the lectern, I peruse a few

Hectoring large-scale verses, and pronounce
"Here endeth" much more loudly than I'd meant.   15
The echoes snigger briefly. Back at the door
I sign the book, donate an Irish sixpence,
Reflect the place was not worth stopping for.

Yet stop I did: in fact I often do,
And always end much at a loss like this,   20
Wondering what to look for, wondering, too,
When churches fall completely out of use
What we shall turn them into, if we shall keep
A few cathedrals chronically on show,
Their parchment, plate and pyx in locked cases,   25
And let the rest rent-free to rain and sheep.
Shall we avoid them as unlucky places?

Or, after dark, will dubious women come
To make their children touch a particular stone;
Pick simples for a cancer; or on some   30
Advised night see walking a dead one?
Power of some sort or other will go on
In games, in riddles, seemingly at random;
But superstition, like belief, must die,
And what remains when disbelief has gone?   35
Grass, weedy pavement, brambles, buttress, sky,

A shape less recognizable each week,
A purpose more obscure. I wonder who
Will be the last, the very last, to seek
This place for what it was; one of the crew   40
That tap and jot and know what rood-lofts were?
Some ruin-bibber, randy for antique,
Or Christmas-addict, counting on a whiff
Of gown-and-bands and organ-pipes and myrrh?
Or will he be my representative,   45

Bored, uninformed, knowing the ghostly silt
Dispersed, yet tending to this cross of ground
Through suburb scrub because it held unspilt
So long and equably what since is found
Only in separation—marriage, and birth,   50
And death, and thoughts of these—for whom was built
This special shell? For though I've no idea
What this accoutered frowsty barn is worth,
It pleases me to stand in silence here;

A serious house on serious earth it is,   55
In whose blent air all our compulsions meet,
Are recognized, and robed as destinies.
And that much never can be obsolete,
Since someone will forever be surprising
A hunger in himself to be more serious,   60
And gravitating with it to this ground,
Which, he once heard, was proper to grow wise in,
If only that so many dead lie round.

Philip Larkin (1922–1985)

QUESTIONS

1. Vocabulary: *Hectoring* (14), *pyx* (25), *dubious* (28), *simples* (30), *accoutered* (53), *frowsty* (53), *blent* (56). *Large-scale* (14) indicates a print size suited to oral reading; an *Irish sixpence* (17) was a small coin not legal tender in England, the scene of the poem; *rood-lofts* (41) are architectural features found in many early Christian churches; *bibber* and *randy* (42) are figurative, literally meaning "drunkard" and "lustful"; *gown-and-bands* (44) are ornate robes worn by church officials in religious ceremonies.
2. Like "Dover Beach" (first published in 1867), "Church Going" (1954) is concerned with belief and disbelief. In modern England the landscape is dotted with small churches, often charming in their combination of stone (outside) and intricately carved wood (inside). Some are in ruins, some are badly in need of repair, and some are well tended by parishioners who keep them dusted and provide fresh flowers for the diminishing attendance at Sunday services. These churches invariably have by the entrance a book that visitors can sign as a record of their having been there and a collection box with a sign urging them to drop in a few coins for upkeep, repair, or restoration. In small towns and villages the church is often the chief or only building of architectural or historical interest, and tourist visitors may outnumber parishioners. To which of the three categories of churches mentioned here does Larkin's poem refer?
3. What different denotations does the title contain?
4. In what activity has the speaker been engaging when he stops to see the church? How is it revealed? Why does he stop? Is he a believer? How involved is he in inspecting this church building?
5. Compare the language used by the speakers in "Dover Beach" and "Church Going." Which speaker is more eloquent? Which is more informal and conversational? Without looking back at the texts, try to assign the following words to one poem or the other: *moon-blanched, cycle-clips, darkling, hath, snigger, whiff, drear, brownish, tremulous, glimmering, frowsty, stuff.* Then go back and check your success.
6. Define the tone (the attitude of the speaker or author toward the subject) of "Church Going" as precisely as possible. Compare this tone to that of "Dover Beach."

128. Getting Out

That year we hardly slept, waking like inmates
who beat the walls. Every night
another refusal, the silent work
of tightening the heart.
Exhausted, we gave up; escaped   5
to the apartment pool, swimming those laps
until the first light relieved us.

Days were different: FM and full-blast
blues, hours of guitar "you gonna miss me
when I'm gone." Think how you tried   10
to pack up and go, for weeks stumbling
over piles of clothing, the unstrung tennis rackets.
Finally locked into blame, we paced
that short hall, heaving words like furniture.

I have the last unshredded pictures   15
of our matching eyes and hair. We've kept
to separate sides of the map,
still I'm startled by men who look like you.
And in the yearly letter, you're sure to say
you're happy now. Yet I think of the lawyer's bewilderment   20
when we cried, the last day. Taking hands
we walked apart, until our arms stretched
between us. We held on tight, and let go.

Cleopatra Mathis (b. 1947)

QUESTIONS

1. Consider the shifting pronouns as you answer the following: Does the
   poem assign blame to one or the other of this couple? Can you tell
   whether either or both were involved in "the silent work / of tightening
   the heart" (3–4)?
2. The poem contains only one detail about the marriage before it began to
   collapse—the "matching eyes and hair" (16) of the two people. Does that
   detail help to explain why the marriage came to seem too confining?
   What kind of emotional maturity does it signify? How does the last line
   contribute to this idea?
3. Should "inmates" (1) be interpreted as imprisonment or confinement to
   a mental hospital? Explain your choice.
4. Explain the shift in tone from line 14 to line 15. What emotions do these
   people feel for each other now? How do you know?

129. A tiny cry within the night

A tiny cry within the night,
A mother's touch, a gentle light,
A rocking chair, a cheek caressed,
A baby to a bosom pressed,
A bundle in a cot replaced,   5
A mother's footsteps, soft, retraced—
She whispers as the shadows creep . . .
"Now let me sleep! Please, let me sleep!!!"

Lynn Johnston (b. 1947)

QUESTION

The radical shift in tone changes the whole meaning of the poem. Without
the last line, what would it mean?

EXERCISES

1. Marvell's "To His Coy Mistress" (No. 56), Herrick's "To the Virgins, to
   Make Much of Time" (No. 64), and Housman's "Loveliest of Trees"
   (No. 104) all treat a traditional poetic theme known as the *carpe diem*
   ("seize the day") theme. They differ sharply, however, in tone. Characterize the tone of each, and point out the differences in poetic technique
   that account for the differences in tone.
2. Describe and account for the differences in tone between the following
   pairs:
   a. "The Lamb" (No. 204) and "The Tiger" (No. 205).
   b. "The Unknown Citizen" (No. 82) and "Departmental" (No. 83).
   c. "It sifts from leaden sieves" (No. 47) and "The Snowstorm" (No. 136).
   d. "Leda and the Swan" (No. 96) and "Leda's Sister and the Geese"
      (No. 97).
   e. "Nothing Gold Can Stay" (No. 141) and "Never Again Would Birds'
      Song Be the Same" (No. 226).
   f. "An altered look about the hills" (No. 98) and "The Sheaves" (No. 272).
   g. "Ballad of Birmingham" (No. 8) and "Southern Cop" (No. 88).
   h. "The Whipping" (No. 5) and "The Beating" (No. 280).

CHAPTER ELEVEN

Musical Devices

Poetry obviously makes a greater use of the "music" of language than does language that is not poetry. The poet, unlike the person who uses language to convey only information, chooses words for sound as well as for meaning, and uses the sound as a means of reinforcing meaning. So prominent is this musical quality of poetry that some writers have made it the distinguishing term in their definitions of poetry. Edgar Allan Poe, for instance, describes poetry as "music . . . combined with a pleasurable idea." Whether or not it deserves this much importance, verbal music, like connotation, imagery, and figurative language, is one of the important resources that enable the poet to do more than communicate mere information. The poet may indeed sometimes pursue verbal music for its own sake; more often, at least in first-rate poetry, it is an adjunct to the total meaning or communication of the poem.

The poet achieves musical quality in two broad ways: by the choice and arrangement of sounds and by the arrangement of accents. In this chapter we will consider the first of these.

An essential element in all music is repetition. In fact, we might say that all art consists of giving structure to two elements: repetition and variation. All things we enjoy greatly and lastingly have these two elements. We enjoy the sea endlessly because it is always the same yet always different. We enjoy a baseball game because it contains the same complex combination of pattern and variation. Our love of art, then, is rooted in human psychology. We like the familiar, we like variety, but we like them combined. If we get too much sameness, the result is monotony and tedium; if we get too much variety, the result is bewilderment and confusion. The composer of music, therefore, repeats certain musical tones; repeats them in certain combinations, or chords; and repeats them in certain patterns, or melodies. The poet likewise repeats certain sounds in certain combinations and arrangements, and thus adds musical meaning to verse. Consider the following short example.

130. The Turtle

> The turtle lives 'twixt plated decks
> Which practically conceal its sex.
> I think it clever of the turtle
> In such a fix to be so fertile.

Ogden Nash (1902–1971)

Here is a little joke, a paradox of animal life to which the author has cleverly drawn our attention. An experiment will show us, however, that much of its appeal lies not so much in what it says as in the manner in which it says it. If, for instance, we recast the verse as prose: "The turtle lives in a shell which almost conceals its sex. It is ingenious of the turtle, in such a situation, to be so prolific," the joke falls flat. Some of its appeal must lie in its metrical form. So now we cast it in unrimed verse:

> Because he lives between two decks,
> It's hard to tell a turtle's gender.
> The turtle is a clever beast
> In such a plight to be so fertile.

Here, perhaps, is *some* improvement over the prose version, but still the piquancy of the original is missing. Much of that appeal must have consisted in the use of rime—the repetition of sound in "decks" and "sex," "turtle" and "fertile." So we try once more.

> The turtle lives 'twixt plated decks
> Which practically conceal its sex.
> I think it clever of the turtle
> In such a plight to be so fertile.

But for perceptive readers there is still something missing—they may not at first see what—but some little touch that makes the difference between a good piece of verse and a little masterpiece of its kind. And then they see it: "plight" has been substituted for "fix."

But why should "fix" make such a difference? Its meaning is little different from that of "plight"; its only important difference is in sound. But there we are. The final x in "fix" catches up the concluding consonant sound in "sex," and its initial f is repeated in the initial consonant sound of "fertile." Not only do these sound recurrences provide a subtle gratification to the ear, but they also give the verse structure; they emphasize and draw together the key words of the piece: "sex," "fix," and "fertile."

Poets may repeat any unit of sound from the smallest to the largest. They may repeat individual vowel and consonant sounds, whole syllables, words, phrases, lines, or groups of lines. In each instance, in a good poem, the repetition will serve several purposes: it will please the ear, it will emphasize the words in which the repetition occurs, and it will give structure to the poem. The popularity and initial impressiveness of such repetitions are evidenced by their becoming in many instances embedded in the language as clichés like "wild and woolly," "first and foremost," "footloose and fancy-free," "penny-wise, pound-foolish," "dead as a doornail," "might and main," "sink or swim," "do or die," "pell-mell," "helter-skelter," "harum-scarum," "hocus-pocus." Some of these kinds of repetition have names, as we will see.

A syllable consists of a vowel sound that may be preceded or followed by consonant sounds. Any of these sounds may be repeated. The repetition of initial consonant sounds, as in "tried and true," "safe and sound," "fish or fowl," "rime or reason," is **alliteration.** The repetition of vowel sounds, as in "mad as a hatter," "time out of mind," "free and easy," "slapdash," is **assonance.** The repetition of final consonant sounds, as in "first and last," "odds and ends," "short and sweet," "a stroke of luck," or Shakespeare's "struts and frets" (No. 91) is **consonance.** *

Repetitions may be used alone or in combination. Alliteration and assonance are combined in such phrases as "time and tide," "thick and thin," "kith and kin," "alas and alack," "fit as a fiddle," and Edgar Allan Poe's famous line, "The viol, the violet, and the vine." Alliteration and consonance are combined in such phrases as "crisscross," "last but not least," "lone and lorn," "good as gold," Housman's "malt does more than Milton can" (No. 11), and Kay's "meanings lost in manners" (No. 25). The combination of assonance and consonance is rime.

Rime is the repetition of the accented vowel sound and all succeeding sounds. It is called **masculine** when the rime sounds involve only one syllable, as in *decks* and *sex* or *support* and *retort.* It is

---

*There is no established terminology for these various repetitions. *Alliteration* is used by some writers to mean any repetition of consonant sounds. *Assonance* has been used to mean the similarity as well as the identity of vowel sounds, or even the similarity of any sounds whatever. *Consonance* has often been reserved for words in which both the initial *and* final consonant sounds correspond, as in *green* and *groan, moon* and *mine. Rime* (or rhyme) has been used to mean any sound repetition, including alliteration, assonance, and consonance. In the absence of clear agreement on the meanings of these terms, the terminology chosen here has appeared most useful, with support in usage. Labels are useful in analysis. However, the student should learn to recognize the devices and, more important, should learn to see their function, without worrying too much over nomenclature.

feminine when the rime sounds involve two or more syllables, as in *turtle* and *fertile* or *spitefully* and *delightfully*. It is referred to as **internal rime** when one or more riming words are *within* the line and as **end rime** when the riming words are at the *ends* of lines. End rime is probably the most frequently used and most consciously sought sound repetition in English poetry. Because it comes at the end of the line, it receives emphasis as a musical effect and perhaps contributes more than any other musical resource except rhythm and meter to give poetry its musical effect as well as its structure. There exists, however, a large body of poetry that does not employ rime and for which rime would not be appropriate. Also, there has always been a tendency, especially noticeable in modern poetry, to substitute approximate rimes for perfect rimes at the ends of lines. **Approximate rimes** (also called slant rimes) include words with any kind of sound similarity, from close to fairly remote. Under approximate rime we include alliteration, assonance, and consonance or their combinations when used at the end of the line; half-rime (feminine rimes in which only half of the word rimes—the accented half, as in *lightly* and *frightful,* or the unaccented half, as in *yellow* and *willow*); and other similarities too elusive to name. "'Twas warm at first like us" (No. 123), "Toads" (No. 54), and "Mr. Z" (No. 87), to different degrees, all employ various kinds of approximate end rime.

131. That night when joy began

That night when joy began
Our narrowest veins to flush,
We waited for the flash
Of morning's leveled gun.

But morning let us pass,   5
And day by day relief
Outgrows his nervous laugh,
Grown credulous of peace,

As mile by mile is seen
No trespasser's reproach,   10
And love's best glasses reach
No fields but are his own.

                                        W. H. Auden (1907–1973)

QUESTIONS

1. What has been the past experience with love of the two people in the poem? What is their present experience? What precisely is the tone of the poem?
2. What basic metaphor underlies the poem? Work it out stanza by stanza. What is "the flash of morning's leveled gun" (3–4)? Does line 10 mean that no trespasser reproaches the lovers or that no one reproaches the lovers for being trespassers? Does "glasses" (11) refer to spectacles, tumblers, mirrors, or field glasses? Point out three personifications.
3. The rime pattern in the poem is intricate and exact. Work it out, considering alliteration, assonance, and consonance.

In addition to the repetition of individual sounds and syllables, the poet may repeat whole words, phrases, lines, or groups of lines. When such repetition is done according to some fixed pattern, it is called a **refrain.** The refrain is especially common in songlike poetry. Shakespeare's "Winter" (No. 2) and "Spring" (No. 4) furnish examples of refrains.

132. Ettrick

When we first rade° down Ettrick,   rode
Our bridles were ringing, our hearts were dancing,
The waters were singing, the sun was glancing,
An' blithely our voices rang out thegither,°   together
As we brushed the dew frae° the blooming heather,   from   5
    When we first rade down Ettrick.

When we next rade down Ettrick,
The day was dying, the wild birds calling,
The wind was sighing, the leaves were falling,
An' silent an' weary, but closer thegither,   10
We urged our steeds thro' the faded heather,
    When we next rade down Ettrick.

When I last rade down Ettrick,
The winds were shifting, the storm was waking,
The snow was drifting, my heart was breaking,   15
For we never again were to ride thegither,
In sun or storm on the mountain heather,
    When I last rade down Ettrick.

Alicia Ann Spottiswood ("Lady John Scott") (1810–1900)

QUESTIONS

1. Ettrick is the name of a small village (and mountain and valley) near Selkirk in the "Border" district of southern Scotland, an area famed for its folk ballads. Some of the characteristics of the **ballad** are the use of refrain, local dialects, and songlike rhythms and rimes, in narratives that show emotional linkages between nature and human emotions and that omit definitive explanations for events. For an example of a true folk ballad, see "Edward" (No. 180). This poem is an imitation or "literary ballad"; discuss the characteristics of the folk ballad that it exhibits.
2. What stages in the development of love are represented in the three stanzas? How does nature reflect those stages? What do the changes in the refrains contribute?

We have not nearly exhausted the possibilities of sound repetition by giving names to a few of the more prominent kinds. The complete study of possible kinds of sound repetition in poetry would be so complex, however, that it would break down under its own machinery. Some of the subtlest and loveliest effects escape our net of names. In as short a phrase as this from the prose of John Ruskin—"ivy as light and lovely as the vine"—we notice alliteration in *light* and *lovely,* assonance in *ivy, light,* and *vine,* and consonance in *ivy* and *lovely,* but we have no name to connect the *v* in *vine* with the *v*s in *ivy* and *lovely,* or the second *l* in *lovely* with the first *l,* or the final syllables of *ivy* and *lovely* with each other; yet these are all an effective part of the music of the line. Also contributing to the music of poetry is the linking of related rather than identical sounds, such as *m* and *n,* or *p* and *b,* or the vowel sounds in *boat, boot,* and *book.*

These various musical repetitions, for trained readers, will ordinarily make an almost subconscious contribution to their reading of the poem: readers will feel their effect without necessarily being aware of what has caused it. There is value, however, in occasionally analyzing a poem for these devices in order to increase awareness of them. A few words of caution are necessary. First, the repetitions are entirely a matter of sound; spelling is irrelevant. *Bear* and *pair* are rimes, but *through* and *rough* are not. *Cell* and *sin, folly* and *philosophy* alliterate, but *sin* and *sugar, gun* and *gem* do not. Second, alliteration, assonance, consonance, and masculine rime are matters that ordinarily involve only stressed or accented syllables; for only such syllables ordinarily make enough impression on the ear to be significant in the sound pattern of the poem. For instance, we should hardly consider *which* and *its* in the second line of "The Turtle" an example of assonance, for neither word is stressed enough in the reading to make it significant as a sound. Third, the words involved in these repetitions must be close enough together that the ear retains the sound, consciously or subconsciously, from its first occurrence to its second. This distance varies according to circumstances, but for alliteration, assonance, and consonance the words ordinarily have to be in the same line or adjacent lines. End rime bridges a longer gap.

133. God's Grandeur

The world is charged with the grandeur of God.
　It will flame out, like shining from shook foil;
　It gathers to a greatness, like the ooze of oil
Crushed. Why do men then now not reck his rod?
Generations have trod, have trod, have trod;　　　　　　　　5
　And all is seared with trade; bleared, smeared with toil;
　And wears man's smudge and shares man's smell: the soil
Is bare now, nor can foot feel, being shod.

And for all this, nature is never spent;
　There lives the dearest freshness deep down things;　　　　10
And though the last lights off the black West went
　Oh, morning, at the brown brink eastward, springs—
Because the Holy Ghost over the bent
　World broods with warm breast and with ah! bright wings.

Gerard Manley Hopkins (1844–1889)

QUESTIONS

1. What is the theme of this sonnet?
2. The image in lines 3–4 possibly refers to olive oil being collected in great vats from crushed olives, but the image is much disputed. Explain the simile in line 2 and the symbols in lines 7–8 and 11–12.
3. Explain "reck his rod" (4), "spent" (9), "bent" (13).
4. Using different-colored pencils, encircle and connect examples of alliteration, assonance, consonance, and internal rime. Do these help to carry the meaning?

　　We should not leave the impression that the use of these musical devices is necessarily or always valuable. Like the other resources of poetry, they can be judged only in the light of the poem's total intention. Many of the greatest works of English poetry—for instance,

Hamlet and *King Lear* and *Paradise Lost*—do not employ end rime. Both alliteration and rime, especially feminine rime, become humorous or silly if used excessively or unskillfully. If the intention is humorous, the result is delightful; if not, fatal. Shakespeare, who knew how to use all these devices to the utmost advantage, parodied their unskillful use in lines like "The preyful princess pierced and pricked a pretty pleasing prickett" in *Love's Labor's Lost* and

> Whereat with blade, with bloody, blameful blade,
> He bravely broached his boiling bloody breast

in *A Midsummer Night's Dream.* Swinburne parodied his own highly alliterative style in "Nephelidia" with lines like "Life is the lust of a lamp for the light that is dark till the dawn of the day when we die." Used skillfully and judiciously, however, musical devices provide a palpable and delicate pleasure to the ear and, even more important, add dimension to meaning.

---

134. We Real Cool

The Pool Players.
Seven At The Golden Shovel.

> We real cool. We
> Left school. We
>
> Lurk late. We
> Strike straight. We
>
> Sing sin. We   5
> Thin gin. We
>
> Jazz June. We
> Die soon.

Gwendolyn Brooks (b. 1917)

QUESTIONS

1. In addition to end rime, what other musical devices does this poem employ?
2. Try reading this poem with the pronouns at the beginning of the lines instead of at the end. What is lost?

3. English teachers in a certain urban school were once criticized for having their students read this poem: it was said to be immoral. Was the criticism justified? Why or why not?

135. Blackberry Sweet

Black girl black girl
lips as curved as cherries
full as grape bunches
sweet as blackberries

Black girl black girl   5
when you walk you are
magic as a rising bird
or a falling star

Black girl black girl
what's your spell to make   10
the heart in my breast
jump   stop   shake

Dudley Randall (b. 1914)

QUESTIONS

1. Refrains traditionally are placed at the ends of stanzas. How does this poem differ? With what effect?
2. Discuss the relation of form and content in the poem. How are the separate stanzas unified in themselves and yet linked to the others? How does each stanza achieve climax? How does the poem as a whole achieve climax?

136. The Snowstorm

Announced by all the trumpets of the sky,
Arrives the snow, and, driving o'er the fields,
Seems nowhere to alight: the whited air
Hides hills and woods, the river, and the heaven,
And veils the farmhouse at the garden's end.   5
The sled and traveler stopped, the courier's feet
Delayed, all friends shut out, the housemates sit
Around the radiant fireplace, enclosed
In a tumultuous privacy of storm.

Come see the north wind's masonry.   10
Out of an unseen quarry evermore
Furnished with tile, the fierce artificer
Curves his white bastions with projected roof
Round every windward stake, or tree, or door.
Speeding, the myriad-handed, his wild work   15
So fanciful, so savage, nought cares he
For number or proportion. Mockingly,
On coop or kennel he hangs Parian wreaths;
A swan-like form invests the hidden thorn;
Fills up the farmer's lane from wall to wall,   20
Maugre the farmer's sighs; and, at the gate,
A tapering turret overtops the work.
And when his hours are numbered and the world
Is all his own, retiring as he were not,
Leaves, when the sun appears, astonished Art   25
To mimic in slow structures, stone by stone,
Built in an age, the mad wind's night-work,
The frolic architecture of the snow.

Ralph Waldo Emerson (1803–1882)

QUESTIONS

1. Vocabulary: *Parian* (18); *thorn* (19); *Maugre* (21); "as he were not" (24) means "as if he had not existed."
2. From line 10 the poem presents an extended metaphor in the form of a personification. As what is the snowstorm personified? How do subsidiary metaphors support that personification (e.g., explain how "quarry" and "tile" [11–12] are used)?
3. The last sentence (23–28) has "he" as an understood subject, and introduces a second personification, "Art." Paraphrase the sentence and discuss how it extends the meaning of this descriptive poem.
4. The poem contains no end rime, but compensates with a richness of alliteration, assonance, consonance, and internal rime. Find as many examples as you can.

137. As imperceptibly as grief

As imperceptibly as grief
The summer lapsed away,
Too imperceptible at last
To seem like perfidy.

A quietness distilled   5
As twilight long begun,
Or nature spending with herself
Sequestered afternoon.

The dusk drew earlier in,
The morning foreign shone —   10
A courteous, yet harrowing grace,
As guest who would be gone.

And thus, without a wing
Or service of a keel,
Our summer made her light escape
Into the beautiful.

Emily Dickinson (1830–1886)

QUESTIONS

1. What are the subject and tone of the poem? Explain its opening simile.
2. Discuss the ways in which approximate rimes, alliteration, and the consonant sounds in the last stanza contribute to the meaning and tone.
3. What possible meanings have the last two lines?

138. Seal Lullaby

Oh! hush thee, my baby, the night is behind us,
    And black are the waters that sparkled so green.
The moon, o'er the combers, looks downward to find us
    At rest in the hollows that rustle between.
Where billow meets billow, there soft be thy pillow;   5
    Ah, weary wee flipperling, curl at thy ease!
The storm shall not wake thee, nor shark overtake thee
    Asleep in the arms of the slow-swinging seas.

Rudyard Kipling (1865–1936)

QUESTIONS

1. Identify speaker, listener, and situation. "[F]lipperling" (6) is a coined
   word; what does it mean?
2. Identify the musical devices (noticing where internal rime is introduced).
3. A feminine rime that involves two syllables is known also as a **double
   rime**. Find examples in the poem of double rimes. Which lines employ
   masculine or **single rimes**?

139. Shut In

Like many of us, born too late,
(like all of us, fenced in by fate),
    the late October fly
    will fondly live and die

insensible of the allure   5
of carrion or cow manure.
    Withindoors day and night,
    propelled by appetite,

he circles with approving hums
a morning's manna-fall of crumbs   10
    hoping to find a smear
    of jelly somewhere near.

In such an easeful habitat
while autumn wanes he waxes fat
    and languorous, but not   15
    enough to let the swat

of hasty, rolled-up magazine
eliminate him from the scene.
    Outside, the air is chill.
    Inside, he's hard to kill.   20

Patrolling with adhesive feet
the ceiling under which we eat,
    he captures at a glance
    the slightest threat or chance,

and flaunts the facets of his eyes   25
that make him prince of household spies.
    And as he watches, we,
    if we look up, will see

a life of limits, like our own,
enclosed within a temperate zone,   30
    not harsh, not insecure,
    no challenge to endure,

but yet, with every buzz of need,
by trifles running out of speed.
    One day he will be gone.   35
    Then the real cold comes on.

Robert B. Shaw (b. 1947)

QUESTIONS

1. What is the central figure of speech? Explain the similarities drawn between the fly and us. What are the two contrasting connotations of the title?
2. Comment on the musical devices. Where is the only approximate rime in
   the poem?

140. Traveling through the dark

Traveling through the dark I found a deer
dead on the edge of the Wilson River road.
It is usually best to roll them into the canyon:
that road is narrow; to swerve might make more dead.

By glow of the tail-light I stumbled back of the car   5
and stood by the heap, a doe, a recent killing;
she had stiffened already, almost cold.
I dragged her off; she was large in the belly.

My fingers touching her side brought me the reason —
her side was warm; her fawn lay there waiting,   10
alive, still, never to be born.
Beside that mountain road I hesitated.

The car aimed ahead its lowered parking lights;
under the hood purred the steady engine.
I stood in the glare of the warm exhaust turning red;   15
around our group I could hear the wilderness listen.

I thought hard for us all — my only swerving —,
then pushed her over the edge into the river.

William Stafford (1914–1993)

QUESTIONS

1. State precisely the speaker's dilemma. What kind of person is he? Does he
   make the right decision? Why does he call his hesitation "my only swerving" (17), and how does this connect with the word "swerve" in line 4?
2. What different kinds of imagery and of image contrasts give life to the
   poem? Do any of the images have symbolic overtones?
3. At first glance this poem may appear to be without end rime. Looking
   closer, do you find any correspondences between lines 2 and 4 in each
   stanza? Between the final words of the concluding couplet? Can you find
   any line-end in the poem without some connection in sound to another
   line-end in its stanza?

141. Nothing Gold Can Stay

Nature's first green is gold,
Her hardest hue to hold.
Her early leaf's a flower;
But only so an hour.
Then leaf subsides to leaf.   5
So Eden sank to grief,
So dawn goes down to day.
Nothing gold can stay.

Robert Frost (1874–1963)

QUESTIONS

1. Explain the paradoxes in lines 1 and 3.
2. Discuss the poem as a series of symbols. What are the symbolic meanings of "gold" in the final line of the poem?
3. Discuss the contributions of alliteration, assonance, consonance, rime, and other repetitions to the effectiveness of the poem.

EXERCISE

Discuss the various ways in which the following poems make use of refrain:
1. "Winter" (No. 2)
2. "Spring" (No. 4)
3. "Southern Cop" (No. 88)
4. "in Just-" (No. 92)
5. "Edward" (No. 180)
6. "The Lamb" (No. 204)
7. "Riddle" (No. 238)
8. "Adieu, farewell, earth's bliss" (No. 256)
9. "Fear no more" (No. 274)
10. "Do Not Go Gentle into That Good Night" (No. 286)

CHAPTER TWELVE

Rhythm and Meter

Our love of rhythm is rooted even deeper in us than our love for musical repetition. It is related to the beat of our hearts, the pulse of our blood, the intake and outflow of air from our lungs. Everything that we do naturally and gracefully we do rhythmically. There is rhythm in the way we walk, the way we swim, the way we ride a horse, the way we swing a golf club or a baseball bat. So native is rhythm to us that we read it, when we can, into the mechanical world around us. Our clocks go tick-tick-tick, but we hear tick-tock, tick-tock. The click of railway wheels beneath us patterns itself into a tune in our heads. There is a strong appeal for us in language that is rhythmical.

The term **rhythm** refers to any wavelike recurrence of motion or sound. In speech it is the natural rise and fall of language. All language is to some degree rhythmical, for all language involves alternations between accented and unaccented syllables. Language varies considerably, however, in the degree to which it exhibits rhythm. Sometimes in speech the rhythm is so unobtrusive or so unpatterned that we are scarcely aware of it. Sometimes, as in rap or in oratory, the rhythm is so pronounced that we may be tempted to tap our feet to it.

In every word of more than one syllable, one or more syllables are **accented** or **stressed;** that is, given more prominence in pronunciation than the rest.* We say toDAY, toMORrow, YESterday, interVENE. These accents within individual words are indicated by stress marks in dictionaries, and with many words of more than two syllables primary and secondary stresses are shown (in'-ter-vene''). When words are arranged into a sentence, we give certain words or syllables more prominence in pronunciation than the rest. We say: "He WENT to the

---

*Though the words *accent* and *stress* generally are used interchangeably, as here, a distinction is sometimes made between them in technical discussions. **Accent,** the relative prominence given a syllable in relation to its neighbors, is then said to result from one or more of four causes: *stress,* or force of utterance, producing loudness; *duration; pitch;* and *juncture,* the manner of transition between successive sounds. Of these, *stress,* in English verse, is the most important.

STORE" or "ANN is DRIVing her CAR." There is nothing mysterious about this; it is the normal process of language. The only difference between prose and verse is that in prose these accents occur more or less haphazardly; in verse the poet may arrange them to occur at regular intervals.

In poetry as in prose, the rhythmic effects depend almost entirely on what a statement means, and different intended meanings will produce different rhythms even in identical statements. If I say "I don't believe YOU," I mean something different from "*I* don't believe you" or from "I don't beLIEVE you." In speech, these are **rhetorical stresses,** which we use to make our intentions clear. Stressing "I" separates me from others who do believe you; stressing "you" separates you from others whom I do believe; stressing "believe" intensifies my statement of disbelief. Such rhetorical stressing comes as naturally to us as language itself, and is at least as important in poetry as it is in expressive speaking. It is also basic to understanding the rhythm of poetry, for poetic rhythm depends on the plain, rhetorical stresses to communicate its meaning. We must be able to recognize the meaning of a line of poetry before we can determine its rhythm.

In addition to accent or stress, rhythm is based on pauses. In poetry as in prose or speech, pauses are the result of natural speech rhythms and the structure of sentences. Periods and commas create pauses, but so does the normal flow of phrases and clauses. Poetry, however, adds another kind of pause arising from the fact that poetry is written in lines. The poetic line is a unit that creates pauses in the flow of speech, sometimes slight and sometimes large. Poets have at their disposal a variety of possibilities when ending a line. An **end-stopped line** is one in which the end of the line corresponds with a natural speech pause; a **run-on line** is one in which the sense of the line hurries on into the next line. (There are of course all degrees of end-stop and run-on. A line ending with a period or semicolon is heavily end-stopped. A line without punctuation at the end is normally considered a run-on line, but it is less forcibly run-on if it ends at a natural speech pause—as between subject and predicate—than if it ends, say, between an article and its noun, between an auxiliary and its verb, or between a preposition and its object.) In addition there are pauses that occur in the middle of lines, either grammatical or rhetorical. These are called **caesuras,** and are another resource for varying the rhythm of lines.

The poetic line is the basic rhythmic unit in **free verse,** the predominating type of poetry now being written. Except for its line arrangement there are no necessary differences between the rhythms of free verse and the rhythms of prose, so our awareness of the line as a rhythmic unit is essential. Consider the rhythmic contrast between end-stopped lines and run-on lines in these two excerpts from poems presented earlier, and notice how the caesuras (marked ‖) help to vary the rhythms:

> A noiseless patient spider,
>
> I marked where on a little promontory it stood isolated,
>
> Marked how to explore the vacant vast surrounding,
>
> It launched forth filament, ‖ filament, ‖ filament, ‖ out of itself,
>
> Ever unreeling them, ‖ ever tirelessly speeding them.
>
> (from Poem No. 61)

> Sorrow is my own yard
>
> where the new grass
>
> flames ‖ as it has flamed
>
> often before ‖ but not
>
> with the cold fire
>
> that closes round me this year.
>
> (from Poem No. 35)

There is another sort of poetry that depends entirely on ordinary prose rhythms—the **prose poem** exemplified by Carolyn Forché's "The Colonel" (No. 222). Having dispensed even with the line as a unit of rhythm, the prose poem lays its claim to being poetry by its attention to many of the poetic elements presented earlier in this book: connotation, imagery, figurative language, and the concentration of meaning in evocative language.

But most often, when people think of poetry they think of the two broad branches, free verse and metrical verse, which are distinguished mainly by the absence or presence of meter. **Meter** is the identifying characteristic of rhythmic language that we can tap our feet to. When verse is metrical, the accents of language are so arranged as to occur at apparently equal intervals of time, and it is this interval we mark off with the tap of a foot.

The study of meter is fascinating but highly complex. It is by no means an absolute prerequisite to an enjoyment, even a rich enjoyment, of poetry, any more than is the ability to identify by name the multiplicity of figures of speech. But a knowledge of the fundamentals of meter does have value. It can make the beginning reader more aware of the rhythmical effects of poetry and of how poetry should be read. It can enable the more advanced reader to analyze how certain effects are achieved, to see how rhythm interacts with meaning, and to explain what makes one poem (in this respect) better than another. The beginning student ought to have at least an elementary knowledge of the subject. And it is not so difficult as its traditional terminology might suggest.

Even for the beginner, one essential distinction must be understood: although the terms *rhythm* and *meter* are sometimes used interchangeably, they mean different things. Rhythm designates the flow of actual, pronounced sound (or sound heard in the mind's ear), whereas meter refers to the patterns that sounds follow when a poet has arranged them into metrical verse. This may be illustrated by an analogy of a well-designed building and the architect's blueprint for its construction. The building, like rhythmic sound, is actual and real; the blueprint for it is an abstract, idealized pattern, like metrical form. When we look at a building, we see the actuality, but we also recognize that it is based on a pattern. The actuality of the building goes beyond the idealized blueprint in a number of ways—it presents us with texture, with color, with varying effects depending upon light and shade, with contrasts of building materials. In poetry, the actuality is language arranged in sentences, with a progression through time, with varying emotions, dramatic contrasts of meaning and tone, the revelation of the speaker's situation, and so forth. All these are expressed through the sounds of language, which are constantly shifting to create meanings and implications.

The word *meter* comes from a word meaning "measure" (the word *rhythm* from a word meaning "flow," as in waves). To measure something we must have a unit of measurement. For measuring length we use the inch, foot, yard; for measuring time we use the second, minute, hour. For measuring verse we use the foot, the line, and (sometimes) the stanza.

One basic unit of meter, the **foot,** consists normally of one accented syllable plus one or two unaccented syllables, though occasionally there may be no unaccented syllables. Determining which syllable in a foot is accented, we compare its sound with that of the other syllables *within the foot,* not with the sounds of syllables in other feet within a line. In fact, because of the varying stresses on syllables in a spoken sentence, it is very unusual for all of the stressed syllables in a line to be equally stressed.

For diagramming the metrical form of verse, various systems of visual symbols have been devised. In this book we shall use a breve (˘) to indicate an unstressed syllable, an ictus (′) to indicate a stressed syllable, and a vertical bar to indicate the division between feet. The basic kinds of feet are as follows:

Examples	Name of foot	Adjectival form*	
to-dáy, thĕ sún	Iamb	Iambic	⎤
dái-lў, wént tŏ	Trochee	Trochaic	⎦ Duple meters
ĭn-tĕr-véne, ĭn thĕ dárk	Anapest	Anapestic	⎤
múl-tĭ-plĕ, cól-ŏr ŏf	Dactyl	Dactylic	⎦ Triple meters
trúe-blúe	Spondee	Spondaic	

Two kinds of examples are given here, whole words and phrases, to indicate the fact that one must not assume that every individual word will be a foot, nor that divisions between feet necessarily fall between words. In actual lines, one might for example find the word *intervene* constituting parts of two different feet:

Ĭ wánt | tŏ ĭn- | tĕr-véne.

As this example demonstrates, in diagramming meters we must sometimes acknowledge the primary and secondary stresses provided by dictionaries: the word *intervene* provides the stresses for two consecutive feet.

The other basic unit of measurement in metrical verse is the line, which has the same properties as in free verse—it may be end-stopped or run-on, and its phrasing and punctuation will create caesuras. The difference between metrical and free verse lines is that

*In the spondee the accent is thought of as being distributed equally or almost equally over the two syllables and is sometimes referred to as a hovering accent. No whole poems are written in spondees. Hence there are only four basic meters: iambic, trochaic, anapestic, and dactylic. Iambic and trochaic are called duple because they employ two-syllable feet, anapestic and dactylic triple because they employ three-syllable feet. Of the four standard meters, iambic is by far the most common, followed by anapestic. Trochaic occurs relatively infrequently as the meter of poems, and dactylic is so rare as to be almost a museum specimen.

metrical lines are measured by naming the number of feet in them. The following names are used to indicate number:

Monometer	one foot	Tetrameter	four feet
Dimeter	two feet	Pentameter	five feet
Trimeter	three feet	Hexameter	six feet

The third unit of measurement, the **stanza,** consists of a group of lines whose metrical pattern is repeated throughout the poem. Since much verse is not written in stanzas, we shall save our discussion of this unit till a later chapter.

Although metrical form is potentially uniform in its regularity, the poet may introduce **metrical variations,** which call attention to some of the sounds because they depart from what is regular. Three means for varying meter are **substitution** (replacing the regular foot with another one), **extra-metrical syllables** added at the beginnings or endings of lines, and **anacrusis** (the omission of an unaccented syllable at the beginning of a line). Because these represent clear changes in the pattern, they are usually obvious and striking. But even metrical regularity rarely creates a monotonous rhythm because rhythm is the actuality in sound, not the pattern or blueprint of meter. The rhythm of a line of poetry, like the actuality of a building, depends on the components of sound mentioned above—stress, duration, pitch, and juncture—as these are presented in rhetorically stressed sentences. We may diagram the metrical form of a line, but because no two sentences in English are identical in sound, there can be no formulas or mechanical systems for indicating rhythm. Rhythm must be described rather than formulated.

The process of defining the metrical form of a poem is called **scansion.** To *scan* any specimen of verse, we do three things: (1) we identify the prevailing foot; (2) we name the number of feet in a line—if this length follows any regular pattern; and (3) we describe the stanzaic pattern—if there is one. We may try out our skill on the following poem:

142. Virtue

Sweet day, so cool, so calm, so bright,
The bridal of the earth and sky;

The dew shall weep thy fall to night,
   For thou must die.

Sweet rose, whose hue, angry and brave,   5
   Bids the rash gazer wipe his eye;
Thy root is ever in its grave,
   And thou must die.

Sweet spring, full of sweet days and roses,
   A box where sweets compacted lie;   10
My music shows ye have your closes,
   And all must die.

Only a sweet and virtuous soul,
   Like seasoned timber, never gives;
But though the whole world turn to coal,   15
   Then chiefly lives.

George Herbert (1593–1633)

QUESTIONS

1. Vocabulary: *bridal* (2), *brave* (5), *closes* (11), *coal* (15).
2. How are the four stanzas interconnected? How do they build to a climax? How does the fourth contrast with the first three?

    The first step in scanning a poem is to read it normally, according to its prose meaning, listening to where the accents fall naturally, and perhaps beating time with the hand. If we have any doubt about how a line should be marked, we should skip it temporarily and go on to lines where we feel greater confidence; that is, to those lines which seem most regular, with accents that fall unmistakably at regular intervals—for we are seeking the poem's pattern, which will be revealed by what is regular in it. In "Virtue" lines 3, 10, and 14 clearly fall into this category, as do the short lines 4, 8, and 12. Lines 3, 10, and 14 may be marked as follows.

The dew | shall weep | thy fall | to night,   3

A box | where sweets | com-pact-ed lie;   10

Like sea- | soned tim- | ber, nev-er gives   14

Lines 4, 8, and 12 are so nearly identical that we may use line 4 to represent all three.

For thŏu╵mŭst díe.╵   4

Surveying what we have done so far, we may with some confidence say that the prevailing metrical foot of the poem is iambic; and we may reasonably hypothesize that the second and third lines of each stanza are tetrameter (four-foot) lines and the fourth line dimeter. What about the first lines? Line 1 contains eight syllables, and since the poem is iambic, we may mark them into four feet. The last six syllables clearly constitute three iambic feet (as a general rule, the last few feet in a line tend to reflect the prevailing meter of a poem).

Swĕet dáy,╵so cóol,╵so cálm,╵so bríght╵   1

This too, then, is a tetrameter line, and the only question is whether to mark the first foot as another iamb or as a spondee—that is, whether it conforms to the norm established by the iambic meter, or is a substituted foot. The adjective "Sweet" is certainly more important in the line than the repeated adverb "so," and ought to receive more stress than the adverbs on the principle of *rhetorical stress,* by which the plain prose sense governs the pronunciation. But we must remember that in marking metrical stresses, we are only comparing the syllables *within a foot,* so the comparison with the repeated "so" is irrelevant. The real question is whether "Sweet" receives as much emphasis as "day."

As another general rule (but by no means an absolute one), a noun usually receives more stress than an adjective that modifies it, a verb more than its adverbs, an adjective more than an adverb that modifies it—except when the modifying word points to an unusual or unexpected condition. If the phrase were "fat day" or "red day," we would probably feel that those adjectives were odd enough to warrant stressing them. "Sweet day" does not strike us as particularly unusual, so the noun ought to receive stress. Further, as we notice that each of the first three stanzas begins with "Sweet" modifying different nouns, we recognize that the statement of the poem is drawing attention to the similarities (and differences) of three things that can be called *sweet*— "day," "rose," and "spring." By its repetition before those three nouns, the word *sweet* may come to seem formulary, and the nouns the object of attention. On the other hand, the repetition of "Sweet" may seem emphatic, and lead us to give approximately equal stress to both the noun and its adjective. As our purpose is to detect the *pattern* of sounds in the poem, the most likely result of this study will be to mark it iambic. However, judging it to be spondaic would not be incorrect, for ultimately we are reporting what we *hear,* and there is room for subjective differences.

The first feet of lines 5 and 9 raise the same problem as line 1 and should be marked in the same way. Choices of a similar sort occur in other lines (15 and 16). Many readers will quite legitimately perceive line 16 as parallel to lines 4, 8, and 12. Others, however, may argue that the world "then"—emphasizing what happens to the virtuous soul when everything else has perished—has an importance that should be reflected in both the reading and the scansion, and will therefore mark the first foot of this line as a spondee:

Then chief-|ly lives.| 16

These readers also will hear the third foot in line 15 as a spondee:

But though|the whole|world turn|to coal| 15

Lines 2 and 7 introduce a different problem. Most readers, if they encountered these lines in a paragraph of prose, would read them thus:

The BRIdal of the EARTH and SKY   2

Thy ROOT is EVer in its GRAVE   7

But this reading leaves us with an anomalous situation. First, we have only three stresses where our pattern calls for four. Second, we have three unaccented syllables occurring together, a situation almost never found in verse of duple meter. From this situation we may learn an important principle. Though normal reading of the sentences in a poem establishes its metrical pattern, the metrical pattern so established in turn influences the reading. An interactive process is at work. In this poem the pressure of the pattern will cause most practiced readers to stress the second of the three unaccented syllables in both lines slightly more than those on either side of it. In scansion, comparing the syllables within the individual foot, we acknowledge that slight increase of stress by marking those syllables as stressed (remember, the marking of the accent does not indicate a *degree* of stress in comparison with other accents in the line). We mark them thus:

The bri-|dal of|the earth|and sky| 2

Thy root|is ev-|er in|its grave   7

Line 5 presents a situation about which there can be no dispute. The word "angry," though it occurs in a position where we would expect an iamb, by virtue of its normal pronunciation *must* be accented on the first syllable, and thus must be marked a trochee:

Sweet rose, | whose hue, | an-gry | and brave | 5

There is little question also that the following line begins with a trochee, but the second foot ("rash gaz-") must be examined, for we may wonder whether the adjective *rash* presents an unexpected modification for the noun *gazer.* Since the possibilities seem about equal, I prefer to let the pattern again take precedence, although a spondee would be acceptable:

Bids the | rash gaz-|er wipe | his eye | 6

Similarly, the word "Only," beginning line 13, must be accented on the first syllable, thus introducing a trochaic substitution in the first foot of the line. Line 13 also presents another problem. A modern reader perceives the word "virtuous" as a three-syllable word, but the poet writing in the seventeenth century when metrical requirements were stricter than they are today would probably have meant the word to be pronounced as two syllables: *ver- tyus.* Following the tastes of this century, I mark it as three syllables, so introducing an anapest instead of the expected iamb in the last foot:

On- ly | a sweet | and vir-| tu-ous soul | 13

In doing this, however, I am consciously modernizing—altering the probable practice of the poet for the sake of a contemporary audience.

One problem of scansion remains: in the third stanza, lines 9 and 11 differ from the other lines of the poem in two respects—(a) they contain an uneven number of syllables (nine rather than the expected eight); (b) they end on unaccented syllables:

Sweet spring, | full of | sweet days | and ros-|es,   9

My mu-| sic shows | ye have | your clos-|es   11

Such leftover unaccented syllables at line ends are examples of extrametrical syllables and are not counted in identifying and naming the meter. These lines are both tetrameter, and if we tap our feet when reading them, we shall tap four times. Metrical verse will often have one and sometimes two leftover unaccented syllables. In iambic and anapestic verse they will come at the end of the lines; in trochaic and dactyllic at the beginning. They never occur in the middle of a line.

Our metrical analysis of "Virtue" is completed. Though (mainly for ease of discussion) we have skipped about, we have indicated a scansion for all its lines. "Virtue" is written in iambic meter (meaning that most of its feet are iambs), and is composed of four-line stanzas, the first three lines tetrameter, the final line dimeter. We are now ready to make a few generalizations about scansion.

1. Good readers will not ordinarily stop to scan a poem they are reading, and they certainly will not read a poem aloud with the exaggerated emphasis on accented syllables that we sometimes give them in order to make the metrical pattern more apparent. However, occasional scansion of a poem has value, as will be indicated in the next chapter, which discusses the relation of sound and meter to sense. Just one example here. The structure of meaning of "Virtue" is unmistakable; three parallel stanzas concerning things that die are followed by a contrasting fourth stanza concerning the one thing that does not die. The first three stanzas all begin with the word "Sweet" preceding a noun, and the first metrical foot in these stanzas is either an iamb or a spondee. The contrasting fourth stanza, however, begins with a trochee, thus departing both from the previous pattern and from the basic meter of the poem. This departure is significant, for the word *only* is the hinge upon which the structure of the poem turns, and the metrical reversal gives it emphasis. Thus meter serves meaning.

2. Scansion only begins to reveal the rhythmical quality of a poem. It simply involves classifying all syllables as either accented or unaccented and ignores the sometimes considerable differences between degrees of accent. Whether we call a syllable accented or unaccented depends only on its degree of accent relative to the other syllable(s) in its foot. In lines 2 and 7 of "Virtue," the accents on "of" and "in" are obviously much lighter than on the other accented syllables in the line. Further, unaccented syllables also vary in weight. In line 5 "whose" is clearly heavier than (-gry) or "and," and is arguably even heavier than the accented "of" and "in" of lines 2 and 7. It is not unusual, either, to find the unaccented syllable of a foot receiving more stress than the accented syllable immediately preceding it in another foot, as in this line by Ben Jonson (No. 245):

Drínk to | me ón- | ly with | thine eýes |

The last four syllables of the line, two perfectly regular iambs, are actually spoken as a sequence of four increasingly stressed accents. A similar sequence of increasing accents occurs in lines 4, 8, and 12 of "Virtue"

For thou⏑́ | must⏑ díe |

since the necessity expressed in the word "must" makes it more heavily stressed than the pronoun "thou." The point is that metrical scansion is incapable of describing subtle rhythmic effects in poetry. It is nevertheless a useful and serviceable tool, for by showing us the metrical *pattern,* it draws attention to the way in which the actuality of sound follows the pattern even while departing from it; that is, recognizing the meter, we can more clearly hear rhythms. The *idea* of regularity helps us be aware of the *actuality* of sounds.

3. Notice that the divisions between feet have no meaning except to help us identify the meter. They do not correspond to the speech rhythms in the line. In the third foot of line 14 of "Virtue," a syntactical pause occurs *within* the foot; and, indeed, feet divisions often fall in the middle of a word. It is sometimes a mistake of beginners to expect the word and the foot to be identical units. We mark the feet divisions only to reveal regularity or pattern, not to indicate rhythm. But in "Virtue," if we examine all of the two-syllable words, we find that all eleven of them as isolated words removed from their lines would be called *trochaic.* Yet only two of them—"angry" (5) and "only" (13)—actually occur as trochaic feet. All the rest are divided in the middle between two iambic feet. This calls for two observations: (a) the rhythm of the poem, the *heard* sound, often runs counter to the meter—iambic feet have what is called a "rising" pattern, yet these words individually and as they are spoken have a "falling" rhythm; and (b) the trochaic hinge word "only" thus has rhythmic echoes throughout the poem, those preceding it yielding a kind of predictive power, and those following it reinforcing the fact that the sense of the poem turns at that word. This rhythmic effect is especially pronounced in the simile of line 14:

Like séa- | soned tím- | ber, név- | er gíves |

Echoing the key word "only," this line contains three disyllabic words, each of them having a falling rhythm running counter to the iambic meter.

4. Finally—and this is the most important generalization of all—perfect regularity of meter is no criterion of merit. Inexperienced readers sometimes get the notion that it is. If the meter is regular, and the rhythm mirrors that regularity in sound, they may feel that the poet has handled the meter successfully and deserves all credit for it. Actually there is nothing easier for any moderately talented versifier than to make language go ta-DUM ta-DUM ta-DUM. But there are two reasons why this is not generally desirable. The first is that, as we have said, all art consists essentially of repetition and variation. If a rhythm alternates too regularly between light and heavy beats, the result is to banish variation; the rhythm mechanically follows the meter and becomes monotonous. But used occasionally or emphatically, a monotonous rhythm can be very effective, as in the triumphant last line of Tennyson's "Ulysses" (No. 67):

To strive, | to seek, | to find, | and not | to yield. |

The second reason is that, once a basic meter has been established, deviations from it become highly significant and are a means by which the poet can reinforce meaning. If a meter is too regular, and the rhythm shows little deviation from it, the probability is that the poet, instead of adopting rhythm to meaning, has simply forced the meaning into a metrical straitjacket.

Actually what gives the skillful use of meter its greatest effectiveness is to be found in the distinction between meter and rhythm. Once we have determined the basic meter of a poem, say iambic tetrameter, we have an expectation that the rhythm will coincide with it—that the pattern will be identical to the actual sound. Thus a silent drumbeat is set up in our minds, and this drumbeat constitutes an expected rhythm. But the actual rhythm of the words—the heard rhythm—will sometimes confirm this expected rhythm and sometimes not. Thus the two, meter and rhythm, are counterpointed, and the appeal of the verse is magnified just as when two melodies are counterpointed in music, or as when we see two swallows flying together and round each other, following the same general course but with individual variations and so making a more eye-catching pattern than one swallow flying alone. If the heard rhythm conforms too closely to the expected rhythm (meter), the poem becomes dull and uninteresting rhythmically. If it departs too far from the meter, there ceases to be an expected rhythm and the result is likely to be a muddle.

There are several ways by which variation can be introduced into a poem's rhythm. The most obvious way, as we have said, is by the substitution of other kinds of feet for the basic foot. Such metrical variation will always be reflected as a rhythmic variation. In our scansion of line 13 of "Virtue," for instance, we found a trochee and an anapest substituted for the expected iambs in the first and last feet. A less obvious but equally important means of variation is through varying degrees of accent arising from the prose meaning of phrases—from the rhetorical stressing. Though we began our scansion of "Virtue" by marking lines 3, 10, and 14 as perfectly regular metrically, there is actually a considerable rhythmic difference between them. Line 3 is quite regular because the rhythmic phrasing corresponds to the metrical pattern, and the line can be read ta-DUM ta-DUM ta-DUM ta-DUM (The DEW shall WEEP thy FALL to NIGHT). Line 10 is less regular, for the three-syllable word "compacted" cuts across the division between two feet. This should be read ta-DUM ta-DUM ta-DUMP-ty DUM (A BOX where SWEETS comPACTed LIE). Line 14 is the least regular of these three because here there is no correspondence between rhythmic phrasing and metrical division. This should be read ta-DUMP-ty DUMP-ty, DUMP-ty DUM (Like SEAsoned TIMber, NEVer GIVES). Finally, variation can be introduced by **grammatical** and **rhetorical pauses,** whether or not signaled by punctuation (punctuated pauses are usually of longer duration than those occasioned only by syntax and rhetoric, and pauses for periods are longer than those for commas). The comma in line 14, by introducing a grammatical pause (in the middle of a foot), provides an additional variation from its perfect regularity. Probably the most violently irregular line in the poem is line 5,

Sweet rŏse, | whŏse húe, | ăn- gry | ănd bráve, |

for here the unusual trochaic substitution in the second from last foot of an iambic line (a rare occurrence) is set off and emphasized by the grammatical pause, and also as we have noted the unaccented "whose" is considerably heavier than the other unaccented syllables in the line. This trochee "angry" is the first unquestionable metrical substitution in the poem. It occurs in a line which, because it opens a stanza, is subconsciously compared to the first line of the first stanza— an example of regularity with its grammatical pauses separating all four of its feet. Once we have noticed that the first line of the second stanza contains a metrical variation, our attention is called to the fact

that after the first, each stanza opens with a line containing a trochee—
and that these trochees are moved forward one foot in each of the successive stanzas, from the third position in stanza two, to the second in
four, and finally to the first in the concluding stanza. This pattern itself tends to add even more emphasis to the climactic change signaled
by the final trochee, "only." Again, meter and rhythm serve meaning.

The effects of rhythm and meter are several. Like the musical repetitions of sound, the musical repetitions of accent can be pleasing for
their own sake. In addition, rhythm works as an emotional stimulus
and heightens our awareness of what is going on in a poem. Finally, a
poet can adapt the sound of the verse to its content and thus make
meter a powerful reinforcement of meaning. We should avoid, however,
the notion that there is any mystical correspondence between certain
meters or rhythms and certain emotions. There are no "happy" meters and no "melancholy" meters. The "falling" rhythm of line 14 of
"Virtue," counterpointed against its "rising" meter, does not indicate
a depression of mood or feeling—the line has quite the opposite emotional tone. Poets' choice of meter is probably less important than how
they handle it after they have chosen it. In all great poetry, meter and
rhythm work intimately with the other elements of the poem to produce the total effect.

And because of the importance of free verse today, we must not
forget that poetry need not be metrical at all. Like alliteration and rime,
like metaphor and irony, like even imagery, meter is simply *one* resource poets may or may not use. Their job is to employ their resources
to the best advantage for the object they have in mind—the kind of
experience they wish to express. And on no other basis should they be
judged.

EXERCISES

1. A term that every student of poetry should know (and should be careful
   not to confuse with *free verse*) is blank verse. **Blank verse** has a very specific meter: it is *iambic pentameter, unrimed.* It has a special name because
   it is the principal English meter; that is, the meter that has been used for
   a large proportion of the greatest English poetry, including the plays of
   Shakespeare and the epics of Milton. Iambic pentameter in English seems
   especially suitable for the serious treatment of serious themes. The natural movement of the English language tends to be iambic. Lines shorter
   than pentameter tend to be songlike, or at least less suited to sustained
   treatment of serious material. Lines longer than pentameter tend to break
   up into shorter units, the hexameter line being read as two three-foot units.

Rime, while highly appropriate to most short poems, often proves a handicap for a long and lofty work. (The word *blank* indicates that the end of the line is "blank," that is, bare of rime.)

Of the following poems, four are in blank verse, two are in other meters, and four are in free verse. Determine in which category each belongs.

a. "Break of Day" (No. 16)
b. "The River-Merchant's Wife: A Letter" (No. 19)
c. "Mirror" (No. 21)
d. "Ulysses" (No. 67)
e. "The Unknown Citizen" (No. 82)
f. "Grace to Be Said at the Supermarket" (No. 85)
g. "'Out, Out—'" (No. 90)
h. "Dover Beach" (No. 126)
i. "Getting Out" (No. 128)
j. "Living in Sin" (No. 268)

2. Examine "My Last Duchess" (No. 89) and "Sound and Sense" (No. 158). Both are written in the same meter (iambic pentameter, rimed in couplets) but their general rhythmical effect is markedly different. What accounts for the difference? How does the contrast support our statement that the way poets handle meter is more important than their choice of a meter?

3. Examine "The Widow's Lament in Springtime" (No. 35), "The Hound" (No. 45), and "The Dance" (No. 167). Which is the most forcibly run-on in the majority of its lines? Describe the differences in effect.

---

143. "Introduction" to *Songs of Innocence*

Piping down the valleys wild,
Piping songs of pleasant glee,
On a cloud I saw a child,
And he laughing said to me:

"Pipe a song about a Lamb."   5
So I piped with merry cheer.
"Piper, pipe that song again."
So I piped; he wept to hear.

"Drop thy pipe, thy happy pipe;
Sing thy songs of happy cheer."   10
So I sung the same again
While he wept with joy to hear.

"Piper, sit thee down and write
In a book that all may read."
So he vanished from my sight,   15
And I plucked a hollow reed,

And I made a rural pen,
And I stained the water clear,
And I wrote my happy songs
Every child may joy to hear.   20

William Blake (1757–1827)

QUESTIONS

1. Poets have traditionally been thought of as inspired by one of the Muses
   (Greek female divinities whose duties were to nurture the arts). Blake's
   Songs of Innocence, a book of poems about childhood and the state of innocence, includes "The Chimney Sweeper" (No. 78) and "The Lamb"
   (No. 204). In this introductory poem to the book, what function is performed by the child upon a cloud?
2. What is symbolized by "a Lamb" (5)?
3. What three stages of poetic composition are suggested in stanzas 1–2, 3,
   and 4–5 respectively?
4. What features of the poems in his book does Blake hint at in this "Introduction"? Name at least four.
5. Mark the stressed and unstressed syllables in lines 1–2 and 9–10. Do
   they establish the basic meter of the poem? If so, is that meter iambic or
   trochaic? Or could it be either? Some metrists have discarded the distinction between iambic and trochaic, and between anapestic and dactylic, as
   being artificial. The important distinction, they feel, is between duple and
   triple meters. Does this poem support their claim?

144. It takes all sorts

It takes all sorts of in and outdoor schooling
To get adapted to my kind of fooling.

Robert Frost (1874–1963)

QUESTIONS

1. What is the poet saying about the nature of his poetry?
2. Scan the poem. Is it iambic or trochaic? Or could it be either? How does
   this poem differ from Blake's "Introduction" in illustrating the ambiguity
   of the distinction between the two meters?

145. Epitaph on an Army of Mercenaries

These, in the day when heaven was falling,
   The hour when earth's foundations fled,
Followed their mercenary calling
   And took their wages and are dead.

Their shoulders held the sky suspended;   5
   They stood, and earth's foundations stay;
What God abandoned, these defended,
   And saved the sum of things for pay.

A. E. Housman (1859–1936)

QUESTIONS

1. The Battle of Ypres (October 31, 1914), early in World War I, pitted a
   small army of British "regulars" against a much larger force of German
   volunteers. German newspapers described the conflict as one between
   young German volunteers and British "mercenaries." Housman first published this poem in the London *Times* on October 31, 1917, the third anniversary of the battle. Who are "These" (1)? Is the tone of the poem one
   of tribute or one of cynical scorn for "These"? How does the poet use the
   word "mercenary" (3)?
2. In scanning Herbert's "Virtue," we discovered two lines that had an unaccented syllable left over at the end that we did not count in determining the meter. How does this poem differ from "Virtue" in its use of such
   lines? The meter of this poem is iambic tetrameter. Does this sufficiently
   describe its metrical form?

146. Had I the Choice

Had I the choice to tally greatest bards,
To limn their portraits, stately, beautiful, and emulate at will,
Homer with all his wars and warriors—Hector, Achilles, Ajax,
Or Shakespeare's woe-entangled Hamlet, Lear, Othello—Tennyson's
      fair ladies,
Meter or wit the best, or choice conceit to wield in perfect rhyme,
      delight of singers;   5
These, these, O sea, all these I'd gladly barter,
Would you the undulation of one wave, its trick to me transfer,
Or breathe one breath of yours upon my verse,
And leave its odor there.

Walt Whitman (1819–1892)

QUESTIONS

1. Vocabulary: *tally* (1), *limn* (2), *conceit* (5).
2. What poetic qualities does Whitman propose to barter in exchange for what? What qualities do the sea and its waves symbolize?
3. Is this free verse, or metrical verse in duple meter? In what way might this be taken as an imitation of the rhythms of the sea?

147. The Aim Was Song

Before man came to blow it right
  The wind once blew itself untaught,
And did its loudest day and night
  In any rough place where it caught.

Man came to tell it what was wrong: 5
  It hadn't found the place to blow;
It blew too hard—the aim was song.
  And listen—how it ought to go!

He took a little in his mouth,
  And held it long enough for north   10
To be converted into south,
  And then by measure blew it forth.

By measure. It was word and note,
  The wind the wind had meant to be—
A little through the lips and throat.   15
  The aim was song—the wind could see.

Robert Frost (1874–1963)

QUESTIONS

1. Frost invents a myth about the origin of poetry. What implications does it suggest about the relation of man to nature and of poetry to nature?
2. Contrast the thought and form of this poem with Whitman's.
3. Scan the poem and identify its meter. How does the poet give variety to a regular metrical pattern?

148. Nevertheless

you've seen a strawberry
  that's had a struggle; yet
    was, where the fragments met,

a hedgehog or a star-
    fish for the multitude   5
    of seeds. What better food

than apple seeds—the fruit
    within the fruit—locked in
    like counter-curved twin

hazelnuts? Frost that kills   10
    the little rubber-plant-
    leaves of *kok-saghyz*-stalks, can't

harm the roots; they still grow
    in frozen ground. Once where
    there was a prickly-pear-   15

leaf clinging to barbed wire,
    a root shot down to grow
    in the earth two feet below;

as carrots form mandrakes
    or a ram's-horn root some-   20
    times. Victory won't come

to me unless I go
    to it; a grape tendril
    ties a knot in knots till

knotted thirty times—so   25
    the bound twig that's under-
    gone and over-gone, can't stir.

The weak overcomes its
    menace, the strong over-
    comes itself. What is there   30

like fortitude! What sap
    went through that little thread
    to make the cherry red!

Marianne Moore (1887–1972)

QUESTIONS

1. Vocabulary: *kok-saghyz* (12), *prickly-pear* (15), *mandrakes* (19).
2. This apparently random collection of examples from botanical nature actually proceeds through a sequence that begins with two types of seed-bearing fruit. Where does it go from there, and what does it end up with?
3. What human meaning does the speaker draw from these botanical examples? How do the examples support that meaning?

4. This poem is an example of **syllabic verse,** which counts only the number of syllables per line regardless of accents. (Sylvia Plath's "Metaphors" [No. 52] is another example.) Describe its formal pattern, including its rime scheme. Although the form appears arbitrary in its line breaks and stanza breaks, it is in fact tightly formalized. How is such a form appropriate to the meaning of the poem?

149. To a Daughter Leaving Home

When I taught you
at eight to ride
a bicycle, loping along
beside you
as you wobbled away   5
on two round wheels,
my own mouth rounding
in surprise when you pulled
ahead down the curved
path of the park,   10
I kept waiting
for the thud
of your crash as I
sprinted to catch up,
while you grew   15
smaller, more breakable
with distance,
pumping, pumping
for your life, screaming
with laughter,   20
the hair flapping
behind you like a
handkerchief waving
goodbye.

Linda Pastan (b. 1932)

QUESTIONS

1. How does the discrepancy between the title and the event create meaning? Which details of the poem take on symbolic meaning?
2. Write out this poem as prose, ignoring line ends. What poetic effect has been lost? Which of the original line ends are particularly important to meaning and feeling?

150. Constantly risking absurdity

Constantly risking absurdity
                          and death
          whenever he performs
                          above the heads
                                          of his audience   5
    the poet like an acrobat
                          climbs on rime
                          to a high wire of his own making
and balancing on eyebeams
                          above a sea of faces   10
          paces his way
                          to the other side of day
          performing entrechats
                          and sleight-of-foot tricks
and other high theatrics   15
                          and all without mistaking
          any thing
                          for what it may not be
          For he's the super realist
                          who must perforce perceive   20
          taut truth
                          before the taking of each stance or step
in his supposed advance
                          toward that still higher perch
where Beauty stands and waits   25
                          with gravity
                          to start her death-defying leap
          And he
          a little charleychaplin man
                          who may or may not catch   30
          her fair eternal form
                          spreadeagled in the empty air
          of existence

Lawrence Ferlinghetti (b. 1919)

QUESTIONS

1. Vocabulary: *entrechats* (13). Explain the meanings of "above the heads" (4), "sleight-of-foot tricks" (14), "high theatrics" (15), and "with gravity" (26).
2. The poet "climbs on rime" (7), the poem asserts. To what extent does this poem utilize rime and other musical devices?
3. What statement does the poem make about poetry, truth, and beauty?

4. How do the rhythms created by the length and placement of lines reinforce the meanings of the poem? Does this poem take poets and poetry seriously? Solemnly?

151. Because I could not stop for Death

Because I could not stop for Death,
He kindly stopped for me;
The carriage held but just ourselves
And Immortality.

We slowly drove; he knew no haste,   5
And I had put away
My labor and my leisure too,
For his civility.

We passed the school, where children strove,
At recess, in the ring,   10
We passed the fields of gazing grain,
We passed the setting sun,

Or rather, he passed us;
The dews drew quivering and chill;
For only gossamer, my gown;   15
My tippet, only tulle.

We paused before a house that seemed
A swelling of the ground;
The roof was scarcely visible.
The cornice, in the ground.   20

Since then, 'tis centuries, and yet
Feels shorter than the day
I first surmised the horses' heads
Were toward eternity.

Emily Dickinson (1830–1886)

QUESTIONS

1. Vocabulary: *gossamer* (15); *tippet, tulle* (16); *surmised* (23).
2. What allegorical meanings are attached to this ride? What does the alliteration in line 7 say about the quality of the speaker's life? Explain the irony of "kindly" (2) and "civility" (8). As what is Death personified? What is the "house" (17)?

3. The fourth stanza alters the metrical pattern of the poem. What aspect of this hypothetical experience is emphasized by the alteration?

152. Break, break, break

> Break, break, break,
>> On thy cold gray stones, O sea!
> And I would that my tongue could utter
>> The thoughts that arise in me.
>
> O, well for the fisherman's boy,   5
>> That he shouts with his sister at play!
> O, well for the sailor lad,
>> That he sings in his boat on the bay!
>
> And the stately ships go on
>> To their haven under the hill;   10
> But O for the touch of a vanished hand,
>> And the sound of a voice that is still!
>
> Break, break, break,
>> At the foot of thy crags, O sea!
> But the tender grace of a day that is dead   15
>> Will never come back to me.

Alfred, Lord Tennyson (1809–1892)

QUESTIONS

1. In lines 3–4 the speaker wishes he could put his thoughts into words. Does he make those thoughts explicit in the course of the poem?
2. What aspects of life are symbolized by the two images in stanza 2? By the image in lines 9–10? How do lines 11–12 contrast with those images?
3. The basic meter of this poem is anapestic, and all but two lines are trimeter. Which two? What other variations from a strict anapestic trimeter do you find? How many lines (and which ones) display a strict anapestic pattern? With this much variation, would you be justified in calling the poem free verse? Do the departures from a strict metrical norm contribute to the meaning?

CHAPTER THIRTEEN

Sound and Meaning

Rhythm and sound cooperate to produce what we call the music of poetry. This music, as we have pointed out, may serve two general functions: it may be enjoyable in itself, or it may be used to reinforce meaning and intensify the communication.

Pure pleasure in sound and rhythm exists from a very early age in the human being—probably from the age the baby first starts cooing in its cradle, certainly from the age that children begin chanting nursery rimes and skipping rope. The appeal of the following verse, for instance, depends almost entirely on its "music":

153.
> Pease porridge hot,
> Pease porridge cold,
> Pease porridge in the pot
> Nine days old.

There is very little sense here; the attraction comes from the emphatic rhythm, the emphatic rimes (with a strong contrast between the short vowel and short final consonant of *hot–pot* and the long vowel and long final consonant combination of *cold–old*), and the heavy alliteration (exactly half the words begin with *p*). From nonsense rimes such as this, many of us graduate to a love of more meaningful poems whose appeal resides largely in the sound they make. Much of the pleasure that we find in poems like Vachel Lindsay's "The Congo" and Edgar Allan Poe's "The Bells" lies in their musical qualities.

The peculiar function of poetry as distinguished from music, however, is to convey not sounds but meaning or experience *through* sounds. In third- and fourth-rate poetry, sound and rhythm sometimes distract attention from sense. In first-rate poetry the sound exists not for its own sake nor for mere decoration, but as a medium of meaning. Its function is to support the leading player, not to steal the scene.

The poet may reinforce meaning through sound in numerous ways. Without claiming to exhaust them, perhaps we can include most of the chief means under four general headings.

First, the poet can choose words whose sound in some degree suggests their meaning. In its narrowest sense this is called onomatopoeia. **Onomatopoeia,** strictly defined, means the use of words which, at least supposedly, sound like what they mean, such as *hiss, snap,* and *bang.*

154. Song: Come unto these yellow sands

Come unto these yellow sands,
    And then take hands.
Curtsied when you have and kissed,
    The wild waves whist,°   being hushed
Foot it featly° here and there,   nimbly 5
And, sweet sprites, the burden° bear.   refrain
    Hark, hark!
      Bow-wow.
    The watch-dogs bark!
      Bow-wow.   10
Hark, hark! I hear
The strain of strutting chanticleer
Cry, "Cock-a-doodle-doo!"

William Shakespeare (1564–1616)

In these lines, "bark," "bow-wow," and "Cock-a-doodle-doo" are onomatopoetic words. In addition, Shakespeare has reinforced the onomatopoetic effect with the repeated use of "hark," which sounds like *bark.* The usefulness of onomatopoeia, of course, is strictly limited, because it can be used only where the poet is describing sound, and most poems do not describe sound. And the use of pure onomatopoeia, as in the preceding example, is likely to be fairly trivial except as it forms an incidental part of a more complex poem. But by combining onomatopoeia with other devices that help convey meaning, the poet can achieve subtle and beautiful effects whose recognition is one of the keenest pleasures in reading poetry.

In addition to onomatopoetic words there is another group of words, sometimes called **phonetic intensives,** whose sound, by a process as yet obscure, to some degree connects with their meaning. An initial *fl-* sound, for instance, is often associated with the idea of moving light, as in *flame, flare, flash, flicker, flimmer.* An initial *gl-* also frequently accompanies the idea of light, usually unmoving, as in *glare, gleam, glint, glow, glisten.* An initial *sl-* often introduces words meaning "smoothly wet," as in *slippery, slick, slide, slime, slop, slosh, slobber, slushy.* An initial *st-* often suggests strength, as in *staunch, stalwart, stout, sturdy, stable, steady, stocky, stern, strong, stubborn, steel.* Short *-i-* often goes with the idea of smallness, as in *inch, imp, thin, slim, little, bit, chip, sliver, chink, slit, sip, whit, tittle, snip, wink, glint, glimmer, flicker, pigmy, midge, chick, kid, kitten, minikin, miniature.* Long *-o-* or *-oo-* may suggest melancholy or sorrow, as in *moan, groan, woe, mourn, forlorn, toll, doom, gloom, moody.* Final *-are* sometimes goes with the idea of a big light or noise, as *flare, glare, stare, blare.* Medial *-att-* suggests some kind of particled movement as in *spatter, scatter, shatter, chatter, rattle, prattle, clatter, batter.* Final *-er* and *-le* indicate repetition, as in *glitter, flutter, shimmer, whisper, jabber, chatter, clatter, sputter, flicker, twitter, mutter,* and *ripple, bubble, twinkle, sparkle, rattle, rumble, jingle.*

None of these various sounds is invariably associated with the idea that it seems to suggest and, in fact, a short *-i-* is found in *thick* as well as *thin,* in *big* as well as *little.* Language is a complex phenomenon. But there is enough association between these sounds and ideas to suggest some sort of intrinsic if obscure relationship. A word like *flicker,* though not onomatopoetic (because it does not refer to sound) would seem somehow to suggest its sense, with the *fl-* suggesting moving light, the *-i-* suggesting smallness, the *-ck-* suggesting sudden cessation of movement (as in *crack, peck, pick, hack,* and *flick*), and the *-er* suggesting repetition. The above list of sound-idea correspondences is only a very partial one. A complete list, though it would involve only a small proportion of words in the language, would probably be a longer list than that of the more strictly onomatopoetic words, to which they are related.

155. Splinter

The voice of the last cricket
across the first frost
is one kind of good-by.
It is so thin a splinter of singing.

Carl Sandburg (1878–1967)

QUESTIONS

1. Why is "so thin a splinter" a better choice of metaphor than *so small an atom* or *so meager a morsel?*
2. How does the poet intensify the effect of the two phonetic intensives in line 4?

A second and far more important way that the poet can reinforce meaning through sound is to choose sounds and group them so that the effect is smooth and pleasant sounding (*euphonious*) or rough and harsh sounding (*cacophonous*). Vowels are in general more pleasing than consonants, for vowels are musical tones, whereas consonants are merely noises. A line with a high percentage of vowel sounds in proportion to consonant sounds will therefore tend to be more melodious than one in which the proportion is low. The vowels and consonants themselves differ considerably in quality. The "long" vowels, such as those in *fate, reed, rime, coat, food,* and *dune* are fuller and more resonant than the "short" vowels, as in *fat, red, rim, cot, foot,* and *dun.* Of the consonants, some are fairly mellifluous, such as the "liquids," *l, m, n,* and *r;* the soft *v* and *f* sounds; the semivowels *w* and *y;* and such combinations as *th* and *wh.* Others, such as the "plosives," *b, d, g, k, p,* and *t,* are harsher and sharper in their effect. These differences in sound are the poet's materials. Good poets, however, will not necessarily seek out the sounds that are pleasing and attempt to combine them in melodious combinations. Rather, they will use **euphony** and **cacophony** as they are appropriate to content. Consider, for instance, the following poem.

156. Upon Julia's Voice

So smooth, so sweet, so silvery is thy voice,
As, could they hear, the Damned would make no noise,
But listen to thee (walking in thy chamber)
Melting melodious words to Lutes of Amber.

Robert Herrick (1591–1674)

QUESTION

Literally, an amber lute is as nonsensical as a silver voice. What connotations do "Amber" and "silvery" have that contribute to the meaning of this poem?

There are no strictly onomatopoetic words in this poem, and yet the sound seems marvelously adapted to the sense. Especially remarkable are the first and last lines, those most directly concerned with Julia's voice. In the first line the sounds that most strike the ear are the unvoiced *s*'s and the soft *v*'s, supported by voiced *th:* "So *smooth,* so *sweet,* so *silvery* is *thy* voice." (A voiced consonant sound is accompanied by vibration of the vocal cords—*then* is voiced, *thin* not. Notice that the terminal *-ce* in "voice" is an example of the unvoiced *s* sound: as with alliteration, spelling is irrelevant.) In the fourth line the predominating sounds are the liquid consonants *m, l,* and *r,* supported by a *w:* "*Melting melodious words* to *Lutes* of *Amber.*" The least euphonious line in the poem, on the other hand, is the second, where the subject is the tormented in hell, not Julia's voice. Here the prominent sounds are the *d*s, supported by a voiced *s* (a voiced *s* buzzes, unlike the sibilant unvoiced *ss* in line 1), and two *k* sounds: "A*s, could* they hear, the *D*amne*d* woul*d* ma*k*e no noi*s*e." Throughout the poem there is a remarkable correspondence between the pleasant-sounding and the pleasant in idea, the unpleasant-sounding and the unpleasant in idea.

A third way in which a poet can reinforce meaning through sound is by controlling the speed and movement of the lines by the choice and use of meter, by the choice and arrangement of vowel and consonant sounds, and by the disposition of pauses. In meter the unaccented syllables usually go faster than the accented syllables; hence the triple meters are swifter than the duple. But the poet can vary the tempo of any meter by the use of substitute feet. Generally, whenever two or more unaccented syllables come together, the effect will be to speed up the pace of the line; when two or more accented syllables come together, the effect will be to slow it down. This pace will also be affected by the vowel lengths and by whether the sounds are easily run together. The long vowels take longer to pronounce than the short ones. Some words are easily run together, while others demand that the position of the mouth be re-formed before the next word is uttered. It takes much longer, for instance, to say, "Watch dogs catch much meat" than to say, "My aunt is away," though the number of syllables is the same. And finally the poet can slow down the speed of a line through the introduction of grammatical and rhetorical pauses. Consider lines 54–56 from Tennyson's "Ulysses" (No. 67):

The lights | be-gin | to twin-|kle from | the rocks; |
The long | day wanes; | the slow | moon climbs; | the deep | 55
Moans round | with man-|y voi-|ces. . . .

In these lines Tennyson wished the movement to be slow, in accordance with the slow waning of the long day and the slow climbing of the moon. His meter is iambic pentameter. This is not a swift meter, but in lines 55–56 he slows it down further, (a) by introducing three spondaic feet, thus bringing three accented syllables together in two separate places; (b) by choosing for his accented syllables words that have long vowel sounds or dipthongs that the voice hangs on to: "long," "day," "wanes," "slow," "moon," "climbs," "deep," "Moans," "round"; (c) by choosing words that are not easily run together (except for "day" and "slow," each of these words begins and ends with consonant sounds that require varying degrees of readjustment of the mouth before pronunciation can continue); and (d) by introducing two grammatical pauses, after "wanes" and "climbs," and a rhetorical pause after "deep." The result is an extremely effective use of the movement of the verse to accord with the movement suggested by the words.*

A fourth way for a poet to fit sound to sense is to control both sound and meter in such a way as to emphasize words that are important in meaning. This can be done by highlighting such words through alliteration, assonance, consonance, or rime; by placing them before a pause; or by skillfully placing or displacing them in the metrical scheme. We have already seen how Ogden Nash uses alliteration and consonance to emphasize and link the three major words ("sex," "fix," and "fertile") in his little verse "The Turtle" (No. 130), and how George Herbert pivots the structure of meaning in "Virtue" (No. 142) on a trochaic substitution in the initial foot of his final stanza. For an additional example, let us look again at "Since there's no help" (No. 118). This poem is a sonnet—fourteen lines of iambic pentameter—in which a lover threatens to leave his sweetheart forever if she will not go to bed with him. In the first eight lines he pretends to be *glad* that they are breaking off their relationship so cleanly. In the last six lines, however, he paints a vivid picture of the death of his personified Love/Passion for her but intimates that even at this last moment ("Now") she could restore it to life again—by satisfying his sexual desires.

Now, at the last gasp of Love's la-test breath,

When, his pulse failing, Passion speechless lies,   10

When Faith is kneeling by his bed of death,

---

*In addition, Tennyson uses one onomatopoetic word ("Moans") and one phonetic intensive ("twinkle").

And In-no-cence is clos-ing up his eyes,
Now, if thou wouldst, when all have given him o-ver,*
From death to life thou mightst him yet re-cov-er.

The emphasis is on *Now*. In a matter of seconds, the speaker indicates, it will be too late: his Love/Passion will be dead, and he himself will be gone. The word "Now" begins line 9. It also begins a new sentence and a new direction in the poem. It is separated from what has gone before by a period at the end of the preceding line. Metrically it initiates a trochee, thus breaking away from the poem's basic iambic meter (line 8 is perfectly regular). In all these ways—its initial position in line, sentence, and thought, and its metrical irregularity—the word "Now" is given extraordinary emphasis appropriate to its importance in the context. Its repetition in line 13 reaffirms this importance, and there again it is given emphasis by its positional and metrical situation. It begins both a line and the final riming couplet, is separated by punctuation from the line before, and participates in a metrical inversion. (The lines before and after are metrically regular.)

While Herbert and Drayton use metrical deviation to give emphasis to important words, Tennyson, in the concluding line of "Ulysses," (No. 67) uses marked regularity, plus skillful use of grammatical pauses, to achieve the same effect.

We are not now that strength which in old days
Moved earth and heav-en, that which we are, we are:
One e-qual tem-per of he-ro-ic hearts,
Made weak by time and fate, but strong in will
To strive, to seek, to find, and not to yield.   70

The blank verse rhythm throughout "Ulysses" is remarkably subtle and varied, but the last line is not only regular in its scansion but heavily regular, for a number of reasons. First, all the words are monosyllables. Second, the unaccented syllables are all very small and unimportant words—four *to*s and one *and*—whereas the accented syllables consist of four important verbs and a very important *not*. Third, each of the verbs is followed by a grammatical pause pointed off by a mark of punctuation. The result is to cause a pronounced alternation between light and heavy syllables that brings the accent

*Drayton probably intended "given" to be pronounced as one syllable (*giv'n*), and most sixteenth-century readers would have pronounced it thus in this poem.

down on the four verbs and the *not* with sledgehammer blows. The line rings out like a challenge, which it is.

157. The Span of Life

The old dog barks backward without getting up.
I can remember when he was a pup.

Robert Frost (1874–1963)

QUESTIONS

1. Is the dog a dog only or also a symbol?
2. The first line presents a visual and auditory image; the second line makes a comment. But does the second line *call up images?* Does it suggest more than it says? Would the poem have been more or less effective if the second line had been, "He was frisky and lively when he was a pup"?

We may well conclude our discussion of the adaptation of sound to sense by analyzing this very brief poem. It consists of one riming anapestic tetrameter couplet. Its content is a contrast between the decrepitude of an old dog and his friskiness as a pup. The scansion is as follows:

The old | dog barks back- | ward with-out | get-ting up.
I can | re-mem- | ber when he | was a pup.

How is sound fitted to sense? In the first place, the triple meter chosen by the poet is a swift meter, but in the first line he has jammed it up in a remarkable way by substituting a kind of foot so rare that English prosody has no name for it (the Greeks, who "measured" their verse by duration of syllables rather than accent, called it a *molussus*); at any rate, it is a foot in which the accent is distributed over three syllables. This foot, following the accented syllable in the first foot, creates a situation where four accented syllables are pushed up together. In addition, each of these accented syllables begins and ends with a strong consonant sound or cluster of consonant sounds, so that they cannot be run together in pronunciation—the mouth must be reformed between syllables: "The ol*d dog barks back*-." The result is to slow down the line drastically, to damage its rhythmical quality severely, and to make it difficult to utter. Indeed, the line is as decrepit as the old dog who turns his head to greet his master but does not get up. When we get to the second line, however, the contrast is startling. The rhythm is swift and regular, the syllables end in vowels or liquid consonants that are easily run together, the whole line ripples fluently off the tongue. In addition, where the first line has a high proportion of explosive and cacophonous consonants—"The old dog barks backward without getting up"—the consonants in the second line are predominantly smoother and more graceful—"I can remember when he was a pup." Thus the motion and the sound of the lines are remarkably in accord with the visual images they suggest. In addition, in the first line the poet has supported the onomatopoetic word barks with a near echo back, so that the sound reinforces the auditory image. If the poem does a great deal in just two lines, this skillful adaptation of sound to sense is one very important reason.

In analyzing verse for correspondence between sound and sense, we need to be very cautious not to make exaggerated claims. A great deal of nonsense has been written about the moods of certain meters and the effects of certain sounds, and it is easy to suggest correspondences that exist only in our imaginations. Nevertheless, the first-rate poet has nearly always an instinctive tact about handling sound so that it in some degree supports meaning; the inferior poet is usually obtuse to these correspondences. One of the few absolute rules that can be applied to the judgment of poetry is that the form should be adequate to the content. This rule does not mean that there must always be a close and easily demonstrable correspondence. It does mean that there will be no glaring discrepancies. Poor poets, and even good poets in their third-rate work, sometimes go horribly wrong.

The two selections that introduce this chapter illustrate, first, the use of sound in verse almost purely for its own sake ("Pease porridge hot") and, second, the use of sound in verse almost purely to imitate meaning ("Hark, hark! Bow-wow"), and they are, as significant poetry, among the most trivial passages in the whole book. But in between these extremes there is an abundant range of poetic possibilities where sound is pleasurable for itself without violating meaning and where sound to varying degrees corresponds with and corroborates meaning; and in this rich middle range lie many of the greatest pleasures of reading poetry.

EXERCISE

In each of the following paired quotations, the named poet wrote the version that more successfully adapts sound to sense. As specifically as possible, account for the superiority of the better version.

1. a. Go forth—and Virtue, ever in your sight,
      Shall be your guide by day, your guard by night.
   b. Go forth—and Virtue, ever in your sight,
      Shall point your way by day, and keep you safe at night.
                                                      Charles Churchill

2. a. How charming is divine philosophy!
      Not harsh and rough as foolish men suppose
      But musical as is the lute of Phoebus.
   b. How charming is divine philosophy!
      Not harsh and crabbed as dull fools suppose
      But musical as is Apollo's lute.   *John Milton*

3. a. All day the fleeing crows croak hoarsely over the snow.
   b. All day the out-cast crows croak hoarsely across the whiteness.
                                                      Elizabeth Coatsworth

4. a. Your talk attests how bells of singing gold
      Would sound at evening over silent water.
   b. Your low voice tells how bells of singing gold
      Would sound at twilight over silent water.   *Edwin Arlington Robinson*

5. a. A thousand streamlets flowing through the lawn,
      The moan of doves in gnarled ancient oaks,
      And quiet murmuring of countless bees.
   b. Myriads of rivulets hurrying through the lawn,
      The moan of doves in immemorial elms,
      And murmuring of innumerable bees.   *Alfred, Lord Tennyson*

6. a. It is the lark that sings so out of tune,
      Straining harsh discords and unpleasing sharps.
   b. It is the lark that warbles out of tune
      In harsh discordant tones with doleful flats. *William Shakespeare*

7. a. "Artillery" and "armaments" and "implements of war"
      Are phrases too severe to please the gentle Muse.
   b. Bombs, drums, guns, bastions, batteries, bayonets, bullets, —
      Hard words, which stick in the soft Muses' gullets.   *Lord Byron*

8. a. The hands of the sisters Death and Night incessantly softly wash
         again, and ever again, this soiled world.
   b. The hands of the soft twins Death and Night repeatedly wash again,
         and ever again, this dirty world.   *Walt Whitman*

9. a. The curfew sounds the knell of parting day,
      The lowing cattle slowly cross the lea,
      The plowman goes wearily plodding his homeward way,
      Leaving the world to the darkening night and me.
   b. The curfew tolls the knell of parting day,
      The lowing herd wind slowly o'er the lea,
      The plowman homeward plods his weary way,
      And leaves the world to darkness and to me.   *Thomas Gray*

10. a. Let me chastise this odious, gilded bug,
       This painted son of dirt, that smells and bites.
    b. Yet let me flap this bug with gilded wings,
       This painted child of dirt, that stinks and stings.   *Alexander Pope*

158. Sound and Sense

True ease in writing comes from art, not chance,
As those move easiest who have learned to dance.
'Tis not enough no harshness gives offense,
The sound must seem an echo to the sense:
Soft is the strain when Zephyr gently blows,   5
And the smooth stream in smoother numbers flows;
But when loud surges lash the sounding shore,
The hoarse, rough verse should like the torrent roar;
When Ajax strives some rock's vast weight to throw,
The line too labors, and the words move slow;   10
Not so, when swift Camilla scours the plain,
Flies o'er the unbending corn, and skims along the main.
Hear how Timotheus' varied lays surprise,
And bid alternate passions fall and rise!

Alexander Pope (1688–1744)

QUESTIONS

1. Vocabulary: *numbers* (6), *lays* (13).
2. This excerpt is from a long poem (called *An Essay on Criticism*) on the arts of writing and judging poetry. Which line states the thesis of the passage?
3. There are four classical allusions: Zephyr (5) was god of the west wind; Ajax (9), a Greek warrior noted for his strength; Camilla (11), a legendary queen reputedly so fleet of foot that she could run over a field of grain without bending the blades or over the sea without wetting her feet; Timotheus (13), a famous Greek rhapsodic poet. How do these allusions enable Pope to achieve greater economy?
4. Copy the passage and scan it. Then, considering both meter and sounds, show how Pope practices what he preaches. (Incidentally, on which syllable should "alternate" in line 14 be accented? Does the meter help you to know the pronunciation of "Timotheus'" in line 13?)

159. I heard a fly buzz when I died

I heard a fly buzz when I died.
The stillness in the room
Was like the stillness in the air
Between the heaves of storm.

The eyes around had wrung them dry,   5
And breaths were gathering firm
For that last onset when the king
Be witnessed in the room.

I willed my keepsakes, signed away
What portion of me be   10
Assignable; and then it was
There interposed a fly

With blue, uncertain, stumbling buzz
Between the light and me;
And then the windows failed, and then   15
I could not see to see.

Emily Dickinson (1830–1886)

QUESTIONS

1. It is important to understand the sequence of events in this deathbed
   scene. Arrange the following events in correct chronological order: (a) the
   willing of keepsakes, (b) the weeping of mourners, (c) the appearance of
   the fly, (d) the preternatural stillness in the room.
2. What or who are the "eyes" and the "breaths" in lines 5–6? What figures
   of speech are involved in these lines? Is the speaker making out her will in
   lines 9–11? What *is* she doing?
3. What sort of expectation is set up by phrases like "last onset" (7), "the
   king" (7), and "be witnessed" (8)?
4. Explain "the windows failed" (15) and "I could not see to see" (16).
5. What is the rime scheme? What kinds of rime are employed? Explain
   the marvelous effectiveness of line 13 in terms of both imagery and
   sound.
6. Explain the point of the poem. How do you interpret the fly?

160. Heaven-Haven

A Nun Takes the Veil

I have desired to go
   Where springs not fail,
To fields where flies no sharp and sided hail
And a few lilies blow.

And I have asked to be   5
   Where no storms come,
Where the green swell is in the havens dumb,
And out of the swing of the sea.

Gerard Manley Hopkins (1844–1889)

QUESTIONS

1. Vocabulary: *blow* (4).
2. Who is the speaker and what is the situation? Explain the metaphors that form the substance of the poem. What things are being compared?
3. Comment on the meaning of "springs" (2) and on the effectiveness of the poet's choice of "lilies" (4).
4. How do the sound repetitions of the title reinforce the meaning? Are there other instances in the poem where sound reinforces meaning?
5. Scan the poem. (The meter is basically iambic, but there is a great deal of variation.) How does the meter reinforce meaning, especially in the last line? What purpose is served by the displacement of "not" (2) from its normal word order?

161. Anthem for Doomed Youth

What passing-bells for these who die as cattle?
Only the monstrous anger of the guns.
Only the stuttering rifles' rapid rattle
Can patter out their hasty orisons.
No mockeries now for them; no prayers nor bells,   5
Nor any voice of mourning save the choirs—
The shrill, demented choirs of wailing shells;
And bugles calling for them from sad shires.

What candles may be held to speed them all?
Not in the hands of boys, but in their eyes   10
Shall shine the holy glimmers of good-byes.
The pallor of girls' brows shall be their pall;
Their flowers the tenderness of patient minds,
And each slow dusk a drawing-down of blinds.

Wilfred Owen (1893–1918)

QUESTIONS

1. Vocabulary: *passing-bells* (1), *orisons* (4), *shires* (8), *pall* (12). It was the custom during World War I to draw down the blinds in homes where a son had been lost (14).
2. How do the octave and the sestet of this sonnet differ in (a) geographical setting, (b) subject matter, (c) kind of imagery used, and (d) tone? Who are the "boys" (10) and "girls" (12) referred to in the sestet?
3. What central metaphorical image runs throughout the poem? What secondary metaphors build up the central one?

4. Why are the "doomed youth" said to die "as cattle" (1)? Why would prayers, bells, and so on, be "mockeries" for them (5)?
5. Show how sound is adapted to sense throughout the poem.

162. Landcrab

A lie, that we come from water.
The truth is we were born
from stones, dragons, the sea's
teeth, as you testify,
with your crust and jagged scissors.   5

Hermit, hard socket
for a timid eye
you're a soft gut scuttling
sideways, a bone skull,
round bone on the prowl.   10
Wolf of treeroots and gravelly holes,
a mount on stilts,
the husk of a small demon.

Attack, voracious
eating, and flight: 15
it's a sound routine
for staying alive on edges.
Then there's the tide, and that dance
you do for the moon
on wet sand, claws raised   20
to fend off your mate,
your coupling a quick
dry clatter of rocks.
For mammals
with their lobes and bulbs,   25
scruples and warm milk,
you've nothing but contempt.

Here you are, a frozen scowl
targeted in flashlight,
then gone: a piece of what   30
we are, not all,
my stunted child, my momentary
face in the mirror,
my tiny nightmare.

Margaret Atwood (b. 1939)

QUESTIONS

1. What theory of the origin of human life is alluded to in line 1? Line 3 alludes to two Greek myths, of Deucalion sowing stones and Cadmus sowing dragon's teeth. If these are unfamiliar, look them up. What do theories
   about the origins of humankind have to do with the speaker's description
   of the landcrab? How do lines 30–34 return to that subject?
2. What do the free-verse rhythms contribute to the experience of the
   poem? Discuss the cacophony and euphony in lines 22–25. Where do
   you find other examples?

163. Eight O'Clock

He stood, and heard the steeple
    Sprinkle the quarters on the morning town.
One, two, three, four, to market-place and people
    It tossed them down.

Strapped, noosed, nighing his hour,   5
    He stood and counted them and cursed his luck;
And then the clock collected in the tower
    Its strength, and struck.

A. E. Housman (1859–1936)

QUESTIONS

1. Vocabulary: *quarters* (2).
2. Eight A.M. was the traditional hour in England for putting condemned men
   to death. Discuss the force of "morning" (2) and "struck" (8). Discuss
   the appropriateness of the image of the clock collecting its strength. Can
   you suggest any reason for the use of "nighing" (5) rather than *nearing?*
3. Scan the poem and note its musical devices. Comment on the adaptation
   of sound to sense.

164. At the round earth's imagined corners

At the round earth's imagined corners, blow
Your trumpets, angels; and arise, arise
From death, you numberless infinities
Of souls, and to your scattered bodies go:
All whom the flood did, and fire shall, o'erthrow,   5
All whom war, dearth, age, agues, tyrannies,

Despair, law, chance hath slain, and you whose eyes
Shall behold God and never taste death's woe.
But let them sleep, Lord, and me mourn a space;
For if above all these, my sins abound,   10
'Tis late to ask abundance of thy grace
When we are there. Here on this lowly ground,
Teach me how to repent; for that's as good
As if thou hadst sealed my pardon with thy blood.

John Donne (1572–1631)

QUESTIONS

1. For a note on the belief in the resurrection of the body, see question 2,
   page 143. The poem contains several allusions to the Bible: line 1, Revelation 7.1; lines 2–4, Job 19.25–26; lines 10–11, Romans 6.1. What is
   the speaker calling for in lines 1–8? Why does he change his plea in lines
   9–12? Where is "there" (12)?
2. Scan lines 1–8. How do the rhythms reinforce the meanings in these
   lines? What is the effect of the placement of "blow" (1)? Scan lines 11–12.
   What do the lack of a caesura in line 11 and the emphatic caesura in line 12
   contribute to meaning? Comment on the trochaic substitution in line 12.

165. Blackberry Eating

I love to go out in late September
among fat, overripe, icy, black blackberries
to eat blackberries for breakfast,
the stalks very prickly, a penalty
they earn for knowing the black art   5
of blackberry-making; and as I stand among them
lifting the stalks to my mouth, the ripest berries
fall almost unbidden to my tongue,
as words sometimes do, certain peculiar words
like *strengths* or *squinched*,   10
many-lettered, one-syllabled lumps,
which I squeeze, squinch open, and splurge well
in the silent, startled, icy, black language
of blackberry-eating in late September.

Galway Kinnell (b. 1927)

QUESTIONS

1. Vocabulary: *black art* (5), *squinched* (10).
2. What comparison does the poet find between "certain peculiar words"
   (9) and blackberries? How appropriate is it?

3. Is the poem free verse or metrical? How do various musical devices reinforce its meaning?

166. The Bench of Boors

In bed I muse on Teniers' boors,
Embrowned and beery losels all:
   A wakeful brain
   Elaborates pain:
Within low doors the slugs of boors   5
Laze and yawn and doze again.

In dreams they doze, the drowsy boors,
Their hazy hovel warm and small:
   Thought's ampler bound
   But chill is found: 10
Within low doors the basking boors
Snugly hug the ember-mound.

Sleepless, I see the slumberous boors
Their blurred eyes blink, their eyelids fall:
   Thought's eager sight   15
   Aches—overbright!
Within low doors the boozy boors
Cat-naps take in pipe-bowl light.

Herman Melville (1819–1891)

QUESTIONS

1. Vocabulary: *boors* (title), *losels* (2), *slugs* (5).
2. David Teniers the Younger, a seventeenth-century Flemish painter, was famous for his genre paintings of peasant life. What was the essential characteristic of this life according to the poem? What symbolism do you find in the fifth line of each stanza?
3. What is the relation of the third and fourth lines of each stanza to the speaker? To the boors? How does the form of the stanza emphasize the contrast in thought?
4. Comment on other correspondences between sound and meaning.

167. The Dance

In Breughel's great picture, The Kermess,
the dancers go round, they go round and
around, the squeal and the blare and the

> tweedle of bagpipes, a bugle and fiddles
> tipping their bellies (round as the thick-   5
> sided glasses whose wash they impound)
> their hips and their bellies off balance
> to turn them. Kicking and rolling about
> the Fair Grounds, swinging their butts, those
> shanks must be sound to bear up under such   10
> rollicking measures, prance as they dance
> in Breughel's great picture, The Kermess.

William Carlos Williams   (1883–1963)

QUESTIONS

1. Peter Breughel the Elder was a sixteenth-century Flemish painter of peas-ant life. A *kermess* is an annual outdoor festival or fair. How do the form, the meter, and the sounds of this poem reinforce its content?
2. Explore the similarities and differences between this poem and the pre-ceding one, both as to form and content.

ADDITIONAL EXERCISE

Follow the instructions for the exercise on page 210.

11. a. Like an iron-clanging anvil banged / With hammers.
    b. Like a massive iron anvil hit / With sledges.   *Alfred, Lord Tennyson*
12. a. I am quiet sand / In an hourglass.
    b. I am soft silt / In an hourglass.   *Gerard Manley Hopkins*
13. a. Dress! arm! mount!—away!
       Save my castle before the day
       Turns to blue from silver gray.
    b. Boot, saddle, to horse, and away!
       Rescue my castle before the hot day
       Brightens to blue from its silvery gray.   *Robert Browning*
14. a. The lilies and languors of virtue,
       . . . the roses and raptures of vice.
    b. The lilies and boredom of virtue,
       . . . the roses and pleasures of evil.   *Algernon Charles Swinburne*
15. a. And still she lulled him to asleep.
    b. And yet she conjured him to sleep.   *Anonymous*

CHAPTER FOURTEEN

Pattern

Art, ultimately, is organization. It is a searching after order, after form. Many consider the primal artistic act to have been God's creation of the universe out of chaos, shaping the formless into form; and every artist since, on a lesser scale, has sought to imitate that act—to reduce the chaotic in experience to a meaningful and pleasing order by means of selection and arrangement. For this reason we evaluate a poem partially by the same criteria that an English instructor uses to evaluate a theme—by its unity, its coherence, and its proper placing of emphasis. A well-constructed poem contains neither too little nor too much; every part of the poem belongs where it is and could be placed nowhere else; any interchanging of two stanzas, two lines, or even two words, would to some extent damage the poem and make it less effective. We come to feel, with a truly first-rate poem, that the choice and placement of every word is inevitable, that it could not be otherwise.

In addition to the internal ordering of materials—the arrangement of ideas, images, and thoughts, which we may refer to as the poem's **structure**—the poet may impose some external pattern on a poem, may give it not only an inside logical order but an outside symmetry, or **form.** Such formality appeals to the human instinct for design, the instinct that has prompted people, at various times, to tattoo and paint their bodies, to decorate their swords and armor with beautiful and complex tracery, and to choose patterned fabrics for their clothing, carpets, curtains, and wallpapers. The poet appeals to our love of the shapely.

In general, a poem may be cast in one of the three broad kinds of form: continuous form, stanzaic form, and fixed form. In **continuous form,** as illustrated by "The Widow's Lament in Springtime" (No. 35), "After Apple-Picking" (No. 38), "Ulysses" (No. 67), and "My Last Duchess" (No. 89), the element of design is slight. The lines follow each other without formal grouping, the only breaks being dictated by units of meaning, as paragraphs are in prose. But even here there are degrees of pattern. "The Widow's Lament in Springtime" has neither regular meter nor rime. "After Apple-Picking," on the other hand, is metrical; it has no regularity in length of line, but the meter is prevailingly iambic; also every line rimes with another, though not according to any fixed pattern. "Ulysses" is regular in both meter and length of line: it is unrimed iambic pentameter, or blank verse. And to these regularities "My Last Duchess" adds regularity of rime, for it is written in riming pentameter couplets. Thus, in increasing degrees, the authors of "After Apple-Picking," "Ulysses," and "My Last Duchess" have chosen a predetermined pattern in which to cast their work.

In **stanzaic form** the poet writes in a series of **stanzas;** that is, repeated units having the same number of lines, usually the same metrical pattern, and often an identical rime scheme. The poet may choose some traditional stanza pattern (poetry, like colleges, is rich in tradition) or invent an original one. The traditional stanza patterns (for example, terza rima, ballad meter, rime royal, Spenserian stanza) are many, and the student specializing in literature will wish to become familiar with some of them; the general student should know that they exist. Often the use of one of these traditional stanza forms constitutes a kind of literary allusion. The reader who is conscious of its traditional use or of its use by a previous great poet will be aware of subtleties in the communication that a less-well-read reader may miss.

Stanzaic form, like continuous form, exhibits degrees of formal pattern. The poem "in Just-" (No. 92) is divided into alternating stanzas of four lines and one line, but neither the four-line stanzas nor the one-line stanzas have any resemblance to each other. In "Poem in October" (No. 174) the stanzas are alike in length of line but are without a regular pattern of rime. In "The Aim Was Song" (No. 147) a rime pattern is added to a metrical pattern. In Shakespeare's "Winter" (No. 2) and "Spring" (No. 4), a refrain is employed in addition to the patterns of meter and rime. The following poem illustrates additional elements of design.

168. These are the days when birds come back

These are the days when birds come back—
A very few—a bird or two—
To take a backward look.

These are the days when skies resume
The old, old sophistries of June—   5
A blue and gold mistake.

Oh fraud that cannot cheat the bee,
Almost thy plausibility
Induces my belief,

Till ranks of seeds their witness bear,   10
And softly through the altered air
Hurries a timid leaf.

Oh sacrament of summer days,
Oh last communion in the haze,
Permit a child to join,   15

Thy sacred emblems to partake,
Thy consecrated bread to take,
And thine immortal wine!

Emily Dickinson (1830–1886)

QUESTIONS

1. Vocabulary: *sophistries* (5). The "fraud that cannot cheat the bee" (6) is probably an allusion to one of the apocryphal tales of Solomon who distinguished between real and artificial flowers by putting a bee into the room; the bee of course flew to the real.
2. If you have difficulty determining the time of year, examine the terms "backward" (3) and "resume" (4), and the evidence provided by "seeds" and "leaf" (10–12). Why is that time of year a "fraud" (7)? What is it pretending to be? In the final metaphor, how is that time of year like a "last communion" (14)?
3. The rime scheme of these stanzas is *aab,* in two lines of iambic tetrameter followed by one of iambic trimeter; several of its rimes are approximate, especially in the first two stanzas. An additional complication is that the first of the stanzas is a variant, riming *aba.* To find the form at its purest, examine stanzas 3 and 4. What you will also notice is that the *b* rimes of those stanzas rime with each other, creating a two-stanza unit. That pattern may then be observed in approximate *b* rimes in stanzas 1–2 and 5–6. How is the *structure* of the poem linked to the formal division into these three two-stanza units? What repetitions other than rime reinforce the meanings?

A stanza form may be described by designating four things: the rime scheme (if there is one), the position of the refrain (if there is one), the prevailing metrical foot, and the number of feet in each line. Rime scheme is traditionally designated by using letters of the alphabet to indicate the riming lines, and *x* for unrimed lines. Refrain lines may be indicated by a capital letter, and the number of feet in the line by a numerical exponent after the letter. Thus the stanza pattern of

Browning's "Meeting at Night" (No. 32) is iambic tetrameter *abccba* (or iambic *abccba⁴*); that of "These are the days when birds come back" is iambic aa^4b^3; that of Donne's "A Hymn to God the Father" (No. 30) is iambic $abab^5A^4B^2$. Stanzaic poetry not written in traditional metrical feet can be described similarly: Moore's "Nevertheless" (No. 148) is syllabic xaa^6.

A **fixed form** is a traditional pattern that applies to a whole poem. In French poetry many fixed forms have been widely used: rondeaus, rondels, villanelles, triolets, sestinas, ballades, double ballades, and others. In English poetry, though most of the fixed forms have been experimented with, perhaps only two—the limerick and the sonnet—have really taken hold.

The **limerick,** though really a subliterary form, will serve to illustrate the fixed form in general. Its pattern is anapestic $aa^3bb^2a^3$. The form freely allows the use of a substitute foot for the first foot in any line but insists as a rule on strict adherence to anapestic meter thereafter:

169. An epicure dining at Crewe

An epᵢ-cure dining at Crewe
Found a rather large mouse in his stew.
Said the waiter, "Don't shout
And wave it a-bout
Or the rest will be wanting one too."   5

Anonymous

The limerick form is used exclusively for humorous and nonsense verse, for which, with its short lines, swift catchy meter, and emphatic rimes, it is particularly suitable. By trying to recast these little jokes and bits of nonsense in a different meter and pattern or into prose, we may discover how much of their effect they owe particularly to the limerick form. There is, of course, no magical or mysterious identity between certain forms and certain types of content, but there may be more or less correspondence. A form may be appropriate or inappropriate. The limerick form is inappropriate for the serious treatment of serious material.

The **sonnet** is less rigidly prescribed than the limerick. It must be fourteen lines in length, and it almost always is iambic pentameter, but in structure and rime scheme there may be considerable leeway. Most sonnets, however, conform more or less closely to one of two general models or types: the Italian and the English.

The **Italian** or *Petrarchan* **sonnet** (so-called because the Italian poet Petrarch practiced it so extensively) is divided usually between eight lines called the **octave,** using two rimes arranged *abbaabba,* and six lines called the **sestet,** using any arrangement of either two or three rimes: *cdcdcd* and *cdecde* are common patterns. The division between octave and sestet in the Italian sonnet (indicated by the rime scheme and sometimes marked off in printing by a space) usually corresponds to a division of thought. The octave may, for instance, present a situation and the sestet a comment, or the octave an idea and the sestet an example, or the octave a question and the sestet an answer. Thus the form reflects the structure.

170. On First Looking into Chapman's Homer

Much have I traveled in the realms of gold,
  And many goodly states and kingdoms seen;
  Round many western islands have I been
Which bards in fealty to Apollo hold.
Oft of one wide expanse had I been told   5
  That deep-browed Homer ruled as his demesne;
  Yet did I never breathe its pure serene
Till I heard Chapman speak out loud and bold:
Then felt I like some watcher of the skies
  When a new planet swims into his ken;   10
Or like stout Cortez when with eagle eyes
  He stared at the Pacific—and all his men
Looked at each other with a wild surmise—
  Silent, upon a peak in Darien.

          John Keats (1795–1821)

QUESTIONS

1. Vocabulary: *fealty* (4), *Apollo* (4), *demesne* (6), *ken* (10). *Darien* (14) is an ancient name for the Isthmus of Panama.
2. John Keats, at twenty-one, could not read Greek and was probably acquainted with Homer's *Iliad* and *Odyssey* only through the translations of Alexander Pope, which to him very likely seemed prosy and stilted. Then

one day he and a friend found a vigorous poetic translation by the Elizabethan poet George Chapman. Keats and his friend, enthralled, sat up late at night excitedly reading aloud to each other from Chapman's book. Toward morning Keats walked home and, before going to bed, wrote the above sonnet and sent it to his friend. What common ideas underlie the three major figures of speech in the poem?

3. What is the rime scheme? What division of thought corresponds to the division between octave and sestet?
4. Balboa, not Cortez, discovered the Pacific. How seriously does this mistake detract from the value of the poem?

The **English** or *Shakespearean* **sonnet** (invented by the English poet Surrey and made famous by Shakespeare) is composed of three quatrains and a concluding couplet, riming *abab cdcd efef gg*. Again, the units marked off by the rimes and the development of the thought often correspond. The three quatrains, for instance, may present three examples and the couplet a conclusion or (as in the following example) the quatrains three metaphorical statements of one idea and the couplet an application.

171. That time of year

That time of year thou mayst in me behold
When yellow leaves, or none, or few, do hang
Upon those boughs which shake against the cold,
Bare ruined choirs where late the sweet birds sang.
In me thou see'st the twilight of such day   5
As after sunset fadeth in the west,
Which by and by black night doth take away,
Death's second self, that seals up all in rest.
In me thou see'st the glowing of such fire,
That on the ashes of his youth doth lie   10
As the deathbed whereon it must expire,
Consumed with that which it was nourished by.
This thou perceivest, which makes thy love more strong,
To love that well which thou must leave ere long.

William Shakespeare (1564–1616)

QUESTIONS

1. What are the three major images introduced by the three quatrains? What do they have in common? Can you see any reason for presenting them in this particular order, or might they be rearranged without loss?

2. Each of the images is to some degree complicated rather than simple. For instance, what additional image is introduced by "Bare ruined choirs" (4)? Explain its appropriateness.
3. What additional comparisons are introduced in the second and third quatrains? Explain line 12.
4. Whom does the speaker address? What assertion does he make in the concluding couplet, and with what degree of confidence? Paraphrase these lines so as to state their meaning as clearly as possible.

Initially, it may seem absurd that poets should choose to confine themselves in an arbitrary fourteen-line mold with prescribed meter and rime scheme. They do so partly from the desire to carry on a tradition, as all of us carry out certain traditions for their own sake, else why should we bring a tree indoors at Christmas time? But, in addition, the tradition of the sonnet has proved useful because, like the limerick, it seems effective for certain types of subject matter and treatment. Though these cannot be as narrowly limited or as rigidly described as for the limerick, the sonnet is usually most effective when used for the serious treatment of love but has also been used for the discussion of death, religion, political situations, and related subjects. Again, there is no magical affinity between form and subject, or treatment, and excellent sonnets have been written outside these traditional areas. The sonnet tradition has also proved useful because it has provided a challenge to the poet. Inferior poets, of course, are often defeated by that challenge: they will use unnecessary words to fill out the meter or inappropriate words for the sake of rime. Good poets are inspired by the challenge: it will call forth ideas and images that might not otherwise have come. They will subdue the form rather than be subdued by it; they will make it do what they require. There is no doubt that the presence of a net makes good tennis players more precise in their shots than they otherwise would be. And finally, there is in all form the pleasure of form itself.

EXERCISES

1. Examine the following sonnets; classify each (when possible) as primarily Italian or primarily English; then specify how closely in form and structure each adheres to or how far it departs from the polarities represented by "On First Looking into Chapman's Homer" and "That time of year":
   a. "The world is too much with us" (No. 28)
   b. "The Caged Skylark" (No. 112)
   c. "Design" (No. 107)
   d. From *Romeo and Juliet* (No. 175)
   e. "Since there's no help" (No. 118)

f. "The Dead" (No. 207)
g. "Batter my heart, three-personed God" (No. 80)
h. "Ozymandias" (No. 79)
i. "Leda and the Swan" (No. 96)
j. "How Annandale Went Out" (No. 111)
k. "Anthem for Doomed Youth" (No. 161)

2. "The Story We Know" (No. 179), "One Art" (No. 31), "The Freaks at Spurgin Road Field" (No. 243), and "Do Not Go Gentle into That Good Night" (No. 286) are all examples of a French fixed form known as the **villanelle.** After studying their formal features, formulate a definition for the villanelle. *Hint:* Start with No. 286, the "purest" example of the form; then examine the extent to which the others conform to or depart from that norm.

---

172. A Handful of Limericks

There was a young lady from Niger
Who smiled as she road on a tiger;
    They returned from the ride
    With the lady inside
And the smile on the face of the tiger.

Anonymous

A tutor who tooted the flute
Tried to teach two young tooters to toot.
    Said the two to the tutor,
    "Is it harder to toot, or
To tutor two tooters to toot?"

Carolyn Wells (1862–1942)

There was a young fellow named Hall
Who fell in the spring in the fall;
    'Twould have been a sad thing
    Had he died in the spring,
But he didn't, he died in the fall.

Anonymous

An amoeba named Sam and his brother
Were having a drink with each other.
    In the midst of their quaffing
    They split themselves laughing,
And each of them now is a mother.

Anonymous

A goat on a stroll near a brook
Found an old movie film and partook.
    "Was it good?" asked his mate.
    Said the goat, "Second-rate!
Not nearly as good as the book!"

Martin Bristow Smith (b. 1916)

A cannibal said to her mate
Who was in a deplorable state
    Of discomfort, "My dear,
    Do you think it's the beer
Or is it just someone you ate?"

A. N. Wilkins (b. 1925)

The limerick's never averse
To expressing itself in a terse
    Economical style
    And yet, all the while,
The limerick's *always* a verse.

Laurence Perrine (1915–1995)

173. Two Japanese Haiku

The lightning flashes!
And slashing through the darkness,
    A night-heron's screech.

A lightning gleam:
    into darkness travels
        a night heron's scream.

Matsuo Bashō (1644–1694)

The falling flower
I saw drift back to the branch
    Was a butterfly.

Fallen flowers rise
    back to the branch—I watch:
        oh . . . butterflies!

Moritake (1452–1540)

QUESTION

The **Haiku,** a Japanese form, consists of three lines of five, seven, and five syllables each. The translators of the versions on the left (Earl Miner and Babette Deutsch respectively) preserve this syllable count; the translator of the right-hand versions (Harold G. Henderson) seeks to preserve the sense of formal structure by making the first and last lines rime. Moritake's haiku, as Miss Deutsch points out, "refers to the Buddhist proverb that the fallen

flower never returns to the branch; the broken mirror never again reflects."
From these two examples, what would you say are the characteristics of
effective haiku?

174. Poem in October

It was my thirtieth year to heaven
Woke to my hearing from harbor and neighbor wood
   And the mussel pooled and the heron
      Priested shore
      The morning beckon   5
With water praying and call of seagull and rook
And the knock of sailing boats on the net webbed wall
    Myself to set foot
     That second
In the still sleeping town and set forth.   10

My birthday began with the water-
Birds and the birds of the winged trees flying my name
   Above the farms and the white horses
     And I rose
     In rainy autumn   15
And walked abroad in a shower of all my days.
High tide and the heron dived when I took the road
    Over the border
     And the gates
Of the town closed as the town awoke.   20

A springful of larks in a rolling
Cloud and the roadside bushes brimming with whistling
   Blackbirds and the sun of October
     Summery
     On the hill's shoulder,   25
Here were fond climates and sweet singers suddenly
Come in the morning where I wandered and listened
    To the rain wringing
     Wind blow cold
In the woods faraway under me.   30

Pale rain over the dwindling harbor
And over the sea wet church the size of a snail
   With its horns through mist and the castle
     Brown as owls
     But all the gardens   35
Of spring and summer were blooming in the tall tales

Beyond the border and under the lark full cloud.
    There could I marvel
      My birthday
Away but the weather turned around.   40

It turned away from the blithe country
And down the other air and the blue altered sky
    Streamed again a wonder of summer
      With apples
      Pears and red currants   45
And I saw in the turning so clearly a child's
Forgotten mornings when he walked with his mother
    Through the parables
      Of sun light
And the legends of the green chapels   50

And the twice told fields of infancy
That his tears burned my cheeks and his heart moved in mine.
    These were the woods the river and sea
      Where a boy
      In the listening   55
Summertime of the dead whispered the truth of his joy
To the trees and the stones and the fish in the tide.
    And the mystery
      Sang alive
Still in the water and singingbirds.   60

And there could I marvel my birthday
Away but the weather turned around. And the true
    Joy of the long dead child sang burning
      In the sun.
      It was my thirtieth   65
Year to heaven stood there then in the summer noon
Though the town below lay leaved with October blood.
    O may my heart's truth
      Still be sung
On this high hill in a year's turning.   70

Dylan Thomas (1914–1953)

QUESTIONS

1. The setting is a small fishing village on the coast of Wales. The poet's first name in Welsh means "water" (12). Trace the poet's walk in relation to the village, the weather, and the time of day.
2. "The weather turned around" (40, 62) is an expression indicating a change in the weather or the direction of the wind. In what psychological

sense does the weather turn around during the poet's walk? Who is "the long dead child" (63), and what kind of child was he? With what wish does the poem close?

3. Explain "thirtieth year to heaven" (1), "horns" (33), "tall tales" (36), "green chapels" (50), "October blood" (67).

4. The elaborate stanza pattern in this poem is based not on the meter (which is very free) but on a syllable count. How many syllables are there in each line of the stanza? (In line 1 "thirtieth" may be counted as only two syllables.) Notice that stanzas 1 and 3 consist of exactly one sentence each.

5. The poem makes considerable use of approximate rime, though not according to a regular pattern. Point out examples.

175. From *Romeo and Juliet*

ROMEO	If I profane with my unworthiest hand
	This holy shrine, the gentle sin is this:
	My lips, two blushing pilgrims, ready stand
	To smooth that rough touch with a tender kiss.
JULIET	Good pilgrim, you do wrong your hand too much, 5
	Which mannerly devotion shows in this;
	For saints have hands that pilgrims' hands do touch,
	And palm to palm is holy palmers' kiss.
ROMEO	Have not saints lips, and holy palmers too?
JULIET	Ay, pilgrim, lips that they must use in prayer. 10
ROMEO	O! then, dear saint, let lips do what hands do;
	They pray, grant thou, lest faith turn to despair.
JULIET	Saints do not move,° though grant for prayer's *propose,*
	sake. *instigate*
ROMEO	Then move not, while my prayer's effect I take.

William Shakespeare (1564–1616)

QUESTIONS

1. These fourteen lines have been lifted out of Act 1, scene 5, of Shakespeare's play. They are the first words exchanged between Romeo and Juliet, who are meeting, for the first time, at a masquerade ball given by her father. Struck by Juliet's beauty, Romeo has come up to greet her. What stage action accompanies this passage?

2. What is the basic metaphor created by such religious terms as "profane" (1), "shrine" (2), "pilgrims" (3), "holy palmers" (8)? How does this metaphor affect the tone of the relationship between Romeo and Juliet?

3. What play on words do you find in lines 8 and 13–14? What two meanings has line 11?

4. By meter and rime scheme, these lines form a sonnet. Do you think this was coincidental or intentional on Shakespeare's part? Discuss.

176. Death, be not proud

Death, be not proud, though some have callèd thee
Mighty and dreadful, for thou art not so;
For those whom thou think'st thou dost overthrow
Die not, poor death, nor yet canst thou kill me.
From rest and sleep, which but thy pictures be,   5
Much pleasure—then, from thee much more must flow;
And soonest° our best men with thee do go,   readiest
Rest of their bones and soul's delivery.
Thou art slave to fate, chance, kings, and desperate men,
And dost with poison, war, and sickness dwell;   10
And poppy or charms can make us sleep as well,
And better than thy stroke. Why swell'st thou then?
One short sleep passed, we wake eternally,
And death shall be no more; death, thou shalt die.

John Donne (1572–1631)

QUESTIONS

1. What two figures of speech dominate the poem?
2. Why should death not be proud? List the speaker's major reasons. Are they consistent? Logical? Persuasive?
3. Discuss the tone of the poem. Is the speaker (a) a man of assured faith with a firm conviction that death is not to be feared or (b) a man desperately trying to convince himself that there is nothing to fear in death?
4. In form this sonnet blends the English and Italian models. Explain. Is its organization of thought closer to the Italian or the English sonnet?

177. A Wreath

A wreathèd garland of deservèd praise,
Of praise deservèd, unto thee I give,
I give to thee, who knowest all my ways,
My crooked winding ways, wherein I live,
Wherein I die, not live: for "live" is straight,   5
Straight as a line, and ever tends to thee,
To thee who art more far above deceit
Than deceit seems above simplicity.
Give me simplicity that I may live,
So live and like, that I may know thy ways,   10
Know them and practise them: then shall I give
For this poor wreath, give thee a crown of praise.

George Herbert (1593–1633)

QUESTIONS

1. The extended metaphor of the poem compares praise for God to a wreath or crown the speaker is twining with his words. Noting the repetition of words or phrases from line to line, trace how the poem finally creates a circle. How are the rimes of the last four lines related to those of the first four?
2. At the center of the poem is an idea that contrasts to the movement of wreathing or twining. What additional meaning is introduced by "Straight as a line" (6)? In what way is "winding" (4) like "deceit" (7)? How are structure, form, and meaning related here?

178. Acquainted with the Night

I have been one acquainted with the night.
I have walked out in rain—and back in rain.
I have outwalked the furthest city light.

I have looked down the saddest city lane.
I have passed by the watchman on his beat   5
And dropped my eyes, unwilling to explain.

I have stood still and stopped the sound of feet
When far away an interrupted cry
Came over houses from another street,

But not to call me back or say good-by;   10
And further still at an unearthly height,
One luminary clock against the sky

Proclaimed the time was neither wrong nor right.
I have been one acquainted with the night.

Robert Frost (1874–1963)

QUESTIONS

1. How does the speaker reveal the strength of his purpose in his night-walking? Can you specify what that purpose is? What symbolic meanings does the night hold?
2. How is the poem structured into sentences? What is the effect of repeating the phrase "I have"? Of repeating line 1 at the conclusion? How do these repetitions affect the tone of the poem?
3. Some critics have interpreted the "luminary clock" (12) literally—as the illuminated dial of a tower clock; others have interpreted it figuratively as the full moon. Of what, in either case, is it a symbol? Does the clock tell accurate chronometric time? What kind of "time" is it proclaiming in line 13? Is knowing *that* kind of time the speaker's quest?

4. The poem contains 14 lines—like a sonnet. But its rime scheme is **terza rima,** an interlocking scheme with the pattern *aba bcb cdc,* etc., a formal arrangement that implies continual progression. How does Frost bring the progression to an end? Terza rima was the form memorably employed by Dante for his *Divine Comedy,* of which the *Inferno* is the best-known section. In what ways does Frost's poem allude to the subject and framework of that poem?

179. The Story We Know

The way to begin is always the same. Hello,
Hello. Your hand, your name. So glad, Just fine,
and Good-bye at the end. That's every story we know,

and why pretend? But lunch tomorrow? No?
Yes? An omelette, salad, chilled white wine?   5
The way to begin is simple, sane, Hello,

and then it's Sunday, coffee, the *Times,* a slow
day by the fire, dinner at eight or nine
and Good-bye. In the end, this is a story we know

so well we don't turn the page, or look below   10
the picture, or follow the words to the next line:
The way to begin is always the same Hello.

But one night, through the latticed window, snow
begins to whiten the air, and the tall white pine.
Good-bye is the end of every story we know   15

that night, and when we close the curtains, oh,
we hold each other against that cold white sign
of the way we all begin and end. *Hello,*
Good-bye is the only story. We know, we know.

Martha Collins (b. 1940)

QUESTIONS

1. What have lines 1, 6, 12, and 18 in common? What have lines 3, 9, 15, and 19 in common?
2. What is the rime scheme?
3. Show how the words "Hello" and "Good-bye" acquire deeper meanings as the poem progresses. What do they refer to or symbolize in the last two lines? Why is the phrase "we know" repeated in the last line?
4. This poem is a villanelle. How closely does it conform to the definition of a villanelle that you formulated on page 226?

180. Edward

"Why does your sword so drip with blood,
    Edward, Edward,
Why does your sword so drip with blood,
    And why so sad go ye, O?"
"O I have killed my hawk so good,   5
    Mother, Mother,
O I have killed my hawk so good,
    And I had no more but he, O."

"Your hawk's blood was never so red,
    Edward, Edward,   10
Your hawk's blood was never so red,
    My dear son, I tell thee, O."
"O I have killed my red-roan steed,
    Mother, Mother,
O I have killed my red-roan steed,   15
    That once was so fair and free, O."

"Your steed was old, and ye have got more,
    Edward, Edward,
Your steed was old, and ye have got more,
    Some other grief ye feel, O."   20
"O I have killed my father dear,
    Mother, Mother,
O I have killed my father dear,
    Alas, and woe is me, O!"

"And what penance will ye do for that,   25
    Edward, Edward,
And what penance will ye do for that,
    My dear son, now tell me, O."
"I'll set my feet in yonder boat,
    Mother, Mother,   30
I'll set my feet in yonder boat,
    And I'll fare over the sea, O."

"And what will ye do with your towers and your hall,
    Edward, Edward,
And what will ye do with your towers and your hall, 35
    That were so fair to see, O?"
"I'll let them stand till they down fall,
    Mother, Mother,
I'll let them stand till they down fall,
    For here nevermore must I be, O."   40

"And what will ye leave to your children and wife,
    Edward, Edward,
And what will ye leave to your children and wife,
    When ye go over the sea, O?"
"The world is large, let them beg through life,   45
    Mother, Mother,
The world is large, let them beg through life,
    For them nevermore will I see, O."

"And what will ye leave to your own mother dear,
    Edward, Edward,   50
And what will ye leave to your own mother dear?
    My dear son, now tell me, O."
"The curse of hell from me shall ye bear,
    Mother, Mother,
The curse of hell from me shall ye bear,   55
    Such counsels you gave to me, O."

Anonymous

QUESTIONS

1. What has Edward done and why? Where do the two climaxes of the poem occur?
2. Tell as much as you can about Edward and his feelings toward what he has done. From what class of society is he? Why does he at first give false answers to his mother's questions? What reversal of feelings and loyalties has he undergone? Do his answers about his hawk and steed perhaps indicate his present feelings toward his father? How do you explain his behavior to his wife and children? What are his present feelings toward his mother?
3. Tell as much as you can about Edward's mother. Why does she ask what Edward has done—doesn't she already know? Is there any clue as to the motivation of her counsel? How skillful is she in her questioning? What do we learn about her from her dismissal of Edward's steed as "old" (17) and only one of many? From her asking Edward what penance *he* will do for his act (25)? From her reference to herself as Edward's "own mother dear" (49)?
4. Structure and form are both important in this poem. Could any of the stanzas be interchanged without loss, or do they build up steadily to the two climaxes? What effect has the constant repetition of the two short refrains, "Edward, Edward" and "Mother, Mother"? What is the effect of the final "O" at the end of each speech? Does the repetition of each question and answer simply waste words or does it add to the suspense and emotional intensity? (Read the poem omitting the third and seventh lines of each stanza. Is it improved or weakened?)
5. Much of what happened is implied; much is omitted. Does the poem gain anything in power from what is *not* told?

181. A Christmas Tree

Star,
If you are
A love compassionate,
You will walk with us this year.
We face a glacial distance, who are here   5
Huddld
At your feet.

William Burford (b. 1927)

QUESTION

Why do you think the author misspelled "Huddled" (6)?

EXERCISE

The typographical shape of a poem on the page (whether, for example, it is printed with a straight left-hand margin or with a system of indentations) is determined sometimes by the poet, sometimes by the printer, sometimes by an editor. Examine each of the following poems and try to deduce what *principle* (if any) determined its typographical design:
1. "The Mill" (No. 20)
2. "To His Coy Mistress" (No. 56)
3. "Dream Deferred" (No. 59)
4. "To a Waterfowl" (No. 106)
5. "Constantly risking absurdity" (No. 150)
6. "Poem in October" (No. 174)
7. "The Lamb" (No. 204)
8. "Offspring" (No. 253)

CHAPTER FIFTEEN

Bad Poetry and Good

The attempt to evaluate a poem should never be made before the poem is understood; and, unless one has developed the capacity to feel some poetry deeply, any judgments one makes will be worthless. A person who likes no wines can hardly be a judge of them. But the ability to make judgments, to discriminate between good and bad, great and good, good and half-good, is surely a primary object of all liberal education, and one's appreciation of poetry is incomplete unless it includes discrimination. Of the mass of verse that appears in print each year, most is "stale, flat, and unprofitable"; a very, very little is of any enduring value.

In judging a poem, as in judging any work of art, we need to ask three basic questions: (1) *What is its central purpose?* (2) *How fully has this purpose been accomplished?* (3) *How important is this purpose?* We need to answer the first question in order to understand the poem. Questions 2 and 3 are those by which we evaluate it. Question 2 measures the poem on a scale of perfection. Question 3 measures it on a scale of significance. The area of a rectangle is determined by multiplying its measurements on two scales, breadth and height; in an analogous way, the greatness of a poem is determined by multiplying its measurements on two scales, perfection and significance. If the poem measures well on the first of these scales, we call it a good-poem, at least of its kind. If it measures well on both scales, we call it a great poem.*

The measurement of a poem is a much more complex process, of course, than is the measurement of a rectangle. It cannot be done as

---

*As indicated in the footnote on page 26, some objection has been made to the use of the term "purpose" in literary criticism. For the two evaluative criteria suggested above may be substituted these two: (1) *How thoroughly are the materials of the poem integrated or unified?* (2) *How many and how diverse are the materials that it integrates?* Thus a poem becomes successful in proportion to the tightness of its organization—that is, according to the degree to which all its elements work together and require each other to produce the total effect—and it becomes great in proportion to its scope—that is, according to the amount and diversity of the material it amalgamates into unity.

exactly. Agreement on the measurements will never be complete. Yet over a period of time the judgments of qualified readers* tend to coalesce: there comes to be more agreement than disagreement. There is almost universal agreement, for instance, that Shakespeare is the greatest of English poets. Although qualified readers might disagree sharply as to whether Donne or Keats is the superior poet—or Wordsworth or Chaucer, or Shelley or Pope—they nearly all agree that each of these is superior to Kipling or Longfellow. And there is almost universal agreement that Kipling and Longfellow are superior to James Whitcomb Riley or Rod McKuen.

But your problem is to be able to discriminate, not between already established reputations, but between poems—poems you have not seen before and of which, perhaps, you do not even know the author. Here, of course, you will not always be right—even the most qualified readers occasionally go badly astray—but you should, we hope, be able to make broad distinctions with a higher average of success than you could when you began this book. And, unless you allow yourself to petrify, your ability to do this should improve throughout your college years and beyond.

For answering the first of our evaluative questions, *How fully has the poem's purpose been accomplished?* there are no easy yardsticks that we can apply. We cannot ask: Is the poem melodious? Does it have smooth meter? Does it use good grammar? Does it contain figures of speech? Are the rimes perfect? Excellent poems exist without any of these attributes. We can judge any element in a poem only as it contributes or fails to contribute to the achievement of the central purpose; and we can judge the total poem only as these elements work together to form an integrated whole. But we can at least attempt a few generalizations. A perfect poem contains no excess words, no words that do not bear their full weight in contributing to the total meaning, and no words that are used just to fill out the meter. Each word is the best word for expressing the total meaning: there are no inexact words forced by the rime scheme or the metrical pattern. The word order is the best order for expressing the author's total meaning; distortions or departures from normal order are for emphasis or some other meaningful purpose. The diction, the images, and the figures of speech are fresh, not trite (except, of course, when the poet uses trite language deliberately for purposes of irony). The sound of the poem

---

*Throughout this discussion the term "qualified reader" is of utmost importance. By a qualified reader we mean briefly a person with considerable experience of literature and considerable experience of life: a person of intelligence, sensitivity, and knowledge.

does not clash with its sense, or the form with its content; and in general both sound and pattern are used to support meaning. The organization of the poem is the best possible organization: images and ideas are so effectively arranged that any rearrangement would be harmful to the poem. Always remember, however, that a good poem may have flaws. We should never damn a poem for its flaws if these flaws are amply compensated for by positive excellence.

If a poem is to have true excellence, it must be in some sense a "new" poem; it must exact a fresh response from the qualified reader. It will neither be merely imitative of previous literature nor appeal to stock, preestablished ways of thinking and feeling that in some readers are automatically stimulated by words like *mother, baby, home, country, faith,* or *God,* much as a vending machine dispenses a product when the right amount is inserted in the slot.

And here, perhaps, we should discuss the kinds of poems that most frequently "fool" inexperienced readers (and occasionally a few experienced ones) and sometimes achieve tremendous popularity without winning the respect of most good readers. These poems are frequently published on greeting cards or in anthologies entitled *Poems of Inspiration, Poems of Courage,* or *Heart-Throbs.* The people who write such poems and the people who like them are often the best of people, but they are not poets or lovers of poetry in any genuine sense. They are lovers of conventional ideas or sentiments or feelings, which they like to see expressed with the adornment of rime and meter, and which, when so expressed, they respond to in predictable ways.

Of the several varieties of inferior poetry, we shall concern ourselves with three: the sentimental, the rhetorical, and the purely didactic. All three are perhaps unduly dignified by the name of poetry. They might more aptly be described as verse.

Sentimentality is indulgence in emotion for its own sake, or expression of more emotion than an occasion warrants. Sentimentalists are gushy, stirred to tears by trivial or inappropriate causes; they weep at all weddings and all funerals; they are made ecstatic by manifestations of young love; they clip locks of hair, gild baby shoes, and talk baby talk; they grow compassionate over hardened criminals when they are punished. Their opposites are callous or unfeeling people. The ideal is the person who responds sensitively on appropriate occasions and feels deeply on occasions that deserve deep feeling, but who has nevertheless a certain amount of emotional reserve, a certain command over feelings. Sentimental *literature* is "tear-jerking" literature. It aims primarily at stimulating the emotions directly rather than at communicating experience truly and freshly; it depends on trite and well-tried formulas for exciting emotion; it revels in old oaken buckets, rocking chairs, mother love, and the pitter-patter of little feet; it over-simplifies; it is unfaithful to the full complexity of human experience. In this book the best example of sentimental verse is the first seven lines of Johnston's "A tiny cry within the night" (No. 129). If this verse had ended as it began, it would have been pure sentimentalism. The eighth line redeems it by making us realize that the speaker is not an idealized mother but a real person and thus transfers the piece from the classification of sentimental verse to that of humorous verse.

Rhetorical poetry uses a language more glittering and high-flown than its substance warrants. It offers a spurious vehemence of language—language without a corresponding reality of emotion or thought underneath. It is oratorical, overelegant, artificially eloquent. It is superficial and, again, often basically trite. It loves rolling phrases like "from the rocky coast of Maine to the sun-washed shores of California" and "our heroic dead" and "Old Glory." It deals in generalities. At its worst it is bombast. In this book an example is offered by the two lines quoted from the play within a play in Shakespeare's *A Midsummer Night's Dream:*

> Whereat with blade, with bloody, blameful blade,
> He bravely broached his boiling bloody breast.

Another example may be found in the player's recitation in *Hamlet* (in Act 2, scene 2):

> Out, out, thou strumpet Fortune! All you gods,
> In general synod take away her power,
> Break all the spokes and fellies from her wheel,
> And bowl the round nave down the hill of heaven
> As low as to the fiends!

Didactic poetry has as a primary purpose to teach or preach. It is probable that all the very greatest poetry teaches in subtle ways, without being expressly didactic; and much expressly didactic poetry ranks high in poetic excellence: that is, it accomplishes its teaching without ceasing to be poetry. But when the didactic purpose supersedes the poetic purpose, when the poem communicates information or moral instruction only, then it ceases to be didactic poetry and becomes di-dactic verse. Such verse appeals to people who read poetry primarily for noble thoughts or inspiring lessons and like them prettily ex-pressed. It is recognizable often by its lack of any specific situation, the flatness of its diction, the poverty of its imagery and figurative lan-guage, its emphasis on moral platitudes, its lack of poetic freshness. It is either very trite or has little to distinguish it from informational prose except rime or meter. Bryant's "To a Waterfowl" (No. 106) is an example of didactic *poetry*. The familiar couplet

> Early to bed and early to rise,
> Makes a man healthy, wealthy, and wise

is more aptly characterized as didactic *verse*.

Undoubtedly, so far in this chapter, we have spoken too categorically, have made our distinctions too sharp and definite. All poetic excellence is a matter of degree. There are no absolute lines between sentimentality and true emotion, artificial and genuine eloquence, didactic verse, and didactic poetry. Though the difference between extreme examples is easy to recognize, subtler discriminations are harder to make. But a primary distinction between the educated person and the ignorant one is the ability to make informed judgments.

A final caution to students: when making judgments on literature, always be honest. Do not pretend to like what you do not like. Do not be afraid to admit a liking for what you do like. A genuine enthusiasm for the second-rate is much better than false enthusiasm or no enthusiasm at all. Be neither hasty nor timorous in making your judgments. When you have attentively read a poem and thoroughly considered it, decide what you think. Do not hedge, equivocate, or try to find out others' opinions before forming your own. But, having formed an opinion and expressed it, do not allow it to petrify. Compare your opinion *then* with the opinions of others; allow yourself to change it when convinced of its error: in this way you learn. Honesty, courage, and humility are the necessary moral foundations for all genuine literary judgment.

In the poems for comparison that follow in this chapter, the distinction to be made is not always between bad and good; it may be between varying degrees of poetic merit.

---

182. God's Will for You and Me

> Just to be tender, just to be true,
> Just to be glad the whole day through,
> Just to be merciful, just to be mild,
> Just to be trustful as a child,
> Just to be gentle and kind and sweet,   5

Just to be helpful with willing feet,
Just to be cheery when things go wrong,
Just to drive sadness away with a song,
Whether the hour is dark or bright,
Just to be loyal to God and right,   10
Just to believe that God knows best,
Just in his promises ever to rest—
Just to let love be our daily key,
That is God's will for you and me.

183. Pied Beauty

Glory be to God for dappled things—
    For skies of couple-color as a brinded cow;
        For rose-moles all in stipple upon trout that swim;
Fresh-firecoal chestnut-falls; finches' wings;
    Landscape plotted and pieced—fold, fallow and plow;   5
    And all trades, their gear and tackle and trim.

All things counter, original, spare, strange;
    Whatever is fickle, freckled (who knows how?)
        With swift, slow; sweet, sour; adazzle, dim;
He fathers-forth whose beauty is past change: 10
                Praise him.

QUESTION

Which is the superior poem? Explain in full.

184. A Poison Tree

I was angry with my friend:
I told my wrath, my wrath did end.
I was angry with my foe:
I told it not, my wrath did grow.

And I watered it in fears,   5
Night and morning with my tears;
And I sunnèd it with smiles,
And with soft deceitful wiles.

And it grew both day and night
Till it bore an apple bright;   10
And my foe beheld it shine,
And he knew that it was mine,

And into my garden stole
When the night had veiled the pole:°   sky
In the morning glad I see   15
My foe outstretched beneath the tree.

185. The Most Vital Thing in Life

When you feel like saying something
    That you know you will regret,
Or keenly feel an insult
    Not quite easy to forget,
That's the time to curb resentment   5
    And maintain a mental peace,
For when your mind is tranquil
    All your ill-thoughts simply cease.

It is easy to be angry
    When defrauded or defied,   10
To be peeved and disappointed
    If your wishes are denied;
But to win a worthwhile battle
    Over selfishness and spite,
You must learn to keep strict silence   15
    Though you know you're in the right.

So keep your mental balance
    When confronted by a foe,
Be it enemy in ambush
    Or some danger that you know.   20
If you are poised and tranquil
    When all around is strife,
Be assured that you have mastered
    The most vital thing in life.

QUESTION

Which poem has more poetic merit? Explain.

186. Longing

Come to me in my dreams, and then
By day I shall be well again!
For then the night will more than pay
The hopeless longing of the day.

Come, as thou cam'st a thousand times,   5
A messenger from radiant climes,
And smile on thy new world, and be
As kind to others as to me!

Or, as thou never cam'st in sooth,
Come now, and let me dream it truth;   10
And part my hair, and kiss my brow,
And say: *My love! why sufferest thou?*

Come to me in my dreams, and then
By day I shall be well again!
For then the night will more than pay   15
The hopeless longing of the day.

187. To Marguerite

Yes! in the sea of life enisled,
With echoing straits between us thrown,
Dotting the shoreless watery wild,
We mortal millions live *alone*.
The islands feel the enclasping flow   5
And then their endless bounds they know.

But when the moon their hollows lights,
And they are swept by balms of spring,
And in their glens, on starry nights,
The nightingales divinely sing;   10
And lovely notes, from shore to shore,
Across the sounds and channels pour—

Oh! then a longing like despair
Is to their farthest caverns sent;
For surely once, they feel, we were   15
Parts of a single continent!
Now round us spreads the watery plain—
Oh might our marges meet again!

Who ordered that their longing's fire
Should be, as soon as kindled, cooled?   20
Who renders vain their deep desire?—
A God, a God their severance ruled!
And bade betwixt their shores to be
The unplumbed, salt, estranging sea.

QUESTION

Both poems are by Matthew Arnold (1822–1888). Which of the two could
have been written only by a great poet? Explain.

188. The Long Voyage

Not that the pines were darker there,
nor mid-May dogwood brighter there,
nor swifts more swift in summer air;
    it was my own country,

having its thunderclap of spring,   5
its long midsummer ripening,
its corn hoar-stiff at harvesting,
    almost like any country,

yet being mine; its face, its speech,
its hills bent low within my reach,   10
its river birch and upland beech
    were mine, of my own country.

Now the dark waters at the bow
fold back, like earth against the plow;
foam brightens like the dogwood now   15
    at home, in my own country.

189. Breathes there the man

Breathes there the man, with soul so dead,
Who never to himself hath said,
    This is my own, my native land!
Whose heart hath ne'er within him burned,
As home his footsteps he hath turned,   5
    From wandering on a foreign strand?
If such there breathe, go, mark him well;

For him no minstrel raptures swell;
High though his titles, proud his name,
Boundless his wealth as wish can claim—   10
Despite those titles, power, and pelf,
The wretch, concentered all in self,
Living, shall forfeit fair renown,
And, doubly dying, shall go down
To the vile dust from whence he sprung,   15
Unwept, unhonored, and unsung.

QUESTION

Which poem communicates the more genuine poetic emotion? Which is
more rhetorical? Justify your answer.

190. The Engine

Into the gloom of the deep, dark night,
    With panting breath and a startled scream,
Swift as a bird in sudden flight
    Darts this creature of steel and steam.

Awful dangers are lurking nigh,   5
    Rocks and chasms are near the track,
But straight by the light of its great white eye
    It speeds through the shadows, dense and black.

Terrible thoughts and fierce desires
    Trouble its mad heart many an hour,   10
Where burn and smoulder the hidden fires,
    Coupled ever with might and power.

It hates, as a wild horse hates the rein,
    The narrow track by vale and hill,
And shrieks with a cry of startled pain,   15
    And longs to follow its own wild will.

191. I like to see it lap the miles

I like to see it lap the miles,
And lick the valleys up,
And stop to feed itself at tanks,
And then, prodigious, step.

Around a pile of mountains,   5
And, supercilious, peer
In shanties by the sides of roads,
And then a quarry pare

To fit its ribs,
And crawl between,   10
Complaining all the while
In horrid, hooting stanza,
Then chase itself down hill

And neigh like Boanerges;
Then, punctual as a star,   15
Stop—docile and omnipotent—
At its own stable door.

QUESTION

Which of these poems is more rhetorical in its language?

192. Little Boy Blue

The little toy dog is covered with dust,
    But sturdy and staunch he stands;
And the little toy soldier is red with rust,
    And his musket moulds in his hands.
Time was when the little toy dog was new,   5
    And the soldier was passing fair;
And that was the time when our Little Boy Blue
    Kissed them and put them there.

"Now, don't you go till I come," he said,
    "And don't you make any noise!"   10
So, toddling off to his trundle-bed,
    He dreamt of the pretty toys;
And, as he was dreaming, an angel song
    Awakened our Little Boy Blue—
Oh! the years are many, the years are long,   15
    But the little toy friends are True!

Ay, faithful to Little Boy Blue they stand
    Each in the same old place—
Awaiting the touch of a little hand,

The smile of a little face;   20
  And they wonder, as waiting the long years through
    In the dust of that little chair,
  What has become of our Little Boy Blue,
    Since he kissed them and put them there.

193. The Toys

My little Son, who looked from thoughtful eyes
And moved and spoke in quiet grown-up wise,
Having my law the seventh time disobeyed,
I struck him, and dismissed
With hard words and unkissed,   5
His Mother, who was patient, being dead.
Then, fearing lest his grief should hinder sleep,
I visited his bed,
But found him slumbering deep,
With darkened eyelids, and their lashes yet   10
From his late sobbing wet.
And I, with moan,
Kissing away his tears, left others of my own;
For, on a table drawn beside his head,
He had put, within his reach,   15
A box of counters and a red-veined stone,
A piece of glass abraded by the beach,
And six or seven shells,
A bottle with bluebells,
And two French copper coins, ranged there with careful art,   20
To comfort his sad heart.
So when that night I prayed
To God, I wept, and said:
Ah, when at last we lie with trancèd breath,
Not vexing Thee in death,   25
And thou rememberest of what toys
We made our joys,
How weakly understood
Thy great commanded good,
Then, fatherly not less   30
Than I whom Thou has moulded from the clay,
Thou'lt leave Thy wrath, and say,
"I will be sorry for their childishness."

QUESTION

One of these poems has an obvious appeal for the beginning reader. The other is likely to have more meaning for the mature reader. Try to explain in terms of sentimentality and honesty.

194. Song: Sweetest love, I do not go

Sweetest love, I do not go
    For weariness of thee,
Nor in hope the world can show
    A fitter love for me;
        But since that I   5
Must die at last, 'tis best
To use my self in jest
    Thus by feigned deaths to die.

Yesternight the sun went hence,
    And yet is here today,   10
He hath no desire nor sense,
    Nor half so short a way:
        Then fear not me,
But believe that I shall make
Speedier journeys, since I take   15
    More wings and spurs than he.

O how feeble is man's power,
    That if good fortune fall,
Cannot add another hour,
    Nor a lost hour recall!   20
        But come bad chance,
And we join it to our strength,
And we teach it art and length,
    Itself o'er us to advance.

When thou sigh'st, thou sigh'st not wind,   25
    But sigh'st my soul away;
When thou weep'st, unkindly kind,
    My life's blood doth decay.
        It cannot be
That thou lov'st me, as thou say'st,   30
If in thine my life thou waste;
    Thou art the best of me.

Let not thy divining° heart   prophetic
      Forethink me any ill;
Destiny may take thy part,   35
      And may thy fears fulfill;
            But think that we
      Are but turned aside to sleep;
      They who one another keep
            Alive, ne'er parted be.   40

195. Song: Sweetest love, return again

Sweetest love, return again,
      Make not too long a stay,
Killing mirth and forcing pain,
      Sorrow leading way.
Let us not thus parted be: 5
Love and absence ne'er agree.

But since you must needs depart,
      And me hapless leave,
In your journey take my heart,
      Which will not deceive.   10
Yours it is, to you it flies,
Joying in those lovèd eyes.

So in part we shall not part,
      Though we absent be:
Time, nor place, nor greatest smart   15
      Shall my bands° make free.   bonds
Tied I am, yet think it gain:
In such knots I feel no pain.

But can I live, having lost
      Chiefest part of me?   20
Heart is fled, and sight is crossed,
      These my fortunes be.
Yet dear heart go, soon return:
As good there as here to burn.

QUESTION

Which is the superior poem, and why?

CHAPTER SIXTEEN

Good Poetry and Great

If a poem has successfully met the test in the question, *How fully has it accomplished its purpose?* we are ready to subject it to our second evaluative question: *How important is its purpose?*

Great poetry must, of course, be good poetry. Noble intent alone cannot redeem a work that does not measure high on the scale of accomplishment; otherwise the sentimental and purely didactic verse of much of the last chapter would stand with the world's masterpieces. But once a work has been judged as successful on the scale of execution, its final standing will depend on its significance of purpose.

Suppose, for instance, we consider three poems in our text: the limerick "A tutor who tooted the flute" by Carolyn Wells (No. 172); the poem "It sifts from leaden sieves" by Emily Dickinson (No. 47), and Shakespeare's sonnet "That time of year" (No. 171). Each of these would probably be judged by critics as highly successful in what it sets out to do. Wells has attempted a tongue-twister in strict limerick form, and she succeeds magnificently. Her poem is filled with a tooting of *oo*s, a clatter of *t*s, and a swarming of *-or*s and *-er*s. Every foot of the poem contains at least one of these sounds; most contain several. Moreover, this astounding feat is accomplished in verse that contains no unnecessary or inappropriate words, no infelicities of grammar or syntax. We are delighted by its sheer technical virtuosity. But what is this limerick *about?* Nothing of the slightest interest. It makes no attempt to communicate significant human experience. Its true subject is the ingenuity of its wordplay. Like an ornately decorated Easter egg, its value lies in its shell rather than in its content. Indeed, we should hardly call it poetry at all; it is highly accomplished, brilliantly clever *verse.* Emily Dickinson's poem, in contrast, *is* poetry, and very good poetry. It appeals richly to our senses and to our imaginations, and it succeeds excellently in its purpose: to convey the appearance and the quality of falling and newly fallen snow as well as a sense of the magic and the mystery of nature. Yet, when we compare this excellent poem with Shakespeare's, we again see important differences. Although the first poem engages the senses and the imagination and may affect us with wonder and cause us to meditate on nature, it does not deeply engage the emotions or the intellect. It does not come as close to the core of human living and suffering as does Shakespeare's sonnet. In fact, it is concerned primarily with that staple of small talk, the weather. On the other hand, Shakespeare's sonnet evokes the universal human concerns of growing old, approaching death, and love. Of these three selections, then, Shakespeare's is the greatest. It "says" more than Emily Dickinson's poem or the limerick; it communicates a richer experience; it successfully accomplishes a more significant purpose. The discriminating reader will get from it a deeper enjoyment because it is nourishing as well as delightful.

Great poetry engages the whole person—senses, imagination, emotion, intellect; it does not touch us merely on one or two sides of our nature. Great poetry seeks not merely to entertain us but to bring us—along with pure pleasure—fresh insights, or renewed insights, and important insights, into the nature of human experience. Great poetry, we might say, gives us a broader and deeper understanding of life, of our fellows, and of ourselves, always with the qualification, of course, that the kind of insight literature gives is not necessarily the kind that can be summed up in a simple "lesson" or "moral." It is *knowledge—felt* knowledge, *new* knowledge—of the complexities of human nature and of the tragedies and sufferings, the excitements and joys, that characterize human experience.

Is Shakespeare's sonnet a *great* poem? It is, at least, a great *sonnet.* Greatness, like goodness, is relative. If we compare any of Shakespeare's sonnets with his greatest plays—*Macbeth, Othello, Hamlet, King Lear, The Tempest*—another big difference appears. What is undertaken and accomplished in these plays is enormously greater, more difficult, and more complex than could ever be undertaken or accomplished in a single sonnet. Greatness in literature, in fact, cannot be entirely dissociated from size. In literature, as in basketball, a good big player is better than a good little player. The greatness of a poem is in proportion to the range and depth and intensity of experience that it brings to us: its amount of life. Shakespeare's plays offer us a multiplicity of life and a depth of living that could never be compressed into the fourteen lines of a sonnet. They organize a greater complexity of life and experience into unity.

Yet, after all, we have provided no easy yardsticks or rule-of-thumb measures for literary judgment. There are no mechanical tests. The final measuring rod can be only the responsiveness, the taste, and the discernment of the cultivated reader. Such taste and discernment are partly a native endowment, partly the product of experience, partly the achievement of conscious study, training, and intellectual effort. They cannot be achieved suddenly or quickly; they can never be achieved in perfection. The pull is a long and a hard one. But success, even relative success, brings enormous rewards in enrichment and command of life.

196. The Canonization

For God's sake, hold your tongue, and let me love!
    Or chide my palsy or my gout,
My five gray hairs or ruined fortune flout;
With wealth your state, your mind with arts improve,
      Take you a course,° get you a place,   career 5
      Observe his honor° or his grace,°   judge; bishop
    Or the king's real or his stamped face°   on a coin
      Contemplate; what you will, approve,°   try out
    So you will let me love.

Alas, alas, who's injured by my love?   10
    What merchant ships have my sighs drowned?
Who says my tears have overflowed his ground?
When did my colds a forward° spring remove?   early
    When did the heats which my veins fill
    Add one more to the plaguy bill?   15
Soldiers find wars, and lawyers find out still
    Litigious men which quarrels move,
      Though she and I do love.

Call us what you will, we are made such by love.
    Call her one, me another fly;°   moth 20
We are tapers too, and at our own cost die;
And we in us find the eagle and the dove;
    The phoenix riddle hath more wit°   meaning
    By us; we two, being one, are it.
So to one neutral thing both sexes fit.   25
    We die and rise the same, and prove
      Mysterious by this love.

We can die by it, if not live by love,
    And if unfit for tombs and hearse
Our legend be, it will be fit for verse;   30

> And if no piece of chronicle° we prove,   history
>   We'll build in sonnets pretty rooms:
>   As well a well-wrought urn becomes
> The greatest ashes as half-acre tombs,
>   And by these hymns all shall approve°   confirm   35
>   Us canonized for love,
>
> And thus invoke us: "You whom reverend love
>   Made one another's hermitage,
> You to whom love was peace, that now is rage,
> Who did the whole world's soul contract, and drove   40
>   Into the glasses of your eyes
>   (So made such mirrors and such spies
> That they did all to you epitomize)
>   Countries, towns, courts: beg from above
>   A pattern of your love!"   45

John Donne (1572–1631)

QUESTIONS

1. Vocabulary: *canonization* (title), *tapers* (21), *phoenix* (23), *invoke* (37), *epitomize* (43). "[R]eal" (7), pronounced as two syllables, puns on *royal*. The "plaguy bill" (15) is a list of plague victims. The word "die" (21, 26, 28) in seventeenth-century slang meant to experience the sexual climax. To understand lines 21 and 28, one also needs to be familiar with the Renaissance superstition that every act of sexual intercourse shortened one's life by one day. The "eagle" and the "dove" (22) are symbols for strength and mildness. "[P]attern" (45) is a model that one can copy.
2. Who is the speaker and what is his condition? How old is he? To whom is he speaking? What has his auditor been saying to him before the opening of the poem? What sort of values can we ascribe to the auditor by inference from the first stanza? What value does the speaker oppose to these? How does the stanzaic pattern of the poem emphasize this value?
3. The sighs, tears, fevers, and chills in the second stanza were commonplace in the love poetry of Donne's time. How does Donne make them fresh? What is the speaker's argument in this stanza? How does it begin to turn from pure defense to offense in the last three lines of the stanza?
4. How are the things to which the lovers are compared in the third stanza *arranged?* Does their ordering reflect in any way the arrangement of the whole poem? Elucidate line 21. Interpret or paraphrase lines 23–27.
5. Explain the first line of the fourth stanza. What status does the speaker claim for himself and his beloved in the last line of this stanza?
6. In what sense is the last stanza an invocation? Who speaks in it? To whom? What powers are ascribed to the lovers in it?
7. What do the following words from the poem have in common: "Mysterious" (27), "hymns" (35), "canonized" (36), "reverend" (37), "hermitage" (38)? What judgment about love does the speaker make by the use of these words?

197. Home Burial

He saw her from the bottom of the stairs
Before she saw him. She was starting down,
Looking back over her shoulder at some fear.
She took a doubtful step and then undid it
To raise herself and look again. He spoke   5
Advancing toward her: "What is it you see
From up there always—for I want to know."
She turned and sank upon her skirts at that,
And her face changed from terrified to dull.
He said to gain time: "What is it you see,"   10
Mounting until she cowered under him.
"I will find out now—you must tell me, dear."
She, in her place, refused him any help
With the least stiffening of her neck and silence.
She let him look, sure that he wouldn't see,   15
Blind creature; and awhile he didn't see.
But at last he murmured, "Oh," and again, "Oh."

"What is it—what?" she said.

              "Just that I see."

"You don't," she challenged. "Tell me what it is."

"The wonder is I didn't see at once.   20
I never noticed it from here before.
I must be wonted to it—that's the reason.
The little graveyard where my people are!
So small the window frames the whole of it.
Not so much larger than a bedroom, is it?   25
There are three stones of slate and one of marble,
Broad-shouldered little slabs there in the sunlight
On the sidehill. We haven't to mind *those*.
But I understand: it is not the stones,
But the child's mound—"

                      "Don't, don't, don't,
don't," she cried.   30

She withdrew, shrinking from beneath his arm
That rested on the banister, and slid downstairs;
And turned on him with such a daunting look,
He said twice over before he knew himself:
"Can't a man speak of his own child he's lost?"   35

"Not you! Oh, where's my hat? Oh, I don't need it!
I must get out of here. I must get air.
I don't know rightly whether any man can."

"Amy! Don't go to someone else this time.
Listen to me. I won't come down the stairs."   40
He sat and fixed his chin between his fists.
"There's something I should like to ask you, dear."

"You don't know how to ask it."

                                        "Help me, then."

Her fingers moved the latch for all reply.

"My words are nearly always an offense.   45
I don't know how to speak of anything
So as to please you. But I might be taught,
I should suppose. I can't say I see how.
A man must partly give up being a man
With women-folk. We could have some arrangement   50
By which I'd bind myself to keep hands off
Anything special you're a-mind to name.
Though I don't like such things 'twixt those that love.
Two that don't love can't live together without them.
But two that do can't live together with them."   55
She moved the latch a little. "Don't—don't go.
Don't carry it to someone else this time.
Tell me about it if it's something human.
Let me into your grief. I'm not so much
Unlike other folks as your standing there   60
Apart would make me out. Give me my chance.
I do think, though, you overdo it a little.
What was it brought you up to think it the thing
To take your mother-loss of a first child
So inconsolably—in the face of love.   65
You'd think his memory might be satisfied—"

"There you go sneering now!"

                                "I'm not, I'm not!
You make me angry. I'll come down to you.
God, what a woman! And it's come to this,
A man can't speak of his own child that's dead."   70

"You can't because you don't know how to speak.
If you had any feelings, you that dug
With your own hand—how could you?—his little grave;

I saw you from that very window there,
Making the gravel leap and leap in air,   75
Leap up, like that, like that, and land so lightly
And roll back down the mound beside the hole.
I thought, Who is that man? I didn't know you.
And I crept down the stairs and up the stairs
To look again, and still your spade kept lifting.   80
Then you came in. I heard your rumbling voice
Out in the kitchen, and I don't know why,
But I went near to see with my own eyes.
You could sit there with the stains on your shoes
Of the fresh earth from your own baby's grave   85
And talk about your everyday concerns.
You had stood the spade up against the wall
Outside there in the entry, for I saw it."

"I shall laugh the worst laugh I ever laughed.
I'm cursed. God, if I don't believe I'm cursed."   90

"I can repeat the very words you were saying:
'Three foggy mornings and one rainy day
Will rot the best birch fence a man can build.'
Think of it, talk like that at such a time!
What had how long it takes a birch to rot   95
To do with what was in the darkened parlor?
You *couldn't* care! The nearest friends can go
With anyone to death, comes so far short
They might as well not try to go at all.
No, from the time when one is sick to death,   100
One is alone, and he dies more alone.
Friends make pretense of following to the grave,
But before one is in it, their minds are turned
And making the best of their way back to life
And living people, and things they understand.   105
But the world's evil. I won't have grief so
If I can change it. Oh, I won't, I won't!"

"There, you have said it all and you feel better.
You won't go now. You're crying. Close the door.
The heart's gone out of it: why keep it up?   110
Amy! There's someone coming down the road!"

"*You*—oh, you think the talk is all. I must go—
Somewhere out of this house. How can I make you—"
"If—you—do!" She was opening the door wider.

"Where do you mean to go? First tell me that.   115
I'll follow and bring you back by force. I *will!*—"

Robert Frost (1874–1963)

QUESTIONS

1. Vocabulary: *wonted* (22).
2. The poem centers on a conflict between husband and wife. What causes the conflict? Why does Amy resent her husband? What is *his* dissatisfaction with Amy?
3. Characterize the husband and wife respectively. What is the chief difference between them? Does the poem take sides? Is either presented more sympathetically than the other?
4. The poem does not say how long the couple have been married or how long the child has been buried. Does it contain suggestions from which we may make rough inferences?
5. The husband and wife both generalize on the other's faults during the course of the poem, attributing them to all men or to all women or to people in general. Point out these generalizations. Are they valid?
6. Finish the unfinished sentences in lines 30, 66, 113, 114.
7. Comment on the function of lines 25, 39, 92–93.
8. Following are three paraphrased and abbreviated versions of statements made in published discussions of the poem. Which would you support? Why?
   a. The young wife is gradually persuaded by her husband's kind yet firm reasonableness to express her feelings in words and to recognize that human nature is limited and cannot sacrifice everything to sorrow. Though she still suffers from excess grief, the crisis is past, and she will eventually be brought back to life.
   b. At the end, the whole poem is epitomized by the door that is neither open nor shut. The wife cannot really leave; the husband cannot really make her stay. Neither husband nor wife is capable of decisive action, of either self-liberation or liberation of the other.
   c. Her husband's attempt to talk, since it is the wrong kind of talk, only leads to her departure at the poem's end.

198. The Love Song of J. Alfred Prufrock

S'io credesse che mia risposta fosse
A persona che mai tornasse al mondo,
Questa fiamma staria senza piu scosse.
Ma perciocche giammai di questo fondo
Non torno vivo alcun, s'i'odo il vero,
Senza tema d'infamia ti rispondo.

Let us go then, you and I,
When the evening is spread out against the sky

Like a patient etherized upon a table;
Let us go, through certain half-deserted streets,
The muttering retreats   5
Of restless nights in one-night cheap hotels
And sawdust restaurants with oyster-shells:
Streets that follow like a tedious argument
Of insidious intent
To lead you to an overwhelming question . . .   10
Oh, do not ask, "What is it?"
Let us go and make our visit.

In the room the women come and go
Talking of Michelangelo.

The yellow fog that rubs its back upon the window-panes,   15
The yellow smoke that rubs its muzzle on the window-panes
Licked its tongue into the corners of the evening,
Lingered upon the pools that stand in drains,
Let fall upon its back the soot that falls from chimneys,
Slipped by the terrace, made a sudden leap,   20
And seeing that it was a soft October night,
Curled once about the house, and fell asleep.

And indeed there will be time
For the yellow smoke that slides along the street,
Rubbing its back upon the window-panes;   25
There will be time, there will be time
To prepare a face to meet the faces that you meet;
There will be time to murder and create,
And time for all the works and days of hands
That lift and drop a question on your plate;   30
Time for you and time for me,
And time yet for a hundred indecisions,
And for a hundred visions and revisions,
Before the taking of a toast and tea.

In the room the women come and go   35
Talking of Michelangelo.

And indeed there will be time
To wonder, "Do I dare?" and "Do I dare?"
Time to turn back and descend the stair,
With a bald spot in the middle of my hair—   40
(They will say: "How his hair is growing thin!")
My morning coat, my collar mounting firmly to the chin,
My necktie rich and modest, but asserted by a simple pin—

(They will say: "But how his arms and legs are thin!")
Do I dare   45
Disturb the universe?
In a minute there is time
For decisions and revisions which a minute will reverse.

For I have known them all already, known them all:—
Have known the evenings, mornings, afternoons,   50
I have measured out my life with coffee spoons;
I know the voices dying with a dying fall
Beneath the music from a farther room.
    So how should I presume?

And I have known the eyes already, known them all—   55
The eyes that fix you in a formulated phrase,
And when I am formulated, sprawling on a pin,
When I am pinned and wriggling on the wall,
Then how should I begin
To spit out all the butt-ends of my days and ways?   60
    And how should I presume?

And I have known the arms already, known them all—
Arms that are braceleted and white and bare
(But in the lamplight, downed with light brown hair!)
Is it perfume from a dress   65
That makes me so digress?
Arms that lie along a table, or wrap about a shawl.
    And should I then presume?
    And how should I begin?

                    *   *   *

Shall I say, I have gone at dusk through narrow streets   70
And watched the smoke that rises from the pipes
Of lonely men in shirt-sleeves, leaning out of windows? . . .

    I should have been a pair of ragged claws
Scuttling across the floors of silent seas.

                    *   *   *

And the afternoon, the evening, sleeps so peacefully!   75
Smoothed by long fingers,
Asleep . . . tired . . . or it malingers,
Stretched on the floor, here beside you and me.
Should I, after tea and cakes and ices,
Have the strength to force the moment to its crisis?   80
But though I have wept and fasted, wept and prayed,
Though I have seen my head (grown slightly bald) brought in upon a platter,
I am no prophet—and here's no great matter;

I have seen the moment of my greatness flicker,
And I have seen the eternal Footman hold my coat, and snicker,   85
And in short, I was afraid.

    And would it have been worth it, after all,
After the cups, the marmalade, the tea,
Among the porcelain, among some talk of you and me,
Would it have been worth while,   90
To have bitten off the matter with a smile,
To have squeezed the universe into a ball
To roll it toward some overwhelming question,
To say: "I am Lazarus, come from the dead,
Come back to tell you all, I shall tell you all"—   95
If one, settling a pillow by her head,
    Should say: "That is not what I meant at all.
    That is not it, at all."

    And would it have been worth it, after all,
Would it have been worth while,   100
After the sunsets and the dooryards and the sprinkled streets,
After the novels, after the teacups, after the skirts that trail along the floor—
And this, and so much more?—
It is impossible to say just what I mean!
But as if a magic lantern threw the nerves in patterns on a screen: 105
Would it have been worth while
If one, settling a pillow or throwing off a shawl,
And turning toward the window, should say:
    "That is not it at all,
    That is not what I meant, at all."   110

        *   *   *

No! I am not Prince Hamlet, nor was meant to be;
Am an attendant lord, one that will do
To swell a progress, start a scene or two,
Advise the prince; no doubt, an easy tool,
Deferential, glad to be of use,   115
Politic, cautious, and meticulous:
Full of high sentence, but a bit obtuse;
At times, indeed, almost ridiculous—
Almost, at times, the Fool.

    I grow old . . . I grow old . . .   120
I shall wear the bottoms of my trousers rolled.°   cuffed

    Shall I part my hair behind? Do I dare to eat a peach?
I shall wear white flannel trousers, and walk upon the beach.
I have heard the mermaids singing, each to each.

I do not think that they will sing to me.   125

I have seen them riding seaward on the waves
Combing the white hair of the waves blown back
When the wind blows the water white and black.

We have lingered in the chambers of the sea
By sea-girls wreathed with seaweed red and brown   130
Till human voices wake us, and we drown.

T. S. Eliot (1888–1965)

QUESTIONS

1. Vocabulary: *insidious* (9), *Michelangelo* (14, 35), *muzzle* (16), *malingers* (77), *progress* (113), *Deferential* (115), *Politic* (116), *meticulous* (116), *sentence* (117).
2. This poem may be for some readers the most difficult in the book because it uses a "stream of consciousness" technique (that is, it presents the apparently random thoughts going through a person's head within a certain time interval), in which the transitional links are psychological rather than logical, and also because it uses allusions you may be unfamiliar with. Even if you do not at first understand the poem in detail, you should be able to get from it a quite accurate picture of Prufrock's character and personality. What kind of person is he (answer this as fully as possible)? From what class of society does he come? What one line especially well sums up the nature of his past life? A brief initial orientation may be helpful: Prufrock is apparently on his way, at the beginning of the poem, to a late afternoon tea, at which he wishes (or does he?) to make a declaration of love to some lady who will be present. The "you and I" of the first line are divided parts of Prufrock's own nature, for he is experiencing internal conflict. Does he or does he not make the declaration? Where does the climax of the poem come? If the portion leading up to the climax is devoted to Prufrock's effort to prepare himself psychologically to make the declaration (or to postpone such effort), what is the portion after the climax devoted to?
3. The poem contains a number of striking or unusual figures of speech. Most of them in some way reflect Prufrock's own nature or his desires or fears. From this point of view discuss lines 2–3; 15–22 and 75–78; 57–58; 73–74; and 124–31. What figure of speech is lines 73–74? In what respect is the title ironic?
4. The poem makes extensive use of literary allusion. The Italian epigraph is a passage from Dante's *Inferno* in which a man in Hell tells a visitor that he would never tell his story if there were a chance that it would get back to living ears. In line 29 the phrase "works and days" is the title of a long poem—a description of agricultural life and a call to toil—by the early Greek poet Hesiod. Line 52 echoes the opening speech of Shakespeare's *Twelfth Night*. The prophet of lines 81–83 is John the Baptist, whose head was delivered to Salome by Herod as a reward for her dancing (Matthew 14.1–11, and Oscar Wilde's play *Salome*). Line 92 echoes the closing six lines of Marvell's "To His Coy Mistress" (No. 56). Lazarus (94–95) may be either the beggar Lazarus (of Luke 16) who was not permitted to return

from the dead to warn a rich man's brothers about Hell, the Lazarus (of John 11) whom Christ raised from death, or both. Lines 111–19 allude to a number of characters from Shakespeare's *Hamlet:* Hamlet himself, the chamberlain Polonius, and various minor characters including probably Rosencrantz, Guildenstern, and Osric. "Full of high sentence" (117) echoes Chaucer's description of the Clerk of Oxford in the Prologue to *The Canterbury Tales.* Relate as many of these allusions as you can to the character of Prufrock. How is Prufrock particularly like Hamlet, and how is he unlike him? Contrast Prufrock with the speaker in "To His Coy Mistress."

199. Sunday Morning

1

Complacencies of the peignoir, and late
Coffee and oranges in a sunny chair,
And the green freedom of a cockatoo
Upon a rug mingle to dissipate
The holy hush of ancient sacrifice. 5
She dreams a little, and she feels the dark
Encroachment of that old catastrophe,
As a calm darkens among water-lights.
The pungent oranges and bright, green wings
Seem things in some procession of the dead, 10
Winding across wide water, without sound.
The day is like wide water, without sound,
Stilled for the passing of her dreaming feet
Over the seas, to silent Palestine,
Dominion of the blood and sepulchre. 15

2

Why should she give her bounty to the dead?
What is divinity if it can come
Only in silent shadows and in dreams?
Shall she not find in comforts of the sun,
In pungent fruit and bright, green wings, or else 20
In any balm or beauty of the earth,
Things to be cherished like the thought of heaven?
Divinity must live within herself:
Passions of rain, or moods in falling snow;
Grievings in loneliness, or unsubdued 25
Elations when the forest blooms; gusty

Emotions on wet roads on autumn nights;
All pleasures and all pains, remembering
The bough of summer and the winter branch.
These are the measures destined for her soul.   30

3

Jove in the clouds had his inhuman birth.
No mother suckled him, no sweet land gave
Large-mannered motions to his mythy mind.
He moved among us, as a muttering king,
Magnificent, would move among his hinds,   35
Until our blood, commingling, virginal,
With heaven, brought such requital to desire
The very hinds discerned it, in a star.
Shall our blood fail? Or shall it come to be
The blood of paradise? And shall the earth   40
Seem all of paradise that we shall know?
The sky will be much friendlier then than now,
A part of labor and a part of pain,
And next in glory to enduring love,
Not this dividing and indifferent blue.   45

4

She says, "I am content when wakened birds,
Before they fly, test the reality
Of misty fields, by their sweet questionings;
But when the birds are gone, and their warm fields
Return no more, where, then, is paradise?"   50
There is not any haunt of prophecy,
Nor any old chimera of the grave,
Neither the golden underground, nor isle
Melodious, where spirits gat them home,
Nor visionary south, nor cloudy palm   55
Remote on heaven's hill, that has endured
As April's green endures; or will endure
Like her remembrance of awakened birds,
Or her desire for June and evening, tipped
By the consummation of the swallow's wings.   60

5

She says, "But in contentment I still feel
The need of some imperishable bliss."

Death is the mother of beauty; hence from her,
Alone, shall come fulfillment to our dreams
And our desires. Although she strews the leaves   65
Of sure obliteration on our paths,
The path sick sorrow took, the many paths
Where triumph rang its brassy phrase, or love
Whispered a little out of tenderness,
She makes the willow shiver in the sun   70
For maidens who were wont to sit and gaze
Upon the grass, relinquished to their feet.
She causes boys to pile new plums and pears
On disregarded plate. The maidens taste
And stray impassioned in the littering leaves.   75

6

Is there no change of death in paradise?
Does ripe fruit never fall? Or do the boughs
Hang always heavy in that perfect sky,
Unchanging, yet so like our perishing earth,
With rivers like our own that seek for seas   80
They never find, the same receding shores
That never touch with inarticulate pang?
Why set the pear upon those river-banks
Or spice the shores with odors of the plum?
Alas, that they should wear our colors there,   85
The silken weavings of our afternoons,
And pick the strings of our insipid lutes!
Death is the mother of beauty, mystical,
Within whose burning bosom we devise
Our earthly mothers waiting, sleeplessly.   90

7

Supple and turbulent, a ring of men
Shall chant in orgy on a summer morn
Their boisterous devotion to the sun,
Not as a god, but as a god might be,
Naked among them, like a savage source.   95
Their chant shall be a chant of paradise,
Out of their blood, returning to the sky;
And in their chant shall enter, voice by voice,
The windy lake wherein their lord delights,
The trees, like serafin, and echoing hills,   100
That choir among themselves long afterward.

They shall know well the heavenly fellowship
Of men that perish and of summer morn.
And whence they came and whither they shall go
The dew upon their feet shall manifest.   105

8

She hears, upon that water without sound,
A voice that cries, "The tomb in Palestine
Is not the porch of spirits lingering.
It is the grave of Jesus, where he lay."
We live in an old chaos of the sun,   110
Or old dependency of day and night,
Or island solitude, unsponsored, free,
Of that wide water, inescapable.
Deer walk upon our mountains, and the quail
Whistle about us their spontaneous cries;   115
Sweet berries ripen in the wilderness;
And, in the isolation of the sky,
At evening, casual flocks of pigeons make
Ambiguous undulations as they sink,
Downward to darkness, on extended wings.   120

Wallace Stevens (1879–1955)

QUESTIONS

1. Vocabulary: *peignoir* (1), *hinds* (35, 38), *requital* (37), *chimera* (52), *consummation* (60), *obliteration* (66), *serafin* (seraphim) (100). "[G]at" (54) is an obsolete past tense of "get."
2. The poem presents a woman meditating on questions of death, mutability, and permanence, beginning with a stanza that sets the stage and shows her being drawn to these questions beyond her conscious will. The meditation proper is structured as a series of questions and answers stated in direct or indirect quotations, with the answer to a preceding question suggesting a further question, and so forth. In reading through the poem, paraphrase the sequence of implied or stated questions, and the answers to them.
3. The opening scene (stanza 1), in a collection of images and details, indicates the means the woman has chosen to avoid thinking of the typical "Sunday morning" topic, the Christian religion. Define the means she employs. Trace the further references to fruits and birds throughout the poem, and explain the ordering principle that ties them together (for example, what development of idea or attitude is implied in the sequence oranges/plums and pears/wild berries?).
4. What symbolic meanings are implied by the images of (a) water, (b) the sun, and (c) birds and other animals?

5. Why does the woman give up her desire for unchanging permanence? With what does she replace it? What is her final attitude toward a world that includes change and death? What is meant by "Death is the mother of beauty" (63, 88)?

6. The poet wrote, "This is not essentially a woman's meditation on religion and the meaning of life. It is anybody's meditation" (*Letters of Wallace Stevens,* ed. Holly Stevens [New York: Knopf, 1966] 250). Can you justify that claim?

7. "The Canonization," "Home Burial," "The Love Song of J. Alfred Prufrock," and "Sunday Morning" are all dramatic poems. "The Canonization" is a dramatic monologue (one person is speaking to another, whose replies we do not hear). Frost's poem (though it has a slight narrative element) is largely a dialogue between two speakers who speak in their own voices. Eliot's poem is a highly allusive soliloquy, or interior monologue. "Sunday Morning" combines descriptive scene-setting with an interior debate of question and answer. In what ways do the dramatic structures of these poems facilitate what they have to say?

PART 2

Poems for Further Reading

200. Woman Work

I've got the children to tend
The clothes to mend
The floor to mop
The food to shop
Then the chicken to fry   5
The baby to dry
I got company to feed
The garden to weed
I've got the shirts to press
The tots to dress   10
The cane to be cut
I gotta clean up this hut
Then see about the sick
And the cotton to pick.

Shine on me, sunshine   15
Rain on me, rain
Fall softly, dewdrops
And cool my brow again.

Storm, blow me from here
With your fiercest wind   20
Let me float across the sky
'Til I can rest again.

Fall gently, snowflakes
Cover me with white
Cold icy kisses and   25
Let me rest tonight.

Sun, rain, curving sky
Mountain, oceans, leaf and stone
Star shine, moon glow
You're all that I can call my own.   30

Maya Angelou (b. 1928)

201. Siren Song

This is the one song everyone
would like to learn: the song
that is irresistible:

the song that forces men
to leap overboard in squadrons   5
even though they see the beached skulls

the song nobody knows
because anyone who has heard it
is dead, and the others can't remember.

Shall I tell you the secret   10
and if I do, will you get me
out of this bird suit?

I don't enjoy it here
squatting on this island
looking picturesque and mythical   15

with these two feathery maniacs,
I don't enjoy singing
this trio, fatal and valuable.

I will tell the secret to you,
to you, only to you.   20
Come closer. This song

is a cry for help: Help me!
Only you, only you can,
you are unique

at last. Alas   25
It is a boring song
but it works every time.

Margaret Atwood (b. 1939)

Siren (title): In Greek mythology, the sirens (sometimes pictured as birds with women's heads) were creatures whose beautiful singing lured sailors to their deaths.

202. Musée des Beaux Arts

About suffering they were never wrong,
The Old Masters: how well they understood
Its human position; how it takes place
While someone else is eating or opening a window or just walking
    dully along;
How, when the aged are reverently, passionately waiting   5
For the miraculous birth, there always must be

Children who did not specially want it to happen, skating
On a pond at the edge of the wood:
They never forgot
That even the dreadful martyrdom must run its course   10
Anyhow in a corner, some untidy spot
Where the dogs go on with their doggy life and the torturer's horse
Scratches its innocent behind on a tree.

In Brueghel's *Icarus,* for instance: how everything turns away
Quite leisurely from the disaster; the plowman may   15
Have heard the splash, the forsaken cry,
But for him it was not an important failure; the sun shone
As it had to on the white legs disappearing into the green
Water; and the expensive delicate ship that must have seen
Something amazing, a boy falling out of the sky,   20
Had somewhere to get to and sailed calmly on.

W. H. Auden (1907–1973)

203. On Reading Poems to a Senior Class at South High

Before
I opened my mouth
I noticed them sitting there
as orderly as frozen fish
in a package.   5

Slowly water began to fill the room
though I did not notice it
till it reached
my ears

and then I heard the sounds   10
of fish in an aquarium
and I knew that though I had
tried to drown them
with my words
that they had only opened up   15
like gills for them
and let me in.

Together we swam around the room
like thirty tails whacking words
till the bell rang   20

puncturing
a hole in the door

where we all leaked out

They went to another class
I suppose and I home   25

where Queen Elizabeth
my cat met me
and licked my fins
till they were hands again.

D. C. Berry (b. 1942)

204. The Lamb

Little Lamb, who made thee?
Dost thou know who made thee?
Gave thee life and bid thee feed
By the stream and o'er the mead;
Gave thee clothing of delight,   5
Softest clothing wooly bright;
Gave thee such a tender voice,
Making all the vales rejoice!
Little Lamb, who made thee?
Dost thou know who made thee?   10

Little Lamb, I'll tell thee,
Little Lamb, I'll tell thee!
He is callèd by thy name,
For he calls himself a Lamb;
He is meek and he is mild,   15
He became a little child;
I a child and thou a lamb,
We are callèd by his name.
Little Lamb, God bless thee.
Little Lamb, God bless thee.   20

William Blake (1757–1827)

205. The Tiger

Tiger! Tiger! burning bright
In the forests of the night,

What immortal hand or eye
Could frame thy fearful symmetry?

In what distant deeps or skies   5
Burnt the fire of thine eyes?
On what wings dare he aspire?
What the hand dare seize the fire?

And what shoulder, and what art,
Could twist the sinews of thy heart?   10
And when thy heart began to beat,
What dread hand forged thy dread feet?

What the hammer? what the chain?
In what furnace was thy brain?
What the anvil? what dread grasp   15
Dare its deadly terrors clasp?

When the stars threw down their spears,
And watered heaven with their tears,
Did he smile his work to see?
Did he who made the Lamb make thee?   20

Tiger! Tiger! burning bright
In the forests of the night,
What immortal hand or eye
Dare frame thy fearful symmetry?

William Blake (1757–1827)

206. Low Barometer

The south wind strengthens to a gale,
Across the moon the clouds fly fast,
The house is smitten as with a flail,
The chimney shudders to the blast.

On such a night, when air has loosed   5
Its guardian grasp on blood and brain,
Old terrors then of god or ghost
Creep from their caves to life again;

And reason kens he herits° in   inherits
A haunted house. Tenants unknown   10
Assert their squalid lease of sin
With earlier title than his own.

Unbodied presences, the packed
Pollution and remorse of time,
Slipped from oblivion, reenact   15
The horrors of unhouseled° crime.   unforgiven

Some men would quell the thing with prayer
Whose sightless footsteps pad the floor,
Whose fearful trespass mounts the stair
Or bursts the locked forbidden door.   20

Some have seen corpses long interred
Escape from hallowing control,
Pale charnel forms—nay, ev'n have heard
The shrilling of a troubled soul,

That wanders till the dawn hath crossed   25
The dolorous dark, or earth hath wound
Closer her storm-spread cloak, and thrust
The baleful phantoms under ground.

Robert Bridges (1844–1930)

207. The Dead

These hearts were woven of human joys and cares,
    Washed marvelously with sorrow, swift to mirth.
The years had given them kindness. Dawn was theirs,
    And sunset, and the colors of the earth.
These had seen movement, and heard music; known   5
    Slumber and waking; loved; gone proudly friended;
Felt the quick stir of wonder; sat alone;
    Touched flowers and furs and cheeks. All this is ended.

There are waters blown by changing winds to laughter
And lit by the rich skies, all day. And after,   10
    Frost, with a gesture, stays the winds that dance
And wandering loveliness. He leaves a white
    Unbroken glory, a gathered radiance,
A width, a shining peace, under the night.

Rupert Brooke (1887–1915)

208. If thou must love me

If thou must love me, let it be for naught
Except for love's sake only. Do not say

"I love her for her smile—her look—her way
Of speaking gently—for a trick of thought
That falls in well with mine, and certes brought   5
A sense of pleasant ease on such a day"—
For these things in themselves, Beloved, may
Be changed, or change for thee—and love, so wrought,
May be unwrought so. Neither love me for
Thine own dear pity's wiping my cheeks dry—   10
A creature might forget to weep, who bore
Thy comfort long, and lose thy love thereby!
But love me for love's sake, that evermore
Thou mayst love on, through love's eternity.

Elizabeth Barrett Browning (1806–1861)

209. Good Times

My Daddy has paid the rent
and the insurance man is gone
and the lights is back on
and my uncle Brud has hit
for one dollar straight   5
and they is good times
good times
good times

My Mama has made bread
and Grampaw has come   10
and everybody is drunk
and dancing in the kitchen
and singing in the kitchen
oh these is good times
good times   15
good times

oh children think about the
good times

Lucille Clifton (b. 1936)

210. The Lost Baby Poem

the time i dropped your almost body down
down to meet the waters under the city
and run one with the sewage to the sea

what did i know about waters rushing back
what did i know about drowning   5
or being drowned

you would have been born into winter
in the year of the disconnected gas
and no car   we would have made the thin
walk over Genesee Hill into Canada wind   10
to watch you slip like ice into strangers' hands
you would have fallen naked as snow into winter
if you were here i could tell you these
and some other things

if i am ever less than a mountain   15
for your definite brothers and sisters
let the rivers pour over my head
let the sea take me for a spiller
of seas   let black men call me stranger
always   for your never named sake   20

Lucille Clifton (b. 1936)

211. Kubla Khan

In Xanadu did Kubla Khan
A stately pleasure-dome decree:
Where Alph, the sacred river, ran
Through caverns measureless to man
  Down to a sunless sea.   5
So twice five miles of fertile ground
With walls and towers were girdled round:
And here were gardens bright with sinuous rills,
Where blossomed many an incense-bearing tree;
And here were forests ancient as the hills,   10
Enfolding sunny spots of greenery.

But oh! that deep romantic chasm which slanted
Down the green hill athwart a cedarn cover!
A savage place! as holy and enchanted
As e'er beneath a waning moon was haunted   15
By woman wailing for her demon-lover!
And from this chasm, with ceaseless turmoil seething,
As if this earth in fast thick pants were breathing,
A mighty fountain momently was forced:

Amid whose swift half-intermitted burst   20
Huge fragments vaulted like rebounding hail,
Or chaffy grain beneath the thresher's flail:
And 'mid these dancing rocks at once and ever
It flung up momently the sacred river.
Five miles meandering with a mazy motion   25
Through wood and dale the sacred river ran,
Then reached the caverns measureless to man,
And sank in tumult to a lifeless ocean:
And 'mid this tumult Kubla heard from far
Ancestral voices prophesying war!   30

   The shadow of the dome of pleasure
   Floated midway on the waves;
   Where was heard the mingled measure
   From the fountain and the caves.
It was a miracle of rare device,   35
A sunny pleasure-dome with caves of ice!

   A damsel with a dulcimer
   In a vision once I saw:
   It was an Abyssinian maid,
   And on her dulcimer she played,   40
   Singing of Mount Abora.
   Could I revive within me
   Her symphony and song,
To such a deep delight, 'twould win me,
That with music loud and long,   45
I would build that dome in air,
That sunny dome! those caves of ice!
And all who heard should see them there,
And all should cry, Beware! Beware!
His flashing eyes, his floating hair!   50
Weave a circle round him thrice,
And close your eyes with holy dread,
For he on honey-dew hath fed,
And drunk the milk of Paradise.

Samuel Taylor Coleridge (1772–1834)

212. Money

   At first it will seem tame,
   willing to be domesticated.

It will nest
in your pocket
or curl up in a corner   5
reciting softly to itself
the names of the presidents.

It will delight your friends,
shake hands with men
like a dog and lick   10
the legs of women.

But like an amoeba
it makes love
in secret
only to itself.   15

Fold it frequently;
it needs exercise.

Water it every three days
and it will repay you
with displays of affection.   20

Then one day when you think
you are its master
it will turn its head
as if for a kiss
and bite you gently   25
on the hand.

There will be no pain
but in thirty seconds
the poison will reach your heart.

                              Victor Contoski (b. 1936)

213. The Listeners

"Is there anybody there?" said the Traveler,
    Knocking on the moonlit door;
And his horse in the silence champed the grasses
    Of the forest's ferny floor:
And a bird flew up out of the turret,   5
    Above the Traveler's head:
And he smote upon the door again a second time;

"Is there anybody there?" he said.
But no one descended to the Traveler;
    No head from the leaf-fringed sill   10
Leaned over and looked into his grey eyes,
    Where he stood perplexed and still.
But only a host of phantom listeners
    That dwelt in the lone house then
Stood listening in the quiet of the moonlight   15
    To that voice from the world of men:
Stood thronging the faint moonbeams on the dark stair,
    That goes down to the empty hall,
Hearkening in an air stirred and shaken
    By the lonely Traveler's call.   20
And he felt in his heart their strangeness,
    Their stillness answering his cry,
While his horse moved, cropping the dark turf,
    'Neath the starred and leafy sky;
For he suddenly smote on the door, even   25
    Louder, and lifted his head:—
"Tell them I came, and no one answered,
    That I kept my word," he said.
Never the least stir made the listeners,
    Though every word he spake   30
Fell echoing through the shadowiness of the still house
    From the one man left awake:
Ay, they heard his foot upon the stirrup,
    And the sound of iron on stone,
And how the silence surged softly backward,   35
    When the plunging hoofs were gone.

Walter de la Mare (1873–1956)

214. A light exists in spring

    A light exists in spring
    Not present on the year
    At any other period.
    When March is scarcely here

    A color stands abroad   5
    On solitary fields
    That science cannot overtake
    But human nature feels.

It waits upon the lawn,
It shows the furthest tree   10
Upon the furthest slope you know.
It almost speaks to you.

Then as horizons step
Or noons report away,
Without the formula of sound   15
It passes, and we stay—

A quality of loss
Affecting our content
As trade had suddenly encroached
Upon a sacrament.   20

Emily Dickinson (1830–1886)

215. A narrow fellow in the grass

A narrow fellow in the grass
Occasionally rides—
You may have met him? Did you not,
His notice instant is:

The grass divides as with a comb,   5
A spotted shaft is seen,
And then it closes at your feet
And opens further on.

He likes a boggy acre,
A floor too cool for corn,   10
But when a boy, and barefoot,
I more than once at noon

Have passed, I thought, a whip-lash
Unbraiding in the sun,
When, stooping to secure it,   15
It wrinkled, and was gone.

Several of nature's people
I know, and they know me;
I feel for them a transport
Of cordiality;   20

But never met this fellow,
Attended or alone,
Without a tighter breathing
And zero at the bone.

Emily Dickinson (1830–1886)

216. There's a certain slant of light

There's a certain slant of light,
Winter afternoons,
That oppresses like the heft
Of cathedral tunes.

Heavenly hurt it gives us.   5
We can find no scar
But internal difference
Where the meanings are.

None may teach it any—
'Tis the seal despair,   10
An imperial affliction
Sent us of the air.

When it comes the landscape listens,
Shadows hold their breath.
When it goes 'tis like the distance   15
On the look of death.

Emily Dickinson (1830–1886)

217. The Lipstick on the Mirror

For years the Mirror reported her doings
With every appearance of respect:
What is the Wicked Queen wearing tonight?
Where did she buy her adorable shoes?
How large are her sapphires? How rare   5
Her pearls? Girls throughout the realm
Would lap it up, gazing in their lesser
Mirrors to see themselves in royal attire,
Diadems of diamonds replacing buns

And braids. Her teeth and décolletage   10
Were the envy of women half her age,
Whose compact mirrors would whisper:
Crone, you'd seem chiseled of the same Parian,
With a milder soap, a better dentrifice.
Try these. Buy this. Inhale her fragrance.   15
Industries sprang up like bramble. Families
Grew rich from the sale of ribbons and laces,
Enhancers and foundation creams,
Hosiery and bras, as consumers, enchanted,
Near and far, lavished endearments   20
On softer skin, more sparkling eyes.
In Bogotá, in Marrakesh, among the Slovaks
and the Esths, the face of the distant
Sovereign began to melt and coalesce
With the faces of all women fair and rich: 25
Movie starlets, heiresses, cruel
Dictatrices,° anchorwomen, teen murderesses   female dictators
Able to sell their tales to Hollywood.
In powders and vials the Wicked Queen's
Essence was suffused like a scentless gas   30
Throughout her realm, democratizing
Vanity. Ah, but still, insatiate,
She sits before her Mirror and crimson lips
Tense in a smile to ask her confidante
Who is fairest of them all, and still the lips   35
In the silvered glass reply, "Thou, Majesty, thou."

Tom Disch (b. 1940)

218. The Good-Morrow

I wonder, by my troth, what thou and I
Did till we loved? were we not weaned till then,
But sucked on country pleasures childishly?
Or snorted we in the seven sleepers' den?
'Twas so; but this, all pleasures fancies be.   5
If ever any beauty I did see,
Which I desired, and got, 'twas but a dream of thee.

And now good-morrow to our waking souls,
Which watch not one another out of fear;
For love all love of other sights controls,   10

And makes one little room an everywhere.
Let sea-discoverers to new worlds have gone;
Let maps to other,° worlds on worlds have shown;   others
Let us possess one world; each hath one, and is one.

My face in thine eye, thine in mine appears,   15
And true plain hearts do in the faces rest;
Where can we find two better hemispheres
Without sharp north, without declining west?
Whatever dies was not mixed equally;
If our two loves be one, or thou and I   20
Love so alike that none can slacken, none can die.

                          John Donne (1572–1631)

(4) *seven sleepers' den:* a cave where, according to Christian legend, seven youths escaped persecution and slept for two centuries.

219. Song: Go and catch a falling star

Go and catch a falling star,
  Get with child a mandrake root,
Tell me where all past years are,
  Or who cleft the devil's foot,
Teach me to hear mermaids singing,   5
  Or to keep off envy's stinging,
      And find
      What wind
Serves to advance an honest mind.

If thou be'st born to strange sights,   10
  Things invisible to see,
Ride ten thousand days and nights,
  Till age snow white hairs on thee,
Thou, when thou return'st, wilt tell me
  All strange wonders that befell thee,   15
      And swear
      No where
Lives a woman true and fair.

If thou find'st one, let me know;
  Such a pilgrimage were sweet.   20
Yet do not; I would not go,
  Though at next door we might meet.

> Though she were true when you met her,
> And last till you write your letter,
>   Yet she   25
>   Will be
> False, ere I come, to two or three.

John Donne (1572–1631)

(2) *mandrake:* supposed to resemble a human being because of its forked root.

220. The Triple Fool

> I am two fools, I know,
>   For loving, and for saying so
>   In whining poetry.
> But where's the wiseman that would not be I
>   If she did not deny?   5
> Then, as the earth's inward, narrow, crooked lanes
> Do purge sea water's fretful salt away,
>   I thought if I could draw my pains
> Through rhyme's vexations, I should them allay.
> Grief brought to numbers° cannot be so fierce,   verse 10
> For he tames it that fetters it in verse.
>
>   But when I have done so,
>   Some man, his art and voice to show,
>   Doth set and sing my pain,
> And by delighting many, frees again   15
>   Grief, which verse did restrain.
> To love and grief tribute of verse belongs,
> But not of such which pleases when 'tis read;°   read aloud
>   Both are increasèd by such songs,
> For both their triumphs so are publishèd.   20
> And I, which was two fools, do so grow three.
> Who are a little wise, the best fools be.

John Donne (1572–1631)

221. Vergissmeinnicht

> Three weeks gone and the combatants gone,
> returning over the nightmare ground
> we found the place again, and found
> the soldier sprawling in the sun.

The frowning barrel of his gun   5
overshadowing. As we came on
that day, he hit my tank with one
like the entry of a demon.

Look. Here in the gunpit spoil
the dishonored picture of his girl   10
who has put: *Steffi.*° *Vergissmeinnicht*   a girl's name
in a copybook gothic script.

We see him almost with content
abased, and seeming to have paid
and mocked at by his own equipment   15
that's hard and good when he's decayed.

But she would weep to see today
how on his skin the swart flies move;
the dust upon the paper eye
and the burst stomach like a cave.   20

For here the lover and killer are mingled
who had one body and one heart.
And death who had the soldier singled
has done the lover mortal hurt.

Keith Douglas (1920–1944)

The German title means "Forget me not." The author, an English poet, fought with a
tank battalion in World War II.

222. The Colonel

What you have heard is true. I was in his house. His wife carried a tray of
coffee and sugar. His daughter filed her nails, his son went out for the
night. There were daily papers, pet dogs, a pistol on the cushion beside
him. The moon swung bare on its black cord over the house. On the tele-
vision was a cop show. It was in English. Broken bottles were embedded
in the walls around the house to scoop the kneecaps from a man's legs or
cut his hands to lace. On the windows there were gratings like those in
liquor stores. We had dinner, rack of lamb, good wine, a gold bell was on
the table for calling the maid. The maid brought green mangoes, salt, a
type of bread. I was asked how I enjoyed the country. There was a brief
commercial in Spanish. His wife took everything away. There was some
talk then of how difficult it had become to govern. The parrot said hello
on the terrace. The colonel told it to shut up, and pushed himself from

the table. My friend said to me with his eyes: say nothing. The colonel returned with a sack used to bring groceries home. He spilled many human
ears on the table. They were like dried peach halves. There is no other way
to say this. He took one of them in his hands, shook it in our faces, dropped
it into a water glass. It came alive there. I am tired of fooling around he
said. As for the rights of anyone, tell your people they can go fuck themselves. He swept the ears to the floor with his arm and held the last of his
wine in the air. Something for your poetry, no? he said. Some of the ears
on the floor caught this scrap of his voice. Some of the ears on the floor
were pressed to the ground.

May 1978

Carolyn Forché (b. 1950)

223. Birches

When I see birches bend to left and right
Across the lines of straighter darker trees,
I like to think some boy's been swinging them.
But swinging doesn't bend them down to stay
As ice-storms do. Often you must have seen them   5
Loaded with ice a sunny winter morning
After a rain. They click upon themselves
As the breeze rises, and turn many-colored
As the stir cracks and crazes their enamel.
Soon the sun's warmth makes them shed crystal shells   10
Shattering and avalanching on the snow-crust—
Such heaps of broken glass to sweep away
You'd think the inner dome of heaven had fallen.
They are dragged to the withered bracken by the load,
And they seem not to break; though once they are bowed   15
So low for long, they never right themselves:
You may see their trunks arching in the woods
Years afterwards, trailing their leaves on the ground
Like girls on hands and knees that throw their hair
Before them over their heads to dry in the sun.   20
But I was going to say when Truth broke in
With all her matter-of-fact about the ice-storm
I should prefer to have some boy bend them
As he went out and in to fetch the cows—
Some boy too far from town to learn baseball,   25
Whose only play was what he found himself,
Summer or winter, and could play alone.

One by one he subdued his father's trees
By riding them down over and over again
Until he took the stiffness out of them,   30
And not one but hung limp, not one was left
For him to conquer. He learned all there was
To learn about not launching out too soon
And so not carrying the tree away
Clear to the ground. He always kept his poise   35
To the top branches, climbing carefully
With the same pains you use to fill a cup
Up to the brim, and even above the brim.
Then he flung outward, feet first, with a swish,
Kicking his way down through the air to the ground.   40
So was I once myself a swinger of birches.
And so I dream of going back to be.
It's when I'm weary of considerations,
And life is too much like a pathless wood
Where your face burns and tickles with the cobwebs   45
Broken across it, and one eye is weeping
From a twig's having lashed across it open.
I'd like to get away from earth awhile
And then come back to it and begin over.
May no fate willfully misunderstand me   50
And half grant what I wish and snatch me away
Not to return. Earth's the right place for love:
I don't know where it's likely to go better.
I'd like to go by climbing a birch tree,
And climb black branches up a snow-white trunk   55
Toward heaven, till the tree could bear no more,
But dipped its top and set me down again.
That would be good both going and coming back.
One could do worse than be a swinger of birches.

                                        Robert Frost (1874–1963)

224. Desert Places

Snow falling and night falling fast, oh, fast
In a field I looked into going past,
And the ground almost covered smooth in snow,
But a few weeds and stubble showing last.

The woods around it have it—it is theirs.   5
All animals are smothered in their lairs.

I am too absent-spirited to count;
The loneliness includes me unawares.

And lonely as it is that loneliness
Will be more lonely ere it will be less—   10
A blanker whiteness of benighted snow
With no expression, nothing to express.

They cannot scare me with their empty spaces
Between stars—on stars where no human race is.
I have it in me so much nearer home   15
To scare myself with my own desert places.

Robert Frost (1874–1963)

225. Mending Wall

Something there is that doesn't love a wall,
That sends the frozen-ground-swell under it,
And spills the upper boulders in the sun;
And makes gaps even two can pass abreast.
The work of hunters is another thing: 5
I have come after them and made repair
Where they have left not one stone on a stone,
But they would have the rabbit out of hiding,
To please the yelping dogs. The gaps I mean,
No one has seen them made or heard them made,   10
But at spring mending-time we find them there.
I let my neighbor know beyond the hill;
And on a day we meet to walk the line
And set the wall between us once again.
We keep the wall between us as we go.   15
To each the boulders that have fallen to each.
And some are loaves and some so nearly balls
We have to use a spell to make them balance: ·
"Stay where you are until our backs are turned!"
We wear our fingers rough with handling them.   20
Oh, just another kind of outdoor game,
One on a side. It comes to little more:
There where it is we do not need the wall:
He is all pine and I am apple orchard.
My apple trees will never get across   25
And eat the cones under his pines, I tell him.
He only says, "Good fences make good neighbors."
Spring is the mischief in me, and I wonder

If I could put a notion in his head:
"*Why* do they make good neighbors? Isn't it   30
Where there are cows? But here there are no cows.
Before I built a wall I'd ask to know
What I was walling in or walling out,
And to whom I was like to give offense.
Something there is that doesn't love a wall,   35
That wants it down." I could say "Elves" to him,
But it's not elves exactly, and I'd rather
He said it for himself. I see him there,
Bringing a stone grasped firmly by the top
In each hand, like an old-stone savage armed.   40
He moves in darkness as it seems to me,
Not of woods only and the shade of trees.
He will not go behind his father's saying,
And he likes having thought of it so well
He says again, "Good fences make good neighbors."   45

Robert Frost (1874–1963)

226. Never Again Would Birds' Song Be the Same

He would declare and could himself believe
That the birds there in all the garden round
From having heard the daylong voice of Eve
Had added to their own an oversound,
Her tone of meaning but without the words.   5
Admittedly an eloquence so soft
Could only have had an influence on birds
When call or laughter carried it aloft.
Be that as may be, she was in their song.
Moreover her voice upon their voices crossed   10
Had now persisted in the woods so long
That probably it never would be lost.
Never again would birds' song be the same.
And to do that to birds was why she came.

Robert Frost (1874–1963)

227. The Oven Bird

There is a singer everyone has heard,
Loud, a mid-summer and a mid-wood bird,
Who makes the solid tree trunks sound again.

He says that leaves are old and that for flowers
Mid-summer is to spring as one to ten.   5
He says the early petal-fall is past,
When pear and cherry blooms went down in showers
On sunny days a moment overcast;
And comes that other fall we name the fall.
He says the highway dust is over all.   10
The bird would cease and be as other birds
But that he knows in singing not to sing.
The question that he asks in all but words
Is what to make of a diminished thing.

Robert Frost (1874–1963)

228. Pushing

Me and my brother would jump off the porch
mornings for a better view of the cars
that raced around the corner up Olds Ave.,
naming the make and year; this was '58
and his voice still young enough to wait for   5
how I'd say the names right to the air.
Cold mornings in Lansing we'd stop the mile
to school in the high-priced grocery nearly there
and the owner, maybe a decent White man
whose heavy dark hair and far Lebanese look   10
had caught too many kids at his candy,
would follow us down the aisles and say,
"I know what you boys is up to, big-eyed
and such, so you better be going your way—
buy something or else you got to leave."   15
We'd rattle the pennies we had and go
but coming home buy some nutchews to stay
and try his nerve again, because we didn't steal
but warmed ourselves till Ray would ask me why—
till, like big brothers will, one day I guessed,   20
"Some things you do because you want to.
Some things you do because you can't."
In what midwest warmth there was we'd laugh,
throw some snowballs high where the sun was
breaking up the clouds.   25

Christopher Gilbert (b. 1945)

229. Nikki-Rosa

childhood remembrances are always a drag
if you're Black
you always remember things like living in Woodlawn
with no inside toilet
and if you become famous or something   5
they never talk about how happy you were to have your mother
all to your self and
how good the water felt when you got your bath from one of those
big tubs that folk in chicago barbecue in
and somehow when you talk about home   10
it never gets across how much you
understood their feelings
as the whole family attended meetings about Hollydale
and even though you remember
your biographers never understand   15
your father's pain as he sells his stock
and another dream goes
and though you're poor it isn't poverty that
concerns you
and though they fought a lot   20
it isn't your father's drinking that makes any difference
but only that everybody is together and you
and your sister have happy birthdays and very good christmasses
and I really hope no white person ever has cause to write about me
because they never understand Black love is Black wealth
    and they'll   25
probably talk about my hard childhood and never understand that
all the while I was quite happy.

Nikki Giovanni (b. 1943)

230. The Allegory of the Wolf Boy

The causes are in Time; only their issue
Is bodied in the flesh, the finite powers.
And how to guess he hides in that firm tissue
Seeds of division? At tennis and at tea
Upon the gentle lawn, he is not ours,   5
But plays us in a sad duplicity.

Tonight the boy, still boy open and blond,
Breaks from the house, wedges his clothes between

Two moulded garden urns, and goes beyond
His understanding, through the dark and dust: 10
Fields of sharp stubble, abandoned by machine
To the whirring enmity of insect lust.

As yet ungolden in the dense, hot night
The spikes enter his feet: he seeks the moon,
Which, with the touch of its infertile light,   15
Shall loose desires hoarded against his will
By the long urging of the afternoon.
Slowly the hard rim shifts above the hill.

White in the beam he stops, faces it square,
And the same instant leaping from the ground   20
Feels the familiar itch of close dark hair;
Then, clean exception to the natural laws,
Only to instinct and the moon being bound,
Drops on four feet. Yet he has bleeding paws.

Thom Gunn (b. 1929)

231. On the Move

The blue jay scuffling in the bushes follows
Some hidden purpose, and the gust of birds
That spurts across the field, the wheeling swallows,
Has nested in the trees and undergrowth.
Seeking their instinct, or their poise, or both,   5
One moves with an uncertain violence
Under the dust thrown by a baffled sense
Or the dull thunder of approximate words.

On motorcycles, up the road, they come:
Small, black, as flies hanging in heat, the Boys,   10
Until the distance throws them forth, their hum
Bulges to thunder held by calf and thigh.
In goggles, donned impersonality,
In gleaming jackets trophied with the dust,
They strap in doubt—by hiding it, robust—   15
And almost hear a meaning in their noise.

Exact conclusion of their hardiness
Has no shape yet, but from known whereabouts
They ride, direction where the tires press.
They scare a flight of birds across the field: 20

Much that is natural, to the will must yield.
Men manufacture both machine and soul,
And use what they imperfectly control
To dare a future from the taken routes.

It is a part solution, after all.   25
One is not necessarily discord
On earth; or damned because, half animal,
One lacks direct instinct, because one wakes
Afloat on movement that divides and breaks.
One joins the movement in a valueless world,   30
Choosing it, till, both hurler and the hurled,
One moves as well, always toward, toward.

A minute holds them, who have come to go:
The self-defined, astride the created will
They burst away; the towns they travel through   35
Are home for neither bird nor holiness,
For birds and saints complete their purposes.
At worst, one is in motion; and at best,
Reaching no absolute, in which to rest,
One is always nearer by not keeping still.   40

Thom Gunn (b. 1929)

232. Snow White and the Seven Deadly Sins

Good Catholic girl, she didn't mind the cleaning.
All of her household chores, at first, were small
And hardly labors one could find demeaning.
One's duty was one's refuge, after all.

And if she had her doubts at certain moments   5
And once confessed them to the Father, she
Was instantly referred to texts in Romans
And Peter's First Epistle, chapter III.

Years passed. More sinful every day, the *Seven*
Breakfasted, grabbed their pitchforks, donned their horns,   10
And sped to contravene the hopes of heaven,
Sowing the neighbors' lawns with tares and thorns.

She set to work. *Pride*'s wall of looking glasses
Ogled her dimly, smeared with prints of lips;
Lust's magazines lay strewn, bare tits and asses   15
Weighted by his "devices"—chains, cuffs, whips.

Gluttony's empties covered half the table,
Mingling with *Avarice*'s cards and chips,
And she'd been told to sew a Bill Blass label
Inside the blazer *Envy*'d bought at Gyp's.   20

She knelt to the cold master bathroom floor as
If a petitioner before the Pope,
Retrieving several pairs of *Sloth*'s soiled drawers,
A sweat-sock and a cake of hairy soap.

Then, as she wiped the Windex from the mirror   25
She noticed, and the vision made her cry,
How much she'd grayed and paled, and how much clearer
Festered the bruise of *Wrath* beneath her eye.

"No poisoned apple needed for this Princess,"
She murmured, making X's with her thumb.   30
A car door slammed, bringing her to her senses:
Ho-hum. Ho-hum. It's home from work we come.

And she was out the window in a second,
In time to see a *Handsome Prince,* of course,
Who, spying her distressed condition, beckoned   35
For her to mount (What else?) his snow-white horse.

Impeccably he spoke. His smile was glowing.
So debonair! So charming! And so *Male.*
She took a step, reversed and without slowing
Beat it to St. Anne's where she took the veil.   40

                                        R. S. Gwynn (b. 1948)

233. The Red Hat

It started before Christmas. Now our son
officially walks to school alone.
Semi-alone, it's accurate to say:
I or his father track him on the way.
He walks up on the east side of West End,   5
we on the west side. Glances can extend
(and do) across the street; not eye contact.
Already ties are feeling and not fact.
Straus Park is where these parallel paths part;
he goes alone from there. The watcher's heart   10
stretches, elastic in its love and fear,

toward him as we see him disappear,
striding briskly. Where two weeks ago,
holding a hand, he'd dawdle, dreamy, slow,
he now is hustled forward by the pull   15
of something far more powerful than school.

The mornings we turn back to are no more
than forty minutes longer than before,
but they feel vastly different—flimsy, strange,
wavering in the eddies of this change,   20
empty, unanchored, perilously light
since the red hat vanished from our sight.

Rachel Hadas (b. 1948)

234. Channel Firing

That night your great guns, unawares,
Shook all our coffins as we lay,
And broke the chancel window-squares,
We thought it was the Judgment-day

And sat upright. While drearisome   5
Arose the howl of wakened hounds:
The mouse let fall the altar-crumb,
The worms drew back into the mounds,

The glebe cow drooled. Till God called, "No;
It's gunnery practice out at sea   10
Just as before you went below;
The world is as it used to be:

"All nations striving strong to make
Red war yet redder. Mad as hatters
They do no more for Christès sake   15
Than you who are helpless in such matters.

"That this is not the judgment-hour
For some of them's a blessed thing,
For if it were they'd have to scour
Hell's floor for so much threatening. . . .   20

"Ha, ha. It will be warmer when
I blow the trumpet (if indeed
I ever do; for you are men,
and rest eternal sorely need)."

So down we lay again. "I wonder,   25
Will the world ever saner be,"
Said one, "than when He sent us under
In our indifferent century!"

And many a skeleton shook his head.
"Instead of preaching forty year,"   30
My neighbor Parson Thirdly said,
"I wish I had stuck to pipes and beer."

Again the guns disturbed the hour,
Roaring their readiness to avenge,
As far inland as Stourton Tower,   35
And Camelot, and starlit Stonehenge.

April 1914

Thomas Hardy (1840–1928)

(35–36) *Stourton Tower:* memorial at the spot where Alfred the Great resisted the invading Danes in 879; *Camelot:* legendary capital of Arthur's kingdom; *Stonehenge:* mysterious circle of huge stones erected in Wiltshire by very early inhabitants of Britain. The three references move backward in time through the historic, the legendary, and the prehistoric.

235. The Darkling Thrush

I leant upon a coppice gate
    When Frost was specter-gray,
And Winter's dregs made desolate
    The weakening eye of day.
The tangled bine-stems scored the sky   5
    Like strings of broken lyres,
And all mankind that haunted nigh
    Had sought their household fires.

The land's sharp features seemed to be
    The Century's corpse outleant,   10
His crypt the cloudy canopy,
    The wind his death-lament.
The ancient pulse of germ and birth
    Was shrunken hard and dry,
And every spirit upon earth   15
    Seemed fervorless as I.

At once a voice arose among
    The bleak twigs overhead

    In a full-hearted evensong
        Of joy illimited;   20
    An aged thrush, frail, gaunt, and small,
        In blast-beruffled plume,
    Had chosen thus to fling his soul
        Upon the growing gloom.

    So little cause for carolings   25
        Of such ecstatic sound
    Was written on terrestrial things
        Afar or nigh around,
    That I could think there trembled through
        His happy good-night air   30
    Some blessed Hope, whereof he knew
        And I was unaware.

31 December 1900

                           Thomas Hardy (1840–1928)

236. Dream of Fair Women

    The lady gave her trust, an apple fell,
    And guilt began, and pain, and death as well,
    In stories that we tell.

    The lady gave her trust, the heavens shone
    Upon a maiden mother, one alone   5
    In ballads we have known.

    O first and second Eve, O dream of men
    Believing life is good or might have been
    And that we live again!

    A sleeping beauty dreams her lover's grace,   10
    Opens her eyes upon a human face,
    Keeps up the human race.

                           Ann Hayes (b. 1924)

237. Redemption

    Having been tenant long to a rich Lord,
        Not thriving, I resolvèd to be bold,
        And make a suit unto him, to afford

A new small-rented lease and cancel the old.
In heaven at his manor I him sought: 5
    They told me there that he was lately gone
    About some land which he had dearly bought
Long since on earth, to take possessiön.
I straight returned, and knowing his great birth,
    Sought him accordingly in great resorts;   10
    In cities, theaters, gardens, parks, and courts:
At length I heard a ragged noise and mirth
    Of thieves and murderers; there I him espied,
    Who straight, "Your suit is granted," said, and died.

George Herbert (1593–1633)

238. Riddle

From Belsen a crate of gold teeth,
from Dachau a mountain of shoes,
from Auschwitz a skin lampshade.
Who killed the Jews?

Not I, cries the typist,   5
not I, cries the engineer,
not I, cries Adolf Eichmann,
not I, cries Albert Speer.

My friend Fritz Nova lost his father—
a petty official had to choose.   10
My friend Lou Abrahms lost his brother.
Who killed the Jews?

David Nova swallowed gas,
Hyman Abrahms was beaten and starved.
Some men signed their papers,   15
and some stood guard,

and some herded them in,
and some dropped the pellets,
and some spread the ashes,
and some hosed the walls,   20

and some planted the wheat,
and some poured the steel,
and some cleared the rails,
and some raised the cattle.

Some smelled the smoke,   25
some just heard the news.
Were they Germans? Were they Nazis?
Were they human? Who killed the Jews?

The stars will remember the gold,
the sun will remember the shoes,   30
the moon will remember the skin.
But who killed the Jews?

William Heyen (b. 1940)

(1–3) *Belsen, Dachau, Auschwitz:* sites of Nazi concentration camps. (7) *Adolf Eichmann* (1906–1962), Nazi official who organized anti-Jewish activities, especially the shipping of Jews to the concentration camps. (8) *Albert Speer* (1905–1981), Hitler's chief architect and later minister of armaments whose efficient methods greatly improved the production of war materials.

239. Two Different Things

A coyote paces the enclosure,
his eyes looking toward the hills.
His paws had been stung by barbed wire and broken
    glass
until the pads were cracked and bloodied.
He was crying to the moon when you found him.   5
You brought fresh water, healed his paws,
And now you say you love him.

While he paces that enclosure
You cannot be free.

Part of his beauty   10
is the dream in his eyes of different places.
Whatever is human feels the need to possess
that, to tame that, to say: *he's mine,*
if only for a moment, and then let go.
He might come back: 15
depending less on gratitude and love
than on nostalgia for old places,
a familiar voice.

In the meantime, there's you on one side,
him on the other,   20
wanting two different things—always.

Something in you wishes he could be free
with your fence still around him.
Something in him will pull and tug
long after he leaves your hills.   25

Michael Hogan (b. 1943)

240. To an Athlete Dying Young

The time you won your town the race
We chaired you through the market-place;
Man and boy stood cheering by,
And home we brought you shoulder-high.

Today, the road all runners come,   5
Shoulder-high, we bring you home,
And set you at your threshold down,
Townsman of a stiller town.

Smart lad, to slip betimes away
From fields where glory does not stay   10
And early though the laurel grows
It withers quicker than the rose.

Eyes the shady night has shut
Cannot see the record cut,
And silence sounds no worse than cheers   15
After earth has stopped the ears:

Now you will not swell the rout
Of lads that wore their honors out,
Runners whom renown outran
And the name died before the man.   20

So set, before its echoes fade,
The fleet foot on the sill of shade,
And hold to the low lintel up
The still-defended challenge-cup.

And round that early-laureled head   25
Will flock to gaze the strengthless dead,
And find unwithered on its curls
The garland briefer than a girl's.

A. E. Housman (1859–1936)

241. Bredon Hill

In summertime on Bredon
  The bells they sound so clear;
Round both the shires they ring them
  In steeples far and near,
  A happy noise to hear.   5

Here of a Sunday morning
  My love and I would lie,
And see the colored counties,
  And hear the larks so high
  About us in the sky.   10

The bells would ring to call her
  In valleys miles away:
"Come all to church, good people;
  Good people, come and pray."
  But here my love would stay.   15

And I would turn and answer
  Among the springing thyme,
"Oh, peal upon our wedding,
  And we will hear the chime,
  And come to church in time."   20

But when the snows at Christmas
  On Bredon top were strown,
My love rose up so early
  And stole out unbeknown
  And went to church alone.   25

They tolled the one bell only,
  Groom there was none to see,
The mourners followed after,
  And so to church went she,
  And would not wait for me.   30

The bells they sound on Bredon,
  And still the steeples hum.
"Come all to church, good people,"—
  Oh, noisy bells, be dumb;
  I hear you, I will come.   35

A. E. Housman (1859–1936)

242. Thistles

Against the rubber tongues of cows and the hoeing hands of men
Thistles spike the summer air
Or crackle open under a blue-black pressure.

Every one a revengeful burst
Of resurrection, a grasped fistful   5
Of splintered weapons and Icelandic frost thrust up

From the underground stain of a decayed Viking.
They are like pale hair and the gutturals of dialects.
Every one manages a plume of blood.

Then they grow grey, like men.   10
Mown down, it is a feud. Their sons appear,
Stiff with weapons, fighting back over the same ground.

Ted Hughes (b. 1930)

243. The Freaks at Spurgin Road Field

The dim boy claps because the others clap.
The polite word, handicapped, is muttered in the stands.
Isn't it wrong, the way the mind moves back.

One whole day I sit, contrite, dirt, L.A.
Union Station, '46, sweating through last night.   5
The dim boy claps because the others clap.

Score, 5 to 3. Pitcher fading badly in the heat.
Isn't it wrong to be or not be spastic?
Isn't it wrong, the way the mind moves back.

I'm laughing at a neighbor girl beaten to scream   10
by a savage father and I'm ashamed to look.
The dim boy claps because the others clap.

The score is always close, the rally always short.
I've left more wreckage than a quake.
Isn't it wrong, the way the mind moves back.   15

The afflicted never cheer in unison.
Isn't it wrong, the way the mind moves back
to stammering pastures where the picnic should have worked.
The dim boy claps because the others clap.

Richard Hugo (1923–1982)

244. The Death of the Ball Turret Gunner

From my mother's sleep I fell into the State,
And I hunched in its belly till my wet fur froze.
Six miles from earth, loosed from its dream of life,
I woke to black flak and the nightmare fighters.
When I died they washed me out of the turret with a hose.   5

Randall Jarrell (1914–1965)

(Title) *Ball Turret:* the poet wrote, "A ball turret was a plexiglass sphere set into the belly of a B-17 or B-24 [bomber during World War II], and inhabited by two .50 caliber machine-guns and one man, a short small man. When this gunner tracked with his machine-guns a fighter [plane] attacking from below, he revolved with the turret; hunched in his little sphere, he looked like the fetus in the womb."

245. Song: To Celia

Drink to me only with thine eyes,
    And I will pledge with mine;
Or leave a kiss but in the cup,
    And I'll not look for wine.
The thirst that from the soul doth rise   5
    Doth ask a drink divine,
But might I of Jove's nectar sup,
    I would not change for thine.

I sent thee late° a rosy wreath,   recently
    Not so much honoring thee   10
As giving it a hope that there
    It could not withered be.
But thou thereon didst only breathe,
    And sent'st it back to me;
Since when, it grows, and smells, I swear,   15
    Not of itself, but thee.

Ben Jonson (1573?–1637)

246. Warning

When I am an old woman I shall wear purple
With a red hat which doesn't go, and doesn't suit me.
And I shall spend my pension on brandy and summer gloves

And satin sandals, and say we've no money for butter.
I shall sit down on the pavement when I'm tired   5
And gobble up samples in shops and press alarm bells
And run my stick along the public railings
And make up for the sobriety of my youth.
I shall go out in my slippers in the rain
And pick the flowers in other people's gardens   10
And learn to spit.

You can wear terrible shirts and grow more fat
And eat three pounds of sausages at a go
Or only bread and pickle for a week
And hoard pens and pencils and beermats and things in boxes.   15

But now we must have clothes that keep us dry
And pay our rent and not swear in the street
And set a good example for the children.
We must have friends to dinner and read the papers.

But maybe I ought to practice a little now?   20
So people who know me are not too shocked and surprised
When suddenly I am old, and start to wear purple.

Jenny Joseph (b. 1932)

247. La Belle Dame sans Merci

A Ballad

> O, what can ail thee, knight-at-arms,
>   Alone and palely loitering?
> The sedge has withered from the lake,
>   And no birds sing.
>
> O, what can ail thee, knight-at-arms,   5
>   So haggard and so woe-begone?
> The squirrel's granary is full,
>   And the harvest's done.
>
> I see a lily on thy brow,
>   With anguish moist and fever dew;   10
> And on thy cheeks a fading rose
>   Fast withereth too.
>
> I met a lady in the meads,
>   Full beautiful—a faery's child,
> Her hair was long, her foot was light,   15
>   And her eyes were wild.

I made a garland for her head,
   And bracelets too, and fragrant zone;
She looked at me as she did love,
   And made sweet moan.   20

I set her on my pacing steed,
   And nothing else saw all day long;
For sidelong would she bend, and sing
   A faery's song.

She found me roots of relish sweet,   25
   And honey wild, and manna dew,
And sure in language strange she said—
   "I love thee true."

She took me to her elfin grot,
   And there she wept and sighed full sore,   30
And there I shut her wild wild eyes
   With kisses four.

And there she lullèd me asleep
   And there I dreamed—Ah! woe betide!
The latest dream I ever dreamed   35
   On the cold hill side.

I saw pale kings and princes too,
   Pale warriors, death-pale were they all;
They cried—"La Belle Dame sans Merci
   Hath thee in thrall!"   40

I saw their starved lips in the gloam
   With horrid warning gapèd wide,
And I awoke and found me here
   On the cold hill's side.

And this is why I sojourn here   45
   Alone and palely loitering,
Though the sedge has withered from the lake,
   And no birds sing.

                     John Keats (1795–1821)

The title means "The beautiful lady without pity."

248. Ode on a Grecian Urn

Thou still unravished bride of quietness,
   Thou foster-child of silence and slow time,

Sylvan historian, who canst thus express
A flowery tale more sweetly than our rhyme:
What leaf-fringed legend haunts about thy shape   5
Of deities or mortals, or of both,
In Tempe or the dales of Arcady?
What men or gods are these? What maidens loth?
What mad pursuit? What struggle to escape?
What pipes and timbrels? What wild ecstasy?   10

Heard melodies are sweet, but those unheard
Are sweeter; therefore, ye soft pipes, play on;
Not to the sensual ear, but, more endeared,
Pipe to the spirit ditties of no tone:
Fair youth, beneath the trees, thou canst not leave   15
Thy song, nor ever can those trees be bare;
Bold lover, never, never canst thou kiss,
Though winning near the goal—yet, do not grieve;
She cannot fade, though thou hast not thy bliss,
For ever wilt thou love, and she be fair!   20

Ah, happy, happy boughs! that cannot shed
Your leaves, nor ever bid the spring adieu;
And, happy melodist, unwearièd,
For ever piping songs for ever new;
More happy love! more happy, happy love!   25
For ever warm and still to be enjoyed,
For ever panting and for ever young;
All breathing human passion far above,
That leaves a heart high-sorrowful and cloyed,
A burning forehead, and a parching tongue.   30

Who are these coming to the sacrifice?
To what green altar, O mysterious priest,
Lead'st thou that heifer lowing at the skies,
And all her silken flanks with garlands drest?
What little town by river or sea shore,   35
Or mountain-built with peaceful citadel,
Is emptied of its folk, this pious morn?
And, little town, thy streets for evermore
Will silent be; and not a soul to tell
Why thou are desolate, can e'er return.   40

O Attic shape! Fair attitude! with brede
Of marble men and maidens overwrought,
With forest branches and the trodden weed;
Thou, silent form, dost tease us out of thought

As doth eternity: Cold Pastoral!   45
  When old age shall this generation waste,
    Thou shalt remain, in midst of other woe
  Than ours, a friend to man, to whom thou say'st,
Beauty is truth, truth beauty,—that is all
  Ye know on earth, and all ye need to know.   50

John Keats (1795—1821)

(40–50) In the 1820 edition of Keats's poems the words "Beauty is truth, truth beauty" were enclosed in quotation marks, and the poem is often reprinted that way. It is now generally agreed, however, on the basis of contemporary transcripts of Keats's poem, that Keats intended the entire last two lines to be spoken by the urn.

249. Ode to a Nightingale

My heart aches, and a drowsy numbness pains
  My sense, as though of hemlock° I had drunk,   a poison
Or emptied some dull opiate to the drains
  One minute past, and Lethe-wards had sunk:
'Tis not through envy of thy happy lot,   5
  But being too happy in thine happiness,—
    That thou, light-wingèd Dryad° of the trees,   wood nymph
      In some melodious plot
  Of beechen green, and shadows numberless,
    Singest of summer in full-throated ease.   10

O for a draught of vintage! that hath been
  Cooled a long age in the deep-delvèd earth,
Tasting of Flora° and the country green,   goddess of flowers
  Dance, and Provençal song, and sunburnt mirth!
O for a beaker full of the warm South,   15
  Full of the true, the blushful Hippocrene,
    With beaded bubbles winking at the brim,
      And purple-stainèd mouth;
  That I might drink, and leave the world unseen,
    And with thee fade away into the forest dim: 20

Fade far away, dissolve, and quite forget
  What thou among the leaves hast never known,
The weariness, the fever, and the fret
  Here, where men sit and hear each other groan;
Where palsy shakes a few, sad, last gray hairs,   25
  Where youth grows pale, and specter-thin, and dies;
    Where but to think is to be full of sorrow

And leaden-eyed despairs,
　　Where Beauty cannot keep her lustrous eyes,
　　　　Or new Love pine at them beyond tomorrow.　　　30

Away! away! for I will fly to thee,
　　Not charioted by Bacchus and his pards,
But on the viewless° wings of Poesy,　　　　　　　　invisible
　　Though the dull brain perplexes and retards:
Already with thee! tender is the night,　　　　　　　35
　　And haply the Queen-Moon is on her throne,
　　　　Clustered around by all her starry Fays;
　　　　　　But here there is no light,
　　Save what from heaven is with the breezes blown
　　　　Through verdurous glooms and winding mossy ways.　　40

I cannot see what flowers are at my feet,
　　Nor what soft incense hangs upon the boughs,
But, in embalmèd° darkness, guess each sweet　　　perfumed
　　Wherewith the seasonable mouth endows
The grass, the thicket, and the fruit-tree wild;　　　45
　　White hawthorn, and the pastoral eglantine;
　　　　Fast fading violets covered up in leaves;
　　　　　　And mid-May's eldest child,
　　The coming musk-rose, full of dewy wine,
　　　　The murmurous haunt of flies on summer eves.　　50

Darkling° I listen; and, for many a time　　　　　in darkness
　　I have been half in love with easeful Death,
Called him soft names in many a musèd rhyme,
　　To take into the air my quiet breath;
Now more than ever seems it rich to die,　　　　　55
　　To cease upon the midnight with no pain,
　　　　While thou art pouring forth thy soul abroad
　　　　　　In such an ecstasy!
　　Still wouldst thou sing, and I have ears in vain—
　　　　To thy high requiem become a sod.　　　　　60

Thou wast not born for death, immortal Bird!
　　No hungry generations tread thee down;
The voice I hear this passing night was heard
　　In ancient days by emperor and clown:
Perhaps the self-same song that found a path　　　65
　　Through the sad heart of Ruth, when, sick for home,
　　　　She stood in tears amid the alien corn;
　　　　　　The same that oft-times hath
　　Charmed magic casements, opening on the foam
　　　　Of perilous seas, in faery lands forlorn.　　　70

Forlorn! the very word is like a bell
 To toll me back from thee to my sole self!
Adieu! the fancy cannot cheat so well
 As she is famed to do, deceiving elf.
Adieu! adieu! thy plaintive anthem fades   75
 Past the near meadows, over the still stream,
  Up the hill-side; and now 'tis buried deep
   In the next valley-glades:
Was it a vision, or a waking dream?
Fled is that music:—Do I wake or sleep?   80

John Keats (1795–1821)

(4) *Lethe:* river of forgetfulness in the Greek underworld. (14) *Provençal:* Provence, a wine-growing region in southern France famous, in the Middle Ages, for troubadours. (16) *Hippocrene:* fountain of the Muses on Mt. Helicon in Greece. (32) *Bacchus . . . pards:* Bacchus, god of wine, had a chariot drawn by leopards. (66) *Ruth:* see Bible, Ruth 2.

250. The warden said to me

The warden said to me the other day
(innocently, I think), "Say, etheridge,
why come the black boys don't run off
like the white boys do?"
I lowered my jaw and scratched my head   5
and said (innocently, I think), "Well, suh,
I ain't for sure, but I reckon it's cause
we ain't got no wheres to run to."

Etheridge Knight (1933–1991)

251. The Sound of Night

And now the dark comes on, all full of chitter noise.
Birds huggermugger crowd the trees,
the air thick with their vesper cries,
and bats, snub seven-pointed kites,
skitter across the lake, swing out,   5
squeak, chirp, dip, and skim on skates
of air, and the fat frogs wake and prink
wide-lipped, noisy as ducks, drunk
on the boozy black, gloating chink-chunk.

And now on the narrow beach we defend ourselves from dark.   10
The cooking done, we build our firework
bright and hot and less for outlook
than for magic, and lie in our blankets
while night nickers around us. Crickets
chorus hallelujahs; paws, quiet   15
and quick as raindrops, play on the stones
expertly soft, run past and are gone;
fish pulse in the lake; the frogs hoarsen.

Now every voice of the hour—the known, the supposed,
    the strange,
the mindless, the witted, the never seen—   20
sing, thrum, impinge, and rearrange
endlessly; and debarred from sleep we wait
for the birds, importantly silent,
for the crease of first eye-licking light,
for the sun, lost long ago and sweet.   25
By the lake, locked black away and tight,
we lie, day creatures, overhearing night.

Maxine Kumin (b. 1925)

252. Aubade

I work all day, and get half drunk at night.
Waking at four to soundless dark, I stare.
In time the curtain-edges will grow light.
Till then I see what's really always there:
Unresting death, a whole day nearer now,   5
Making all thought impossible but how
And where and when I shall myself die.
Arid interrogation: yet the dread
Of dying, and being dead,
Flashes afresh to hold and horrify.   10

The mind blanks at the glare. Not in remorse
—The good not done, the love not given, time
Torn off unused—nor wretchedly because
An only life can take so long to climb
Clear of its wrong beginnings, and may never;   15
But at the total emptiness for ever,
The sure extinction that we travel to
And shall be lost in always. Not to be here,
Not to be anywhere,
And soon; nothing more terrible, nothing more true.   20

This is a special way of being afraid
No trick dispels. Religion used to try,
That vast moth-eaten musical brocade
Created to pretend we never die,
And specious stuff that says *No rational being*   25
Can fear a thing it will not feel, not seeing
That this is what we fear—no sight, no sound,
No touch or taste or smell, nothing to think with,
Nothing to love or link with,
The anaesthetic from which none come round.   30

And so it stays just on the edge of vision,
A small unfocused blur, a standing chill
That slows each impulse down to indecision.
Most things may never happen: this one will,
And realization of it rages out   35
In furnace-fear when we are caught without
People or drink. Courage is no good:
It means not scaring others. Being brave
Lets no one off the grave.
Death is no different whined at than withstood.   40

Slowly light strengthens, and the room takes shape.
It stands plain as a wardrobe, what we know,
Have always known, know that we can't escape,
Yet can't accept. One side will have to go.
Meanwhile telephones crouch, getting ready to ring   45
In locked-up offices, and all the uncaring
Intricate rented world begins to rouse.
The sky is white as clay, with no sun.
Work has to be done.
Postmen like doctors go from house to house.   50

Philip Larkin (1922–1985)

253. Offspring

I tried to tell her:
        This way the twig is bent.
        Born of my trunk and strengthened by my roots,
        you must stretch newgrown branches
        closer to the sun   5
        than I can reach.

I wanted to say:
    Extend my self to that far atmosphere
    only my dreams allow.

But the twig broke,   10
and yesterday I saw her
walking down an unfamiliar street,
    feet confident
    face slanted upward toward a threatening sky,
and   15
    she was smiling
    and she was
    her very free,
    her very individual,
    unpliable   20
    own.

Naomi Long Madgett (b. 1923)

254. Life with Father

Sunday meant sleeping in,
time to pull another quilt
and hide from whiskey
in our daddy's snoring.

Only the Sunday funnies saved us   5
after last night's raving,
proof there was a demon.
Under covers we traded peeks

at Maggie giving Jiggs
the devil, Dagwood   10
bumbling about insanely sober,
tiny Wash Tubbs with twins

he doted over. At dawn
we folded the quilts
and funnies, crept softly   15
through our chores

as if in church,
soothing the fi-foe-fum
of his slumber, fearing
the thrum of his boots   20

descending the heavy
stalk of his stupor,
fierce when he found
his dreamed gold gone.

Walter McDonald (b. 1934)

(9–12) *Maggie . . . Tubbs:* characters in comic strips called, respectively, "Bringing Up Father," "Blondie," and "Captain Easy."

255. What Are Years?

What is our innocence,
what is our guilt? All are
    naked, none is safe. And whence
is courage: the unanswered question,
the resolute doubt,—   5
dumbly calling, deafly listening—that
in misfortune, even death,
    encourages others
    and in its defeat, stirs

    the soul to be strong? He   10
sees deep and is glad, who
    accedes to mortality
and in his imprisonment rises
upon himself as
the sea in a chasm, struggling to be   15
free and unable to be,
    in its surrendering
    finds its continuing.

    So he who strongly feels,
behaves. The very bird,   20
    grown taller as he sings, steels
his form straight up. Though he is captive,
his mighty singing
says, satisfaction is a lowly
thing, how pure a thing is joy.   25
    This is mortality,
    this is eternity.

Marianne Moore (1887–1972)

256. Adieu, farewell, earth's bliss

Adieu, farewell, earth's bliss;
This world uncertain is;
Fond° are life's lustful joys;   foolish
Death proves them all but toys;°   trifles
None from his darts can fly;   5
I am sick, I must die.
     Lord, have mercy on us!

Rich men, trust not in wealth,
Gold cannot buy you health;
Physic° himself must fade.   medicine   10
All things to end are made.
The plague full swift goes by;
I am sick, I must die.
     Lord, have mercy on us!

Beauty is but a flower   15
Which wrinkles will devour;
Brightness falls from the hair;
Queens have died young and fair;
Dust hath closed Helen's eye.
I am sick, I must die.   20
     Lord, have mercy on us!

Strength stoops unto the grave,
Worms feed on Hector brave;
Swords may not fight with fate,
Earth still holds ope her gate.   25
"Come, come," the bells do cry.
I am sick, I must die.
     Lord, have mercy on us!

Wit° with his wantonness   intelligence
Tasteth death's bitterness;   30
Hell's executioner
Hath no ears for to hear
What vain art can reply.
I am sick, I must die.
     Lord, have mercy on us!   35

Haste, therefore, each degree,°   social rank
To welcome destiny;
Heaven is our heritage,
Earth but a player's stage;

Mount we unto the sky.   40
I am sick, I must die.
　　Lord, have mercy on us.

Thomas Nashe (1567–1601)

257. what gramma said about her grandpa

he was white grandpa
his name jim butler
he's good irish man
he was nice talk our
language   5
big man with moustache
boss of town
tonopah°   in southwest Nevada
he found silver mine
we still on reservation they   10
come tell us "your grandpa
found mine" so
we move to tonopah
he say "buy anything you want
don't buy just little things   15
don't buy just candy
buy something big"
that's what he used to say
4th of july he make
a great long table   20
put sheet over it
then put all kinds of food on it
he say "get your plate &
help yourselves"
he fed all the indians   25
he was good man
but then
he marry white woman
& we go back to reservation

nila northSun (b. 1951)

258. The Victims

When Mother divorced you, we were glad. She took it and
took it, in silence, all those years and then

kicked you out, suddenly, and her
kids loved it. Then you were fired, and we
grinned inside, the way people grinned when   5
Nixon's helicopter lifted off the South
Lawn for the last time. We were tickled
to think of your office taken away,
your secretaries taken away,
your luncheons with three double bourbons,   10
your pencils, your reams of paper. Would they take your
suits back, too, those dark
carcasses hung in your closet, and the black
noses of your shoes with their large pores?
She had taught us to take it, to hate you and take it   15
until we pricked with her for your
annihilation, Father. Now I
pass the bums in doorways, the white
slugs of their bodies gleaming through slits in their
suits of compressed silt, the stained   20
flippers of their hands, the underwater
fire of their eyes, ships gone down with the
lanterns lit, and I wonder who took it and
took it from them in silence until they had
given it all away and had nothing   25
left but this.

Sharon Olds (b. 1942)

259. Speaking

I take him outside
under the trees,
have him stand on the ground.
We listen to the crickets,
cicadas, million years old sound.   5
Ants come by us.
I tell them,
"This is he, my son.
This boy is looking at you.
I am speaking for him."   10

The crickets, cicadas,
the ants, the millions of years
are watching us,
hearing us.
My son murmurs infant words,   15

speaking, small laughter
bubbles from him.
Tree leaves tremble.
They listen to this boy
speaking for me.   20

Simon J. Ortiz (b. 1941)

260. The Sad Children's Song

This house is a wreck said the children
when they came home with their children
Your papers are all over the place
The chairs are covered with books
and look   brown leaves are piled on the floor   5
under the wandering Jews

Your face is a wreck said the children
when they came home with their children
There are lines all over your face
your necks like curious turtles   10
Why did you let yourself go?
Where are you going without us?

This world is a wreck said the children
When they came home with their children
There are bombs all over the place   15
There's no water   the fields are all poisoned
Why did you leave things like this
Where can we go said the children
what can we say to our children?

Grace Paley (b. 1922)

261. The Hat Lady

In a childhood of hats—
my uncles in homburgs and derbies,
Fred Astaire in high black silk,
the yarmulke my grandfather wore
like the palm of a hand   5
cradling the back of his head—
only my father went hatless,
even in winter.

And in the spring,
when a turban of leaves appeared   10
on every tree, the Hat Lady came
with a fan of pins in her mouth
and pins in her sleeves,
the Hat Lady came—
that Saint Sebastian of pins,   15
to measure my mother's head.

I remember a hat of dove-grey felt
that settled like a bird
on the nest of my mother's hair.
I remember a pillbox that tilted   20
over one eye—pure Myrna Loy,
and a navy straw with cherries caught
at the brim that seemed real enough
for a child to want to pick.

Last year when the chemicals   25
took my mother's hair, she wrapped
a towel around her head. And the Hat Lady came,
a bracelet of needles on each arm,
and led her to a place
where my father and grandfather waited,   30
head to bare head, and Death
winked at her and tipped his cap.

Linda Pastan (b. 1932)

(3) *Fred Astaire* and (21) *Myrna Loy:* popular film stars of the mid-twentieth century.

262. The Imperfect Paradise

If God had stopped work after the fifth day
With Eden full of vegetables and fruits,
If oak and lilac held exclusive sway
Over a kingdom made of stems and roots,
If landscape were the genius of creation   5
And neither man nor serpent played a role
And God must look to wind for lamentation
And not to picture postcards of the soul,
Would he have rested on his bank of cloud
With nothing in the universe to lose,   10
Or would he hunger for a human crowd?

Which would a wise and just creator choose:
The green hosannas of a budding leaf
Or the strict contract between love and grief?

Linda Pastan (b. 1932)

263. A Work of Artifice

The bonsai tree
in the attractive pot
could have grown eighty feet tall
on the side of a mountain
till split by lightning.   5
But a gardener
carefully pruned it.
It is nine inches high.
Every day as he
whittles back the branches   10
the gardener croons,
It is your nature
to be small and cozy,
domestic and weak;
how lucky, little tree,   15
to have a pot to grow in.
With living creatures
one must begin very early
to dwarf their growth:
the bound feet,   20
the crippled brain,
the hair in curlers,
the hands you
love to touch.

Marge Piercy (b. 1934)

264. Spinster

Now this particular girl
During a ceremonious April walk
With her latest suitor
Found herself, of a sudden, intolerably struck
By the birds' irregular babel   5
And the leaves' litter.

By this tumult afflicted, she
Observed her lover's gestures unbalance the air,
His gait stray uneven
Through a rank wilderness of fern and flower.   10
She judged petals in disarray,
The whole season, sloven.

How she longed for winter then!—
Scrupulously austere in its order
Of white and black   15
Ice and rock, each sentiment within border,
And heart's frosty discipline
Exact as a snowflake.

But here—a burgeoning
Unruly enough to pitch her five queenly wits   20
Into vulgar motley—
A treason not to be borne. Let idiots
Reel giddy in bedlam spring:
She withdrew neatly.

And round her house she set   25
Such a barricade of barb and check
Against mutinous weather
As no mere insurgent man could hope to break
With curse, fist, threat
Or love, either.   30

Sylvia Plath (1932–1963)

265. Getting Through

Like a car stuck in gear,
a chicken too stupid to tell
its head is gone,
or sound ratcheting on
long after the film   5
has jumped the reel,
or a phone
ringing and ringing
in the house they have all
moved away from,   10
through rooms where dust

is a deepening skin,
and the locks unneeded,
so I go on loving you,
my heart blundering on,   15
a muscle spilling out
what is no longer wanted,
and my words hurtling past,
like a train off its track,
toward a boarded-up station,   20
closed for years,
like some last speaker
of a beautiful language
no one else can hear.

Deborah Pope

266. Bells for John Whiteside's Daughter

There was such speed in her little body,
And such lightness in her footfall,
It is no wonder her brown study
Astonishes us all.

Her wars were bruited in our high window.   5
We looked among orchard trees and beyond
Where she took arms against her shadow,
Or harried unto the pond

The lazy geese, like a snow cloud
Dripping their snow on the green grass,   10
Tricking and stopping, sleepy and proud,
Who cried in goose, Alas,

For the tireless heart within the little
Lady with rod that made them rise
From their noon apple-dreams and scuttle   15
Goose-fashion under the skies!

But now go the bells, and we are ready,
In one house we are sternly stopped
To say we are vexed at her brown study,
Lying so primly propped.   20

John Crowe Ransom (1888–1974)

267. Aunt Jennifer's Tigers

Aunt Jennifer's tigers prance across a screen,
Bright topaz denizens of a world of green.
They do not fear the men beneath the tree;
They pace in sleek chivalric certainty.

Aunt Jennifer's fingers fluttering through her wool   5
Find even the ivory needle hard to pull.
The massive weight of Uncle's wedding band
Sits heavily upon Aunt Jennifer's hand.

When Aunt is dead, her terrified hands will lie
Still ringed with ordeals she was mastered by.   10
The tigers in the panel that she made
Will go on prancing, proud and unafraid.

Adrienne Rich (b. 1929)

268. Living in Sin

She had thought the studio would keep itself;
no dust upon the furniture of love.
Half heresy, to wish the taps less vocal,
the panes relieved of grime. A plate of pears,
a piano with a Persian shawl, a cat   5
stalking the picturesque amusing mouse
had risen at his urging.
Not that at five each separate stair would writhe
under the milkman's tramp; that morning light
so coldly would delineate the scraps   10
of last night's cheese and three sepulchral bottles;
that on the kitchen shelf among the saucers
a pair of beetle-eyes would fix her own—
envoy from some village in the moldings . . .
Meanwhile, he, with a yawn,   15
sounded a dozen notes upon the keyboard,
declared it out of tune, shrugged at the mirror,
rubbed at his beard, went out for cigarettes;
while she, jeered by the minor demons,
pulled back the sheets and made the bed and found   20
a towel to dust the table-top,
and let the coffee-pot boil over on the stove.
By evening she was back in love again,
though not so wholly but throughout the night

she woke sometimes to feel the daylight coming   25
like a relentless milkman up the stairs.

Adrienne Rich (b. 1929)

269. Nani

Sitting at her table, she serves
the sopa de arroz° to me   rice soup
instinctively, and I watch her,
the absolute *mamá,* and eat words
I might have had to say more   5
out of embarrassment. To speak,
now-foreign words I used to speak,
too, dribble down her mouth as she serves
me albóndigas.° No more   spiced meatballs
than a third are easy to me.   10
By the stove she does something with words
and looks at me only with her
back. I am full. I tell her
I taste the mint, and watch her speak
smiles at the stove. All my words   15
make her smile. Nani° never serves   granny
herself, she only watches me
with her skin, her hair. I ask for more.

I watch the *mamá* warming more
tortillas for me. I watch her   20
fingers in the flame for me.
Near her mouth, I see a wrinkle speak
of a man whose body serves
the ants like she serves me, then more words
from more wrinkles about children, words   25
about this and that, flowing more
easily from these other mouths. Each serves
as a tremendous string around her,
holding her together. They speak
nani was this and that to me   30
and I wonder just how much of me
will die with her, what were the words
I could have been, was. Her insides speak
through a hundred wrinkles, now, more
than she can bear, steel around her,   35
shouting, then, What is this thing she serves?

She asks me if I want more.
I own no words to stop her.
Even before I speak, she serves.

Alberto Ríos (b. 1952)

270. Mr. Flood's Party

Old Eben Flood, climbing alone one night
Over the hill between the town below
And the forsaken upland hermitage
That held as much as he should ever know
On earth again of home, paused warily.   5
The road was his with not a native near;
And Eben, having leisure, said aloud,
For no man else in Tilbury Town to hear:

"Well, Mr. Flood, we have the harvest moon
Again, and we may not have many more;   10
The bird is on the wing, the poet says,
And you and I have said it here before.
Drink to the bird." He raised up to the light
The jug that he had gone so far to fill,
And answered huskily: "Well, Mr. Flood,   15
Since you propose it, I believe I will."

Alone, as if enduring to the end
A valiant armor of scarred hopes outworn,
He stood there in the middle of the road
Like Roland's ghost winding a silent horn.   20
Below him, in the town among the trees,
Where friends of other days had honored him,
A phantom salutation of the dead
Rang thinly till old Eben's eyes were dim.

Then, as a mother lays her sleeping child   25
Down tenderly, fearing it may awake,
He set the jug down slowly at his feet
With trembling care, knowing that most things break;
And only when assured that on firm earth
It stood, as the uncertain lives of men   30
Assuredly did not, he paced away,
And with his hand extended, paused again:

"Well, Mr. Flood, we have not met like this
In a long time; and many a change has come
To both of us, I fear, since last it was   35
We had a drop together. Welcome home!"
Convivially returning with himself,
Again he raised the jug up to the light;
And with an acquiescent quaver said:
"Well, Mr. Flood, if you insist, I might.   40

"Only a very little, Mr. Flood—
For auld lang syne. No more, sir; that will do."
So, for the time, apparently it did,
And Eben evidently thought so too;
For soon amid the silver loneliness   45
Of night he lifted up his voice and sang,
Secure, with only two moons listening,
Until the whole harmonious landscape rang—

"For auld lang syne." The weary throat gave out,
The last word wavered, and the song was done.   50
He raised again the jug regretfully
And shook his head, and was again alone.
There was not much that was ahead of him,
And there was nothing in the town below—
Where strangers would have shut the many doors   55
That many friends had opened long ago.

Edwin Arlington Robinson (1869–1935)

(11) *bird:* Mr. Flood is quoting from *The Rubáiyát of Omar Khayyám,* "The bird of
Time . . . is on the wing." (20) *Roland:* hero of the French epic poem *The Song of Roland.* He
died fighting a rearguard action for Charlemagne against the Moors in Spain; before his
death he sounded a call for help on his famous horn, but the king's army arrived too late.

271. Richard Cory

Whenever Richard Cory went down town,
We people on the pavement looked at him:
He was a gentleman from sole to crown,
Clean favored, and imperially slim.

And he was always quietly arrayed,   5
And he was always human when he talked;
But still he fluttered pulses when he said,
"Good-morning," and he glittered when he walked.

And he was rich—yes, richer than a king—
And admirably schooled in every grace: 10
In fine, we thought that he was everything
To make us wish that we were in his place.

So on we worked, and waited for the light,
And went without the meat, and cursed the bread;
And Richard Cory, one calm summer night,   15
Went home and put a bullet through his head.

Edwin Arlington Robinson (1869–1935)

272. The Sheaves

Where long the shadows of the wind had rolled,
Green wheat was yielding to the change assigned;
And as by some vast magic undivined
The world was turning slowly into gold.
Like nothing that was ever bought or sold   5
It waited there, the body and the mind;
And with a mighty meaning of a kind
That tells the more the more it is not told.

So in a land where all days are not fair,
Fair days went on till on another day   10
A thousand golden sheaves were lying there,
Shining and still, but not for long to stay—
As if a thousand girls with golden hair
Might rise from where they slept and go away.

Edwin Arlington Robinson (1869–1935)

273. I knew a woman

A knew a woman, lovely in her bones,
When small birds sighed, she would sigh back at them;
Ah, when she moved, she moved more ways than one:
The shapes a bright container can contain!
Of her choice virtues only gods should speak,   5
Or English poets who grew up on Greek
(I'd have them sing in chorus, cheek to cheek).

How well her wishes went! She stroked my chin,
She taught me Turn, and Counter-turn, and Stand;
She taught me Touch, that undulant white skin;   10
I nibbled meekly from her proffered hand;
She was the sickle; I, poor I, the rake,
Coming behind her for her pretty sake
(But what prodigious mowing we did make).

Love likes a gander, and adores a goose: 15
Her full lips pursed, the errant note to seize;
She played it quick, she played it light and loose;
My eyes, they dazzled at her flowing knees;
Her several parts could keep a pure repose,
Or one hip quiver with a mobile nose   20
(She moved in circles, and those circles moved).

Let seed be grass, and grass turn into hay:
I'm martyr to a motion not my own;
What's freedom for? To know eternity.
I swear she cast a shadow white as stone.   25
But who would count eternity in days?
These old bones live to learn her wanton ways:
(I measure time by how a body sways).

Theodore Roethke (1908–1963)

274. Fear no more

Fear no more the heat o' the sun,
   Nor the furious winter's rages;
Thou thy worldly task hast done,
   Home art gone, and ta'en thy wages.
Golden lads and girls all must,   5
As chimney-sweepers, come to dust.

Fear no more the frown o' the great;
   Thou art past the tyrant's stroke;
Care no more to clothe and eat;
   To thee the reed is as the oak.   10
The scepter, learning, physic,° must   art of healing
All follow this, and come to dust.

Fear no more the lightning-flash,
   Nor the all-dreaded thunder-stone;°   thunderbolt

Fear not slander, censure rash;   15
   Thou hast finished joy and moan.
All lovers young, all lovers must
Consign to thee,° and come to dust.   yield to your condition

William Shakespeare (1564–1616)

275. Let me not to the marriage of true minds

Let me not to the marriage of true minds
Admit impediments. Love is not love
Which alters when it alteration finds,
Or bends with the remover to remove.
O no! it is an ever-fixèd mark   5
That looks on tempests and is never shaken;
It is the star to every wandering bark,
Whose worth's unknown, although his height be taken.
Love's not Time's fool, though rosy lips and cheeks
Within his bending sickle's compass come;   10
Love alters not with his brief hours and weeks,
But bears it out even to the edge of doom.
If this be error and upon me proved,
I never writ, nor no man ever loved.

William Shakespeare (1564–1616)

276. My mistress' eyes

My mistress' eyes are nothing like the sun;
Coral is far more red than her lips' red;
If snow be white, why then her breasts are dun;
If hairs be wires, black wires grow on her head.
I have seen roses damasked,° red and white,   of different colors
But no such roses see I in her cheeks;   6
And in some perfumes is there more delight
Than in the breath that from my mistress reeks.°   exhales
I love to hear her speak, yet well I know
That music hath a far more pleasing sound;   10
I grant I never saw a goddess go,—
My mistress, when she walks, treads on the ground.
And yet, by heaven, I think my love as rare
As any she belied with false compare.

William Shakespeare (1564–1616)

277. Shall I compare thee to a summer's day?

Shall I compare thee to a summer's day?
Thou art more lovely and more temperate:
Rough winds do shake the lovely buds of May,
And summer's lease hath all too short a date.
Sometimes too hot the eye of heaven shines,   5
And often is his gold complexion dimmed;
And every fair° from fair sometimes declines   beauty
By chance or nature's changing course untrimmed°;   stripped
But thy eternal summer shall not fade   bare
Nor lose possession of that fair thou ow'st°,   own 10
Nor shall death brag thou wand'rest in his shade
When in eternal lines to time thou grow'st.
So long as men can breathe or eyes can see,
So long lives this°, and this gives life to thee.   this poem

William Shakespeare (1564–1616)

278. The Fly

O hideous little bat, the size of snot,
With polyhedral eye and shabby clothes,
To populate the stinking cat you walk
The promontory of the dead man's nose,
Climb with the fine leg of a Duncan-Phyfe   5
    The smoking mountains of my food
        And in a comic mood
    In mid-air take to bed a wife.

Riding and riding with your filth of hair
On gluey foot or wing, forever coy,   10
Hot from the compost and green sweet decay,
Sounding your buzzer like an urchin toy—
You dot all whiteness with diminutive stool,
    In the tight belly of the dead
        Burrow with hungry head   15
    And inlay maggots like a jewel.

At your approach the great horse stomps and paws
Bringing the hurricane of his heavy tail;
Shod in disease you dare to kiss my hand
Which sweeps against you like an angry flail;   20
Still you return, return, trusting your wing

To draw you from the hunter's reach
That learns to kill to teach
Disorder to the tinier thing.

My peace is your disaster. For your death   25
Children like spiders cup their pretty hands
And wives resort to chemistry of war.
In fens of sticky paper and quicksands
You glue yourself to death. Where you are stuck
You struggle hideously and beg,
You amputate your leg
Imbedded in the amber muck.

But I, a man, must swat you with my hate,
Slap you across the air and crush your flight,
Must mangle with my shoe and smear your blood,   35
Expose your little guts pasty and white,
Knock your head sidewise like a drunkard's hat,
Pin your wings under like a crow's,
Tear off your flimsy clothes,
And beat you as one beats a rat.   40

Then like Gargantua I stride among
The corpses strewn like raisins in the dust,
The broken bodies of the narrow dead
That catch the throat with fingers of disgust.
I sweep. One gyrates like a top and falls   45
And stunned, stone blind, and deaf
Buzzes its frightful F
And dies between three cannibals.

Karl Shapiro (b. 1913)

279. Small Town with One Road

We could be here. This is the valley
And its black strip of highway, big-eyed
With rabbits that won't get across.
Kids could make it, though.
They leap barefoot to the store—   5
Sweetness on their tongues, red stain of laughter.
They are the spectators of fun.
Hot dimes fall from their palms,
Chinks of light, and they eat

Candies all the way home   10
Where there's a dog for each hand,
Cats, chickens in the yard.
A pot bangs and water runs in the kitchen.
Beans, they think, and beans it will be,
Brown soup that's muscle for the field   15
And crippled steps to a ladder.
Okie or Mexican, Jew that got lost,
It's a hard life where the sun looks.
The cotton gin stands tall in the money dream
And the mill is a paycheck for   20
A wife—and perhaps my wife
Who, when she was a girl,
Boxed peaches and plums, hoed
Papa's field that wavered like a mirage
That wouldn't leave. We could go back.   25
I could lose my job, this easy one
That's only words, and pick up a shovel,
Hoe, broom that takes it away.
Worry is my daughter's story.
She touches my hand. We suck roadside   30
Snowcones in the shade
And look about. Behind sunglasses
I see where I stood: a brown kid
Getting across. "He's like me,"
I tell my daughter, and she stops her mouth.   35
He looks both ways and then leaps
Across the road where riches
Happen on a red tongue.

Gary Soto (b. 1952)

280. The Beating

The first blow caught me sideways, my jaw
Shifted. The second beat my skull against my
Brain. I raised my arm against the third.
Downward my wrist fell crooked. But the sliding

Flood of sense across the ribs caught in   5
My lungs. I fell for a long time,
One knee bending. The fourth blow balanced me.
I doubled at the kick against my belly.

The fifth was light. I hardly felt the
Sting. And down, breaking against my side, my   10
Thighs, my head. My eyes burst closed, my
Mouth the thick blood curds moved through. There

Were no more lights. I was flying. The
Wind, the place I lay, the silence.
My call came to a groan. Hands touched   15
My wrist. Disappeared. Something fell over me.

Now this white room tortures my eye.
The bed too soft to hold my breath,
Slung in plaster, caged in wood.
Shapes surround me.   20

No blow! No blow!
They only ask the thing I turn
Inside the black ball of my mind,
The one white thought.

Ann Stanford (1916–1987)

281. The Death of a Soldier

Life contracts and death is expected,
As in a season of autumn.
The soldier falls.

He does not become a three-days personage,
Imposing his separation,   5
Calling for pomp.

Death is absolute and without memorial,
As in a season of autumn,
When the wind stops,

When the wind stops and, over the heavens,   10
The clouds go, nevertheless,
In their direction.

Wallace Stevens (1879–1955)

282. Disillusionment of Ten O'Clock

The houses are haunted
By white night-gowns.
None are green,

Or purple with green rings,
Or green with yellow rings,   5
Or yellow with blue rings.
None of them are strange,
With socks of lace
And beaded ceintures.°   sashes
People are not going   10
To dream of baboons and periwinkles.
Only, here and there, an old sailor,
Drunk and asleep in his boots,
Catches tigers
In red weather.   15

Wallace Stevens (1879–1955)

283. The Snow Man

One must have a mind of winter
To regard the frost and the boughs
Of the pine-trees crusted with snow;

And have been cold a long time
To behold the junipers shagged with ice,   5
The spruces rough in the distant glitter

Of the January sun; and not to think
Of any misery in the sound of the wind,
In the sound of a few leaves,

Which is the sound of the land   10
Full of the same wind
That is blowing in the same bare place

For the listener, who listens in the snow,
And, nothing himself, beholds
Nothing that is not there and the nothing that is.   15

Wallace Stevens (1879–1955)

284. A Description of the Morning

Now hardly here and there a hackney-coach
Appearing, showed the ruddy morn's approach.
Now Betty from her master's bed had flown,
And softly stole to discompose her own.
The slip-shod 'prentice from his master's door   5

Had pared the dirt, and sprinkled round the floor.
Now Moll had whirled her mop with dextrous airs,
Prepared to scrub the entry and the stairs.
The youth with broomy stumps began to trace
The kennel's edge, where wheels had worn the place.   10
The small-coal man was heard with cadence deep,
Till drowned in shriller notes of chimney-sweep.
Duns at his lordship's gate began to meet;
And Brickdust Moll had screamed through half the street.
The turnkey now his flock returning sees,   15
Duly let out a-nights to steal for fees.
The watchful bailiffs take their silent stands;
And schoolboys lag with satchels in their hands.

Jonathan Swift (1667–1745)

(9) *youth:* he is apparently searching for salvage. (10) *kennel:* gutter. (14) *Brickdust:* red-complexioned.

285. From *In Memoriam A. H. H.*

Dark house, by which once more I stand
    Here in the long unlovely street,
    Doors, where my heart was used to beat
So quickly, waiting for a hand,

A hand that can be clasped no more—   5
    Behold me, for I cannot sleep,
    And like a guilty thing I creep
At earliest morning to the door.

He is not here; but far away
    The noise of life begins again,   10
    And ghastly through the drizzling rain
On the bald street breaks the blank day.

Alfred, Lord Tennyson (1809–1892)

This poem is part of a sequence composed after the death at age twenty-two of the poet's closest friend, the fiancé of his sister.

286. Do Not Go Gentle into That Good Night

Do not go gentle into that good night,
Old age should burn and rave at close of day;
Rage, rage against the dying of the light.

Though wise men at their end know dark is right,
Because their words had forked no lightning they   5
Do not go gentle into that good night.

Good men, the last wave by, crying how bright
Their frail deeds might have danced in a green bay,
Rage, rage against the dying of the light.

Wild men who caught and sang the sun in flight,   10
And learn, too late, they grieved it on its way
Do not go gentle into that good night.

Grave men, near death, who see with blinding sight
Blind eyes could blaze like meteors and be gay,
Rage, rage against the dying of the light.   15

And you, my father, there on the sad height,
Curse, bless, me now with your fierce tears, I pray.
Do not go gentle into that good night.
Rage, rage against the dying of the light.

Dylan Thomas (1914–1953)

287. Fern Hill

Now as I was young and easy under the apple boughs
About the lilting house and happy as the grass was green,
   The night above the dingle starry,
    Time let me hail and climb
   Golden in the heydays of his eyes,   5
And honored among wagons I was prince of the apple towns
And once below a time I lordly had the trees and leaves
    Trail with daisies and barley
   Down the rivers of the windfall light.

And as I was green and carefree, famous among the barns   10
About the happy yard and singing as the farm was home,
   In the sun that is young once only,
    Time let me play and be
   Golden in the mercy of his means,
And green and golden I was huntsman and herdsman, the calves 15
Sang to my horn, the foxes on the hills barked clear and cold,
    And the sabbath rang slowly
   In the pebbles of the holy streams.

All the sun long it was running, it was lovely, the hay
Fields high as the house, the tunes from the chimneys, it was air 20

And playing, lovely and watery
    And fire green as grass.
And nightly under the simple stars
As I rode to sleep the owls were bearing the farm away,
All the moon long I heard, blessed among stables, the nightjars   25
    Flying with the ricks, and the horses
        Flashing into the dark.

And then to awake, and the farm, like a wanderer white
With the dew, come back, the cock on his shoulder: it was all
    Shining, it was Adam and maiden,   30
        The sky gathered again
And the sun grew round that very day.
So it must have been after the birth of the simple light
In the first, spinning place, the spellbound horses walking warm
    Out of the whinnying green stable   35
        On to the fields of praise.

And honored among foxes and pheasants by the gay house
Under the new made clouds and happy as the heart was long,
    In the sun born over and over,
        I ran my heedless ways,   40
    My wishes raced through the house high hay
And nothing I cared, at my sky blue trades, that time allows
In all his tuneful turning so few and such morning songs
    Before the children green and golden
        Follow him out of grace,   45

Nothing I cared, in the lamb white days, that time would take me
Up to the swallow thronged loft by the shadow of my hand,
    In the moon that is always rising,
        Nor that riding to sleep
    I should hear him fly with the high fields   50
And wake to the farm forever fled from the childless land.
Oh as I was young and easy in the mercy of his means,
        Time held me green and dying
    Though I sang in my chains like the sea.

Dylan Thomas (1914–1953)

288. The Virgins

Down the dead streets of sun-stoned Frederiksted,
the first free port to die for tourism,
strolling at funeral pace, I am reminded
of life not lost to the American dream;

but my small-islander's simplicities   5
can't better our new empire's civilized
exchange of cameras, watches, perfumes, brandies
for the good life, so cheaply underpriced
that only the crime rate is on the rise
in streets blighted with sun, stone arches   10
and plazas blown dry by the hysteria
of rumor. A condominium drowns
in vacancy; its bargains are dusted,
but only a jeweled housefly drones
over the bargains. The roulettes spin   15
rustily to the wind—the vigorous trade
that every morning would begin afresh
by revving up green water round the pierhead
heading for where the banks of silver thresh.

Derek Walcott (b. 1930)

---

(1) *Frederiksted:* chief port of St. Croix, largest of the American Virgin Islands, a free port where goods can be bought without payment of customs duties and therefore at bargain prices. The economy of St. Croix, once based on sugar cane, is now chiefly dependent on tourism. Like the other American Virgin Islands, St. Croix has suffered from uncontrolled growth, building booms, unevenly distributed prosperity, destruction of natural beauty, and pollution. (5) *my . . . simplicities:* The poet is a native of St. Lucia in the West Indies. (16) *trade:* cf. trade wind.

289. When I Heard the Learn'd Astronomer

When I heard the learn'd astronomer,
When the proofs, the figures, were ranged in columns before me,
When I was shown the charts and diagrams, to add, divide,
    and measure them,
When I sitting heard the astronomer where he lectured with much
    applause in the lecture-room,
How soon unaccountable I became tired and sick,   5
Till rising and gliding out I wandered off by myself,
In the mystical moist night-air, and from time to time,
Looked up in perfect silence at the stars.

Walt Whitman (1819–1892)

290. The Writer

In her room at the prow of the house
Where light breaks, and the windows are tossed with linden,
My daughter is writing a story.

I pause in the stairwell, hearing
From her shut door a commotion of typewriter-keys   5
Like a chain hauled over a gunwale.

Young as she is, the stuff
Of her life is a great cargo, and some of it heavy:
I wish her a lucky passage.

But now it is she who pauses,   10
As if to reject my thought and its easy figure.
A stillness greatens, in which

The whole house seems to be thinking,
And then she is at it again with a bunched clamor
Of strokes, and again is silent.   15

I remember the dazed starling
Which was trapped in that very room, two years ago;
How we stole in, lifted a sash

And retreated, not to affright it;
And how for a helpless hour, through the crack of the door,   20
We watched the sleek, wild, dark

And iridescent creature
Batter against the brilliance, drop like a glove
To the hard floor, or the desk-top,

And wait then, humped and bloody,   25
For the wits to try it again; and how our spirits
Rose when, suddenly sure,

It lifted off from a chair-back,
Beating a smooth course for the right window
And clearing the sill of the world.   30

It is always a matter, my darling,
Of life or death, as I had forgotten. I wish
What I wished you before, but harder.

                                        Richard Wilbur (b. 1921)

291. Poem

As the cat
climbed over
the top of

              the jamcloset
              first the right   5
              forefoot

              carefully
              then the hind
              stepped down

              into the pit of   10
              the empty
              flowerpot

                     William Carlos Williams (1883–1963)

292. Spring and All

        By the road to the contagious hospital
        under the surge of the blue
        mottled clouds driven from the
        northeast—a cold wind. Beyond, the
        waste of broad, muddy fields   5
        brown with dried weeds, standing and fallen

        patches of standing water
        the scattering of tall trees

        All along the road the reddish
        purplish, forked, upstanding, twiggy   10
        stuff of bushes and small trees
        with dead, brown leaves under them
        leafless vines—

        Lifeless in appearance, sluggish
        dazed spring approaches—   15

        They enter the new world naked,
        cold, uncertain of all
        save that they enter. All about them
        the cold, familiar wind—

        Now the grass, tomorrow   20
        the stiff curl of wildcarrot leaf
        One by one objects are defined—
        It quickens: clarity, outline of leaf

But now the stark dignity of
entrance—Still, the profound change   25
has come upon them: rooted they
grip down and begin to awaken

William Carlos Williams (1883–1963)

293. To Waken an Old Lady

Old age is
a flight of small
cheeping birds
skimming
bare trees   5
above a snow glaze.
Gaining and failing
they are buffeted
by a dark wind—
But what?   10
On harsh weedstalks
the flock has rested,
the snow
is covered with broken
seedhusks   15
and the wind tempered
by a shrill
piping of plenty.

William Carlos Williams (1883–1963)

294. Composed upon Westminster Bridge, September 3, 1802

Earth has not anything to show more fair:
Dull would he be of sight who could pass by
A sight so touching in its majesty:
This City now doth, like a garment, wear
The beauty of the morning; silent, bare,   5
Ships, towers, domes, theaters, and temples lie
Open unto the fields, and to the sky,
All bright and glittering in the smokeless air.
Never did sun more beautifully steep
In his first splendor, valley, rock, or hill;   10

Ne'er saw I, never felt, a calm so deep!
The river glideth at his own sweet will:
Dear God! the very houses seem asleep,
And all that mighty heart is lying still!

William Wordsworth (1770–1850)

295. I wandered lonely as a cloud

I wandered lonely as a cloud
That floats on high o'er vales and hills,
When all at once I saw a crowd,
A host, of golden daffodils;
Beside the lake, beneath the trees,   5
Fluttering and dancing in the breeze.

Continuous as the stars that shine
And twinkle on the milky way,
They stretched in never-ending line
Along the margin of a bay: 10
Ten thousand saw I at a glance,
Tossing their heads in sprightly dance.

The waves beside them danced; but they
Outdid the sparkling waves in glee;
A poet could not but be gay,   15
In such a jocund company;
I gazed—and gazed—but little thought
What wealth the show to me had brought:

For oft, when on my couch I lie
In vacant or in pensive mood,   20
They flash upon that inward eye
Which is the bliss of solitude;
And then my heart with pleasure fills,
And dances with the daffodils.

William Wordsworth (1770–1850)

296. The Solitary Reaper

Behold her, single in the field,
Yon solitary Highland lass!
Reaping and singing by herself;

Stop here, or gently pass!
Alone she cuts and binds the grain, 5
And sings a melancholy strain;
O listen! for the vale profound
Is overflowing with the sound.

No nightingale did ever chant
More welcome notes to weary bands 10
Of travelers in some shady haunt
Among Arabian sands.
A voice so thrilling ne'er was heard
In springtime from the cuckoo-bird,
Breaking the silence of the seas 15
Among the farthest Hebrides.

Will no one tell me what she sings?—
Perhaps the plaintive numbers° flow   measures
For old, unhappy, far-off things,
And battles long ago. 20
Or is it some more humble lay,°   song
Familiar matter of today?
Some natural sorrow, loss, or pain
That has been, and may be again?

Whate'er the theme, the maiden sang 25
As if her song could have no ending;
I saw her singing at her work,
And o'er the sickle bending—
I listened, motionless and still;
And, as I mounted up the hill, 30
The music in my heart I bore
Long after it was heard no more.

William Wordsworth (1770–1850)

297. Sailing to Byzantium

That is no country for old men. The young
In one another's arms, birds in the trees
—Those dying generations—at their song,
The salmon-falls, the mackerel-crowded seas,
Fish, flesh, or fowl, commend all summer long 5
Whatever is begotten, born, and dies.
Caught in that sensual music all neglect
Monuments of unaging intellect.

An aged man is but a paltry thing,
A tattered coat upon a stick, unless   10
Soul clap its hands and sing, and louder sing
For every tatter in its mortal dress,
Nor is there singing school but studying
Monuments of its own magnificence;
And therefore I have sailed the seas and come   15
To the holy city of Byzantium.

O sages standing in God's holy fire
As in the gold mosaic of a wall,
Come from the holy fire, perne° in a gyre,   spin
And be the singing-masters of my soul.   20
Consume my heart away; sick with desire
And fastened to a dying animal
It knows not what it is; and gather me
Into the artifice of eternity.

Once out of nature I shall never take   25
My bodily form from any natural thing,
But such a form as Grecian goldsmiths make
Of hammered gold and gold enameling
To keep a drowsy Emperor awake;
Or set upon a golden bough to sing   30
To lords and ladies of Byzantium
Of what is past, or passing, or to come.

William Butler Yeats (1865–1939)

Byzantium: Ancient eastern capital of the Roman Empire; in this poem symbolically a
holy city of the imagination. (1) *That:* Ireland, or the ordinary sensual world. (27–31)
such . . . Byzantium: The Byzantine Emperor Theophilus had made for himself mechanical golden birds which sang upon the branches of a golden tree.

298. The Second Coming

Turning and turning in the widening gyre
The falcon cannot hear the falconer;
Things fall apart; the center cannot hold;
Mere anarchy is loosed upon the world,
The blood-dimmed tide is loosed, and everywhere   5
The ceremony of innocence is drowned;
The best lack all conviction, while the worst
Are full of passionate intensity.

Surely some revelation is at hand;
Surely the Second Coming is at hand.   10
The Second Coming! Hardly are those words out
When a vast image out of *Spiritus Mundi*
Troubles my sight: somewhere in sands of the desert
A shape with lion body and the head of a man,
A gaze blank and pitiless as the sun,   15
Is moving its slow thighs, while all about it
Reel shadows of the indignant desert birds.
The darkness drops again; but now I know
That twenty centuries of stony sleep
Were vexed to nightmare by a rocking cradle,   20
And what rough beast, its hour come round at last,
Slouches towards Bethlehem to be born?

William Butler Yeats (1865–1939)

In Christian legend the prophesied "Second Coming" may refer either to Christ or to Antichrist. Yeats believed in a cyclical theory of history in which one historical era would be replaced by an opposite kind of era every two thousand years. Here, the anarchy in the world following World War I (the poem was written in 1919) heralds the end of the Christian era. (12) *Spiritus Mundi:* the racial memory or collective unconscious mind of mankind (literally, world spirit).

299. The Wild Swans at Coole

The trees are in their autumn beauty,
The woodland paths are dry,
Under the October twilight the water
Mirrors a still sky;
Upon the brimming water among the stones   5
Are nine-and-fifty swans.

The nineteenth autumn has come upon me
Since I first made my count;
I saw, before I had well finished,
All suddenly mount   10
And scatter wheeling in great broken rings
Upon their clamorous wings.

I have looked upon those brilliant creatures,
And now my heart is sore,
All's changed since I, hearing at twilight,   15
The first time on this shore,
The bell-beat of their wings above my head,
Trod with a lighter tread.

Unwearied still, lover by lover,
They paddle in the cold   20
Companionable streams or climb the air;
Their hearts have not grown old;
Passion or conquest, wander where they will,
Attend upon them still.

But now they drift on the still water,   25
Mysterious, beautiful;
Among what rushes will they build,
By what lake's edge or pool
Delight men's eyes when I awake some day
To find they have flown away?   30

William Butler Yeats (1865–1939)

Coole Park, in County Galway, Ireland, was the estate of Lady Augusta Gregory, Yeats's patroness and friend. Beginning in 1897, Yeats regularly summered there for many years.

Writing about Poetry

I. WHY WRITE ABOUT LITERATURE?

Written assignments in a literature class have two purposes: (1) to give you additional practice in writing clearly and persuasively, and (2) to deepen your understanding of literary works by leading you to read and think about a few works more searchingly than you might otherwise do. But these two purposes are private. To be successful, your paper must have a public purpose as well: it should be written to enlighten others besides yourself. Even if no one else ever reads your paper, you should never treat it as a private note to your instructor. You should write every paper as if it were intended for publication.

II. FOR WHOM DO YOU WRITE?

The audience for whom you write will govern both the content and expression of your paper. You need to know something about your readers' backgrounds—national, racial, social, religious—and be able to make intelligent guesses about their knowledge, interests, and previous reading. In writing about George Herbert's "Peace" (No. 65) for a Hindu audience, you would need to include explanations of Christian belief and biblical stories that would be unnecessary for a Western European or American audience. But the most crucial question about an audience is: *Has it read the work you are writing about?* The book reviewer in your Sunday paper generally writes about a newly published book that the audience has not read. A reviewer's purpose is to let readers know something of what the book is about and to give them some notion of whether they will enjoy or profit from reading it. At an opposite extreme, the scholar writing in a specialized scholarly journal can generally assume an audience that *has* read the work, that has a knowledge of previous interpretations of the work, and that is familiar with other works in its period or genre. The scholar's purpose, not infrequently, is to persuade this audience that some new information or some new way of looking at the work appreciably deepens or alters its meaning or significance.

Clearly, essays written for such different audiences and with such different purposes differ considerably in content, organization, and style. Book reviewers reviewing a new novel will include a general idea of its plot while being careful not to reveal the outcome. Scholars will assume that readers already know the plot and will have no compunction about discussing its outcome. Reviewers will try to write interestingly and engagingly about the novel and to persuade readers that they have valid grounds for their opinions of its worth, but their manner will generally be informal. Scholars are more interested in presenting a cogent argument, logically arranged, and solidly based on evidence. They will be more formal, and may use critical terms and refer to related works that would be unfamiliar to nonspecialized readers. In documentation the two types of essays will be quite different. Reviewers' only documentation is normally the identification of the novel's title, author, publisher, and price, at the top of the review. For other information and opinions they hope that a reader will rely on their intelligence, knowledge, and judgment. Scholars, on the other hand, may furnish an elaborate array of citations of other sources of information, allowing the reader to verify the accuracy or basis of any important part of their argument. Scholars expect to be challenged, and they see to it that all parts of their arguments are buttressed.

For whom, then, should *you* write? Unless your instructor stipulates (or you request) a different audience, the best plan is to assume that you are writing for the other members of your class. Pretend that your class publishes a journal of which it also constitutes the readership. Your instructor is the editor and determines editorial policy. If you write on a poem that has been assigned for class reading, you assume that your audience is familiar with it. (This kind of paper is generally of the greatest educational value, for it is most open to challenge and class discussion, and places on you a heavier burden of proof.) If you compare an assigned poem with one that has not been assigned, you must gauge what portion of your audience is familiar with the unassigned poem, and proceed accordingly. If the unassigned poem is a later sonnet in the Shakespearean form, which you are comparing to one by Shakespeare, you will not need to provide a definition of the rime scheme of the form, for you can assume that *this* audience is familiar with the form of a sonnet; but you cannot assume familiarity with all of the sonnets of Shakespeare. You know that, as members of the same class, your readers have certain backgrounds and interests in common and are at comparable levels of education. Anything you know about your audience may be important for how you write your paper and what you put in it.

Assuming members of your class as your audience carries another advantage: you can also assume that they are familiar with the definitions and examples given in this book, and therefore you can avoid wasting space by quoting or paraphrasing the book. There will be no need to tell them that blank verse is unrimed iambic pentameter, or that Emily Dickinson's poems are untitled, or that Tennyson is a nineteenth-century poet.

III. CHOOSING A TOPIC

As editor of this imaginary publication, your instructor is responsible for the nature of its contents. Instructors may be very specific in their assignments, or they may be very general, inviting you to submit a paper on any subject within a broadly defined area of interest. They will also have editorial policies concerning length of papers, preparation of manuscripts, and deadlines for submission (all of which should be meticulously heeded). Instructors may further specify whether the paper should be entirely the work of your own critical thinking, or whether it is to be an investigative assignment—that is, one involving research into what other writers have written concerning your subject and the use of their findings, where relevant, to help you support your own conclusions.

Let us consider four kinds of papers you might write: (1) papers that focus on a single poem; (2) papers of comparison and contrast; (3) papers on a number of poems by a single author; and (4) papers on a number of poems having some feature other than authorship in common.

1. Papers that Focus on a Single Poem

If your assignment is a specific one (Who are the speakers in Mari Evans's "When in Rome" [No. 18] and what is the relationship between them? What does personification add to Tennyson's "The Eagle" [No. 1]? How is structure fitted to form in Shakespeare's "That time of year" [No. 171]?), your task is clear-cut. You have only to read the selection carefully (obviously more than once), formulate your answer, and support it with corroborating evidence from within the text as cogently and convincingly as possible. In order to convince your readers that your answer is the best one, you will need to examine and account for apparently contrary evidence as well as clearly supportive evidence; otherwise skeptical readers, reluctant to change their minds, might simply refer to "important points" that you have "overlooked."

Specific questions like these, when they are central to the poem and may be a matter of dispute, make excellent topics for papers. You may discover them for yourself when you disagree with a classmate about the interpretation of a poem. The study questions following many of the selections in this anthology frequently suggest topics of this kind.

If your assignment is more general, and if you are given some choice as to which poem you wish to write on, it is usually best to choose one you enjoyed, whether or not you entirely understood it. (You are more likely to write a good paper on a selection you liked than on one you disliked, and you should arrive at a fuller understanding of it while thinking through your paper.) You must then decide what kind of paper you will write, taking into account the length and kind of selection you have chosen and the amount of space at your disposal. Probably your paper will be either an *explication* or an *analysis*.

An *explication* (literally, an "unfolding") has been defined as "an examination of a work of literature for a knowledge of each part, for the relations of these parts to each other, and for their relations to the whole."* It is a detailed elucidation of a work, sometimes line by line or word by word, which is interested not only in *what* that work means but in *how* it means what it means. It thus considers all relevant aspects of a work—speaker, connotative words and double meanings, images, figurative language, allusions, form, structure, sound, rhythm—and discusses, if not all of these, at least the most important. (There is no such thing as exhausting the meanings and the ways to those meanings in a really rich piece of literature, and the explicator must settle for something less than completeness.) Explication follows from what we sometimes call "close reading"—looking at a piece of writing, as it were, through a magnifying glass.

Clearly, the kinds of literature for which an explication is appropriate are limited. First, the work must be rich enough to repay the kind of close attention demanded. One would not think of explicating "Thirty days hath September" (unless for purposes of parody), for it has no meanings that need elucidation and no "art" worthy of comment. Second, the work must be short enough to be encompassed in a relatively brief discussion. A thorough explication of *Othello* would be longer than the play itself and would tire the patience of the most dogged reader. Explications work best with short poems. (Sonnets like Shakespeare's "That time of year" [No. 171] and Frost's "Design" [No. 107] almost beg for explication.) Explication sometimes may also be appropriate for passages in long poems as, for example, the lines spoken by Macbeth after the death of his wife (No. 91) or the "sonnet" from *Romeo and Juliet* (No. 175). But explication as a critical form should perhaps be separated from explication as a method. Whenever you elucidate even a small part of a literary work by a close

*George Arms, "A Note on Explication," *Western Review* 15 (1950): 57.

examination that relates it to the whole, you are essentially explicating (unfolding). For example, if you elaborate at length on the multiple denotations and connotations of the title of Langston Hughes's "Cross" (No. 27) as they relate to that poem's central purpose, you are explicating the title.

For a sample of an explication, see "A Study of Reading Habits," page 382. The text of this book uses the explicative method frequently, but has no pure examples of explication. The discussions of "A Noiseless Patient Spider" (No. 61) and "Digging" (No. 63) come close to being explications, and might have been so designated had they included discussions of other relevant aspects of the poems (connotative language, imagery, structure and form, and so forth). The General Exercises for Analysis and Evaluation of poetry on page 29 should be helpful to you in writing an explication of a poem. Not all the questions will be applicable to every poem, and you need not answer all those that are applicable, but you should begin by considering all that apply and then work with those that are central and important for your explication.

An *analysis* (literally a "breaking up" or separation of something into its constituent parts), instead of trying to examine all parts of a work in relation to the whole, selects for examination *one* aspect or element or part that relates to the whole. Clearly, an analysis is a better approach to longer works and to prose works than is an explication. A literary work may be usefully approached through almost any of its elements, so long as you relate this element to the central meaning or the whole. (An analysis of meter is pointless unless it shows how meter serves the meaning.) As always, it is important to choose a topic appropriate to the space available. "Visual and auditory imagery in 'The Love Song of J. Alfred Prufrock'" (No. 198) is too large a topic to be usefully treated in one or two pages, but the irony of the refrain about the women talking of Michelangelo could be suited to such a length. Conversely, it might be too great a challenge to write a ten-page essay on so limited a topic, though the Michelangelo refrain could contribute a valuable page or two of discussion in a longer essay about Eliot's irony, or about the various effects of the refrains in the poem.

2. Papers of Comparison and Contrast

The comparison and contrast of two poems having one or more features in common may be an illuminating exercise because the similarities highlight the differences, or vice versa, and thus lead to a better understanding not only of both pieces but of literary processes in general. The works selected may be similar in subject but different in tone, similar in meaning but different in literary value, similar in means but different in the ends they achieve or, conversely, similar in tone but different in subject, similar in literary value but different in meaning, and so on. In writing such a paper, it is usually best to decide first whether the similarities or the differences are more significant, begin with a brief summary of the less significant, and then concentrate on the more significant.*

3. Papers on a Number of Poems by a Single Author

Most readers, when they discover a poem they particularly like, look for other works by the same author. The paper that focuses on a single author rather than a single work is the natural corollary of such an interest. The most common concern in a paper of this type is to identify the characteristics that make this author different from other authors and therefore of particular interest to the writer. What are the poet's characteristic subjects, attitudes, or themes? With what kinds of life does the poet characteristically deal? What are the poet's preferred literary forms? What tones does the poet favor? Is the poet ironic, witty, serious, comic, tragic? Is the poet's vision directed principally inward or outward? In short, what configuration of patterns makes the poet's fingerprints unique? Your paper may consider one or more of these questions.†

A more ambitious type of paper on a single poet examines the poems for signs of development. The attitudes that any person, especially a poet, takes toward the world, may change with the passing from adolescence to adulthood to old age. So also may a poet's means of expressing attitudes and judgments. Though some authors are

---

*A number of selections in this book have been "paired" to encourage just this kind of study: "Ulysses" and "Curiosity," "Dust of Snow" and "Soft Snow" in Chapter 6; "The Unknown Citizen" and "Departmental" in Chapter 7; "Abraham to kill him" and "An altered look about the hills" in Chapter 8; except for "Little Jack Horner," all six pairs of poems in Chapter 9; "For a Lamb" and "Apparently with no surprise," "One dignity delays for all" and " 'Twas warm at first like us," "Crossing the Bar" and "The Oxen," "The Apparition" and "The Flea," "Dover Beach" and "Church Going," in Chapter 10; "Had I the Choice" and "The Aim Was Song" in Chapter 12; and all seven pairs of poems in Chapter 15.

†John Donne, Emily Dickinson, and Robert Frost are represented in this anthology by a sufficient number of poems to support such a paper without turning to outside sources.

remarkably consistent in outlook and expression throughout their careers, others manifest surprising changes. What are the differences between early Yeats, middle Yeats, and late Yeats? To write such a paper, you must have accurate information about the dates when works were written, and the works must be read in chronological order. When you have mastered the differences, you may be able to illustrate them through close examination of two or three poems—one for each stage.

When readers become especially interested in the works of a particular poet, they may develop a curiosity about the poet's life as well. This is a legitimate interest and, if there is sufficient space and your editor/instructor permits it, you may want to incorporate biographical information into your paper. If so, however, you should heed three caveats. First, your main interest should be in the literature itself; the biographical material should be subordinated to and used in service of your examination of the work. In general, discuss only those aspects of the poet's life that bear directly on the work: biography should not be used as "filler." Second, you should be extremely cautious about identifying an event in a work with an event in the life of the author. Almost never are poems exact transcriptions of the writers' personal experiences. Authors fictionalize themselves when they put themselves into imaginative works. If you consider that even in autobiographies (where they intend to give accurate accounts of their lives) writers must select incidents from the vast complexity of their experiences, that the memory of past events may be defective, and that at best writers work from their own points of view—in short, when you realize that even autobiography cannot be an absolutely reliable transcription of historical fact—you should be more fully prepared not to expect such an equation in works whose object is imaginative truth. Third, you must document the sources of your information about the author's life (see pages 368–73, 384).

4. Papers on a Number of Poems with Some Feature Other than Authorship in Common

Papers on poems by various poets that have some feature in common—subject, form, poetic devices, and the like—where the purpose is to discover different ways that different works may use or regard that common feature, are often illuminating. Probably the most familiar paper of this type is the one that treats works having a similar thematic concern (love, war, religious belief or doubt, art, adolescence, initiation, maturity, old age, death, parents and children, racial conflict, social injustice). But a paper may also examine particular forms of literature, for example, the Italian sonnet, the dramatic monologue, the descriptive lyric. Topics of this kind may be further limited by time or place or number—Elizabethan love lyrics, poetry of the Vietnam War, four attitudes toward death, satires of bureaucracy.

IV. PROVING YOUR POINT

In writing about literature, your object generally is to convince your readers that your understanding of a work is valid and important and to lead them to share that understanding. When writing about other subjects, it may be appropriate to persuade your readers through various rhetorical means—through eloquent diction, devices of suspense, analogies, personal anecdotes, and the like. But readers of essays about literature usually look for "proof." They want you to show them *how* the work, or the element you are discussing, does what you claim it does. Like scientists who require proof of the sort that they can duplicate in their own laboratories, readers of criticism want access to the process of inference, analysis, and deduction that has led to your conclusions, so that they may respond as you have done.

To provide this proof is no easy task, for it depends on your own mastery of reading and of writing. You must understand what a poem means and what its effects are; you must be able to point out precisely how it communicates that meaning and how it achieves those effects; and you must be able to present your experience of it clearly and directly. When you have spent considerable time in coming to understand and respond to a work of literature, it may become so familiar that it seems self-evident to you, and you will need to "back off" sufficiently to be able to put yourself in your readers' position—they may have vague feelings about the poem ("I like it" or "It moves me deeply"), without knowing what it is that produced those feelings. It is your job to refine the feelings and define away the vagueness.

Some forms of "proof" rarely do the job. Precision does not result from explaining a metaphor metaphorically ("When Shakespeare's Juliet calls parting from Romeo a 'sweet sorrow,' the reader is reminded of taking bitter-tasting medicine"). Nor can you prove anything about a work by hypothesizing about what it might have been if it did not contain what it does ("If Dickinson had concluded 'A narrow fellow in the grass' by writing 'Without gasping for breath / And feeling chilled,' the poem would be much less effective"—this is equivalent to saying "If the poem were not what it is, it would not be what it is"). Your own personal experiences will rarely help your readers ("My anxiety, excitement, and awkwardness at my first skiing lesson were like the mixed feelings Prufrock imagines for himself at the tea party"—*your* reader hasn't shared your experience of that lesson). Even your personal history of coming to understand a literary work will seldom help ("At a first reading, Williams's 'The Red Wheelbarrow' seems empty and pointless, until one realizes its meaning"—most literature does not yield up its richness on a first reading, so this approach has nothing to add to your reader's understanding). Just as in formal logic, argument by analogy is not regarded as valid, so in critical discourse analogies are usually unconvincing ("The rhythm of this sonnet is like the trot of a three-legged racehorse"). These strategies all have in common the looseness and vagueness of trying to define something by saying what it is not, or what it is like, rather than dealing with what it *is*.

"Proof" in writing about literature is primarily an exercise in strict definition. Juliet's phrase "sweet sorrow" (quoted in the preceding paragraph) derives its feeling from the paradoxical linking of sweetness and grief as a representation of the conflicting emotions of love. To provide an appropriate definition of the effect of the phrase, you would need to identify the figure of speech as paradox, and to investigate the way in which love can simultaneously inflict pain and give pleasure, and you might find it useful to point to the alliteration that ties these opposites together. Obviously, comparing this kind of proof to that required by science is inexact, since what you are doing is reminding your readers, or perhaps informing them, of feelings that are associated with language, not of the properties of chemical compounds. Furthermore, a scientific proof is incomplete if it does not present every step in a process. If that requirement were placed on literary analysis, a critical essay would be interminable, since more can always be said about any interpretive point. So, rather than attempting to prove every point that you make, you should aim to demonstrate that your *method* of analysis is valid by providing persuasive proof of your major point or points. If you have shown that your handling of a major point is sound, your readers will tend to trust your judgment on lesser matters.

V. WRITING THE PAPER

The general procedures for writing a good paper on literature are much the same as the procedures for writing a good paper on any subject.

1.   As soon as possible after receiving the assignment, read carefully and thoughtfully the literary materials on which it is based, mulling over the problem to be solved or—if the assignment is general—a good choice of subject, jotting down notes, and sidelining or underlining important passages with a pencil if the book is your own.* If possible, read the material more than once.

2.   Then, rather than proceeding directly to the writing of the paper, put the materials aside for several days and let them steep in your mind. The advantage of this is that your subconscious mind, if you have truly placed the problem in it, will continue to work on the problem while you are engaged in other activities, indeed even while you are asleep. Repeated investigations into the psychology of creativity have shown that great solutions to scientific and artistic problems frequently occur while the scientist or artist is thinking of something else; the answer pops into consciousness as if out of nowhere but really out of the hidden recesses of the mind where it has been quietly incubating. Whether this apparent "miracle" happens to you or not, it is probable that you will have more ideas when you sit down to write after a period of incubation than you will if you try to write your paper immediately after reading the material.

3.   When you are ready to write (allow yourself as long an incubation period as possible, but also allow ample time for writing, looking things up, revising, copying your revision, and correcting your final copy), jot down a list of the ideas you have, select connecting ideas relevant to your problem or to a single acceptable subject, and formulate a thesis statement that will clearly express in one sentence what you wish to say about that subject. Make a rough outline, rearranging your ideas in the order that will best support your thesis. Do they make a coherent case? Have you left out anything necessary to demonstrate your thesis? If so, add it in the proper place. Then begin to write, using your rough outline as a guide. Write this first draft as swiftly as possible, not bothering about sentence structure, grammar, diction, spelling, or verification of sources. Concentrate on putting on paper what is in your head and on your outline without interrupting the flow of thought for any other purpose. If alternative ways of expressing a thought occur to you, put them all down for a later decision. Nothing is more unprofitable than staring at a blank sheet of paper, chewing on a pencil—or staring at a blank monitor, hearing the word processor's hum—wondering, "How shall I begin?" Just begin.

---

*If you use a library book, make notes of the page or line numbers of such passages so that you can readily find them again.

Get something down on paper. It may look awful, but you can shape and polish it later.

4. Once you have something on paper, it is much easier to see what should be done with it. The next step is to revise. Does your paper proceed from an introductory paragraph that either defines the problem to be solved or states your thesis, through a series of logically arranged paragraphs that advance toward a solution of the problem or demonstrate your thesis, to a final paragraph that either solves the problem or sums up and restates your thesis but in somewhat different words? If not, analyze the difficulty. Do the paragraphs need reorganization or amplification? Are more examples needed? Does the thesis itself need modification? Make whatever adjustments are necessary for a logical and convincing demonstration. This may require a rewriting of the paper, or it may call only for a few deletions, insertions, and circlings with arrows showing that a sentence or paragraph should be shifted from one place to another.

Notice that you are expected to organize your paper according to *your* purpose or thesis. This frequently will mean that you will not be moving line-by-line and stanza-by-stanza through a poem, following the structure that the poet created, but rather ordering your paper in the most effective way to make your point. If you do discuss the poem in the order in which its materials are presented, your reader will naturally expect your thesis to include some comment on the poem's structure. The exception to this is a paper devoted entirely to explication, since in that case you will be expected to follow the structure of the poem.

5. In your revision (if not earlier), be sure that the stance expressed in your statements and judgments is firm and forthright, not weak and wishy-washy. Don't allow your paper to become a sump of phrases like "it seems to me that," "I think [or feel] that," "this word might connote," "this line could mean," and "in my opinion." Your readers know that the content of your paper expresses your thoughts; you need to warn them only when it expresses someone else's. And don't be weak-kneed in expressing your opinion. Even though you are not 100 percent sure of your rightness, write as if you are presenting a truth. Realizing beforehand that you will need to state your interpretations and conclusions confidently should also help you to strive for a greater degree of certainty as you read and interpret.

6. Having revised your paper for the logic, coherence, confidence, and completeness of its argument, your next step is to revise it for effectiveness of expression. Do this slowly and carefully. How many words can you cut out without loss of meaning? Are your sentences constructed for maximum force and economy? Are they correctly punctuated? Do the pronouns have clear antecedents? Do the verbs agree with their subjects? Are the tenses consistent? Have you chosen the most exact words and spelled them correctly? Now is the time to use the dictionary, to verify quotations and other references, and to supply whatever documentation is needed. A conscientious writer may put a paper through several revisions.

7. After all is in order, write or type your final copy, being sure to follow the editorial policies of your instructor for the submission of manuscripts.

8. Read over your final copy slowly and carefully, and correct any mistakes (omissions, repetitions, typographical errors) you may have made in copying from your draft. This final step—too often omitted due to haste or fatigue—is extremely important and may make the difference between an A or a C paper, or between a C paper and an F. It is easy to make careless mistakes in copying, but your editor should not be counted on to recognize the difference between a copying error and one of ignorance. Moreover, the smallest error may utterly destroy the sense of what you have written: omission of a "not" may make your paper say the exact opposite of what you meant it to say. Few editors require or want you to recopy or retype a whole page of your paper at this stage. It is enough to make neat corrections in ink on the paper itself.

VI. INTRODUCING QUOTATIONS

In writing about literature it is often desirable, sometimes imperative, to quote from the work under discussion. Quoted material is needed (a) to provide essential evidence in support of your argument, and (b) to set before your reader any passage that you are going to examine in detail. It will also keep your reader in contact with the text and allow you to use felicitous phrasing from the text to enhance your own presentation. You must, however, be careful not to overquote. If a paper consists of more than 20 percent quotation, it loses the appearance of closely knit argument and seems instead merely a collection of quotations strung together like clothes hung out on a line to dry. Avoid, especially, unnecessary use of long quotations. Readers tend to skip them. Consider carefully whether the quoted material may not be more economically presented by paraphrase or effectively shortened by ellipsis (see Q9 below). Readers faced with a long quotation may reasonably expect you to examine it in some detail; that is, the longer your quotation, the more you should do with it.

As a general rule in analytical writing, quotation should be included for the purpose of supporting or proving a point, not for the purpose of re-creating the experience of the poem for your reader. You may assume that your reader has already read the poem and does not need to have it summarized—but on the other hand, you should not send your reader back to the book to re-read in order to understand what you are referring to. Analysis is the process of demonstrating how the parts work together to create the whole; it requires both the details and the way they work together. Quoting presents details, and analysis shows how the details do what you claim they do. If a quotation seems entirely self-evident to you so that you have nothing to explain about it, then it is not really worth quoting. If it is self-evident, your reader has already understood all there is to know about it.

As with every other aspect of good writing, the amount of quotation one uses and the explanation of how the quoted material works are matters of intelligence and tact and cannot be decreed. Effective use of quotation is an art.

Principles and "Rules"

There is no legislative body that establishes laws governing the formal aspects of quoting, documenting, or any other aspect of writing. The only "rules" are the editorial policies of the publisher to whom you submit your work. There is, however, a national organization—the Modern Language Association of America—that is so influential that its policies for its own publications and its recommendations for others are adopted by most journals of literary criticism and scholarship. The instructions below are in general accord with those stated in the *MLA Handbook for Writers of Research Papers,* 4th edition, by Joseph Gibaldi (New York: MLA, 1995). In your course, your instructor will inform you of any editorial policies in effect that differ from those given here or in the *MLA Handbook.* The examples used in this section are all drawn from Housman's "Terence, this is stupid stuff" (No. 11).

Q1. If the quotation is short (normally not more than two or three lines of verse), put it in quotation marks and introduce it directly into the text of your essay.

> Terence, in a rejoinder to his friend's complaint about
> the melancholy sobriety of his poetry, reminds him,
> a "There's brisker pipes than poetry," and the English
> b gentry "brews / Livelier liquor than the Muse"
> (16, 19–20).

Q2. If the quotation is long (normally more than three lines of verse), begin it on a new line (and resume the text of your essay on a new line also); double-space it (like the rest of your paper); and indent it twice as far from the left margin (ten spaces or one inch) as you do for a new paragraph (five spaces or one-half inch). If a ten-space indentation is unsuitable because the verse lines are either too long or too short, center the quotation between the margins. *Do not enclose it in quotation marks.* Since the indentation and the line arrangement both signal a quotation, the use of quotation marks would be redundant.

> In the final verse paragraph, Terence describes the
> terror of Mithridates's would-be assassins:
>> They poured strychnine in his cup
>> And shook to see him drink it up:
>> They shook, they stared as white's
>>   their shirt:
>> Them it was their poison hurt. (71–74)

The two boxed examples illustrate (Q1) the "run-in" quotation, where the quotation is "run in" with the writer's own text, and (Q2) the "set-off" or "block" quotation, which is separated from the writer's text.

Q3. In quoting verse, it is extremely important to preserve the line arrangement of the original because the verse line is a rhythmical unit and thus affects meaning. When more than one line of verse is run in, the lines are separated by a virgule (or diagonal slash with one letter-space on each side), and capitalization after the first line follows that of the original (see Q1.b. above).

Q4. In general, sentences containing a quotation are punctuated as they would be if there were no quotation. In Q1.a above, a comma precedes the quoted sentence as it would if there were no quotation marks. In Q2, a colon precedes the quoted sentence because it is long and complex. In Q1.b, there is no punctuation at all before the quotation. Do not put punctuation before a quotation unless it is otherwise called for.

Q5. Your quotation must combine with its introduction to make a grammatically correct sentence. The normal processes of grammar and syntax, like the normal processes of punctuation, are unaffected by quoting. Subjects must agree with their verbs, verbs must be consistent in tense, pronouns must have their normal relation with antecedents.

WRONG	Terence says, "And I myself a sterling lad" (34).
	(Incomplete sentence)
RIGHT	Terence calls himself "a sterling lad" (34).

WRONG	Terence's friend complains, "'tis our turn now / To hear such tunes as killed the cow'" (9–10).
	(The pronoun "our" does not agree in number or person with its antecedent "friend.")
RIGHT	Terence's friend, on behalf of the others, complains: "'We poor lads, 'tis our turn now / To hear such tunes as killed the cow'" (9–10).

WRONG	Terence says that "The world, it was the old world yet" (39).
	(Incorrect mixture of direct and indirect quotation)
RIGHT	Terence says, "The world, it was the old world yet" (39).

WRONG	Terence says that he "have been to Ludlow fair" (29). (Subject and verb of subordinate clause lack agreement.)
RIGHT	Terence says that he has "been to Ludlow fair" (29).

Q6. Your introduction must supply enough context to make the quotation meaningful. Be careful that all pronouns in the quotation have clearly identifiable antecedents.

WRONG	Terence begins his narration by saying, "Why, if 'tis dancing you would be, / There's brisker pipes than poetry" (15–16). (Who wants to dance?)
RIGHT	Terence begins his reply to his friend by saying, "Why, if 'tis dancing you would be, / There's brisker pipes than poetry" (15–16).

Q7. The words within your quotation marks must be quoted *exactly* from the original.

WRONG	Terence confesses that "in lovely muck he's lain," where he slept "happily till he woke again" (35–36).

Q8. It is permissible to insert or supply words in a quotation *if* you enclose them within brackets. Brackets (parentheses with square corners) are used to indicate *editorial* changes or additions. If parentheses were used, the reader might interpret the enclosed material as *authorial* (as part of the quotation). Since brackets do not appear on all typewriters, you may have to put them in with pen or pencil. Avoid excessive use of brackets: they have a pedantic air. Find other solutions. Often paraphrase will serve as well as quotation.

CORRECT	Terence confesses that "in lovely muck [he's] lain," where he slept "Happ[ily] till [he] woke again" (35–36).
BETTER	Terence confesses that when drunk he's slept in muck--and happily, until he woke up.

Notice that a word or letters within brackets can either replace a word in the original (as in the substitution of *he's* for the original "I've") or be added to explain or complete the original (as with *-ily*). Since a reader understands that brackets signal either substitution or additions, it is superfluous to include the words for which the substitutions are made.

WRONG	Terence confesses that "in lovely muck I've [he's] lain" (35).

Your sentences, including bracketed words, must read as if there were no brackets:

RIGHT	Terence summarizes his philosophy when he advises his friend:
	Therefore, since the world has still
	Much good, but much less good than ill,
	And . . . Luck's a chance, but trouble's sure,
	[You should] face it as a wise man would,
	And train for ill and not for good. (43–48)

Q9.   It is permissible to omit words from quoted material, but *only* if the omission is indicated. Three *spaced* periods are used to indicate the omission (technically they are called "ellipsis points"). The third line in the preceding quotation is an example. If there are four periods, one is the normal period at the end of a sentence; the other three indicate the ellipsis.

The statement just concluded, if quoted, might be shortened in the following way: "It is permissible to omit words . . . if the omission is indicated. Three *spaced* periods are used to indicate the omission. . . . If there are four periods, one is the normal period at the end of a sentence."

It is usually not necessary to indicate ellipsis at the beginning or ending of a quotation (the very act of quoting implies that something precedes and follows)—unless what you quote is in some way contradicted by its original context, as for example by a "not" preceding the material you quote.

Q10.   Single quotation marks are used for quotations within quotations. Thus, if double quotes occur *within* a run-in quotation, they should be reduced to single quotes. (In a block quotation, the quotation marks would remain unchanged.)

> Terence (who speaks the whole poem) begins by quoting a complaining friend. To the demand for "'a tune to dance to,'" Terence instead offers a defense of sober poetry that will "do good to heart and head" (14, 55).

Single quotation marks are not used for any other purposes and should not be substituted for double quotes.

Q11.   At the conclusion of a run-in quotation, commas and periods are conventionally placed *within* quotation marks; semicolons and colons are placed outside. (The convention is based on appearance, not on logic.) Question marks and exclamation points are placed inside if they belong to the quoted sentence, outside if they belong to your sentence. (This is logic.) Special rules apply when the quotation is followed by parenthetical documentation (see PD4, page 372). The following examples are all correct:

> "Mithridates, he died old," Terence concludes (76).
>
> Terence concludes, "Mithridates, he died old" (76).
>
> "[W]hy was Burton built on Trent?" Terence asks (18).
>
> Does Housman endorse the friend's preference for "a tune to dance to" (14)?

VII. DOCUMENTATION

Documentation is the process of identifying the sources of materials used in your paper. The sources are of two kinds: primary and secondary. *Primary* sources are materials written *by* the author being studied, and may be confined to the single work being discussed. *Secondary* sources are materials by other writers *about* the author or work being discussed, or materials having some bearing on that work. Documentation serves two purposes: (1) it enables your readers to check any material they may think you have misinterpreted; (2) it enables you to make proper acknowledgment of information, ideas, opinions, or phraseology that are not your own.

It is difficult to overemphasize the second of these purposes. The use of someone else's ideas or insights in your own words, since it does not require quotation marks, makes an even heavier demand for acknowledgment than does quoted material. Although you need not document matters of common knowledge, your use without acknowledgment of material that is uniquely someone else's is not only dishonest but illegal (plagiarism), and could result in penalties ranging from an F on the paper through expulsion from school to a term in jail, depending on the magnitude of the offense.

Documentation may be given in (a) the text of your essay; (b) parenthesis placed within the text of your essay; or (c) a list of Works Cited placed at the end of your essay but keyed to parenthetical references within the essay. The three methods are progressively more formal.

Documentation by a list of Works Cited is required when several sources have contributed to an essay—and is necessary in a research paper or term paper for which you have consulted a number of works. If you are assigned such a project in conjunction with studying this book, your instructor will supply you with information about the method to use. The *MLA Handbook for Writers of Research Papers* (mentioned earlier) provides a full account of the appropriate method, in the event that your instructor does not supply you with other information.

In any case, the type of documentation required in your class will be chosen by your instructor, who may wish to have you practice several methods so that you will learn their use.

1. Textual Documentation

Every literary essay contains textual documentation. A title like "Dramatic Irony in 'My Last Duchess'" identifies the poem that will furnish the main materials in a paper. A paragraph beginning "In the second verse paragraph . . ." locates more specifically the source of what follows. An informally documented essay is one that relies on textual documentation exclusively. Perhaps the majority of articles published in newspapers and periodicals with wide circulation are of this kind. Informal documentation works best for essays written on a single short work, without use of secondary sources, for readers without great scholarly expectations. A first-rate paper could be written on Wallace Stevens's "Sunday Morning" using only textual documentation. The poet's name and the title of the poem mentioned somewhere near the beginning of the essay, plus a few phrases like "In the opening stanza" or "In the vision of the orgiastic future" or "The final image of the pigeons" might provide all the documentation needed for this audience. The poem is short enough that the reader can easily locate any detail within it. If the essay is intended for our hypothetical journal published by your literature class (all of whose members are using the same anthology), its readers can readily locate the poem. But the informal method, although less appropriate, can also be used for more complex subjects, and can even accommodate secondary sources with phrases like "As Helen Vendler points out in her study of Stevens's longer poems . . ."

Principles and "Rules"

TD1. Enclose titles of short stories, articles, and poems (unless they are book-length) in quotation marks; underline titles of plays, magazines, newspapers, and books. Do not underline or put the title of your own paper in quotation marks. The general principle is that titles of separate publications are underlined; titles of selections or parts of books are put within quotation marks. Full-length plays, like *Othello* and *Oedipus Rex,* though often reprinted as part of an anthology, are elsewhere published as separate books and should be underlined. Underlining, in manuscripts, is equivalent to italics in printed matter. Many word-processing programs allow the use of italics, so you should check with your instructor for the preferred style.

TD2.   Capitalize the first word and all important words in titles. Do not capitalize articles, prepositions, and conjunctions except when they begin the title ("The Unknown Citizen," "To the Virgins, to Make Much of Time," "A Study of Reading Habits").

TD3.   When the title above a poem is identical with its first line or a major part of its first line, there is a strong presumption that the poet left the poem untitled and the editor or anthologist has used the first line or part of it to serve as a title. In such a case you may *use* the first line as a title, but should not *refer* to it as a title (don't write: "The poet's repetition of his title in his first line emphasizes . . ."). In using it as a title, capitalize only those words that are capitalized in the first line.

TD4.   Never use page numbers in the body of your discussion because a page is not a structural part of a poem. You may refer in your discussion to verse paragraphs, sections, stanzas, and lines, as appropriate, but use page numbers *only* in parenthetical documentation where a specific edition of the work has been named.

TD5.   Spell out numerical references when they precede the unit they refer to; use numbers when they follow the unit (the second paragraph, or paragraph 2; the fourth line, or line 4; the tenth stanza, or stanza 10). Use the first of these alternative forms sparingly, and only with small numbers. Never write "In the thirty-fourth and thirty-fifth lines . . . ," for to do so is to waste good space and irritate your reader; write "In lines 34–35. . . ."

2. Parenthetical Documentation

Parenthetical documentation makes possible fuller and more precise accrediting without a forbidding apparatus of footnotes or an extensive list of Works Cited. It is the method most often required for a paper using only the primary source or, at most, two or three sources— as, for example, most of the writing assigned in an introductory

literature course. The information given in parenthetical documentation should enable your reader to turn easily to the exact source of a
quotation or a reference. At the first mention of a work (which may
well precede the first quotation from it), full publishing details should
be given, but parenthetical documentation should supplement textual
documentation; that is, information provided in the text of your essay
should not be repeated within the parentheses. For the readers of our
hypothetical journal, the first reference to a poem might look like this:

> In "Home Burial" (Robert Frost, reprinted in Thomas R. Arp,
> *Perrine's Sound and Sense,* 9th ed. [Fort Worth: Harcourt, 1997]
> 255–258), the poet examines . . .

Notice in this entry that brackets are used for parentheses within
parentheses. In subsequent references only inclusive line numbers
need be given:

> Amy's silent gesture underscores her sense that her husband
> cannot understand her feelings: "Her fingers moved the latch for
> all reply" (44).

If more than one source is used, each must be identified, if referred to
a second time, by an abbreviated version of the main entry, normally
the author's last name or, if several works by a single author are cited,
by the title of the work; in any case, use the shortest identification that
will differentiate the source from all others.

Principles and "Rules"

PD1.   For the first citation from a book, give the author's name;
the title of the selection; the name of the book from which it is taken;
the editor (preceded by the abbreviation ed. for "edited by") or the
translator (preceded by the abbreviation trans. for "translated by");
the edition (designated by an Arabic number) if there has been more
than one; the city of publication (the first one will suffice if there is
more than one); the publisher (this may be given in shortened form,
dropping all but the first name named); the year of publication or of
most recent copyright; and the page number. The following example
correctly combines textual with parenthetical documentation.

In "Home Burial," Frost has a husband complain, "'A man must partly give up being a man / With women-folk'" (The Poetry of Robert Frost, ed. Edward Connery Latham [New York: Holt, 1969] 52).

PD2.   For your principal primary source, after the first reference, only a page number is required. For long poems, however, it may be more useful, if easily available, to give line numbers or stanza numbers rather than page numbers. If the poem is short, line numbers are unnecessary and should be omitted, nor is there any need to cite a page number after the first documentation. For plays in verse also, citation by line number (preceded by act and scene number) will often be more useful than by page; for example, *Othello* (5.2.133).

PD3.   Documentation for run-in quotations always follows the quotation marks. If the quotation ends with a period, move it to the end of the documentation. If it ends with an exclamation point or question mark, leave it, but put a period after the documentation as well. The following examples are from "Home Burial" (No. 197):

"She moved the latch a little. 'Don't--don't go'" (56).

"'There you go sneering now!'" (67).

PD4.   With block quotations, parenthetical documentation follows the last mark of punctuation without further punctuation after the parentheses:

He saw her from the bottom of the stairs

Before she saw him. She was starting down,

Looking back over her shoulder at some fear. (1-3)

PD5.   Avoid cluttering your paper with excessive documentation. When possible, use one note to cover a series of short quotations. (See example, Q1.) Remember that short poems need no parenthetical documentation at all after the first reference. Do not document well-known sayings or proverbs that you use for stylistic purposes and that form no part of the substance of your investigation (and of course be wary of including hackneyed commonplaces in your formal writing).

PD6. It is customary in a formal paper to document all quoted materials. Do not, however, fall victim to the too frequent delusion that *only* quotations need documentation. The first purpose of documentation (see page 368) implies that any major or possibly controversial assertion concerning interpretation may need documentation. If you declare that the climax of a long poem occurs with an apparently insignificant passage that you choose not to quote for full analysis, it may be more important for the reader to have line numbers for that passage than for any quotations from the poem. Judgment must be exercised.

> The vividness with which Amy recalls her husband's remark the morning of the burial is evidence that the words have been preying on her mind (92-93).

VIII. STANCE AND STYLE

In section II, "For Whom Do You Write?" we discussed the assumed audience for your critical writing. Now we must consider the other half of the reader/writer equation. We might ask the parallel question "Who Are You?" except that that would imply that we are asking about your own personal identity. Rather, since we defined your audience hypothetically as members of your class, we need to define "you" in terms of the voice that your audience will expect and respond to. There are certain conventional expectations that are aroused when we read critical analyses of literature, and what follows are a few suggestions that may lead you to adopt the stance that your readers will expect. If these sound prescriptive (or if your instructor suggests others), remember that writing about literature is essentially persuasive writing, its purpose being to persuade your readers to agree with your interpretation; the means of persuasion are many, and the writer's stance is only one of them. What we provide here are a few "hints" that have been valuable to students in the past, and may be helpful to you.

S1. *Keep out!* This injunction warns you away from unnecessarily intruding yourself into your critical statements, with a consequent loss of power and precision. Consider the relative force of these approaches:

POOR	It seems to me that Owen captures the horror of war by describing a man dying of poison gas.
GOOD	Owen captures the horror of war by describing a man dying of poison gas.
BETTER	The image of a man dying of poison gas evokes the horror of war.

The first example dilutes the statement by making it sound tentative and opinionated. It allows your reader to respond, "Why should I consider that seriously, since the writer confesses that it's only a private opinion rather than a fact?" As a critic, you should adopt the stance of the sensitive person who is confident of the accuracy of her or his insights—even when in your heart you may *feel* tentative or unsure. Say it with an air of confidence.

The third example is "better" because it observes the following suggestion.

S2. *Write about the poem.* When analyzing a poem or some aspect of it, you should be sure that the thesis or topic of a paragraph or essay (and its thesis sentences) focuses on your topic. You will usually not be writing about a *poet* but about a *poem,* so try to avoid using the poet's name as the subject.

POOR	Tennyson uses personification when he refers to the eagle's talons as "hands." (This focuses on *Tennyson* [subject] and *uses* [verb].)
GOOD	The word "hands" describing the eagle's talons personifies him. (Subject, *word;* verb, *personifies.*)

Try also to avoid the verb *uses,* since your focus is not on a poet using a poetic device but on the result of that use, not on an author selecting a device to achieve a purpose but on the result of that selection. The easiest way to get rid of the word *use* or the idea of *using* is simply to delete them:

POOR	The speaker uses the word "green" to suggest freshness.
GOOD	The word "green" suggests freshness.

The revised version cuts the wordiness and is more direct.

S3. *Avoid passive constructions.* In analyzing literature, the passive voice presents three potential problems: (a) it may fail to identify its subject and thus (b) may introduce vagueness, and (c) it is often a weak and wordy way to say something that can be said directly and forcefully. It may also be a roundabout way to write about an author rather than a work.

POOR	Soldiers with their packs are used as a comparison to beggars with sacks.
POOR	Owen uses the comparison of soldiers to beggars . . . (Passive voice is eliminated, but a problem with S2.)
GOOD	Soldiers with their packs resemble beggars with sacks.

S4. *Omit praise.* Praising a poet or a poem with such adverbs as *cleverly, carefully, remarkably, beautifully,* and so forth, usually sounds a little condescending and fatuous when you are analyzing established literature (as distinct from writing a review of a new book). It suggests that *your* estimation of the quality of Shakespeare's or Dickinson's poetry will tip the balance in favor of immortality for them.

S5. *Avoid preparatory circumlocution.* Don't write a "table of contents" as an introductory paragraph, and eliminate such phrases as "in order to understand X we must examine Y." Just go ahead and examine Y, and trust your reader to recognize its relevance. Another example: "Z is a significant aspect of the poem" (or, even worse, "It is interesting to note that Z is a significant aspect"). If Z is significant, just go ahead and say what it signifies; if it is interesting, let what is interesting about it be your topic.

Such circumlocution is sometimes called "treading water," since it is generally only a way of keeping afloat on the page until you get a good idea of the direction you really want to swim. You wouldn't walk into a room and announce, "I am now going to tell you that I'm here," or "I will tell you how interested you'll be to notice that I'm here." You'd say, "Here I am!"

It is perfectly all right to use such space-wasters in preliminary drafts—as ways of keeping your pen or keyboard in action while you are figuring out which way you are going to swim. Just be sure to edit them out of your finished text.

S6.   *Avoid negative hypotheses.* An example of negative hypothesis is introduced with an example on p. 357, "Proving Your Point." Here's another: "If Shakespeare had made 'Winter' into a sermon, all of the poem's best features would have been lost." But he *didn't*, so a critical analysis can neither speculate about what he might have done had he done otherwise, or prove that what he did do is better by comparison—there is nothing to compare.

IX. GRAMMAR, PUNCTUATION, AND USAGE: SPECIAL PROBLEMS

1. Grammar

G1.   In discussing the action of a literary work, rely primarily on the present tense (even when the work itself uses the past), keeping the past, future, and perfect tenses available for prior or subsequent actions; for example,

> When Amy withdraws from her husband and slides downstairs
> "beneath his arm / That [rests] on the banister" (31-32), the
> references to sliding, a staircase, and a banister create an ironic
> allusion to what will be revealed as their central concern, the
> dead child.

G2.   Do not let pronouns refer to nouns in the possessive case. Antecedents of pronouns should always hold a strong grammatical position: a possessive is a mere modifier, like an adjective.

WRONG	In Frost's poem "Home Burial," he writes . . .
	(Antecedent of "he" is in possessive case.)
RIGHT	In his poem "Home Burial," Frost writes . . .
	(Antecedent of "his" is the subject of the sentence.)

2. Punctuation

P1.   The insertion of a parenthetical phrase in your sentence structure (as, for example, in parenthetical documentation) does not alter the normal punctuation of the rest of the sentence. Do not, as the preceding sentence doesn't, place a comma after a parenthetical phrase unless it belonged there before the parenthesis was inserted. You wouldn't write, "Owen's poem, is about the horror of war," so don't include that comma when you insert a parenthesis.

WRONG	Owen's poem (repr. in Thomas R. Arp, *Perrine's Sound and Sense,* 9th ed. [Fort Worth: Harcourt, 1997] 7-8), is about the horror of war.
	(Delete the comma after the parenthesis.)

And it is an inflexible rule of punctuation: never place a comma immediately before a parenthesis.

P2.   Do not set off restrictive appositives with commas. A "restrictive" appositive is one necessary to the meaning of the sentence; a "nonrestrictive" appositive could be left out without changing the meaning.

WRONG	In his book, *A Boy's Will,* Robert Frost . . .
	(Without the title we do not know which of Frost's books is referred to. As punctuated, the sentence falsely implies that Frost wrote only one book.)
RIGHT	In his book *A Boy's Will,* Robert Frost . . .
RIGHT	In his first book, *A Boy's Will,* Robert Frost . . .
	(The adjective *first* identifies the book. The title simply supplies additional information and could be omitted without changing the meaning.)

P3. Words used simply as words should be underlined, italicized, or put in quotation marks.

WRONG	The sixth word in "The Road Not Taken" is yellow.
	(This statement is false; all the words in the poem are black.)
RIGHT	The sixth word in "The Road Not Taken" is "yellow."

Since the word "yellow" is quoted from the poem, it has here been put in quotation marks. However, if you list a series of words from the poem, you may prefer underlining for the sake of appearance. Whichever system you choose, be consistent throughout your paper.

P4. Observe the conventions of typed manuscripts: (1) put a space after an abbreviating period (p. 7, not p.7; pp. 10–13, not pp.10–13); (2) use two hyphens to represent a dash -- and do not put spaces before or after them.

P5. Observe the standard for forming possessives. For a singular noun, add an apostrophe and an *s* (a student's duty, yesterday's mail, the dress's hemline). For a plural noun, add only an apostrophe (the students' duties, seven days' mail). For proper nouns, the same rules apply (Keats's odes, Donne's sonnets. Evans's poem).

Do not confuse the contraction *it's* (it is) with the possessive *its* (belonging to it). *Its* is an exception to the general rule requiring apostrophes for possessives.

3. Usage

U1.   Though accepted usage changes with time, and the distinctions between the following pairs of words are fading, many instructors will bless you if you try to preserve them.

convince, persuade   *Convince* pertains to belief (conviction); *persuade* pertains to either action or belief. The following sentences observe the distinction. "In 'To His Coy Mistress' the speaker tries to persuade a young woman to sleep with him." "In 'To His Coy Mistress' the speaker tries to convince a young woman that she has nothing to lose by sleeping with him." "I persuaded him to have another drink though he was convinced he ought not to."

describe, define   *Describe* means to delineate the visual appearance of something; *define* means to state the meaning of a word or phrase, or to explain the essential quality of something. Reserve *describe* and *description* for talking about how things look.

disinterested, uninterested   A disinterested judge is one who has no "stake" or personal interest in the outcome of a case and who can therefore judge fairly; an uninterested judge goes to sleep on the bench. A good judge is interested in the case but disinterested in its outcome. An uninterested reader finds reading boring. A disinterested reader? Perhaps one who can enjoy a book whatever its subject matter.

imply, infer   A writer or speaker implies; a reader or listener infers. An implication is a meaning hinted at but not stated outright. An inference is a conclusion drawn from evidence not complete enough for proof. If you imply that I am a snob, I may infer that you do not like me.

lover, beloved   In older literature, the word *lover* usually meant one of two things—a man who is sexually involved, or any person who feels affection or esteem for another person or persons. In the case of the former, *lover* generally designated the male partner and *beloved* his female partner. In the case of the latter usage, no sexual implications are involved.

sensuous, sensual   *Sensuous* normally pertains to the finer senses, *sensual* to the appetites. Good poetry is sensuous: it appeals through the imagination to the senses. A voluptuous woman, an attractive man, or a rich dessert may have a sensual appeal that stirs a desire for possession.

quote, quotation   *Quote* was originally used only as a verb. Today the use of "single quotes" and "double quotes" in reference to quotation marks is almost universally accepted; but, although the use of "quote" for "quotation" is common in informal speech, it is still unacceptable in formal writing.

Note also that quoting is an act performed by the writer about literature, not by the writer of literature.

WRONG	Shakespeare's famous quotation "To be or not to be" . . .
RIGHT	The famous quotation from Shakespeare, "To be or not to be" . . .
RIGHT	Shakespeare's famous line "To be or not to be" . . .
BETTER	Hamlet's famous line "To be or not to be" . . .
BEST	Probably the most-quoted line by Shakespeare is Hamlet's "To be or not to be" . . .

U2.   Some words and phrases to be avoided are the following.

center around   A geometrical impossibility. A story may perhaps center *on* a certain feature, but to make it center *around* that feature is to make the hub surround the wheel.

just as   This phrase as a term of comparison is too precise for discussing literature because the adjective *just* means *exactly* or *identical in every possible way,* almost an impossibility in comparing literary works. You should take the trouble to establish the points of similarity and dissimilarity between things that you are comparing.

lifestyle   An overused neologism, especially inappropriate for use with older literature, that is too general to mean much. One dictionary defines it as "a person's typical approach to living, including his moral attitudes, preferred entertainment, fads, fashions, etc." If you wish to define someone's moral attitudes, do so; if you try to define a person's "lifestyle," you have a monumental task of all-inclusive definition. It's easier just to avoid it.

society   The problem with this word is that it is too often used only vaguely as a substitute for some more precise idea. Any poem that does deal with "society" will clearly indicate a *particular* society—the world of servants and workers in sixteenth-century England (Shakespeare's "Winter," No. 2) or the world of racial and class distinctions that Mari Evans evokes in "When in Rome" (No. 18). In those cases, once one has defined the particular society and its characteristics, the term might legitimately be used. But don't use it simply to mean "people in general at that time in that place." And it is important to avoid the glib assumption that *society* makes a person do something. A person's desire to be a member of a social group may lead to actions that appear to be imposed or forced, but what makes a person conform is the desire to be or remain a member, not the fact that there are codes of behavior. See Ellen Kay's "Pathedy of Manners" (No. 25).

somewhat (also *rather, more or less, as it were, in a manner*) All of these terms are specifically designed to avoid or evade precision—to create a sense of vagueness. Since clarity and precision are the goals of critical analysis, these terms should be avoided. They also sound wishy-washy, while you should strive to sound firm and convinced.

upset   As an adjective to define an emotional condition, the word is just too vague. Your dictionary will tell you that its synonyms are "distressed, disturbed, agitated, perturbed, irritated," and so forth. All of those terms are more precise than *upset,* and the one that most nearly indicates your meaning should be chosen.

what the author is trying to say is   The implication of this expression is that the author *failed* to say it. You don't say "I'm trying to get to Boston" if you are already there; give the author credit for having got where he or she was going.

Others suggested by your instructor:

_____   _____

_____   _____

_____   _____

X. A SAMPLE EXPLICATION

"A Study of Reading Habits"

The first noteworthy feature of Philip Larkin's "A Study of Reading Habits" (reprinted in Thomas R. Arp, *Perrine's Sound and Sense*, 9th ed. [Fort Worth: Harcourt, 1997] 23) is the ironic discrepancy between the formal language of its title and the colloquial, slangy, even vulgar language of the poem itself. The title by its tone implies a formal sociological research paper, possibly one that samples a cross section of a population and draws conclusions about people's reading. The poem presents, instead, the confessions of one man whose attitudes toward reading have progressively deteriorated to the point where books seem to him "a load of crap." The poem's real subject, moreover, is not the man's reading habits but the revelation of life and character they provide.

The poem is patterned in three stanzas having an identical rime scheme (*abcbac*) and the same basic meter (iambic trimeter). The stanzaic division of the poem corresponds to the internal structure of meaning, for the three stanzas present the speaker at three stages of his life: as schoolboy, adolescent, and adult. The chronological progression is signaled in the first lines of the stanzas by the words "When," "Later," and "now." The "now" is the present out of which the adult speaks, recalling the two earlier periods.

The boy he remembers in stanza 1 was unhappy, both in his home and, even more so, at school. Perhaps small and bullied by bigger boys, probably an indifferent student, making poor grades, and scolded by teachers, he found a partial escape from his miseries through reading. The books he read--tales of action and adventure, pitting good guys against bad buys, full of physical conflict, and ending with victory for the good guys--enabled him to construct a fantasy life in which he identified with the virtuous hero and in his imagination beat up villains twice his size, thus reversing the situations of his real life.

In stanza 2 the speaker recalls his adolescence, when his dreams were of sexual rather than muscular prowess. True to the prediction of "ruining [his] eyes" in stanza 1, he had to wear spectacles, which he describes hyperbolically as "inch-thick"--a further detriment to his social life. To compensate for his lack of success with girls, he envisioned himself as a Dracula-figure with cloak and fangs, enjoying a series of sexual triumphs. His reading continued to feed his fantasy life, but, instead of identifying with the virtuous hero, he identified with the glamorous, sexually ruthless villain. The poet puns on the word "ripping" (the speaker "had ripping times in the dark"), implying both the British slang meaning of "splendid" and the violence of the rapist who rips the clothes off his victim.

In stanza 3 the speaker, now a young adult, confesses that he no longer reads much. His accumulated experience of personal failure and his long familiarity with his shortcomings have made it impossible for him to identify, even in fantasy, with the strong virtuous hero or the viciously potent villain. He can no longer hide from himself the truth that he resembles more closely the weak secondary characters of the escapist tales he picks up. He recognizes himself in the undependable dude who fails the heroine, or the cowardly storekeeper who knuckles under to the bad guys. He therefore has turned to a more powerful means of escape, one that protects him from dwelling on what he knows about himself: drunkenness. His final words are memorable-- so "unpoetical" in a traditional sense, so poetically effective in characterizing this speaker. "Get stewed," he says, "Books are a load of crap."

It would be a serious mistake to identify the speaker of the poem, or his attitudes or his language, with the poet. Poets, writers of books themselves, do not think that "books are a load of crap." Philip Larkin, moreover, an English poet and a graduate of Oxford, was for many years until his death a university librarian (Ian Hamilton, ed., *Oxford Companion to Twentieth-Century Poetry* [Oxford: Oxford UP, 1994] 288). "A Study of Reading Habits" is both dramatic and ironic. It presents a first-person speaker who has been unable to cope with the reality of his life in any of its stages and has therefore turned toward various means of escaping it. His confessions reveal a progressive deterioration of values (from good to evil to sodden indifference) and a decline in reading tastes (from adventure stories to prurient sexual novels to none) that reflect his downward slide.

COMMENTS

The title of this paper is enclosed in quotation marks because the writer has used the title of the poem for the title of the paper. The paper uses textual and parenthetical documentation. Line numbers for quotations from the poem are not supplied because the poem is too short to require them: they would serve no useful purpose. Notice that in quoting from stanza 1, the writer has changed the phrase "ruining my eyes" to fit the essay's syntax, but has indicated the alteration by putting the changed word within brackets. The paper is written for an American audience; if it had been written for an English audience the writer would not have needed to explain that "ripping" is British slang or to have made it a point that the poet is English. The paper is documented for an audience using this textbook. If it were directed toward a wider audience, the writer would make reference for the text of the poem not to a textbook or anthology but to the volume of Larkin's poetry containing this poem (*Collected Poems,* ed. Anthony Thwaite [London: Faber, 1988] 131). Also, the writer would probably wish to include the poet's name in his title: Philip Larkin's "A Study of Reading Habits" (or) An Explication of Larkin's "A Study of Reading Habits." Since Larkin's nationality and his profession as a librarian are not common knowledge, the paper documents a biographical source where that information is found.

Glossary of Terms

The definitions in this glossary sometimes repeat and sometimes differ in language from those in the text. Where they differ, the intention is to give a fuller sense of the term's meaning by allowing the reader a double perspective on it. Page numbers refer to discussion in the text, which in most but not all cases is fuller than that in the glossary.

Accent In this book, the same as *stress*. A syllable given more prominence in pronunciation than its neighbors is said to be accented. 177

Allegory A narrative or description having a second meaning beneath the surface one. 89

Alliteration The repetition at close intervals of the initial consonant sounds of accented syllables or important words (for example, *m*ap–*m*oon, *k*ill–*c*ode, *p*reach–ap*p*rove). Important words and accented syllables beginning with vowels may also be said to alliterate with each other inasmuch as they all have the same lack of an initial consonant sound (for example, "*I*nebriate of *a*ir am *I*"). 165

Allusion A reference, explicit or implicit, to something in literature or history. (The term is reserved by some writers for implicit references only, such as those in "in Just-" [No. 92], and in "On His Blindness" [No. 93]; but the distinction between the two kinds of reference is not always clear-cut.) 122

Anacrusis In metrical verse, the omission of an unaccented syllable at the beginning of a line. 182

Anapest A metrical foot consisting of two unaccented syllables followed by one accented syllable (for example, un-der-stánd). 181

Anapestic meter A meter in which a majority of the feet are anapests. (But see *Triple meter.*) 181

Apostrophe A figure of speech in which someone absent or dead or something nonhuman is addressed as if it were alive and present and could reply. 66

Approximate rime (also known as *imperfect rime, near rime, slant rime,* or *oblique rime*)   A term used for words in a riming pattern that have some kind of sound correspondence but are not perfect rimes. See *Rime.* Approximate rimes occur occasionally in patterns where most of the rimes are perfect (for example, push–rush in "Leda and the Swan" [No. 96], and sometimes are used systematically in place of perfect rime (for example, "Mr. Z" [No. 87]). 166

Assonance   The repetition at close intervals of the vowel sounds of accented syllables or important words (for example, hat–ran–amber, vein–made). 165

Aubade   A poem about dawn; a morning love song; or a poem about the parting of lovers at dawn. 312

Ballad   A fairly short narrative poem written in a songlike stanza form. Examples: "Ballad of Birmingham" (No. 8), "Ettrick" (No. 132), "Edward" (No. 180), "La Belle Dame sans Merci" (No. 247). 168

Blank verse   Unrimed iambic pentameter. 191

Cacophony   A harsh, discordant, unpleasant-sounding choice and arrangement of sounds. 204

Caesura   See *Grammatical pause* and *Rhetorical pause.* 178

Connotation   What a word suggests beyond its basic definition; a word's overtones of meaning. 37

Consonance   The repetition at close intervals of the final consonant sounds of accented syllables or important words (for example, book–plaque–thicker). 165

Continuous form   That form of a poem in which the lines follow each other without formal grouping, the only breaks being dictated by units of meaning. 219

Couplet   Two successive lines, usually in the same meter, linked by rime. 224

Dactyl   A metrical foot consisting of one accented syllable followed by two unaccented syllables (for example, mér-ri-ly). 181

Dactylic meter   A meter in which a majority of the feet are dactyls. (But see *Triple meter.*) 181

Denotation   The basic definition or dictionary meaning of a word. 37

Didactic poetry   Poetry having as a primary purpose to teach or preach. 240

Dimeter   A metrical line containing two feet. 182

Double rime   A rime in which the repeated vowel is in the second last syllable of the words involved (for example, politely–rightly–spritely); one form of *feminine rime.* 166, 173

Dramatic framework The situation, whether actual or fictional, realistic or fanciful, in which an author places his or her characters in order to express the theme. 25–26

Dramatic irony See *Irony*. 107

Duple meter A meter in which a majority of the feet contain two syllables. Iambic and trochaic are both duple meters. 181

End rime Rimes that occur at the ends of the lines. 166

End-stopped line A line that ends with a natural speech pause, usually marked by punctuation. 178

English (or *Shakespearean*) *sonnet* A sonnet riming *ababcdcdefefgg*. Its content or structure ideally parallels the rime scheme, falling into three coordinate quatrains and a concluding couplet; but it is often structured, like the Italian sonnet, into octave and sestet, the principal break in thought coming at the end of the eighth line. 224, 225–26 (Exercise 1)

Euphony A smooth, pleasant-sounding choice and arrangement of sounds. 204

Expected rhythm The rhythmic expectation set up by the basic meter of a poem. 189

Extended figure (also known as *sustained figure*) A figure of speech (usually metaphor, simile, personification, or apostrophe) sustained or developed through a considerable number of lines or through a whole poem. 71, 72

Extra-metrical syllables In metrical verse, extra unaccented syllables added at the beginnings or endings of lines; these may be either a feature of the metrical form of a poem (example, "Epitaph on an Army of Mercenaries," [No. 145], even-numbered lines) or occur as exceptions to the form (example, "Virtue," [No. 142], lines 9 and 11). In iambic lines, they occur at the end of the line; in trochaic, at the beginning. 182, 186–87, 195 (Question 2)

Feminine rime A rime in which the repeated accented vowel is in either the second or third last syllable of the words involved (for example, *ceil*ing–ap*peal*ing, *hur*rying–*scur*rying). 166, 173

Figurative language Language employing figures of speech; language that cannot be taken literally or only literally. 62

Figure of speech Broadly, any way of saying something other than the ordinary way; more narrowly (and for the purposes of this book), a way of saying one thing and meaning another. 62

Fixed form Any form of poem in which the length and pattern are prescribed by previous usage or tradition, such as *sonnet, limerick, villanelle, haiku,* and so on. 222

Folk ballad   A narrative poem designed to be sung, composed by an anonymous author, and transmitted orally for years or generations before being written down. It has usually undergone modification through the process of oral transmission. 168 (Question 1)

Foot   The basic unit used in the scansion or measurement of metrical verse. A foot usually contains one accented syllable and one or two unaccented syllables (the *spondaic foot* is a modification of this principle). 180

Form   The external pattern or shape of a poem, describable without reference to its content, as *continuous form, stanzaic form, fixed form* (and their varieties), *free verse,* and *syllabic verse.* 219 See *Structure.*

Free verse   Nonmetrical poetry in which the basic rhythmic unit is the line, and natural speech rhythms replace metrical regularity as a formal device. 178

Grammatical pause (also known as *caesura*)   A pause introduced into the reading of a line by a mark of punctuation. 178, 190

Haiku   A three-line poem, Japanese in origin, narrowly conceived of as a fixed form in which the lines contain respectively five, seven, and five syllables (in American practice this requirement is frequently dispensed with). Haiku are generally concerned with some aspect of nature and present a single image or two juxtaposed images without comment, relying on suggestion rather than on explicit statement to communicate their meaning. 227

Heard rhythm   The actual rhythm of a metrical poem as we hear it when it is read naturally. The heard rhythm mostly conforms to but sometimes departs from or modifies the *expected rhythm.* 189

Hexameter   A metrical line containing six feet. 182

Hyperbole   See *Overstatement.* 102

Iamb   A metrical foot consisting of one unaccented syllable followed by one accented syllable (for example, re-hearse). 181

Iambic meter   A meter in which the majority of feet are iambs. The most common English meter. 181

Imagery   The representation through language of sense experience. 49

Internal rime   A rime in which one or both of the rime words occur(s) *within* the line. 166

Irony   A situation, or a use of language, involving some kind of incongruity or discrepancy. 105–110 Three kinds of irony are distinguished in this book:

Verbal irony   A figure of speech in which what is meant is the opposite of what is said. 105

Dramatic irony   A device by which the author implies a different meaning from that intended by the speaker (or by *a* speaker) in a literary work. 107

Irony of situation (or *situational irony*)   A situation in which there is an incongruity between actual circumstances and those that would seem appropriate or between what is anticipated and what actually comes to pass. 109

Italian (or *Petrarchan*) *sonnet*   A sonnet consisting of an octave riming *abbaabba* and of a sestet using any arrangement of two or three additional rimes, such as *cdcdcd* or *cdecde*. 223, 225–26 (Exercise 1)

Limerick   A fixed form consisting of five lines of anapestic meter, the first two trimeter, the next two dimeter, the last line trimeter, riming *aabba;* used exclusively for humorous or nonsense verse. 222

Masculine rime (also known as *single rime*)   A rime in which the repeated accented vowel sound is in the final syllable of the words involved (for example, dance–pants, scald–recalled). 165, 173

Metaphor   A figure of speech in which an implicit comparison is made between two things essentially unlike. It may take one of four forms: (1) that in which the literal term and the figurative term are *both named;* (2) that in which the literal term is *named* and the figurative term *implied;* (3) that in which the literal term is *implied* and the figurative term *named;* (4) that in which *both* the literal and the figurative terms are *implied.* 62–65

Meter   The regular patterns of accent that underlie metrical verse; the measurable repetition of accented and unaccented syllables in poetry. 179

Metonymy   A figure of speech in which some significant aspect or detail of an experience is used to represent the whole experience. In this book the single term *metonymy* is used for what are sometimes distinguished as two separate figures: *synecdoche* (the use of the part for the whole) and *metonymy* (the use of something closely related for the thing actually meant). 67

Metrical variations   Departures from the basic metrical pattern (see *anacrusis, substitution, extra-metrical syllables*). 182

Monometer   A metrical line containing one foot. 182

Octave   (1) An eight-line stanza. (2) The first eight lines of a sonnet, especially one structured in the manner of an Italian sonnet. 223

Onomatopoeia   The use of words that supposedly mimic their meaning in their sound (for example, *boom, click, plop*). 202

Onomatopoetic language   Language employing *onomatopoeia.*

Overstatement (or *hyperbole*)   A figure of speech in which exaggeration is used in the service of truth. 102

Paradox   A statement or situation containing apparently contradictory or incompatible elements. 101

Paradoxical situation   A situation containing apparently but not actually incompatible elements. The celebration of a fifth birthday anniversary by a twenty-year-old man is paradoxical but explainable if the man was born on February 29. The Christian doctrines that Christ was born of a virgin and is both God and man are, for a Christian believer, paradoxes (that is, apparently impossible but true). 101

Paradoxical statement (or *verbal paradox*)   A figure of speech in which an apparently self-contradictory statement is nevertheless found to be true. 101

Paraphrase   A restatement of the content of a poem designed to make its *prose meaning* as clear as possible. 23–25

Pentameter   A metrical line containing five feet. 182

Personification   A figure of speech in which human attributes are given to an animal, an object, or a concept. 65

Petrarchan sonnet   See *Italian sonnet.* 223

Phonetic intensive   A word whose sound, by an obscure process, to some degree suggests its meaning. As differentiated from *onomatopoetic words,* the meanings of phonetic intensives do not refer explicitly to sounds. 202

Prose   Nonmetrical language; the opposite of *verse.*

Prose meaning   That part of a poem's *total meaning* that can be separated out and expressed through paraphrase. 133

Prose poem   Usually a short composition having the intentions of poetry but written in prose rather than verse. 179

Quatrain   (1) A four-line stanza. (2) A four-line division of a sonnet marked off by its rime scheme. 224

Refrain   A repeated word, phrase, line, or group of lines, normally at some fixed position in a poem written in stanzaic form. 167, 221

Rhetorical pause (also known as *caesura*)   A natural pause, unmarked by punctuation, introduced into the reading of a line by its phrasing or syntax. 178, 190

Rhetorical poetry   Poetry using artificially eloquent language; that is, language too high-flown for its occasion and unfaithful to the full complexity of human experience. 240

Rhetorical stress   In natural speech, as in prose and poetic writing, the stressing of words or syllables so as to emphasize meaning and sentence structure. 178

Rhythm   Any wavelike recurrence of motion or sound. 177

Rime (or *rhyme*)   The repetition of the accented vowel sound and all succeeding sounds in important or importantly positioned words (for example, old–cold, vane–reign, court–report, order–recorder). The above definition applies to *perfect rime* and assumes that the accented vowel sounds involved are preceded by differing consonant sounds. If the preceding consonant sound is the same (for example, manse–romance, style–stile), or if there is no preceding consonant sound in either word (for example, aisle–isle, alter–altar), or if the same word is repeated in the riming position (for example, hill–hill), the words are called *identical rimes*. Both *perfect rimes* and *identical rimes* are to be distinguished from *approximate rimes*. 165

Rime scheme   Any fixed pattern of rimes characterizing a whole poem or its stanzas. 220–22

Run-on line   A line which has no natural speech pause at its end, allowing the sense to flow uninterruptedly into the succeeding line. 178

Sarcasm   Bitter or cutting speech; speech intended by its speaker to give pain to the person addressed. 105

Satire   A kind of literature that ridicules human folly or vice with the purpose of bringing about reform or of keeping others from falling into similar folly or vice. 105

Scansion   The process of measuring metrical verse, that is, of marking accented and unaccented syllables, dividing the lines into feet, identifying the metrical pattern, and noting significant variations from that pattern. 182

Sentimental poetry   Poetry aimed primarily at stimulating the emotions rather than at communicating experience honestly and freshly. 239

Sestet   (1) A six-line stanza. (2) The last six lines of a sonnet structured on the Italian model. 223

Shakespearean sonnet   See *English sonnet.* 224

Simile   A figure of speech in which an explicit comparison is made between two things essentially unlike. The comparison is made explicit by the use of some such word or phrase as *like, as, than, similar to, resembles,* or *seems.* 62–65

Single rime　See *Masculine rime.* 173

Situational irony　See *Irony.*

Sonnet　A fixed form of fourteen lines, normally iambic pentameter, with a rime scheme conforming to or approximating one of two main types—the *Italian* or the *English.* 223–24

Spondee　A metrical foot consisting of two syllables equally or almost equally accented (for example, true–blue). 181

Stanza　A group of lines whose metrical pattern (and usually its rime scheme as well) is repeated throughout a poem. 182, 220

Stanzaic form　The form taken by a poem when it is written in a series of units having the same number of lines and usually other characteristics in common, such as metrical pattern or rime scheme. 220

Stress　In this book, the same as *Accent.* But see 177 (footnote).

Structure　The internal organization of a poem's content. See *Form.* 219

Substitution　In metrical verse, the replacement of the expected metrical foot by a different one (for example, a trochee occurring in an iambic line). 182

Sustained figure　See *Extended figure.*

Syllabic verse　Verse measured by the number of syllables rather than the number of feet per line. 197 Also see *Haiku.*

Symbol　A figure of speech in which something (object, person, situation, or action) means more than what it is. A symbol, in other words, may be read both literally and metaphorically. 81

Synecdoche　A figure of speech in which a part is used for the whole. In this book it is subsumed under the term *Metonymy.* 67

Terza rima　An interlocking rime scheme with the pattern *aba bcb cdc,* etc. 233

Tetrameter　A metrical line containing four feet. 181

Theme　The central idea of a literary work. 23

Tone　The writer's or speaker's attitude toward the subject, the audience, or herself or himself; the emotional coloring, or emotional meaning, of a work. 146

Total meaning　The total experience communicated by a poem. It includes all those dimensions of experience by which a poem communicates—sensuous, emotional, imaginative, and intellectual—and it can be communicated in no other words than those of the poem itself. 133

Trimeter   A metrical line containing three feet. 181

Triple meter   A meter in which a majority of the feet contain three syllables. (Actually, if more than 25 percent of the feet in a poem are triple, its effect is more triple than duple, and it ought perhaps to be referred to as triple meter.) Anapestic and dactylic are both triple meters. 181

Trochaic meter   A meter in which the majority of feet are trochees. 181

Trochee   A metrical foot consisting of one accented syllable followed by one unaccented syllable (for example, bár-tĕr). 181

Understatement   A figure of speech that consists of saying less than one means, or of saying what one means with less force than the occasion warrants. 103

Verbal irony   See *Irony.* 105

Verse   Metrical language; the opposite of *prose.*

Villanelle   See 226 (Exercise 2).

Copyrights and
Acknowledgments

ploughing," "To an Athlete Dying Young," "Terence, this is stupid stuff," "Loveliest of Trees" "Bredon Hill," "Eight O'Clock," and "Epitaph on an Army of Mercenaries."

LANGSTON HUGHES   "Cross" from *Selected Poems* by Langston Hughes. Copyright 1926 by Alfred A. Knopf, Inc. and renewed 1954 by Langston Hughes. "Dream Deferred" from *The Panther and the Lash* by Langston Hughes. Copyright 1951 by Langston Hughes. Reprinted by permission of Alfred A. Knopf, Inc.

TED HUGHES   "Thistles" from *Wodwo* by Ted Hughes. Copyright © 1961 by Ted Hughes. Reprinted by permission of HarperCollins Publishers, Inc. and by permission of Faber & Faber Limited, London. "Hawk Roosting" from *Lupercal*. Reprinted by permission of Faber & Faber Limited, London.

RICHARD HUGO   "The Freaks at Spurgin Road Field" from *Making Certain It Goes On: The Collected Poems of Richard Hugo*. Copyright © 1975 by W.W. Norton & Company, Inc. Reprinted by permission of W.W. Norton & Company, Inc.

RANDALL JARRELL   "The Death of the Ball Turret Gunner" and "The State" from *The Complete Poems* by Randall Jarrell. Copyright © 1969 by Mrs. Randall Jarrell. Reprinted by permission of Farrar, Straus & Giroux, Inc.

LYNN JOHNSTON   "A tiny cry within the night" from *For Better or For Worse*. Copyright Lynn Johnston Production Inc. Reprinted by Permission of Universal Press Syndicate.

JENNY JOSEPH   "Warning" from *Selected Poems,* published by Bloodaxe Books Ltd. Copyright © 1992 by Jenny Joseph. Reprinted by permission of John Johnson, Author's Agent: London.

ELLEN KAY   "Pathedy of Manners" from *A Local Habitation* (The Swallow Press, 1958). Reprinted with the permission of The Ohio University Press and the author.

JANE KENYON   "The Letter" from *Let Evening Come*. Copyright 1990 by Jane Kenyon. Reprinted by permission of Graywolf Press, Saint Paul, Minnesota.

GALWAY KINNELL   "Blackberry Eating" from *Mortal Acts, Mortal Words* by Galway Kinnell. Copyright © 1980 by Galway Kinnell. Reprinted by permission of Houghton Mifflin Co. All rights reserved.

ETHERIDGE KNIGHT   "The warden said to me" from *Poems from Prison*. Copyright © 1968 by Broadside Press. Reprinted by permission of Broadside Press.

MAXINE KUMIN   "The Sound of Night" from *Halfway*. Copyright © 1961 by Maxine Kumin. Reprinted by permission of Curtis Brown Ltd.

PHILIP LARKIN   "A Study of Reading Habits" from *The Whitsun Weddings* by Philip Larkin. "Aubade" from *Collected Poems*. Reprinted by permission of Faber and Faber Limited. "Church Going" and "Toads" by Philip Larkin from *The Less Deceived*. Reprinted by permission of The Marvell Press, England and Australia.

WALTER McDONALD   "Life With Father" from *Counting Survivors* by Walter McDonald. Copyright © 1995 by Walter McDonald. Reprinted by permission of the University of Pittsburgh Press.

KATHARYN HOWD MACHAN   "Leda's Sister and the Geese" from *Sometime the Cow Kick Your Head: Light Year '88/9* (Cleveland: Bits Press, 1988). Reprinted by permission of the author.

ARCHIBALD MacLEISH   "Ars Poetica" from *Collected Poems 1917–1982* by Archibald MacLeish. Copyright © 1985 by The Estate of Archibald MacLeish. Reprinted by permission of Houghton Mifflin Co. All rights reserved.

NAOMI LONG MADGETT   "Offspring" from *Pink Ladies in the Afternoon* (Detroit: Lotus, 1972, 1990). Reprinted by permission of the author.

Index of Authors, Titles, and First Lines

Author's names appear in capitals, titles of poems in italics, and first lines of poems in roman type. A number in bold face is the page of the selection, and roman numbers are pages where the poem is discussed.